History and the Cult

Colonialism denied Algeria its own history; nationalism reinvented it. James McDougall's book charts the creation of that history through colonialism to independence, exploring the struggle to define Algeria's past and determine the meaning of its nationhood. Through local histories and individual experiences, McDougall analyses the relationship between history, Islamic culture and nationalism in Algeria. In so doing, he confronts prevailing notions that nationalism emancipated Algerian history, and that Algeria's past has somehow determined its present, violence breeding violence, tragedy repeating itself. Instead, he argues, nationalism was a new kind of domination, in which multiple memories and possible futures were effaced. But the histories hidden by nationalism remain below the surface, and can be recovered to create alternative visions for the future. This is an exceptional and engaging book, rich in analysis and documentation. It will be read by colonial historians and social theorists as well as by scholars of the Middle East and North Africa.

JAMES MCDOUGALL is Assistant Professor of History at Princeton University. He has edited *Nation, Society and Culture in North Africa* (2003).

Cambridge Middle East Studies 24

Cambridge Middle East Studies has been established to publish books on the modern Middle East and North Africa. The aim of the series is to provide new and original interpretations of aspects of Middle Eastern societies and their histories. To achieve disciplinary diversity, books will be solicited from authors writing in a wide range of fields including history, sociology, anthropology, political science and political economy. The emphasis will be on producing books offering an original approach along theoretical and empirical lines. The series is intended for students and academics, but the more accessible and wide-ranging studies will also appeal to the interested general reader.

A list of books in the series can be found after the index.

History and the Culture of Nationalism in Algeria

James McDougall
Princeton University

CAMBRIDGE
UNIVERSITY PRESS

CAMBRIDGE UNIVERSITY PRESS
Cambridge, New York, Melbourne, Madrid, Cape Town, Singapore, São Paulo, Delhi

Cambridge University Press
The Edinburgh Building, Cambridge CB2 8RU, UK

Published in the United States of America by Cambridge University Press, New York

www.cambridge.org
Information on this title: www.cambridge.org/9780521103671

First published 2006
Reprinted 2007
This digitally printed version 2009

A catalogue record for this publication is available from the British Library

Library of Congress Cataloguing in Publication data
McDougall, James, 1974–
History and the culture of nationalism in Algeria / James McDougall –
1st ed.
p. cm. – (Cambridge Middle East studies; 23)
Includes bibliographical references and index.
ISBN-13: 978-0-521-84373-7 (hardback)
ISBN-10: 0-521-84373-1 (hardback)
1. Nationalism – Algeria – History. I. Title. II. Series.
DT294.5.M45 2006
320.540965 – dc22 2005029331

ISBN 978-0-521-84373-7 hardback
ISBN 978-0-521-10367-1 paperback

Would it exceed the bounds of legitimate doubt if we were to place our emphasis on the part of purely linguistic play in these spiritual, or religious, variations, which constitute the ancient history of the Maghrib? This history is, perhaps, nothing but a study in heresy. The Maghribis, we are told, apostatized as many as twelve times. In this they pursued a search for their own identity which has probably not yet ceased today. As we know, in matters of schism and sect it is the verbal label, the classification by name, or by epithet, which plays the primary role. It is by this that the personalities of individuals, or of groups, situate, recognise, or affirm themselves relative to one another. Do we not see, throughout recent centuries, Islamic religious brotherhoods – just like the Wahhabi movement that today, in turn, attacks them – constantly renewing against one another the same struggle in the name of authenticity and purism? Indeed, throughout North African history, people may always have been labelled as 'puritan' or 'heretic', just as they have been as 'nomad' or 'peasant'. Or even 'Arab' or 'Berber' . . . This, surely, is to carry our doubts too far. I have merely wished to show to what extent, in North Africa, this land par excellence of the search for oneself . . . a part of things is held in their sign. A part of history, as of the morphology of groups, hangs on the life of words.

Jacques Berque
'Qu'est-ce qu'une "tribu" nord-africaine?'

Contents

Illustrations

Every effort has been made to secure necessary permissions to reproduce copyright material in this work, though in some cases it has proved impossible to trace copyright holders. Omissions brought to the publisher's notice will be appropriately rectified in future editions wherever possible.

Preface

This book examines the place of cultural authority and historical imagination in nationalism. My aim has been to move beyond the tropes of awakening and consciousness still common in writing on this subject with regard to the Maghrib, and to put the cultural history of nationalism back into a critical, materialist discursive history of changing forms of social power and modes of domination. I do not pretend to have exhausted this subject; there are many important aspects of the issue not addressed here. Limits of space, competence and material have defined what I have, and have not, been able to discuss.

This study is based primarily on two sets of documentary sources: French colonial archives that chronicle the development of new cultural dynamics in Algerian society through the first two-thirds of the twentieth century; and published periodicals and books in French and Arabic that both constitute and reflect on these same developments. I particularly have to thank the directors and staff of archives and libraries in Aix-en-Provence, Nantes, Tunis, Algiers, Oran and Constantine, the School of Oriental and African Studies, London, the Bibliothèque nationale de France and the Centre culturel algérien, Paris, the National Library and the Institut supérieur de l'histoire du mouvement national, Tunis, the Firestone library at Princeton and the various libraries of the University of Oxford.

In transliterating from Arabic, I have aimed for clarity overall. Place names are given in the most familiar form (Oran not Wahrān). For proper names of persons, I have given Arabic transliterations for people who wrote primarily in Arabic, and established French forms for individuals who themselves wrote in French. Personal names are transliterated on their first appearance, following the system of the *International Journal of Middle East Studies* (with word-final *hamza* omitted), and thereafter given in a simplified transliteration without diacritics. Less commonly known Arabic terminology (e.g. *dhikr*) is transliterated, but words familiar in English (e.g. sufi) are not. All unattributed translations are my own.

Some of this material first appeared elsewhere. I thank the following for permission to reproduce parts of the work: Duke University Press for parts of chapter 5 which appeared as 'Myth and counter-myth: "The Berber" as national signifier in Algerian historiographies', *Radical History Review* 86 (Spring 2003), 66–88; Nebraska University Press, for part of the epilogue appearing in 'Authenticity/Alienation: the cultural politics of rememoration in post-colonial Algeria', in William B. Cohen and James D. le Sueur (eds.), *France and Algeria: From Colonial Conflicts to Postcolonial Memories*; and Indiana University Press, for parts of chapters 4 and 5 appearing in 'Martyrdom and destiny: the inscription and imagination of Algerian history', in Ussama Makdisi and Paul Silverstein (eds.), *Memory and Violence in the Middle East and North Africa*.

It is a pleasure to acknowledge my many debts. The British Academy, latterly the Arts and Humanities Research Board, made my graduate education possible, and I was fortunate to pursue it at the Oriental Institute and St Antony's College, Oxford. I was lucky again to receive a post-doctoral award from the Leverhulme Trust, to be able to hold that award at St Antony's Middle East Centre through the generosity of Jack McCrane and the Hadid Fund, and to be elected to a research fellowship by the Warden and Fellows of St Antony's. It is a privilege to have been part of such a distinguished, stimulating and supportive institution. The book was finished in my first year as a member of another extraordinary institution, the history department at Princeton. It would never have been written without the welcome afforded me by the Institut de Recherches et d'Etudes sur le Monde arabe et musulman at the Maison méditerranéenne des Sciences de l'Homme in Aix-en-Provence, the Institut de Recherches sur le Maghreb contemporain, Tunis, and the Centre de Recherches en Anthropologie sociale et culturelle in Oran. To the wonderful faculty and staff of all of these I am greatly indebted. My thanks go especially to Mastan Ebtehaj, Elizabeth Anderson and Collette Caffrey.

Eugene Rogan's encouragement, guidance and generous enthusiasm have been with this project since its inception. Charles-Robert Ageron and Benjamin Stora reassured me early on that I was doing something interesting, and Robin Ostle and Jean-Claude Vatin gave both heartening encouragement and helpful criticism.

I am grateful to many people for support, criticism, encouragement, advice, hospitality and friendship: in Aix and Marseille, Isabelle Grangaud and Randi Deguilhem, and their families, Jean-Robert Henry and Françoise Lorcerie, Ahmed Mahiou, Bernard Botiveau, Isabelle Merle, Ali Bensaad and Abderrahmane Moussaoui; in Paris, Omar Carlier, Sylvie Thénault, Raphaëlle Branche, Anne-Marie Pathé, Ouarda

Tengour, Laure Blévis, Marianne Boucheret, Marie Colonna and Marcel, and Kamel Chachoua; in Tunis, Odile Moreau, Anne-Marie Planel, Kmar Bendana, Habib Belaïd and Mohamed Aziz Ben Achour; in Oran, Fouad Soufi, Sadek Benkada, Nouria and Hassan Remaoun, and Abed and Ina Bendjelid; in Algiers, Jean-Paul and Marie-France Grangaud and their family, Daho Djerbal, Fatiha Loualich, Mustafa Haddab, Anissa Amziane, Joseph Rivat and everyone at CIARA; in Constantine, Abdelmajid Merdaci, Zeyneb and Meriem, Khadija Adel, Lazhar Othmani, Bouba Medjani and Badreddine Chaabani. Mohamed Harbi and Mostefa Lacheraf generously gave interviews that clarified a number of issues. Without Fanny Colonna, I would never have understood anything.

Judith Scheele, Mohand Akli Hadibi, Tewfik Sahraoui and Hichem El-Fekair shared travels in Algeria and conversations on the issues addressed here as well as much else. David Lambert and Marie-Anne Marchal, Michael Willis, Cathie Lloyd, John King, James Onley, Michael Collyer, Paul Silverstein, Susan Miller, Geoff Porter, Ben White and Dan Gordon have all discussed parts of this work, or related questions, in Tunisia, France, Morocco, England and America. I have had more sympathetic hearings than I usually deserved from participants in seminars and conferences in Houston, San Francisco, Tunis, Rabat, Aix, Oxford, Exeter, Anchorage, Chicago, Oran, London, Paris, Georgetown, Princeton and Harvard.

The manuscript was read in part, or in its entirety, with extraordinary generosity of time and energy by Michael Cook, Julia Clancy-Smith, Michael Laffan, Molly Greene, Gyan Prakash, and two readers for the Press. The book has far fewer errors, and greater clarity, than it would have had without their incisive and detailed comments; remaining errors and obscurity are my own responsibility. Marigold Acland's enthusiasm and patience have been wonderful. My thanks to her, to Isabelle Dambricourt, Liz Davey and Mary Starkey.

Finally and most of all, I have to thank our friends in Oxford and Princeton, and our families, both for supporting this project and for taking me away from it regularly. My father's voyages to far-off places were early inspirations for my own. My mother, grandmother, sisters and aunts have for years been consistently and lovingly supportive of my interest in questions very distant from home. What I owe to Anna, who has lived with this study from beginning to end and in several places, who puts up with my presence and my absences, and who is the reason I always come home, is more than I can put into words.

Abbreviations and acronyms

AAN	*Annuaire de l'Afrique du Nord*
ADA	Archives du Département d'Alger
ADC	Archives du Département de Constantine
ADN	Archives diplomatiques, Nantes
AESC	*Annales: Economies, Sociétés, Civilisations*
AGGA	Archives du Gouvernement Général de l'Algérie
AHR	*American Historical Review*
AHSS	*Annales: Histoire, Sciences sociales* (formerly *AESC*)
ALN	Armée de libération nationale
AML	Amis du manifeste et de la liberté
ANT/AGGT	Archives nationales, Tunis; Archives générales du Gouvernement Tunisien
AUMA	Association des *'ulamā* musulmans algériens
AWC	Archives of the *wilaya* of Constantine
AWO	Archives of the *wilaya* of Oran
BCAF	*Afrique française. Bulletin du Comité de l'Afrique française*
BnF	Bibliothèque nationale de France, Paris
BNT	Bibliothèque nationale, Tunis
BSGA	*Bulletin de la Société de Géographie d'Alger*
BSOAS	*Bulletin of the School of Oriental and African Studies*
CANA	Centre des archives nationales, Algiers
CAOM	Centre des archives d'outre mer, Aix-en-Provence
CFLN	Comité français de libération nationale (1944)
CIE	Centre d'information et d'études (created May 1935)
CM	Commune mixte
Comm. div.	Commissaire divisionnaire
CPE	Commune de plein exercice
CRUA	Comité révolutionnaire d'unité et d'action
C/SIDM	Centre/Service d'information et de documentation musulmane (succeeds CIE, 1945)
CSSH	*Comparative Studies in Society and History*

EI2	*Encyclopaedia of Islam* (2nd edn)
ENA	Etoile nord-africaine
FADRL	Front algérien pour la défense et le respect de la liberté
FLN	Front de libération nationale
GPRA	Gouvernement provisoire de la République algérienne
GPRF	Gouvernement provisoire de la République française
IBLA	*Revue de l'Institut des belles lettres arabes* (Tunis)
IJMES	*International Journal of Middle East Studies*
ISHMN	Institut supérieur de l'histoire du mouvement national, La Manouba, Tunis
JAH	*Journal of African History*
J. Hist. Sociol.	*Journal of Historical Sociology*
JORA	*Journal officiel de la République algérienne*
MAE	Ministère des affaires étrangères
MES	*Middle East Studies*
MNA	Mouvement national algérien
MS(S)	manuscript(s)
MTLD	Mouvement pour le triomphe des libertés démocratiques
OS	Organisation spéciale (PPA/MTLD paramilitary wing, 1947–50)
PCA	Parti communiste algérien
PCF	Parti communiste français
PE	Police d'Etat
PPA	Parti du peuple algérien
PRG	Police des renseignements généraux
RA	*Revue africaine*
RASJEP	*Revue algérienne des sciences juridique, économique et politique*
REMMM	*Revue des mondes musulmans et de la Méditerannée* (formerly *ROMM*)
Rev. Hist. Maghr.	*Revue d'histoire maghrébine*
ROMM	*Revue de l'Occident musulman et de la Méditerannée*
SAINA	Service des affaires indigènes nord-africaines (Paris Police Prefecture)
SD	Sûreté départementale
SEGLNA	Service des études générales et des liaisons nord-africaines (1958–9)
SLNA	Service des liaisons nord-africaines (succeeds C/SIDM, 1947–57)
tr. extr.	translated extract
UDMA	Union démocratique du manifeste algérien

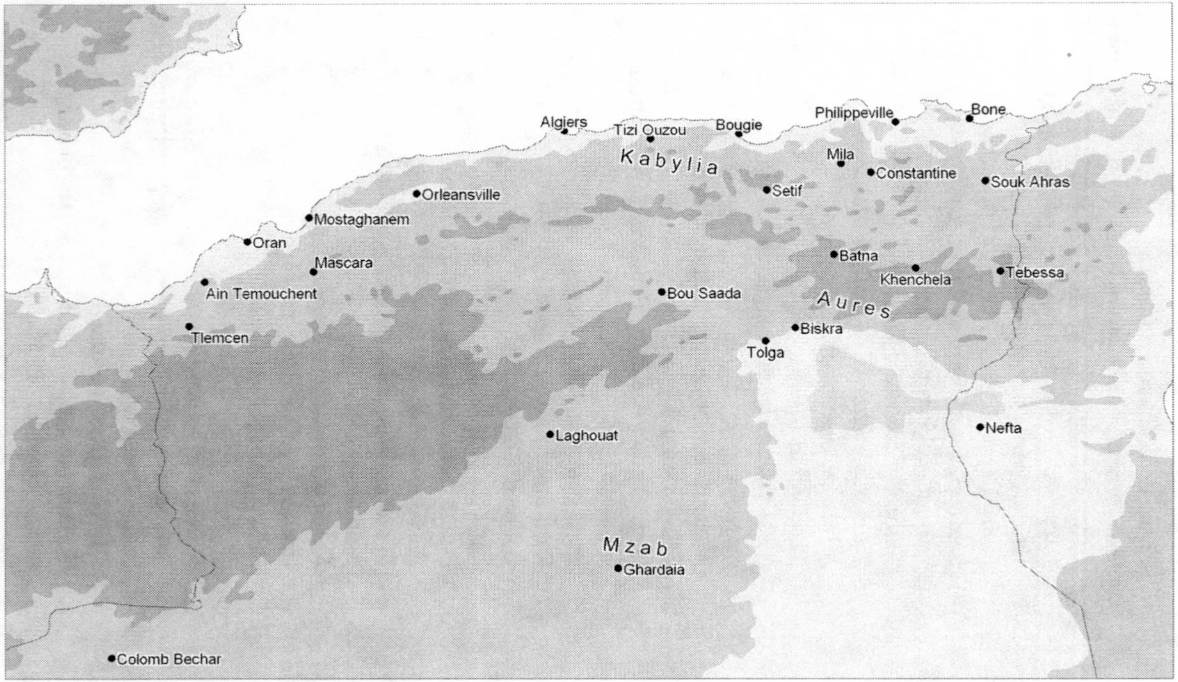

Colonial Algeria *(By permission of HarperCollins Ltd)*

The language of history

Closures of violence

> The tradition of all the dead generations weighs like a nightmare on the mind of the living.
> Karl Marx[1]

There is a short drama in Kateb Yacine's cycle for theatre, *Le Cercle des représailles*,[2] whose title has become a lapidary phrase in writing on Algeria: *Les Ancêtres redoublent de férocité*, 'the ancestors redouble their ferocity'. A disturbing focus of the play, hovering insistently in the background, is the nightmarish presence of a vulture, 'the bird of death', messenger of the ancestors. At the play's end, Nedjma, the female embodiment of Algeria, lies dead, only to be (re-)'incarnated in war'.

Lifted from the playwright's astonishing poetic talent, his gift for haunting and – frequently, in its very resonant obscurity – eloquent expression, this title has become a recurrent theme in the depiction of Algeria's contemporary history. In few places is the temptation so strong to see a society and culture 'inhabited by violence',[3] a history composed of recurrent, inescapable cycles of terror. The tortured history of modern Algeria's dead generations, it might appear, does in a terribly active sense weigh 'like a nightmare on the mind of the living'. From the cataclysm of the forty years' war of conquest (1830–70) through the repressive, everyday violence of an exceptionally intense colonialism, to the atrocious seven years' war of liberation (1954–62), and then the civil turmoil of the twentieth century's bloody final decade, violence weighs so heavy in this history that it seems to repeat itself endlessly, with past tragedies on perpetual, grotesque replay as each new moment unfolds. Nor is this perception limited to the easy racist stereotype of 'Algerian savagery' – long-lived and insidious though this is. Respectable

1 *The Eighteenth Brumaire of Louis Bonaparte.*
2 Paris, Seuil, 1959.
3 Youssef Nacib, quoted in Remaoun, 'La Question de l'histoire', 32.

commentators have underscored the significance of a 'superabundance' of social memory, steeped in an epic national history of perennial revolt and revolution, as a significant force in the 1990s, shaping those conditions, not of their own choosing, under which 'men make their history'.[4] Thus, Algeria in the mid-1990s was said to be 'in the process of reinvoking its dreaded past'.[5]

This is not a study of Algeria's supposedly 'dreaded past'. Monolithic and endlessly reinvoked ancestral violence is much too superficial an image of Algeria's rich and complex history. Too often related, by colonialists and nationalists alike, in mythical form, whether as the miraculous progress of divine revelation or the patient process of natural evolution, the cyclical repetition of rising hope (colonial or revolutionary hubris) and spiralling, catastrophic nemesis, Algerian history has been ill-served by the closures of violent destiny imposed upon it, whether these have been heroic, as in the halcyon, revolutionary 1950s and 1960s, or dreadful, in the disenchanted and distraught 1990s. An alternative approach to the presence of the past, to the meaning of the 'nightmarish weight' of history in Algeria, is possible. If Algerians' histories have been filled with the closures imposed by violence – 'civilising' violence and its 'maintenance of order', 'redeeming' violence and the martyrology of each new order – it is emphatically not the task of historiography to naturalise these murderous tropologies in the violence of new closures, in writing the Algerian past as if all of this were somehow inevitable, thus doing new abuse to the past in its very inscription. On the contrary, historical writing must endeavour both to uncover the ways in which this trope of 'destiny', this image of a unitary and undifferentiated, linear and epic or cyclical and tragic, history came to appear as such, and to see beyond it, to the deeper social, political and cultural processes at work in shaping Algerian history, and perceptions of that history.

The ends of history

This book examines the place of historical imagination and cultural authority in the making of nationalism. Focusing on the role of Islamic teachers and writers through whom a new vision of Algeria's history and

[4] Remaoun, 'La Question de l'histoire'; Stora, 'Algérie: absence et surabondance de mémoire'; Ained-Tabet, 'Manuels d'histoire et discours idéologique'; Carlier, *Entre nation et jihad*, 25–6, 393, 399; Martinez, *La Guerre civile en Algérie*, 14–15, 28, 376. A careful discussion is Carlier, 'D'une guerre à l'autre'.

[5] Entelis, 'Islam, democracy and the state', 248.

culture coalesced in the first half of the twentieth century, I trace the history of the articulation of a modernist discourse which would come to define Algeria's history and 'national identity'. I examine some of the transformations wrought in Algerian culture by the ascendancy of this reimagined history, and show how those who articulated it, in a series of struggles for the power to represent their community's past and future, became the spokesmen of a sovereign vision of national 'authenticity', but were reduced, along with that vision, to an instrumental status in a revolutionary political order whose emergence, through the resort to arms, they had hoped to avoid. At the same time, however, they had themselves unwittingly ensured the cultural legitimisation of the unitary, undifferentiated and exalted model of community upon which the revolutionary order would come to rest; and in doing so they had also, as it would turn out, begun to prepare the ground for a much later, religiously imagined revolt against that order. Their success and their failures were constitutive of the modern culture of nationalism in Algeria. Their visions of history provide a particularly good ground on which to trace the development of both.

As a first step towards delineating this story, we need to dispense with the closed narrative of ancestral violence. 'The presence of the past' means something more complex than the persistence of atavistic memory, immutable laws or determining cultural structures of thought and action. It is not the ancestors who 'redouble their ferocity'; they are dead and gone. The injustice and suffering inflicted upon them can never be righted, revenged, or removed in any subsequent present. Only in the minds of their descendants do shades rise up and demand justice, or inspire retribution, and these ghosts, as Michel de Certeau reminds us, are faceless and silent. Their silence, indeed, is the necessary condition of their entry into History, their memorialisation in text.[6] Their form and voice are given them by historical imagination in the present. This, to be sure, is shaped and coloured by conditions which the past has produced, but historical understanding and imagination are never simply transmissions from the past. They are, rather, appropriations of it. As Ricoeur puts it, 'What does it mean [for a past event, or a historical person] to survive? Nothing . . . All that is finally meaningful is *the current possession of* the activity of the past . . . Survival and inheritance are

[6] 'The dear departed enter the text because they can neither hurt nor speak. These ghosts find a welcome in writing only on condition that they *are silent* forever . . . The People, too, is the silent object of the poem which speaks of it. Certainly, only the People can "authorise" the historian's writing – but even this is on condition of its being *absent*': de Certeau, *L'Ecriture de l'histoire*, 7–8, original emphasis.

natural processes. Historical knowledge begins with the way in which we enter into possession of them.'[7]

The formulation of historical knowledge is an active production of meaning in which, at every new historical moment, a conception of the past is continually reconnected to the constantly vanishing present. This production of meaning is itself a complex social process, answering certain social needs. The tradition of all the dead generations weighs on the mind of the living, not as a *dead* weight, predetermining the present in a closed, unidirectional path (the Salvation of Man or Manifest Destiny), but rather because meaningful self-location in, and interpretation of, the world, and the possibility of acting in and upon that world, requires that a certain sense be made of the past.[8] I emphasise that it must be *made*: history (as socially institutionalised knowledge of the past) is not of itself immanent in the practical structures of social life, nor in people's minds. 'Social memory' is not simply spontaneously 'shared' memory, but a cultural artefact, constructed through a creative project, a certain kind of socio-cultural work. Systematised and articulated in speech and writing, historical knowledge is above all a particular *language* of the past, a discourse on the past in which events are systematically ordered in knowable form and in which that order is expressed as meaningful – as the *sens de l'histoire*, the meaning, and direction, of history.

Under the modern political conditions of nationalism, the formation of 'national' states and of 'national' culture, the public definition of such meaning is, as we know, of considerable importance. Historical discourse, as a constitutive part of the culture of nationalism, is a cultural product which itself, in a very material way, 'makes sense' (that is, produces meaning and explanation) in the present. Historical discourse constitutes an ordering representation of past and present social reality that has its own conceptual, textual and, ultimately, institutionalised ideological weight in society.[9] Narratives of the true order and meaning of the past, informing the social world of the present and pointing the way to the future, claim a particular kind of social authority, both for themselves as statements of the truth and for their speakers, as those who authoritatively represent that truth.

In any attempt at writing a critical history, such discourses need to be interrogated as to their own social and political meanings, not faithfully transcribed as the truths they claim to be. In accounting for the

[7] Ricoeur, *Reality of the Historical Past*, 11, emphasis added.
[8] Duby, 'Histoire sociale et idéologies des sociétés'.
[9] De Certeau, 'L'Opération historique', 7ff., for 'the historical institution'.

particular form of a community's historical self-conception, we cannot assume simply that it speaks the truth because we (think we) detect some unexamined 'emotive resonance' that it seems to excite among 'the people'.[10] This would amount merely to accepting and re-transcribing a particular worldview, and self-view, on and in its own terms. We must, instead, investigate the social–historical location of such claims. This, in turn, is found in social conflicts expressed as struggles over the cultural and political power of authoritative representation, i.e. to speak the past and, through it, the present, of community and culture with legitimate authority – to produce a dominant definition of social reality.

The institution of particular narratives, particular patterns and figures of history giving 'authentic' meaning to the social world – ancestry, community, destiny; past, present and future – highlights certain conceptions and effaces others. When these authoritative definitions are reproduced in later scholarship (as, in the case of Algeria, they generally have been) the complexities and alternatives that were effaced in the course of the inscription of 'the nation and its truth' are left uninterrogated. But things could always have been different. As Algerian sociologist Fanny Colonna rightly insists, one could always 'have imagined a history quite other than that which is related here'.[11] Part of the task of dismantling the linear certainties of foundational master-narratives[12] must be the attempt to reveal the suppressed alternatives effaced or condemned by authoritative histories, in attempting to offer an equitable account of those who are shouted down in the courts of Final Judgement, abusively condemned in terms of, or equally abusively 'rehabilitated' into, ineluctable schemes in whose construction they had no part. It is just as necessary to do this as it is to examine and account for those forces that coalesced to make the actual outcomes that *have* occurred, without falling again into the determinist mode of thinking that creates the necessity of 'what really happened' while purporting merely to describe it.

The history investigated here, then, is not the closed narrative of Algeria's 'national destiny', but the still unfinished history of how such a notion has come to have particular meaning, of what that meaning has been, and what were, and might remain, its suppressed and potential alternatives. By investigating the ends – the purposes and consequences – of

[10] *Pace*, most notably, the work of Anthony D. Smith.

[11] Colonna, *Versets de l'invincibilité*, 357.

[12] That is, the 'grand narratives' of colonialism and nationalism, which, as Edmund Burke has pointed out, the historiography of the Maghrib has yet to 'go beyond' in a sustained and serious way (Burke, 'Theorizing the histories of colonialism and nationalism'); cf. Prakash, 'Writing post-Orientalist histories'.

transformations in historical imagination, the role they have played in the production of meaning in Algeria, and how they have shaped the dominant meanings *of* 'Algeria', I hope to move beyond the closed, univocal images of destiny, however imagined, that have consistently plagued our understanding of this part of the world. The mode of the presence of the past in Algeria, that mythologised place which came to stand, in the latter half of the twentieth century, as the epitome of both hope and horror, was not predestined to be that of a nightmare, an endless recurrence of the same hard, oppressive realities, the same impoverishment, the same convulsive extremes of atrocity. It could have been otherwise, and can be again.

Colonial modernity, culture and the nation

The colonial encounter, in Algeria as elsewhere, was constitutively marked by violence. But far from being a simple matter of the 'monologic' imposition of an unchanging European will on similarly unchanging, perennially passive or unyieldingly resisting others, colonialism was a relationship within which new, dialogical discursive practices of self-fashioning emerged.[13] A brief detour through the meanings of colonial modernity elsewhere in the world should elucidate this point.

Studying China, Mark Elvin suggested that 'modernity' be located in a distinctively new 'ability to create power', where power is understood, firstly as 'a capacity to direct energy' (in thermodynamics, factories, bureaucracy or the military), and, through the application of that power, as 'the capacity to change the structure of systems' – in nature, social organisation, economic production, or the worlds of thought and belief.[14] As recent work on colonialism and empire has shown, the process of generating and applying this power played out, not within an internal 'great transformation' of European societies, from which Europe would emerge as the torchbearer of civilisation throughout the world, but rather from the worldwide expansion and uneven impact of capitalism itself, to which all the barbarisms of empire, from slave-ships to napalm, as well as steam engines and rational-bureaucratic 'good government', were integral. Rather than being 'native' to Europe, and (more or less unsuccessfully) transplanted elsewhere, modernity was *inherently* colonial, the product of the uneven development of capitalist penetration, extraction, production and circulation right across the globe. Correlatively, in the

[13] Wolfe, 'History and imperialism', on 'monologic' accounts; for 'dialogic', Washbrook, 'Orients and Occidents'.
[14] Elvin, 'A working definition of "modernity"?'.

cultural as well as in the economic sphere, and in Algeria as throughout the Middle East, North Africa and elsewhere, the development of nationalism and contemporary forms of Islam cannot be understood as integrally oppositional resistance to the imposition of 'modern, Western civilisation'. On the contrary, contemporary cultures of nationalism and Islam are themselves the products of the profound, global transformations effected in the imperial interrelationships of societies and cultures throughout the modern world.

Modernity, then, is unevenly played out in different settings. Examining its impact on structures of thought and belief in the dominated majority of the world, Donald Donham, an anthropologist of east Africa, writes of the ways in which 'vernacular modernisms' emerged among the colonised and dominated themselves – how the dislocating impact of modern power produced, in the minds of Ethiopians as of others, judgements on their own society and culture which articulated, in locally specific cultural terms, visions of that culture as being, or as having become, 'backward'.[15] Donham writes: 'By "modernism", I mean a local, culturally encoded stance toward history, one that yearns to bring things "up to date".'[16] What the onset of such locally conceived modernism effects is not the appearance of globally homogeneous, universally 'modernised' societies in the sense classically given that term by Huntington or Lerner, or by more recent apostles of triumphant global capitalism,[17] but the transformation of peoples' views of themselves and their histories, the consequences of which are unpredictable: 'In a phrase, what has been altered are people's imaginations – their sense of their place in the world and the shape of their pasts and their futures.' From this profound change emerge complex local struggles over the meaning and direction of the past and future, and 'what is needed to follow them is . . . an ethnography of local historical imaginations'.[18]

This book traces just such a struggle over local historical imaginations, engaged in by an Algerian 'vernacular modernism' articulated in the

[15] It should be emphasised that European experiences and expressions of modernity too are, in this sense, 'vernacular'. In the relatively privileged zone of imperial interaction (including the metropolitan working classes), of course, the forms taken by the vernacular-modern historical imaginary were quite different. I am grateful to Gyan Prakash for discussion of this point.

[16] Donham, *Marxist Modern*, 185.

[17] Huntington, *Political Order in Changing Societies*; Lerner, *Passing of Traditional Society*. Universal modernisation narratives of the left, too, are rightly criticised for ignoring indigenous agency and the culturally specific forms taken by processes such as commodification, or the reification of value in cash. (See Feierman, 'Africa in history', commenting on Wolf, *Europe and the People Without History*.)

[18] Donham, *Marxist Modern*, xviii.

interrelated (indeed, indissociable) fields of culture, religion and history. The new visions of Algerian history and culture played a substantial, though never straightforward, part in the shaping of Algerian nationalism, endowing it with a particular cultural doctrine and thus framing what would become the dominant, newly legitimate definition of Algerian social reality, denoting the 'truth' of Algerian history and the meaning of 'national identity' – of what it meant to *be* 'Algerian'. In accounts of twentieth-century Algeria, this process has generally been considered simply in the terms in which its proponents themselves conceived it, as the 'recovery' and 'reassertion' of national selfhood. But like other, similar movements elsewhere in the colonial world, Algerian nationalism's social and cultural project did not, contrary to its own self-view, constitute a rebirth or recovery, the 'renaissance' of a self-contained civilisational character, an original 'national genius'. Its dominant historical imagination was not the simple restitution of a glorious national past freed from the falsifications of colonial ideology. Nor, contrary to certain scholars' views on nationalisms in Arab and Islamic societies, was it a 'failed modernism' or an 'anti-modernism', an inappropriately derivative effort crippled by its own ideological prejudice and 'resentment' of the dominant West. In Foucault's terms, nationalist discourse in colonial Algeria was a new kind of 'practice imposed on things', a new disciplinary order, changing the structures of thought about and practice of Islam and 'Algerian' culture and history, and imposing on them a new 'principle of their regularity'. This practice was also, both symbolically and physically, 'a violence'.[19] In this, though, it was not the expression (again) of some Algerian pathology, but rather the repercussion, mediated through and taken up in the self-fashioning practices of Algerians themselves, of the impact of colonialism's own relentless modernity.

This process involved nothing less than a seizure of symbolic power in the cultural realm, an attempt to reinvent Algerians' historical imaginations. In a much-quoted and influential passage, Partha Chatterjee observes what he calls a 'fundamental feature of anticolonial nationalisms in Asia and Africa': the division of the social world into two separate domains, the material and the spiritual, 'outside' and 'inside'. In the material realm of statecraft, economy, science and technology, the West reigns supreme and must be emulated; in the spiritual domain lie language, religion, the practices of family and communal life, 'the

19 'We must conceive of discourse as a violence that we do to things, or at least as a practice that we impose upon them; it is in this practice that the events of a discourse find the principle of their regularity': Foucault, *L'Ordre du discours*, 55.

"essential" marks of cultural identity', which must be preserved. Nationalism must create 'its own domain of sovereignty within colonial society well before it begins its political battle with the imperial power'. The colonial state

> is kept out of the 'inner' domain of national culture; but it is not as though this so-called spiritual domain is left unchanged. In fact, here nationalism launches its most powerful, creative, and historically significant project: to fashion a 'modern', national culture that is nevertheless not Western . . . *In this, its true and essential domain, the nation is already sovereign*, even when the state is in the hands of the colonial power.[20]

This 'inner domain', however, is neither impervious to assault from the 'outside' realm of new political, economic and scientific technologies of power[21] nor, within its own confines, is it the domain of sovereign selfhood that cultural nationalists themselves see in it. It too is a field of social struggle. Like any historically occurring form of human community, its boundaries and bonds created in the social imaginary,[22] a 'nation' is never an entity that can be positively, 'objectively' identified and defined, its 'natural' boundaries and internal characteristics fixedly described, but a field of rival representations, each claiming to articulate its 'authenticity'. This does not imply that 'nation' has no meaning, nor that it is somehow capable of 'an infinity of meanings'. The suggestion is rather that, in that it exists meaningfully at all, 'nation' *exists in the contests over meaning* engaged in by specifiable social actors, in particular historical conjunctures, with specific symbolic, linguistic and material resources present in the social world at a given moment in time. The nation only exists meaningfully in the struggle to 'hegemonise' its meaning; in contests over the symbolic power to name and represent the community. Nationalism, as Prasenjit Duara writes of China, 'is rarely the nationalism *of the nation* [hypostatised], but rather marks the site where different representations of the nation contest and negotiate with each other'.[23]

20 Chatterjee, *Nation and its Fragments*, 6, emphasis added.

21 Prakash, *Another Reason*, 201–3.

22 Clearly conceiving of the locus of community in social meaning, i.e. as a social imaginary, obviates the sterile recent argument in nationalism studies, centred on the non-question of whether 'nations' are 'real or imagined'. The point is that *only* imagined communities *are* 'real'; the only 'reality' – the only possible mode of existence – of any 'community' is *as* an imaginary (e.g. Cohen, *Symbolic Construction of Community*).

23 Duara, *Rescuing History*, 27. Recent historiography of the Maghrib has lagged, in this respect, far behind that of areas such as South Asia or China. Recent work on Egypt, Lebanon, Syria, Palestine, Jordan, Yemen, Iraq and Israel has also been more consistently engaged with these questions.

Such contests may be more or less democratic, or they may not be democratic at all. What is certain is that they are part of a broader field of social struggles, since, throughout the world, the politics of nationalism have, since the late eighteenth century, condensed both powerful discourses of emancipation and powerful systems of subjection. Like 'the state', in fact, I would argue that 'the nation', even in colonial contexts where it most clearly vehicled an ostensible project of liberation, 'never emerges except as a claim to domination'[24] – even 'national liberation' can only occur (or at least, in the Middle East and elsewhere in Africa and Asia, has in general only yet actually occurred) through the transformation of a subjugated 'native'-colonial society into a differently subjugated 'national' one. Sartre's apothegm is particularly relevant to the Algerian revolutionary and post-revolutionary experience: 'Never has *homo faber* better understood that he has made history – and never has he felt so powerless before history.'[25]

The thrust of this line of thinking is to insist on the social–historical embeddedness of the national imaginary; 'the nation-itself' does not exist separately, transhistorically, in any ontological sense, from these contests over representation and the actual socially and historically located people who engage in them. Nations, in short, exist only in their naming. Like other products of ideology, they *are real* only because they are *invoked* – called into existence and believed in – by human actors who order their lives, their sentiments and their sense of themselves and their pasts around them. 'The priest, says Nietzsche, is the one who "calls his own will God." The same could be said of the politician when he calls his own will "people", "opinion" or "nation." . . . The "people" is used these days just as in other times God was used – to settle accounts between clerics.'[26] 'Nations' (and 'Peoples') neither act nor speak; people do, and their acts of speaking are always grounded in the very practical, actual social life of struggles over production, appropriation,

[24] Abrams, 'Difficulty of studying the state', 77. 'The nation', in late eighteenth-century bourgeois liberal thought, marked the bourgeoisie's claim to domination over the popular masses, even as they were supposedly incorporated into the body of the self-manifesting sovereign People. In the colonial New World, late eighteenth-century nationalism is more visible as a mode of domination in the racialised divisions it drew between incorporated and subject populations. The new American nation as 'bearer of the rights of man' was conceived within the same process as the expansion of black slavery, and the decline of white indentured labour (Wolfe, 'Land, labor, and difference', 874ff.). In the 'pioneer' nationalisms of Latin America, creole élites were motivated to independence from Spain by 'the fear of "lower-class" political mobilizations: . . . Indian or Negro-slave uprisings' (Anderson, *Imagined Communities*: 48).

[25] *What is Literature?* quoted in Young, *White Mythologies*, 31.

[26] Bourdieu, *Language and Symbolic Power*, 210, 214.

expression and domination. Nor is this simply a case of restating a tired argument on the reality of class struggle against the false consciousness of nationalism. Rather, the approach to 'nation' here is the same as that of Stedman Jones to 'class', that is, 'as a discursive rather than as an ontological reality', it being impossible to ascertain 'what sort of substantive reality [it] might have possessed outside the particular historical idioms in which it has been ascribed meaning'.[27]

If, then, a domain of 'sovereign' national culture is created within colonial society, and this creation is a new historical process emerging from the experience of colonialism, the 'sovereign' culture thus produced is itself a product of struggles for dominance in the cultural field. Rather than an uncoerced expression of the already-homogeneous whole of colonial society, it is, first of all, the domain of those who most effectively assert themselves as spokesmen for 'the nation'. This does not mean that the objects of such struggle remain abstract – on the contrary, what is at stake is the outcome of the very practical social struggle over which of many imaginable realities will actually be inscribed into real life, into people's minds, bodies, behaviours and perceptions, and the laws governing them. As Balibar puts it: 'The fundamental problem is . . . *to produce the people*. More exactly, it is to make the people produce itself continually as national community.'[28] It is not so much, then, that '*the nation* is already sovereign' in '*its* inner domain', as that those particular social actors who hold the symbolic capital of what emerges as the legitimate, modern national culture exercise a certain sovereignty over that domain, over the legitimate 'self-expression' of the community – that is, they exercise ownership of the means of production of community itself.

This is an entirely different proposition from the more conventional (and conservative) assertion that a necessary part of national development lies in the 'renewal' of 'authentic national selfhood' by a class of intellectuals, notably historians, philologists and clerics. It is one thing to claim that nationalist intellectuals 'saved national culture' from oppression and thus contributed to the achievement (or recovery) of sovereignty. It is quite another to interrogate such claims, the acts of cultural

[27] Stedman Jones, *Languages of Class*, 1–2. Cf., for contemporary Egypt, Amr Ibrahim's emphasis on the importance in social competition of 'those entitled to speak in the name of the symbolic law which is constitutive of the community' (Ibrahim, 'Egypte: luttes pour l'appropriation', 80), and for Morocco, Mohamed Tozy's study of 'the mode of production of symbolic values and their investment in the political' (Tozy, 'Monopolisation de la production symbolique').

[28] Balibar, 'The nation form', 94, emphasis added. Cf. Renan's notion of the nation as a 'daily plebiscite': *Qu'est-ce qu'une nation?*

production engaged in by social actors who thereby constitute themselves as spokesmen for 'the nation', appropriating to themselves the symbolic goods of social truth.

Salafī modernism

The ultimate realisation of Algerian statehood in 1962 was the work of the militant, populist, revolutionary avant-garde that created the FLN and embarked, against overwhelming odds and the reason of their elders, on armed struggle. Their history has generally been understood within a wider, totalising narrative, that of 'the national movement', which has subsumed all of colonial Algeria's political struggles into a neat and coherent story typical of nationalist historiographies. A clearer understanding of the culture of nationalism, and of the relation of the cultural work of national self-fashioning to the political field, requires a disaggregation of this totalising scheme, and the teasing out of its separate, conflicting histories. Recent scholarship on the social and political history of Algerian nationalism has greatly elucidated the internal complexities of the revolutionary populist movement.[29] The cultural history of nationalism, however, has not received the same attention, and the story told in this book, that of the reformist *'ulamā*,[30] has arguably been long in need of re-examination.[31]

The modernist movement for the reform (*iṣlāḥ*) of Islam, also referred to as the *salafiyya* movement (since its members posited a return to the supposed purity of the earliest Islamic tradition, that of the 'pious ancestors', *al-salaf al-ṣāliḥ*), coalesced in Algeria in the early 1920s, in a group of *'ulamā* around shaykh 'Abd al-Ḥamīd Ben Bādīs (1889–1940), the most prominent exponent of reformed Sunni Islam in North Africa. Ben Badis and his colleagues organised themselves in the Association of Algerian Muslim *'ulamā*, (*jam'īyat al-'ulamā al-muslimīn al-jazā'iriyyīn*, in French

[29] Especially the work of Harbi, Carlier, Meynier and Stora.

[30] Sing. *'ālim*: a learned scholar of Islam.

[31] The best general study of the movement in Algeria is still Merad, *Réformisme*. Ending with the death of Ben Badis (1940), his work is a study of the movement's origins and diffusion written (in the 1960s) very much in the light of the movement itself and its assumed contribution to a 'national awakening'. Fanny Colonna's *Versets de l'invincibilité* and Kamel Chachoua's *Islam kabyle* are important recent revisions which also consider the movement's later, and long-term, consequences, as well as reconsidering its relation to 'local knowledge' in two berberophone regions (the Aurès and Kabylia respectively). A detailed sociological study for the region of Oran (concluding in the mid-1940s) is Mohammed el-Korso, 'Politique et religion en Algérie'. Recent contributions in Arabic are Zerrūqī, *Jihād ibn Bādīs*, Muṭabbaqānī, *Jam'iyat al-'ulamā'*, and Sa'd, *Ḥarakat 'Abd al-Ḥamīd ibn Bādīs*; all focus on Ben Badis as a national figurehead.

Figure 1. 'Abd al-Hamid Ben Badis (1889–1940). (Reproduced from Ageron, *Histoire de l'Algérie contemporaine*, vol. II. By permission of Presses universitaires de France.)

the Association des *'ulamā* musulmans algériens, hence the acronym AUMA), founded in Algiers in May 1931.

The Association's activities in the field of intellectual and cultural production constituted a significant socio-cultural and, implicitly, political project. This project participated in a double contest, both against the monopolisation of legitimate knowledge and cultural superiority by colonial France and against the competing projects of rival Algerian spokesmen for the 'authentic' representation of the indigenous Algerian community. From 1931 until the end of the Association's independent existence in 1956–7, the AUMA provided the organisational base for a campaign to gain exclusive control of the cultural authority to define 'the true religion' in Algeria, an aim that would be ratified after independence when the reformists' Islam became the religion of state.[32] Their objective in the religious field was part of a total social project that placed the *'ulamā* at the heart of the task of 'resurrecting' Algerian Muslim society, a task in which education was the central theme. Within this 'work of renewal' through proselytism and pedagogy, history played a significant role – indeed, the reformists' 'contribution' to Algerian nationalism is often situated specifically in their historiographic production.[33] It was the reformists, with their drive for modern societal education in Arabic and Islam, who first provided Algerians with a nationalist history intended to map out, in Arabic, their community's glorious past and the way to the future they saw as necessary for it.

It has often been supposed that the reformist *'ulamā* thus made a crucial, constitutive contribution to the dynamic growth of 'the national movement' leading inexorably to the revolution. This has particularly been the case where schematic models of 'national development' have cast around for cultural 'awakeners', who in every case are expected to arouse the masses from their slumbers, and have found them, for Algeria, in the *salafīs*.[34] In the context of debate on the political Islam of the 1980s, Jean-Claude Vatin provided a timely counter to this assumption:

> One need not delve deep into history to see the reduced role of Islam in the struggle for national independence in North Africa. At the end of the colonial period, the Muslim cultural and religious code *did not* underpin the resistance, *whatever governments and official commentators may have later claimed.* In the case of Algeria, the *'ulamā* were said to have infused the nationalist discourse with religious slogans and Qur'anic quotations. At that time all political movements (most of which had secular programs) had to submit to the terms of the *'ulamā*'s requirements . . . [But] Islam did not, in fact, provide the ideological foundation of the war.[35]

[32] Article 4 of the 1963 Constitution (*JORA* 63, 10 Sept. 1963, 888ff., repr. *AAN* 2 (1963), 852ff.), which included the guarantee of freedom of opinion and belief; art. 2 of the 1976 Constitution (*JORA* XV/94, 24 Nov. 1976, 1042ff., repr. *AAN* 15 (1976), 770ff.) dissociated the official status of Islam from this guarantee, which was demoted to art. 53.

[33] Touati, 'Algerian historiography'; Haddab, 'Histoire et modernité'; Kaddache, *Nationalisme algérien*, 226–7; Ruedy, *Modern Algeria*, 136.

[34] This is Merad's position, echoed by Christelow (*Muslim Law Courts*, introduction) and most other scholars.

[35] Vatin, 'Seduction and sedition', 161, emphasis added.

The debate on the role of the reformists has, in fact, been vigorous, with positions ranging from assertions that the AUMA had 'a key role in awakening nationalist consciousness'[36] and the claim that 'without the Association of '*ulamā*, Algeria in 1954 would have been [powerless as] a feather swept away by the wind'[37] through Mahfoud Kaddache's evaluation of their political ambivalence,[38] to Abdelkader Djeghloul's contention that it is in a travesty of their true historical significance that 'the '*ulamā* . . . are sometimes bizarrely considered as nationalists'.[39]

The terms of this discussion reflect a tendency still dominant in the historiography of modern Algeria, assuming as its metanarrative the teleological development of a unified and unifying 'national movement', in terms of whose single, coherent story every other aspect of Algerian history and each constituent part of society are judged according to what might be reckoned as their 'contribution' to the eventual and predestined freedom of the nation. In fact, however, what was actually going on, in Algeria as elsewhere, was a continuous struggle among competing actors and their different visions and aspirations for the cultural and political power to create 'the nation' as an effective ideological form, one which has always been (and which, as yet, generally remains) as much an instrument of domination as a means of emancipation. To specify the position of the '*ulamā* in this contest, a clearer appreciation of the significance of 'nation' in the political context of colonial Algeria is required.

There was a fundamental, though unacknowledged, tension in Algerian nationalism between a conception of the nation as *will*, a dream to be inscribed in reality through human agency, and as *essence*, a prior, deep truth requiring revelation to those who have not known it, and recognition by those who deny it. The former, voluntarist notion was that of Algeria's populist, revolutionary nationalism embodied in the emigrant workers' party, the PPA (Parti du peuple algérien) whose internal strife eventually gave birth to the FLN. Mohamed Harbi, a veteran militant of the party, writes:

> In fact, the Algerian nation – and the old nationalists themselves are beginning to realise this – never existed save as the will of a minority of *étatistes*, the militants of the PPA. Blocked in their development, a group of them [would] decide to force the course of history, unify the Algerians through the FLN, here by persuasion,

36 Christelow, 'Ritual, culture, and politics', 255; Merad, *Réformisme, passim.*

37 Sa'adallah, 'Jam'īyat al-'ulamā wa'l-siyāsa', in his *Abḥāth wa-ārā fī ta'rīkh al-Jazā'ir*, IV, 147.

38 Kaddache, *Nationalisme algérien*, 223.

39 Djeghloul, 'Formation des intellectuels', 657.

there by violence, bringing them to see themselves as belonging to *Algeria* rather than to a party or a region.[40]

The second, essentialist conception was that promoted by the *salafī* reformists from the mid-1920s, and which would dominate political culture and cultural politics in Algeria after independence. Their project, however, was by no means uncontested in the later colonial period in which it arose, and the struggle for its implementation did not suddenly end after independence, when it reached its fullest development. Although the reformists' message did, after 1962, and especially after 1967,[41] achieve a considerable hegemony in the state's institutions of cultural, educational and religious policy, the struggle would remain an ongoing hegemonic process in which Algerians are still both creatively and destructively engaged.

What was certainly achieved, however, between the 1920s and the 1950s was the appropriation by the reformists of a certain cultural capital, the occupation of ground to which their rivals in speaking for 'Algeria' could not, for one reason or another, lay claim. After the revolution, to which, as Vatin observed, their message was instrumental, not fundamental, the reformists' nation-as-essence was retroactively projected into an eternal Algeria, recast in the nationalist imaginary as a unified community of faith and resistance. This integrative national imaginary was precisely what the adoption of the reformists' worldview by the 'unanimist' (or 'monist'[42]) state of the 1960s and 1970s was intended to achieve. Only thus could the bloody internecine history of the revolution, and the violent struggle of the revolutionaries (against the French, against recalcitrant Algerians and against each other) to impose themselves as the nation's only legitimate representatives, be rendered invisible, 'forgotten' like Renan's St Bartelémy and the Albigensian crusade.[43]

But what did this mean for the *'ulamā* themselves? What was the significance of their project, if their relation to the revolution was not that of causal contribution ascribed to them in the smoothly unifying teleology of 'the national movement'? What had they really intended,

[40] Harbi, *L'Algérie et son destin*, 24.

[41] Harbi (interview, Paris, 2004) points out that it was in the aftermath of Tahar Zbiri's attempted coup of December 1967 that the reformists and their heirs gained significant power within the regime. Their prominence, and that of more radical Islamists sometimes claiming their inheritance *against* the regime, became more pronounced from 1970 onwards (cf. Rouadjia, *Frères et la mosquée*, esp. pp. 20–3, ch. 6).

[42] The term is Sami Zubaida's.

[43] Anderson, *Imagined Communities* (2nd edn), ch. 11. On the internecine struggles in the FLN, see Harbi, *FLN: mirage et réalité* and Meynier, *Histoire intérieure du FLN*.

and what became of these intentions? And in what sense, and why, if the *'ulamā* were not its inspiration, did the revolution nonetheless, in Vatin's telling phrase, have to 'submit to the terms of [their] requirements'? This book is about their limited success, and the failures that went with it.

In the process of examining this history, it also becomes clear that the crucial question in Algeria, again, as elsewhere in Africa and Asia, has not (despite mountainous literature to the contrary) been about a perpetual conflict between 'tradition' or 'authenticity' – or 'Islam' – vs. 'modernity', but about an ongoing struggle over what *kind* of modernity, and what kind of modern politics and culture, should be assumed – among other things, over the extent to which they will be pluralist or exclusionary, consensual or unanimist, more or less democratic, or not democratic at all. It is necessary to resist the idea that the roles of history and Islam in the creation of national and revolutionary imaginaries in the Middle East and North Africa have been as forces of 'tradition' acting against 'modernity'. On the contrary, and in contrast with the reformist movements of the eighteenth century (which had nothing to do with nationalism) such as those of Muḥammmad ibn 'Abd al-Wahhāb in Nejd, or Muḥammad al-Shawkānī in Yemen, those who saw themselves as the reformists (*muṣliḥīn*) of Islam in the nineteenth and twentieth centuries were strictly unable to escape the ubiquitous presence of Europe, which by the time this story begins, in 1899, had already been in almost total physical possession of Algeria for a half-century. As Ahmad Dallal points out:

> The problems that informed eighteenth-century [Islamic] reform ideas bore no resemblance whatsoever to those that inspired and drove later reforms . . . Europe is notably absent from the thought of all the major thinkers of the eighteenth century . . . For most eighteenth century thinkers, the Islamic past was still a continuous reality . . . For the thinkers of [the] late nineteenth and early twentieth centuries . . . this past had to be rediscovered and reconstructed.[44]

This recomposition of the past, and the reconfiguration of contemporary, colonially transformed societies' relationship to it, took place in a profoundly restructured world in which the violent embrace of Europe and the saturating power of modernity could no longer be ignored.

The social life of words

I began with a passage from Jacque Berque's 1953 lecture, 'What is a North African "tribe"?', a title that clearly echoed Renan's famous address of 1882, 'What is a nation?' In addressing the subject, Berque

[44] Dallal, 'Appropriating the past', 333–4.

highlighted, in a characteristic flight of intensely incisive speculation that, even to his mind, was 'surely to carry our doubts too far', the role of words, of 'purely linguistic play', in the formation of histories and of the morphology of social groups. It has since become commonplace to discuss the ways in which naming and representation – as 'heretic' or 'orthodox', 'nomadic' or 'sedentary', 'Oriental' or 'Western' – function in the creation and institutionalisation of groups and identities. And in North Africa and the Middle East, as elsewhere throughout the world, ordinary people are still faced daily with social conflicts that manifest themselves (whatever other causes they may in fact, or also, express) as religious struggles over what Berque called 'the themes of authenticity and purism', with 'the search for oneself,' the legitimate shape of cultural, and political, community. In Algeria, this has been precisely the idiom of expression of an unimaginably atrocious war that tore the country asunder in the final decade of the twentieth century.

In this context, Berque's notion that we might examine that part of history and social morphology that 'hangs on the life of words' – mere words – may seem to offer little. The suggestion, though, appears to me to be a suitably modest, suitably quiet point of departure, well away from endless clichés of 'fury' and 'revenge', for a critical exploration of the relationship between forms of historical self- perception, Islamic culture, and the nationalist struggle in colonial Algeria. Berque's insight is an appropriate starting-point for a rereading of nationalism as the attempt to create and impose a dominant language of Algeria's cultural and historical reality. This study explores the ways in which a particular discourse of Islam and the Algerian past sought to establish a dominant representation of 'Algeria'; how particular spokesmen articulated this language, how they presented a newly invented form of self-understanding as a 'restoration', a return to the 'authenticity' of changeless truth; and how they sought to constitute themselves, in a frequently bitter struggle against their rivals, as the pre-eminent spokesmen for that truth. Central to their story is the dialogic relationship of colonialism in which they found themselves, a relationship whose consequences belie their own, and their subsequent interpreters', attempts to characterise them as that which they claimed to be: the guardians and revivifiers of a pristine, inviolate national selfhood. For their supposedly pristine language of national history spoke irredeemably colonial words.

This, precisely, was the irony of colonialism's ruthless assertion of its own self-assured dominance. Not only the politics but also the culture of nationalism, and the imagination of a 'national' past, would appear, not against and in spite of colonialism and from the depths of an inviolate self, but out of the very transformations wrought by colonial power.

nationalism: by-product of Colonialism

Despite the claims so often made today, in the name on the one hand, of ethno-linguistic or religious particularisms of 'identity', and on the other, of the fundamentally irreconcilable and geopolitically determining nature of sharply divided 'civilisations', the last two centuries' history remains one of the worldwide, radical transformation of social and cultural forms in an increasingly, inescapably interconnected and massively unequal relationship of subjection and domination. Even a colonised society's 'own' languages could not escape the invasive transformations wrought by its enforced dialogue with colonial modernity. No more could the language of 'its own' history. Nothing, though, in the distant past or the colonial present, predetermined what the new words would be that would make sense of it all, nor what new worlds such words would eventually conjure up and fill.

Prologue: Tunis, 1899

As the nineteenth century drew to a close, and France's North African empire seeped slowly in at the borders of the Moroccan sultanate, the scholar Aḥmad al Nāṣirī, writing in the long-established Islamic historical idiom of the dynastic chronicle, completed his history of the 'Alawi rulers of Morocco:

> Know too that during these years the power of these Europeans has advanced to a shocking and reprehensible height, and has manifested itself in a manner the like of which has never before been seen. The progress and improvement in their condition of life have accelerated at an ever-growing pace . . . Indeed, we are on the brink of a time of utter corruption.[1]

This was in 1897. Two years later, at the other extremity of the Maghrib, in a narrow lane in the heart of the old city of Tunis, a son was born to an Algerian family who, like many others, had fled their lands over the previous sixty years to escape from the manifest power of Europe and the 'utter corruption' it had wrought. The view of the world into which he was born as one of 'shocking and reprehensible' change, as 'a time of corruption', was impressed early upon the boy's mind, along with a highly religious sense of a duty not to endure such change. Growing up in Tunis after the turn of the century, Aḥmad Tawfīq al-Madanī saw in the world around him the effects of unbridled and illegitimate changes in social and cultural order, the 'corruption' of truths that had to be recovered in their original purity.

The remedy for this corruption, however, was to him not spiritual retrenchment and isolation from the world, nor illuminary and 'cleansing' jihad, as older forms of Maghribi Islam might have proposed, but an intellectual search for, and return to, the enlightenment of origins (*uṣūl*), and faithfulness to a discoverable, and essentially unalterable, condition of 'authenticity' (*aṣāla*), an underlying and inalienable true selfhood which must, as he saw it, lie in the history of his community. It

[1] Al-Nasiri, *Kitāb al-istiqṣā*, IX, 208.

was to the writing of this history that he would devote much of his life, and in terms of the same belief that he would tell his own life's story.

Al-Madani opens his autobiography, *Ḥayāt Kifāḥ*[2] ('A Life of Struggle'), a monument in three volumes composed in Algiers in the mid-1970s, with a verse from the thirty-third chapter of the Qur'ān, *Sūrat al-Aḥzāb*:

Some were there among the faithful who made good what they had promised to God. Some have fulfilled their course, and others await [its fulfilment], and have not been changelings who change.[3]

Changelessness and continuity, faithfulness to a 'life of struggle', is the theme of his memoir, a model of nationalist self-representation. 'This is a blessed child,' he reports his maternal grandfather, 'Omar Boyrâz, telling his mother. 'I hope he may live a *mujāhid*, and die a martyr.'[4] At the very beginning of the first chapter of his life-story, al-Madani identifies himself with a tradition of unyielding resistance and struggle which had led his grandparents, both maternal and paternal, to perform *hijra* (emigration) from Algeria after the collapse of the last great anti-colonial uprising of the nineteenth century, the insurrection of 1871 led in Kabylia by a rural notable, the *bachaga* al-Moqrānī, and a religious leader, shaykh al-Ḥaddād of the Raḥmāniyya brotherhood.[5] To escape the increasingly coercive occupation of the capital, his father, Muḥammad ibn Aḥmad, and grandfather had left their home in Algiers and travelled east, to the Djurdjura mountains of Kabylia, in 1870. Having participated in Moqrani's revolt until its defeat, they moved on eastwards in the company of Si 'Omar ibn Muṣṭafa Boyrâz al-Turkī, whose father, in 1830, had commanded the Algerian cavalry at the battle of Staouëli (an attempt to prevent the French marching inland from their beachhead towards Algiers) and whose daughter would be Muhammad al-Madani's wife. It is thus only after the last gasp of 'primary' resistance that the families of the writer's parents, having fought the French from the first, are supposed to have left Algeria. They settled in Tunis, where Ahmad Tawfiq's father and mother were married and where, he says,

2 Hereafter *HK*.
3 Q 33:23 (tr. Rodwell).
4 *HK*, I, 6–7 (*mujāhid:* a fighter for the faith).
5 On the doctrine and practice of *hijra* from colonised territory: Clancy-Smith, *Rebel and Saint*; Masud, 'Obligation to migrate'; Ageron, 'L'émigration des musulmans algériens'. *Bachaga* (Turkish *bāsh-āghā*) was an Ottoman title for a senior provincial governor, preserved in the indirect rule system of rural French North Africa. The Rahmaniyya *ṭarīqa* (sufi brotherhood) was one of the most extensive and popular networks of Islam in nineteenth-century Algeria.

'I was born on 1 November 1899 (24 Jumada II 1317),[6] the son of two noble Algerian families of faithful combatants and émigrés.'[7]

Tawfiq al-Madani, around whose individual history much of the wider story of this book will be told, is an intriguingly marginal figure in the history of the contemporary Maghrib. In some respects well known, he certainly left behind, at his death in Algiers in November 1983, a large number of traces to mark his passing through his turbulent century. A substantial body of writing in the Arabic press, political speeches and memoranda, and interventions in public life, many of them preserved, in necessarily distorted fragments, in the archives of France's colonial governments, exist alongside a dozen or so works of history and geography, and the more than 1,300 pages in which he set down his own narrative of himself as he wished his compatriots and their children to read it. In the words of one Algerian historian, he is 'an emblematic figure of our history'.[8] Others – particularly the younger generation, the vast majority of Algeria's population – have never heard of him. He is often briefly quoted and accorded passing reference in scholarly works on North African history, but his own historiography, and his own story, and the ways they might relate to contemporary Algerian history more broadly, have not hitherto been seriously examined.

This book, however, is in no sense a biography. Rather, in order to articulate my exploration of the relationship between history, culture and nationalism in Algeria, I have chosen to tell a series of short stories which move in time and space between and around the cities of Tunis, Algiers and Constantine, and from the mid-nineteenth century to the mid-twentieth. There are forays, too, beyond these limits, when the sense of the story demands it. The cast of characters is quite large, and the detail of the narrative necessarily inconsistent – it has been necessary sometimes to give very 'thick' descriptions of apparently minuscule events, while momentous developments are sometimes passed over in a few lines. To give a 'centre' to the enquiry overall – a deliberately shifting, unstable centre, a mobile pivot around which a series of stories turn – I therefore periodically refer back to the itinerary of Ahmad Tawfiq al-Madani.

This choice is deliberate, a conscious artifice of my own, but it is neither fortuitous nor unwarranted. One of the most prolific writers and

[6] The second Arabic edition, referred to here, has 1889, and the French translation has 1898. The *hijri* date, internal indications in the text and other sources concur on 1899. A more intriguing question concerns the proleptic date of 1 November.

[7] 'Salīl 'ā'ilatayn min kirām al-muhājirīn al-mujāhidīn al-jazā'iriyyīn.' (*HK*, I, 13).

[8] Personal communication. The official *Majallat al-ta'rikh* (Algiers) 18 (1985) was a commemorative volume dedicated to al-Madani.

Figure 2. Call for subscribers for the publication of al-Madani's first historical work, *Qarṭājanna fī arbaʿat ʿuṣūr*, a history of North Africa from the Stone Age to the Islamic conquest. Seized by French officials at Tozeur. (ADN.)

intellectuals associated with Algerian Islamic reformism in the colonial period, al-Madani was responsible for the largest corpus of specifically historical writing in Arabic produced in this period of Algerian history. Where his name is known, it is generally as one of two with whom modern Algerian historiography in Arabic (and Algerian 'national history') is considered to have begun, the second being his colleague, shaykh Mubārak ibn Muḥammad al-Mīlī, whom we shall also meet in the course of our story.[9] Both are important figures in the intellectual and cultural history of Algeria in the first half of the twentieth century, associated with the Islamic reformist movement both in its informal stage prior to 1931 and in the Association of Algerian Muslim *'ulamā* thereafter. While al-Mili died prematurely, nine years before the beginning of his country's war of liberation, al-Madani would go on to become secretary-general of the Association of *'ulamā* in the first years of the revolution, and then to play a prominent role as accredited Arabic-language spokesman of, and ambassador for, Algeria in the countries of the Middle East. At independence, he would be the Republic's first minister of *habous* (with responsibility for culture and religious affairs[10]), a post he had already held in the first revolutionary provisional government of 1958.

Al-Madani's political role, like his part in the Algerian *salafiyya* movement, was decided by his mastery of language. Editor of the reformists' newspaper, *al-Baṣā'ir*, author of the nationalist history *Kitāb al-Jazā'ir*, one of Algeria's finest public speakers, he was one of the reformists' foremost writers and orators, and is generally referred to as such in histories of the movement – as 'the historian' of Algerian nationalism's intellectual wing,[11]

9 Desparmet, 'Naissance d'une histoire "nationale"'; Bencheneb, 'Quelques historiens'; Lanasri, *Littérature algérienne*; Murtāḍ, *Nahḍat al-adab*; Kaddache, *Nationalisme algérien*; Haddab, 'Histoire et modernité'; Touati, 'Algerian historiography'. Al-Mili was born in el-Milia in 1897, and died in Constantine in 1945. Although al-Mili's single historical work, *Ta'rīkh al-Jazā'ir fī 'l-qadīm wa-'l-ḥadīth*, is frequently cited as the first modern, national history of Algeria, it was in fact preceded by two years by al-Madani's first sustained historical text (*Qarṭājanna fī arba'at 'uṣūr*), which, though apparently concentrating on Ifriqiya (Tunisia), is presented as a history of the whole of North Africa in antiquity. The latter's most significant contribution (and also his one work which is frequently cited), *Kitāb al-Jazā'ir*, an encyclopaedia of Algerian history, geography and politics, appeared in 1932, the same year as al-Mili's second volume.

10 *Habous* (*ḥubūs*, in the Mashriq *waqf*, pl. *awqāf*), property endowed for the maintenance of religious establishments. The cabinet of September 1962 had no separate culture portfolio.

11 Where he is mentioned in the literature, it is for his best-known text, *Kitāb al-Jazā'ir*, invariably considered as evidence of 'Algeria's national awakening': e.g. Bencheneb, 'Quelques historiens', 499, and after him Ruedy, *Modern Algeria*, 134–5; Vatin, 'Conditions et formes', 896; W. Rollman, 'Introduction', in Le Gall and Perkins (eds.), *Maghrib in Question*.

one of 'the great auxiliaries' of Ben Badis.[12] His own, self-ascribed, role was as spokesman and representative of Algerian nationalism, and especially – among the revolution's francophone politicians and hard-bitten guerrilla chiefs – of the *culture* of Algerian nationalism, both during the revolution, when he wrote and broadcast on behalf of the FLN, and in his self-presentation to posterity through the three volumes of his autobiography.

This position he wished for himself, as a pre-eminent representative of the 'national identity', the 'authentic' culture and historical 'personality' of Algeria – singular, essentially changeless and reaffirmed through continuous struggle – he was never quite able to establish. His works circulated among a very small audience and, even as a government minister, he was far from exercising any great intellectual, political or cultural influence. But the principal elements of this self-view, and of the view of Algeria and its history which is condensed into it, have been enormously powerful, in Algerian nationalism's own official histories and also in many accounts of that history.[13] The dominance of this trope of singular destiny, of nationalism as the recovery of an unchanged, authentic selfhood, has obscured the extraordinary complexity of what actually occurred in the making of the discourse of the nation, the struggles it occasioned, the cultural diversity it effaced and the political possibilities it ultimately obliterated.

All this is highly ironic when one considers al-Madani himself, his own complicated, cross-border and even cosmopolitan trajectory, his tarbush-and-tie-wearing modernism, his identification with a movement of religious intellectuals whose own canonical forms of knowledge and communication had so little in common with his work, which ranged from the theatre to commentary on international affairs; his claimed association with anyone and everyone, from Abdülmecit II, the last Ottoman caliph, and Shakīb Arslān, the Druze notable and interwar pan-Islamist, to Gamāl 'Abd al-Nāṣir and 'Abd al-Karīm Qāsim, secular pan-Arab presidents of revolutionary Egypt and Iraq. Far from being representative of a singular immutability, he was distinctively *not* 'one thing only'. And although his writings receive more attention in this book than they have generally hitherto been accorded, he is interesting

[12] Merad, *Réformisme*, 116–18.

[13] E.g. in French, Ghalem and Remaoun (eds.), *Comment on enseigne l'histoire en Algérie*; Koulakssis and Meynier, *Emir Khaled*; in English, Le Gall and Perkins (eds.), *Maghrib in Question*; in Arabic, the works of the doyen of contemporary Algerian historians, Abū 'l-Qāsim Sa'adallah (e.g. *Abḥāth wa ārā fi ta'rīkh al-Jazā'ir*, *al-Ḥaraka 'l-waṭaniyya 'l-jazā'iriyya*).

not as an 'author', as the independently creative consciousness at the origin of forces shaping the nationalist history and culture of Algeria, but as a product of those forces, whose imprint is legible both in the works he composed and in the refiguring of his actual life to meet the requirements of their narrative scheme. I do not mean by this that the nationalist culture and the national past of Algeria were themselves impersonal, metahistorical and outside human agency. Nor, however, do they originate in one creative genius or national hero-saviour. The aim here is to discern, in part through al-Madani, the broader social process of the production of the discourse of Algeria's national selfhood, in which he participated and which reshaped him. It is because, despite himself, he stands so well for the very complexity of historical experience which his own self-presentation to posterity as the incarnation of the history of nationalism ultimately seeks to efface that he seems to me precisely *not* 'representative', but an appropriately 'emblematic' figure. Emblematic, that is, of the irrevocable complexity of history and culture brought about by colonialism and modernity, and of the ultimate impossibility of simply rejecting such complexity as 'corruption', of simply 'returning' to an imagined condition of singular, self-sufficient purity.

Al-Madani's birthplace was 'one of those Arab houses built at the end of the Hafsid period, at number four, rue de la Noria; the street that runs between the rue du Pasha and the rue du Tribunal'.[14] Twisting awkwardly between the two smart, principal arteries of the patrician, *beldi* quarter of late-nineteenth century Tunis, the nahj al-Nā'ūra is the narrowest lane in this part of the city.[15] On the edge of the heart of upper-bourgeois Tunis, the hub of Tunisian anti-colonialism in the early 1920s, the unremarkable alley where al-Madani was born is a peculiarly marginal, liminal place. A son of combative exiles, he would retrace his grandparents' steps when he was himself exiled, in June 1925, from the country of his birth to that of his forebears. He settled in Algiers, 'the city of my ancestors',[16] where he lived the rest of his life.[17] Asked about him, Tunisians not uncommonly think of him as an Algerian, and Algerians as a Tunisian. In a sense, Tawfiq al-Madani,

[14] *HK*, I, 13.

[15] In contrast to its usual usage elsewhere, *beldi* in Tunis refers to the old-established, patrician urban class. On the nahj el-Bācha quarter, the importance it retained into the 1920s and its subsequent decline, see Berque, *Maghreb entre deux guerres*, 205–21.

[16] *HK*, I, 340.

[17] Save for the years of the revolution from 1956 to 1962, when he joined the FLN's External Delegation in Cairo, and his various missions as ambassador to Iran, Iraq, Turkey and Pakistan from the mid-1960s to early 1970s.

the self-declared spokesman of history as permanence, of the return to an essentially changeless selfhood, was himself emblematic of the coerced shifts and transformations, the endless exiles and alienated homecomings, the irremediable 'corrupting' change and the reimagined, 'authentic' changelessness that colonialism forced on Algeria, and through which Algeria had to reconquer itself.

1 The margins of a world in fragments Maghribi voices in exile: Algeria, Tunisia, Europe and the East

Controlled movements

1830 was an end of the world. The Ottoman Regency of Algiers was the first of the caliph's Mediterranean Muslim domains to fall decisively to a modern European power, and the consequences were such that the Europeans, indeed, did not know quite how to proceed and were drawn into expansive conquest more by the maelstrom of conjunctural forces unleashed by the epochal event of the fall of Algiers itself than by any deliberate, considered policy.[1] For conquerors and conquered this was 'an event of a different kind',[2] one that would profoundly influence the whole shape and meaning of the modern world in French and North African eyes, and that would have far-reaching echoes throughout the Mediterranean world and beyond through the end of the nineteenth century and well into the second half of the twentieth.

Nationalist history tells a story of restoration, of recovery or 'renewal'[3] of the world and the community lost, at a moment of interruption in 'natural' historical time, by the unnatural irruption of foreign domination into the space of national evolution. Such tropes have been remarkably resilient in writing about the Maghrib. Critical historiography of nationalism, including perforce of anti-colonial nationalisms, perhaps too often romanticised, has elsewhere long sought to situate nationalisms and their visions of history within the social-historical contexts of their own production, to see nationalist discourses and practices, and the nations constituted by them, as problematic artefacts created in a field of conflict,

[1] Despite protests to the contrary (e.g. Sahli, *Décoloniser l'histoire*), France's new imperialism proceeded 'piecemeal and haphazardly' and not according to a premeditated 'master plan' (Clancy-Smith, *Rebel and Saint*, 258; Andrew and Kanya-Forstner, 'Centre and periphery').

[2] Hourani, *History of the Arab Peoples*, 269.

[3] Smith, 'Golden Age and national renewal'.

and not as natural products of unilinear evolution. Modern Algerian history, however, has continued to be narrated in 'evolutionary' terms: the canonical narrative moves from conquest and primary resistance (1830–70), through quietism (1870–1919), to a 'reawakening' (1919–45) which leads, through political reformism, to the armed revolution whose first shots are fired in the aborted insurrection, and subsequent massacres, of Sétif and Guelma in May 1945. 'Precocious' reformist demands are said to have prepared the ground for later independentist radicalism, which develops only with the 'maturity' of the movement.[4] In dealing with the terrible memory of the revolutionary war of national liberation, the predominant strategy has been to treat the cataclysm that unfolded from November 1954 to March 1962 as the result of the proverbial meeting of an immovable object (the intransigence of the European colonial settlers) with an irresistible force (the manifest destiny and will of the Algerian nation). The story, in these terms, is well known, and many of its long-suppressed details, on both sides of the Mediterranean, have also been illuminated in the rush of new scholarship on Algeria, and especially its war of independence, since the 1980s.

However, the political projects, and the historical worldviews which both inform and are shaped by them, which have generally taken 'Algeria' and 'France', or 'France' and 'the Maghrib', 'colonialism' and 'the nation' as stable, bounded categories, trans-historical subjects moving through time, might better be seen as having created these 'subjects' as such, through their own, dualistic narrative structuring of colonial history as static antagonism, as total response to total aggression. Such conceptions (and this is, of course, their unspoken intention) leave little room for the complexity of relations between and even within societies and individuals, for the fluidity and adaptability of cultural systems, the inventiveness of life-strategies, the daily work of inflecting and contesting domination by 'working the system to one's least disadvantage'.[5] They have often been reduced to dealing in normative terms of resistance and heroism, collaboration and treachery, speaking (as élite nationalism does) of the people's 'sleep', 'passivity', 'indifference' and incapacity to see 'clearly'[6] or (as populist nationalism does) of the

4 A neat summary of this view is Heggoy, 'Origins of Algerian nationalism'.

5 Hobsbawm, 'Peasants and politics', 13; Scott, *Weapons of the Weak*.

6 Cf. al-Madani, *Kitāb al-Jazā'ir*, 93, evoking the nation which must 'awaken from its sleep, shake off from itself the obscuring dust of its indifferent languor' and Merad, 'Islam et nationalisme arabe', 217, who considers that 'the masses ['le menu peuple'], absorbed in their misery, were hardly capable of clearly envisioning their problems, nor able to conceive the reforms necessary for the improvement of their moral and material conditions'. The shared presumptions of elite nationalism and of colonialism in respect of 'the people' are strikingly evident in the latter passage.

people's heroic and unending struggle with which the élites, after losing themselves in assimilationist illusions for a while, eventually reconnect.[7] 'The people', in either case, are objectified in a voiceless, anonymous totality spoken of and for, whether as crushed, incapable and ignorant, or as *un seul héros,*[8] a single hero unanimous in exaltation, but never really permitted to speak.

The overwhelming tendency in narrating the history of 'the Algerian national movement', by which has been meant, consciously or not, history as the *movement* through time *of the Algerian nation*, has thus been to treat the various socio-political and cultural forces of Algerian society, particularly in the period from the First World War through to the 1950s, as essentially complementary, as 'three strands' of a common thread, each contributing a distinctive element to the eventual unity and reality of the nation. Political enlightenment (liberal-democratic principles of equality, liberty and 1789) came from the so-called *évolués,*[9] the French-schooled notables. Cultural enlightenment (scripturalist, 'high-culture', Islam) was the gift of the reformist *'ulamā*. The dynamic will of popular revolution was mustered by the proletarian current manifested through the successive 'prestigious acronyms': ENA, PPA/MTLD, FLN.[10] Historiographical dispute has centred mainly on the relative merits of each constituent current, the worth of each contribution to the singular, common effort.[11]

[7] Kaddache, 'La Résistance politique', in Kaddache and Sari, *L'Algérie dans l'histoire*; Kaddache, *Nationalisme algérien*. For Amin, the urban 'nationalist' leaders were 'completely ignorant of the stubborn resistance among the peasantry . . . They remained preoccupied by their own relatively paltry problems as second-class citizens' (*Maghreb in the Modern World*, 107. For a corrective, see the constant – if paternalistic – concern with the conditions of the peasantry in Ferhat Abbas's own writings).

[8] Post-1962 slogan in Algeria.

[9] The assumptions behind this term are all too eloquent as to the categorisation of individuals and cultural systems, and the particular conception of *legitimate movement*, from 'backwardness' to 'civilisation', that dominated colonial discourse, and unhappily survives in its historiography.

[10] The Etoile nord-africaine was an association founded in 1926 by Maghribi migrant workers in Paris. Dissolved by the French authorities on 20 November 1929 and relaunched in May 1933, it was finally banned on 26 January 1937 and replaced by the Parti du peuple algérien (founded in March 1937 and banned in 1939). The Mouvement pour le triomphe des libertés démocratiques was constituted as the legal cover of the clandestine PPA in October 1946. It was ex-members of the paramilitary wing (OS) of the PPA/MTLD, established in 1947 but broken up by the police in 1950, who were responsible for the opening of hostilities on 1 November 1954 and the creation of the FLN/ALN.

[11] Compare, in particular, the different positions of Sa'adallah (a pupil of the AUMA) and Kaddache (a former PPA militant, schooled in the nationalist Scout movement); on this point see Carlier, 'Scholars and politicians'.

The broader framework of the nationalist story, too, is conceived in stable, clearly bounded terms. The history of colonial Algeria is, first (and still, for example, in the work of the anti-colonialist Charles-André Julien[12]) primarily French history, and then the history of France-and-Algeria (the title of Charles-Robert Ageron's monumental work, *Les Algériens musulmans et la France*, marks the crucial shift in this regard). The legitimate subjects of colonial history and the frame within which they are perceived have thus been dictated by definitions and relations that are the translation into historiography of the categorising and communicative practices of colonial order itself. The invariable frame of reference is traced along the vertical, face-to-face diagram of colonial communication between colony and metropole, fixed periphery and fixed centre. The actors and processes involved are similarly those constituted by the categories of colonial domination, which fix a complex range of possibilities, positions and strategies into easily policed terms of loyalty or treason, dividing populations, like the spaces they inhabit, into bureaucratically systematised order, and maintaining order through the extraordinary power of the colonial state: guns, police, repressive tribunals; civil registers, census data and numbered correspondence on headed notepaper. This ordering of colonial history along the lines of colonialism's own legitimate axes of movement, metropole–colony/centre–periphery/loyalty–treason, is unsurprising. Historiography, especially the historiography of so terribly divisive and traumatic a recent past, necessarily seeks order and understanding out of the chaotic horror of repression and revolution. The writing of history, like that of colonial legislation, seeks to 'fix' in text, to order and limit, to control, the movement of history and of people in history.

The stories told in this chapter are of people who escaped being 'fixed' in these familiar patterns. By straying beyond the paths of controlled movement, they have also fallen out of the frame of familiar narratives of nationalism. But their itineraries suggest that we ought to look beyond the closed and controlling teleologies of colonial and nationalist history, as a first step towards deconstructing 'the nation' as a single subject, and 'nationalism' as a unitary, irresistible force, in linear, progressive movement. Beyond these simple schemata lies a much more complex story of overlapping, shifting patterns of resistance and strategies of negotiation, of social conflicts and cultural change, of attempts to assert authority and speak for one's community, which have eluded both the geographies and the chronologies of canonical linearity.

[12] Julien, *Histoire de l'Algérie contemporaine*, vol. I.

Contrary to the 'happy story' of 'national renewal', the world that began to end in 1830 was irretrievable forever after, and the world replacing it was one of a new disorder, of the loss of sovereignty and sacred assurance, of the destabilisation of systems that had ensured meaningful self-location, self-recognition, the understanding of the social and political world, and the relationships of community and territory along established circuits of pilgrimage, travel and exchange, and in familiar narratives of ancestry, sanctity and immunity. These circuits and stories were now, and thereafter increasingly, reinscribed in a new and distinctively different order which is sometimes said to have 'turned the world upside down', but might equally well be described as having shattered it into fragments. The world remade in colonial (dis) order was one of radically new 'fields of force',[13] of redefined social relations and geographical spaces of domination, where the location of individuals, and their margins of manoeuvre, their possibilities of action, were shaped in new ways, in new terms. This occurred, too, not in a coherent way, but according to profoundly ambiguous logics and contradictory aims, the mass of 'disunited, fragmented attempts at domination' which constituted colonialism.[14] Algerians' attempts at self-expression within colonised spaces were, inevitably, caught up in these contradictions and shaped by them, as we shall see in the following chapters. The violent, disorderly remaking of the world also produced important shifts in the patterns and meanings of physical movement both within and outside the immediate territory of the colony. Such movement, the control of which was a persistent obsession of colonial government, came to constitute newly significant boundary-crossings.[15]

Historically, the routes of migration and exchange between the major cities of central and eastern Algeria – Algiers, Bejaïa, Sétif, Constantine – and, laterally, the eastern face of the Maghrib, Tunis, opening onto the Mediterranean and the Mashriq (Istanbul, Izmir, Beirut, Alexandria) and, transversally, southwards through the Atlas to the oases of the Mzab, the Sūf and Zibān, and thence out across the desert – west to Morocco, the *seguia al-ḥamra* and the old trans-Saharan gold and slave

13 The metaphor is originally E. P. Thompson's ('Class struggle without class?', quoted in Roseberry, 'Hegemony and the language of contention', 356–7). I am using it here as a suggestive image for thinking about multidimensional relations of power which must be envisaged as operating 'horizontally', across geographic, as well as 'vertically', through social, space.

14 Sayer 'Some dissident remarks', 371, referring to Abrams, 'Difficulty of studying the state'.

15 See the important place that Anderson, following Turner, accords to new types of journey or 'pilgrimage' in colonial spaces for the formation of nationalisms (*Imagined Communities*, 53–8, 123–31; Turner, *Dramas, Fields and Metaphors*, ch. 5).

routes, or east to the Tripolitanian coast, Egypt, the Red Sea and the *ḥaramayn* (Mecca and Medina) – were well-established lines of communication along which the economic, intellectual and spiritual life of the region was channelled. The colonial systematisation of space imposed other logics. The mapping of colonised Algeria into three French provinces, and then three metropolitan *départements*,[16] plus the vast residual *territoires du sud*, produced a neat reordering of northern Algeria in a tricolour regime (conventionally, on nineteenth-century maps, blue for Oran in the west, pink for Algiers and yellow for Constantine) closed off along its pre-conquest borders from Tunisian and Moroccan territory, and from the shores of the desert to the south.

Adaptation to this new order would eventually mean the reorientation of the dominant channels of physical movement and the transfer of resources along new lines of legitimate transmission – of labour to French factories, intellectual talent to French universities and Paris publishers – while movement across these lines, to Morocco, Tunisia and the Ottoman east, became suspect and subversive. This was especially true, up to the end of the First World War, which is thus an important watershed in this regard, of travel to the Ottoman Empire.[17] Travel to Muslim countries was strictly regulated by colonial legislation[18] which, as of 1846, sequestered the property of emigrants to Morocco,[19] restricted the delivery of passports for the Levant, Morocco and the Regencies of Tunis and Tripoli to the prerogative of the governor-general in person,[20] and then, in 1858, prescribed that no passport for Ottoman territory should be granted 'save after the most searching inquiry into the morality, means, and origin of the interested party'.[21]

It was therefore in movements between Algeria and France that, from the late nineteenth century, the most visible dynamics of Algerian history

[16] An ordinance of 22 July 1834 initially organised the 'French possessions in North Africa' with legislation by royal decree; 'civilian territory' was later organised into three provinces, under the same regime as the metropole (18 April 1845), before becoming three *départements* after the February revolution of 1848 reinstated republican government (constitution of November 1848). Algeria was declared 'an integral part of French territory' by a decree of 4 March 1848.

[17] Some families who had left Algeria for Syria, between the conquest and the First World War, returned after the establishment of the Middle Eastern mandates. The script of one of the first plays performed in Arabic in Algiers, appropriately entitled *Fi sabīl al-waṭan* (lit. 'On the road of the homeland'; idiomatically, 'In the cause of the homeland'), first performed in December 1922, was brought from Beirut by one such returning émigré (Bachetarzi, *Mémoires*, 42).

[18] The discussion here draws on Collot, *Institutions*, 294–312.

[19] *Arrêté* of the governor-general, 28 April 1846.

[20] *Arrêté* of 20 March 1854.

[21] Collot, *Institutions*, 306.

new movement
reclamation of (margin note)
shared condition (margin note)

would develop: the 'Young Algerians' movement, and then the labour migration which would see proletarised workers of rural origin move into the marginal zones of Algeria's interior cities, to Algiers, and thence to Marseille, Lyon, Paris and Lille. There they would become involved in organised labour, would experience the development of a new vision of themselves as 'Algerians' – and more broadly as North Africans, as Africans, as *colonisés* – with a shared condition and shared motivation to liberty. This movement, initiated substantially by the exigencies of the First World War,[22] led to the foundation of revolutionary-populist nationalism embodied in the workers' organisation, the ENA, and its successor the PPA, under the charismatic leadership of Messali Hadj, an émigré from Tlemcen, wherein lie the origins of the FLN.[23]

worked in vital (margin note)

It is these later patterns of movement that have most held scholars' attention. The appearance of Algerians' nationalist demands is generally dated to proletarian engagement in political organisations, especially the PCF and ENA, in interwar emigration to France. The importance of these dynamics, however, ought to be understood within a longer-term and wider-angle view, one looking back to the first decades after the conquest and out well beyond the cut-off lines which isolate the obsessive couple of 'France-and-Algeria' from the rest of the Mediterranean, Arab and Muslim worlds. Produced at the limits of shifting centres of power, the margins of the colonially disordered world – for which the Madani family's Hafsid house in the rue de la Noria stands as an appropriate symbol – became important spaces. Beyond the colonially policed boundary lines, new liminal areas for speech and action opened up; not 'free' spaces of liberty (since the forms of expression were newly constrained, as well as enabled, by new forms of legitimate language), but spaces of lesser constraint, where voices in exile could formulate radical demands, constituting themselves as representatives of the people apparently reduced to silence, in the colonial territories, by the colonisers' massive apparatus of expropriative language.

---

[22] In 1912, there were around three thousand Algerian workers in France. Between 1915 and 1919, there were 78,000, of whom 10,000 were employed in agriculture. Thereafter, the demands of post-war reconstruction brought 20,000 migrants in 1920, 60,000 in 1923 and 70,000 in 1924. Control over migration to France was reimposed in 1924, and, with the exception of a brief interlude from July to December 1936, it was not until 1946 that Algerians, though 'French', could travel freely from the French port of Algiers to the French port of Marseille without some kind of passport.

[23] On Messali, see Stora, *Messali Hadj*, and Haroun et al., *Messali Hadj, 1898–1998*. It cannot be too strongly stressed that the actual chain of events leading to the revolutionary action of 1 November 1954 is above all a matter of the internal history of the PPA/MTLD, its crisis and factional split of April 1953 through the summer of 1954 (Harbi, *Aux origines du FLN* and *Vie debout*, ch. 4).

Attempts at speaking out from such temporary, marginal locations were, at least superficially, all short-lived and unsuccessful. They are also, however, the first historical examples of Maghribis articulating demands for national independence in the arena of world politics. They mark a watershed in which faltering attempts to reassert the established cultural authority of religious notables, articulated through an 'unbroken' inheritance of resistance, met new, modernist and reformist expressions of Islam and the nation. And despite their apparent failure, they constitute a link across the century after the conquest between successive struggles to speak for the people. This link is not the direct one of the unflinching revolution, the continuous resistance of 132 years fabricated as national memory after 1962. On the contrary, the long trajectories traced by the biographies in the rest of this chapter moved in anything but straight lines. They illustrate the massive, complex shifts as well as the continuities in practices of resistance that originated in Algeria immediately after 1830.

Transgressive movements of people and of language, from before the First World War into the 1920s, continued in the paths of early forms of resistance by avoidance and self-exile, and attempted to preserve the authority of religious notables as spokesmen for their people. As colonial power expanded, however, the places of refuge became fewer, until even the spaces of subversion were sucked into the metropole itself, unwittingly creating new networks and new kinds of solidarity and resistance within the strictly controlled movements of its migrant workers. The radical nationalism of the post-1919 migrant proletarians was developed and diffused through the very paths of transmission that the colonial state had established for its own exercise of control and exploitation – ultimately, Algerian nationalism too would come to Algeria *from France*, in the person of Messali, in 1936. Rather than emerging into a void of resigned quietism, or simply reiterating a perennially unflinching revolt, however, it replaced, and in certain places made connections to the surviving spokesmen of, earlier itineraries sketched out across a much wider map of space and time. The existence of these other, marginal stories reveals shifting dynamics of attempts at authoritative representation, occurring in a much wider range of spaces and registers, and on the part of a wider range of personalities, than have generally been recognised by dualistic and linear narratives of 'France-and-Algeria', or by the salvation history of the FLN. Stepping outside these conventional narrative frames reveals a complex field of struggle over the representation of 'the nation' that it would, eventually, be precisely the FLN's major achievement to swallow up in itself, in the necessary and terrible violence of an enforced revolutionary unity. For a broader understanding of the history of nationalism, we need to recover this complexity of voices, existing in the spaces before and outside the imposition of linearity, at the margins of the colonial world-in-fragments.

Transgressive itineraries (i): the shaykh in the trenches

self-imposed exile

The family of Si Muhammad al-Madani was by no means alone. There were some sixteen thousand Algerians in the Regency of Tunis in 1876–8, the vast majority of whom had emigrated without the assent of the French colonial authorities,[24] particularly after 1871. A further movement of emigration, east to Syria and Turkey, in some cases an extension of exile from Algeria self-imposed as far back as the 1830s, followed the French occupation of Tunisia in 1881. Such an experience was that of shaykh Ṣāliḥ ibn al-Mukhṭār ibn al-ʻArabī al-Sharīf,[25] grandson of emigrants from Kabylia, who left Tunis for Istanbul, Damascus and, eventually, Berlin and Lausanne, and of his associate shaykh Muḥammad al-Khiḍr Ben al-Ḥusayn,[26] grandson of a prominent Algerian religious notable who had arrived in Tunisia in 1844. Among their companions in exile and in their anti-colonial activities was al-Madani's maternal uncle, Muḥammad Boyrâz al-Jazāʼirī.[27] A man of whom little is otherwise known,[28] he figures prominently in al-Madani's account of his formative childhood. Boyrâz's house was 'the school that enlightened my thought, awakened my sentiments and stirred up my feelings . . . I observed the developments of public life with the greatest assiduity, and came to realise that the salvation of Islam and of the nation was an absolute duty that had been laid upon my shoulders.'[29] It was this uncle who apparently impressed upon the young al-Madani a militant vision of the state of the world of Islam; while his grandfather lamented 'every night, the French occupation of Algeria, its sorrows, atrocities, massacres and squalid impurity',[30] Muhammad Boyrâz,

24 Collot, *Institutions*, 307.

25 Born Tunis, 1869; d. Lausanne (not, as Green, *Tunisian ʻUlamā*, 287, Damascus), 1920.

26 Born Nefta, July 1873 (or 18 August 1876/26 Rajab 1293); d. Cairo, (Feb.?) 1958 or 1959.

27 *HK*, I, 74. His sobriquet is rendered 'Poyraz' in Merabet's French translation, and appears as 'Biraz' in the signature appended to the text of the Algero-Tunisian committee's 1919 declaration to the Versailles peace conference.

28 I have come across no explicit references to him in the archives relating to Salih al-Sharif and his activities in Istanbul, Germany or Switzerland. He appears in the literature only as the 'Biraz' who co-signed the 1919 declaration (Ageron, *Algériens musulmans*, 1182) – presumably from Switzerland, where the other members of the group were all to be found after November 1918. Notes on al-Madani in Tunisian archives do mention his Turkish family connections, but without details.

29 *HK*, I, 24.

30 *Ibid.*, 22.

in furious words, spoke to us of the condition of Islam and the Muslims, the passive inertia that shackled the hands of the Muslims, of the aggression committed by the enemies of Islam against its domains, [saying that] what was to come in future would be more calamitous and more bitter still, *since the Islamic lands had been emptied of their true guides*, and all the Muslims busied themselves with mere private concerns . . . Then [he spoke of] the tyranny of the Sultan, Abdülhamid . . . of the Greek worms who bore into the bones of the Ottoman state, of the injustice, dissolution, obscenity and wickedness in Algeria and Tunisia.[31]

This uncle, an assiduous reader of the Egyptian press and of *al-'Urwa 'l-wuthqā*, the important journal published in Paris by Jamāl al-Dīn al-Afghānī and Muḥammad 'Abduh in the 1880s,[32] and whom al- Madani describes as having been 'fire and light' to him, seems to have left Tunis for Istanbul prior to 1914, and reappears among the group of Maghribis who constituted themselves, in a joint Ottoman and German propaganda effort, as spokesmen for Maghribi independence during the First World War. This interrelated group of individual and family histories, pursuing exile as a strategy of resistance and places of exile as spaces for the self-constitution of representative voices, also illustrates the complex relationships between representatives of Algerian and Tunisian nationalism, and different forms of Islamic thought, developing from the 1890s into the first quarter of the twentieth century.

The principal figure of the group was shaykh Salih al-Sharif. Born in Tunis shortly before the arrival there of al-Madani's grandparents, his family had emigrated from Algeria, apparently in the 1830s.[33] Claiming descent from the Prophet, the family was quickly established among the religious notability of Tunis. Salih's grandfather, shaykh al-'Arabi al-Sharif, was among the thirty scholars recruited by Aḥmad Bey for the reformed professorial corps of the Zaytūna, Tunis's great mosque and university, in 1842[34] and his father, Mukhtar, also taught there. In 1889

31 *Ibid.*, emphasis added.

32 The pan-Islamic secret society of the same name is known to have had a section in Tunis (Hourani, *Arabic Thought*, 109); perhaps Boyrâz was a member, or perhaps al-Madani would wish us to think so.

33 Heine, 'Salih ash-Sharif', 89, for their emigration from Algeria c. the 1830s. Green does not mention his Algerian origins, but fixes his birth in 1869. The Kabyle origin of the family is asserted in a note (a/s Salah Chérif), Residence-General, Tunis, 15 January 1916 (4 pp.), which mentions only a 'somewhat distant date that we are unable to verify' for their arrival in the Regency (ISHMN/MAE/Guerre 14–18/P76/1655/1/82–86 and Telegram, Resident General, Tunis to Sous-Direction Afrique, Quai d'Orsay, 13 Jan. 1916 no. 13, ISHMN/MAE/Guerre 14–18/P76/1655/1). The sources on the family to be found in Tunisian archives all begin with the paternal grandfather, shaykh al-'Arabi, and it seems reasonable to suppose that they had arrived in Tunis during his lifetime.

34 Green, *Tunisian 'Ulamā*, 286; al-Temimi, 'Min a'lāminā 'l-bārizīn', 350.

Salih al-Sharif completed his own studies at the Zaytuna, and five years later became a Maliki *mudarris* (professor). He first came to political notice as a member of the protectorate's commission for the reform of Zaytuna education in 1898, a body whose fractious deliberations crystallised the rivalry emerging in Tunisia at this time between the conservative Islamic scholars of the Zaytuna, on the one hand, and a modernist alliance of young Tunisian intellectuals and liberal colonial officials, on the other.[35] The administration, supported by the leading 'Young Tunisian' (intellectual, journalist, president of the Khaldūniyya society[36] and teacher of history) Bachir Sfar,[37] hoped *inter alia* to introduce modern, secular disciplines to the Zaytuna curriculum. Salih al-Sharif contributed a lengthy response to the proposals of the commission's *de facto* president, the protectorate's Director of Public Instruction, Louis Machuel, which reinforced the conservative position of the Zaytuna's governing council, the *niẓāra 'ilmiyya*: salvation rests on the *sharī'a*, which could not be adequately transmitted if the curriculum were expanded to include secular subjects. The outcome of the commission's deliberations was a victory for the conservative *'ulamā*, among whom shaykh Salih appears to have been particularly vocal.

Muhammad 'Abduh himself, mufti of Egypt and figurehead of reformed Sunni Islam, came under attack from Salih during the great scholar's second visit to Tunis, 6–24 September 1903, when, at a luncheon held at the home of a Tunisi *'ālim*, 'Abduh expressed his dissatisfaction at what he apparently considered the 'archaic' texts and pedagogy employed in Maghribi institutions of Islamic learning. It was, he said, an advantage to students at the Zaytuna that they could supplement their religious instruction with the modern subjects taught at the Khalduniyya.[38] There followed a discussion of the dissident fourteenth-century Islamic thinker Ibn Taymiyya, opposing 'Abduh to Salih Sharif, who apparently accused the former of 'expounding Wahhabi views'.[39] Four days later, 'Abduh gave a public lecture at the Khalduniyya library

[35] Green *Tunisian 'Ulamā*, 178.

[36] Founded in 1896 by an association of liberal protectorate officials, notably Louis Machuel, and Sadiqi College-educated Tunisian intellectuals who were already (since 1888) grouped around the newspaper *al-Ḥāḍira*, the Khalduniyya was a major foyer of modernist thought and education, with premises opposite the Zaytuna in the centre of the Tunis medina.

[37] Born Tunis 1863; d. 1 March 1917.

[38] The question of making classes at the Khalduniyya in history, geography and mathematics obligatory for Zaytuna students had been a major stumbling-block in Machuel's 1898 proposals. The *'ulamā* resisted any attempt to take the transmission of 'legitimate knowledge' outside their purview.

[39] Green, *Tunisian 'Ulamā*, 184.

in the sūq al-ʻAṭṭārīn, in which he urged the acquisition of secular, as well as religious, knowledge, and criticised certain conservative teachings. It seems likely that shaykh Salih was among those 'ultra-conservatives' (*al-jāmidīn*) who, according to the account given by the reformist shaykh al-Ṭāhir ibn ʻAshūr, took strong exception to these statements.[40]

The shaykh clearly belonged to the dominant tendency among Tunisian *ʻulamā* at this time: anti-reformist, retrenching in the face of both the colonial government and their younger, modernist compatriots, determined to preserve their monopoly over legitimate knowledge (*'lā ʻilm illa mā yuqra' fi 'l-zaytūna'*, it was said – 'There is no knowledge save that taught at the Zaytuna') and their role as guides of and spokesmen for the Tunisian people. Ironically, this very concern – and their concomitant failure to achieve any sort of alliance with the Young Tunisians and then, after 1919, with the nationalists grouped in the reformist ʻAbd al-ʻAzīz al-Thaʻālibī's Destour,[41] or *a fortiori* with the later, yet more francophone and anti-establishment neo-Destour – made the Tunisian *ʻulamā*, alone in North African countries, 'a negligible factor' in anti-colonial nationalism.[42] They have thus frequently been regarded, like the heads of the Sufi brotherhoods in Algeria, as having capitulated to colonialism. The crucial exception to this judgement is the small group of émigré *ʻulamā* whose activities in Europe and the Mashriq were pointedly more outspoken than those of their colleagues remaining in Tunis. The greater scope for radical demands opened up to the exiles demonstrates the significance of the spaces into which transgressive movement to the East and to Europe took them, once they had left their homes (or initial places of exile) in Tunisia.

Of course, these spaces were created not only in the realignments of geography but by the conjuncture of space with time. It would be the Italian invasion of Libya in 1911, and then the First World War, that would catapult Salih al-Sharif and his associates onto the stage of international politics in a significant way. He left Tunis in 1906,[43] having obtained a passport for the Hijaz on the pretext of performing the *ḥajj*. He went first to Tripoli and then to Istanbul, and was teaching at the Umayyad Mosque in Damascus in 1909. A member of the Rifāʻī *ṭarīqa*, headed by Abu 'l-Hudā al-Sayyādi (the vehement enemy of al-Afghani and 'spiritual director' to Sultan Abdülhamid II) shaykh Salih appears quickly to have developed some standing in Ottoman circles of power.[44]

[40] Quoted in *ibid.*
[41] Al-Ḥizb al-ḥurr al-dustūrī al-tūnisī, the Tunisian Liberal Constitutional Party.
[42] Green, *Tunisian ʻUlamā*, 235.
[43] Note, a/s Salah Chérif, 15 Jan. 1916 (n. 33), p. 3; Green, *Tunisian ʻUlamā*, 287; Temimi, 'Min aʻlāminā 'l-bārizīn', 351; not, *pace* Heine, 'Salih ash-Sharif', 89, in 1900.
[44] Note, a/s Salah Chérif (n. 33), p. 4; Heine, 'Salih ash-Sharif', 90.

He managed to maintain this position after the Young Turks' revolution ousted Abdülhamid in 1908, and became a close associate of Enver Pasha, whom he accompanied to Tripolitania in 1911, where he preached jihad against the Italian aggression.

Apparently on the basis of this experience, he found his way into the Ottoman intelligence service personally patronised by Enver, the *teşkilāt-ı mahsuse*,[45] and as of 1914, he assumed a leading role in the German–Ottoman propaganda effort. He founded a Committee for the Independence of Tunisia and Algeria (*Jam'īyat istiqlāl Tūnis wa-'l-Jazā'ir)*,[46] and, as early as November 1914, the French authorities in Tunis were concerned at the possible diffusion in the Regency of a pamphlet, written by him, and apparently entitled *Jihad is an Obligation.*[47] Attacking France 'for repressing Islamic culture in the Maghrib and for disrespecting the personal status of its Muslim subjects', the pamphlet already called for Algerian and Tunisian independence. Other tracts written by Salih al-Sharif and his associates – particularly the former Hanafi *qāḍī* of Tunis and colleague of Salih al-Sharif on the 1898 Zaytuna commission, Ismā'īl al- Safā'iḥī, who had also emigrated to Istanbul, in October 1906[48] – were dropped over trenches occupied by Maghribi contingents of the French army, and introduced into Tunisia and Algeria via Switzerland, Spain or the Spanish zone in Morocco, or through Tripolitania.[49]

At the end of 1914, Salih al-Sharif was in Berlin, drafting pamphlets and representing the Turkish Minister for War. He clearly enjoyed considerable official regard as the representative of an allied power. He was received by notable establishment families, meeting, among others, Gustav Stresemann, future foreign minister of the Weimar Republic; he was shown the secret Fokker aircraft factory at Schwerin and Krupps's

[45] The origins of this service are unclear, but it 'appears to have been formed out of those Ottoman officers and servicemen who were sent to Tripolitania to combat the Italians' (Lüdke, 'Jihad made in Germany', 100).

[46] Telegram, Pascal, Consul in Geneva, to MAE, 25 Jan. 1916 no. 15, ISHMN/MAE/Guerre14–18/P76/1655/1; Resident General, Tunis, to Briand, 31 Jan. 1916 no. 53, ISHMN/MAE/Guerre 14–18/P76/1655/1/117; *Bayān tawaḥḥush firansā* p. 21 (See n. 56 below); Green, *Tunisian 'Ulamā*, 223.

[47] Green, *Tunisian 'Ulamā*, 223.

[48] Born in Tunis, 1 January 1856, he was thought 'a model *qadi*' before his emigration. Note, a/s 'Cheikh Ismail Sefaïhi, ancien cadhi hanéfite de Tunis', Residence General, Tunis, Jan. 1916, ISHMN/MAE/Guerre 14–18/P76/1655/1/118–123; Notice, ISHMN/MAE/Tunisie 17–1940/623/319/1/55–58; Pelle, Haut Commissaire de la République française en Orient, Constantinople, to Briand, 23 May 1921 no. 185, ISHMN/MAE/Tunisie 1917–1940/623/319/1/82–3; Saint, Resident General, Tunis to Briand, 26 Feb. 1921 no. 179, ISHMN/MAE/Tunisie 1917–1940/623/319/1/54; Green, *Tunisian 'Ulamā*, 179–80, 223, 281.

[49] Heine, 'Salih ash-Sharif', 90; Meynier, *Algérie révélée*, 509.

armament works at Essen; he went aboard a submarine at Wilhelmshafen and was received by the Kaiser.[50] On the German home front he wrote a treatise on jihad, translated into German as *Die Wahrheit über den Glaubenskrieg* ('The Truth about Holy War'), a riposte to the eminent Dutch Orientalist C. Snouck Hurgronje's *Heilige Oorlog Made in Germany*, which first appeared in a Dutch magazine in January 1915[51] and attracted much attention in Germany, as well as among French colonial officials. Salih's tract defined jihad as 'struggle against the declared enemies of Turkey and Islam, alongside the friends and allies of the Ottoman Empire'[52] – a German newspaper could thus conclude that 'holy war is not, as our enemies allege, *Made in Germany*; it issues, on the contrary, from the true spirit of Islam'.[53]

The same emphasis on Germany as friend and ally, and the insistence that the Ottoman war effort and jihad proclaimed by the caliph was not, as the French alleged, a German machination, but the necessary assertion of the caliph's duty to protect the domains of Islam, undertaken in a freely chosen alliance with Germany, 'the protector of the Turkish Empire',[54] are the key themes of extant texts by Salih al-Sharif. *Sharḥ dasā'is al-firansiyyīn ḍidd al-islām wa-khalīfatihi* ('A Declaration on the Machinations of the French against Islam and its Caliph') expounds the role of the caliphate, the legitimacy of the House of Osman, and the duty of Muslims to obey the caliph's commands.[55] A longer text, *Bayān tawaḥḥush firansā fi 'l-quṭr al-tūnisī al-jazā'irī wa-'l-istinjād ilayhi*[56] ('An Account of the Savagery of France in the Land of Tunisia and Algeria, and an Appeal for Aid'), presents a brief geographical and historical description of 'the Algero-Tunisian land' before enumerating the various (mainly juridical and institutional) infringements perpetrated by the French regime in North Africa, and particularly in Tunisia.

The shaykh, though, was not simply an Ottoman ideologue in German service (as French proposals for counter-propaganda tried to portray him and his fellows[57]). His consistently vocal self-assertion, whether in uncompromising and anti-reformist positions in Tunis, a bellicose

[50] Heine, 'Salih ash-Sharif' 92, n. 23.
[51] French tr. of Snouck Hurgronje in ISHMN/MAE/Fonds Augustin Bernard/500/13; note on *Die Wahrheit*, 'Résumé de la presse allemande', no. 17, 7 Dec. 1915, p. 29 (ISHMN/MAE/Fonds Augustin Bernard/500/13/31); Heine, 'Salih ash-Sharif', 95, n. 21.
[52] *Vossische Zeitung*, 6 Jan. 1916, tr. extr., 'Presse allemande', Quai d'Orsay, ISHMN/MAE/Guerre 14–18/P76/1655/1/88.
[53] *Ibid.*
[54] *Ibid.*
[55] Text published in Temimi, 'Min a'lāminā 'l-bārizīn', 354–62.
[56] Published in *Rawāfid* (Tunis) 4 (1998): 231–51.
[57] MS counter-propaganda proposal, n.d., n.p. [Residence General, Tunis, 1916(?)] 34 pp., ANT/AGGT/MN16.1/43.

insistence on Ottoman caliphal sovereignty over the Islamic world[58] as a relevant principle after 1914, or, in 1919, the right of 'the Algero-Tunisian people', having contributed to Allied victory, to independence, is not easily reconciled with any notion of him as merely some other powers' 'agent'. Whether in the prime minister's office in Tunis on Machuel's reform commission, in a trench on the Western Front, or in a Swiss retreat after the war, his consistent personal agenda was to demand the right for Maghribi Muslims to speak for and regulate themselves – or rather, for their legitimate guides, namely the *'ulamā*, and himself as one of them, to speak authoritatively for, and of, 'Algeria' and 'Tunisia'. It is not unreasonable to suppose that his particular activism in the service of his notion of legitimate Muslim sovereignty and unity (whether caliphal or Maghribi), in large part prefiguring the interwar activity of Shakib Arslan[59] – who in turn would be a significant influence on Messali Hadj – can be somewhat illuminated by the fact of his threefold exile. The successive displacements shaping his immediate family history and his own life, from Kabylia to Tunis, from Tunis to the Mashriq, and from there to Germany and Switzerland, combined with direct involvement in war in Tripolitania and Europe, perhaps imposed on him an intense experience of the fragmentation and disorder of the world. The assurance of divine order embodied in the caliphate, it seems perfectly reasonable to believe, was for him, as for many others, a necessary anchor in turbulent times.

We might justifiably take these marginal claims to representative status seriously.[60] Shaykh Salih exerted particular efforts in his work among Muslim prisoners of war in Germany, particularly in camps set aside for Muslims such as the 'Halbmondlager' at Zossen, some eighty kilometres

[58] He may not necessarily have envisaged a revived political caliphate. Perhaps, as Heine suggests, his revived caliphate would exercise spiritual authority over a number of independent Muslim countries. Such would be the aim of al-Madani's Tunisian Committee of the Caliphate in the early 1920s. He omits, evidently, from the tracts which emphasise the authority and responsibility of the Ottoman sultan, references to Morocco. A text entitled *Kitāb maftūḥ li-mūlay Yūsuf sulṭān al-maghrib* apparently exhorted the Moroccan ruler to remember and conform to 'the honour of his lineage and the merits of his forebears in the defence of the realm of Islam' (Hafnawi, 'Ṣāliḥ al-Sharīf', 229).

[59] It seems likely that Salih al-Sharif himself had at least some contact with Arslan, in Switzerland in 1919–20, if not earlier. According to Ageron, *Algériens musulmans*, 1179, Arslan lent direct support to Salih and Safa'ihi.

[60] Meynier, *Algérie révélée*, 515–16 and Ageron, *Algériens musulmans*, 1179–82, dismiss the credentials of shaykh Salih et al. and find their pretension to represent Algerians surprising. Both appear unaware of the origins of their families in exile from Algeria. The exiles' 1919 declaration specifically draws attention to the many Algerians who left for Tunis after 1830. Meynier contrasts the lack of influence of these committees in Europe with the political success of 'authentic Algerians', notably 'Abd al-Qādir's grandson, the Emir Khāled, after 1919; but Khaled was born even further afield, in Damascus, also of exiled grandparents. Perkins, 'Tunisia, Islam and the Ottoman empire' considers al-Sharif and al-Safa'ihi only within the context of Tunisian–Ottoman relations.

from Berlin. This went well beyond the propaganda effort to preach jihad and induce Maghribi soldiers to enlist for the Ottoman army; he drafted camp orders to regulate the daily life of the prisoners, led them at prayer, and interceded with the German authorities to ensure respect for Islamic observances – being concerned, as Heine notes, 'in every possible way' with both the spiritual and physical welfare of his congregation.[61]

In short, shaykh Salih fulfilled, in this strange space of prison camps and trenches, amongst the field grey and industry of total, mechanical warfare, the very role he had considered himself fitted for in the halls of the Zaytuna: a figure invested with legitimate authority for the leadership and regulation of the community, in matters ritual or mundane. It is notable that he appears, according to written and photographic portraits, never to have abandoned his traditional dress. With a certain show of courage, he went in person to the front to appeal to the Maghribi Muslim soldiers in the French ranks opposite, standing above the parapet of a German trench in turban and *burnūs* (the traditional Maghribi hooded cloak) and making a lengthy speech in classical Arabic to exhort his compatriots and coreligionists to desert. With comparable efficacy, perhaps, but no less self-assurance, he apparently wrote a letter to Wilhelm II, recommending that, if the Germans desired to increase their prestige among oppressed peoples, they should liberate their own colonial territories, thereby inciting unrest in the empires of their enemies.[62]

Transgressive itineraries (ii): vanguards and founding fathers

Calls for independence are easy historical markers to use for charting nationalism. Their significance, though, is too easily presupposed by unspoken assumptions about the place of individual actors and enunciations within a prescribed historical scheme. The dynamic that ultimately eventuated in Algeria's revolution and statehood began with the ENA in Paris and its programme for total independence, adopted in 1926. In the context of the historiographical proscription of Messali in Algeria after independence (and until the late 1980s) it has been important to assert the origins of the FLN in the radical nationalism of the migrant workers and the stormy internal history of the PPA/MTLD.[63] In this context, the

[61] Heine, 'Salih ash-Sharif', 91. [62] *Ibid.*, 93.

[63] The schism in the PPA/MTLD, leading to the formation of the CRUA and the FLN, and to the fratricidal struggle of the FLN with Messali's rival MNA, led to Messali's eviction from legitimate history for almost three decades; in a widely circulated tag, originally derived from a colonial officer's misplaced boast, Messali was even libelled as 'the last trump card' of colonialism.

call for Maghribi independence launched publicly by Messali on 10 February 1927, at the 'Congress of Eastern Peoples' held in Brussels under the aegis of the Third International, has become a historical founding event, the first enunciation of modern Algerian nationalism. 'The import of Messali's speech . . . was very great,' writes Stora. 'The programme was striking in the originality of its themes, notably that of independence, *which Messali was the first to demand*.'[64]

As we have seen, calls for Maghribi independence were being made by religious notables in Europe and the Mashriq as early as November 1914. They would be made again by Salih al-Sharif and his colleagues, at the height of the German–Turkish effort in January 1916, at a high-level, staged event at Berlin's Esplanade Hotel, and, after the central powers' defeat, in a declaration drafted in the exiles' Swiss refuge and presented by their 'Algero-Tunisian committee' to the Versailles peace conference in January 1919. In 1916 they declared: 'France respects nothing of the culture, the property, or the personal status of Muslims . . . The time has come to reclaim our independence. *The representatives of the indigenous people of Tunisia and Algeria* have therefore resolved to address themselves to the caliph, to the Emperor of Germany and the Emperor of Austria, to solicit their aid in this effort.'[65] In 1919, the logic necessarily shifted. The history of Tunisia and Algeria showed its people to be one nation, and the right of nations to self-determination was the principal gain of the war. 'The Algero-Tunisian people has abundantly poured out its blood in this war; it has contributed to the deliverance of the invaded lands of France and Belgium and to the liberation of oppressed peoples . . . It participated from the first day in the World War; it has the right to participate in the Peace.'[66] These earlier declarations have remained historiographically marginal for a number of reasons that deserve further reflection.

[64] Stora, *Messali Hadj*, 71, emphasis added; Nouschi, *Naissance du nationalisme*, 62.

[65] Quoted in Allizé, Minister in the Netherlands, The Hague, to Briand, 10 Jan. 1916 no. 48 (emphasis added); also telegram, Allizé to MAE, 9 Jan. 1916 no. 30; *Vossische Zeitung*, 7 January 1916, tr. extr. (Quai d'Orsay); Resident General, Tunis to Briand, 31 Jan. 1916 no. 53 (all in ISHMN/MAE/Guerre 14–18/P76/1655/1). The meeting, under the auspices of Salih and al-Safa'ihi's committee for the independence of Tunisia and Algeria, was held on 7 January and attended by the full senior staff of the Turkish embassy, as well as by a representative of the German chancellor, the under-secretary of the German Foreign Ministry, the vice-president of the Prussian upper chamber, two representatives of the Austrian government, and a large number of army officers.

[66] This text is reproduced in Collot and Henry (eds.), *Mouvement national*, 25–30, from a secondary source. I have been unable to find a copy of the original. The published version carries the signatures of 'Cheikh Salah Cherif Ettounsi', 'Cheikh Mohammed Elkhedir Ben el Houssine', 'Mohammed Biraz Eldjazairi', 'Mohammed Bach Hamba', and three others. Isma'il al-Safa'ihi had died in Istanbul on 27 December 1918.

On the one hand, there is the obvious point that the Algerian–Tunisian exiles founded no movement, played no part in the dynamic process that would eventually produce the FLN and 1 November 1954. Ageron is doubtless correct to evaluate the influence in Algeria of the exiles' activities as weak and without echo.[67] The evaluation of their efficacy, if by this is meant influencing movements of dissent and insurrection in North Africa, seems to be negative.

Conversely, there is little to be gained from reinscribing them as hero-leaders, a 'vanguard' of later nationalism. Hailing Salih al-Sharif as 'al-za'īm al-tūnisī al-abraz',[68] 'the most outstanding Tunisian leader' of this period, only restates the presentation made of him to the German public in 1916, when a magazine cover illustrated him as 'Vorkämpfer für die Befreiung Tunesiens und Algeriens vom französischen Joch'[69] ('Pioneer of the struggle for the freedom of Tunisia and Algeria from the French yoke'). The sterile search for 'founding father' figures[70] – dictated by a perceived need to attribute legitimate paternity, another example of the persistence of genealogy and linearity – is, again, a categorising practice seeking to fix historical actors in prescribed roles.

'Who was the first nationalist?', a question constantly asked of modern Algeria, is perhaps the wrong question. It is more productive to ask how, and where, different nationalist enunciations were produced. The durably marginal figures of Salih al-Sharif et al. deserve consideration, not so that exalted places might be reclaimed for them in a reiterated teleology, but because their existence reveals the un-predetermined plurality of attempts to recreate representative authority in a world torn apart. Far from being identifiably central actors in a stable, progressive story, they deserve attention precisely because their constant dislocation and relocation, in an extraordinary variety of spaces – from the Zaytuna and the protectorate to the Umayyad Mosque and the *teşkilāt-ı mahsuse*, to Berlin's Esplanade Hotel and the prison camp at Zossen, to post-war refuges in Geneva and Lausanne – illustrate the extent of displacement and change experienced by individuals who attempted to find, in shifting configurations of power and circumstance, space from which to speak, to constitute themselves as representative voices in a bid to gain a grasp on the world. It is important to note that they did so in the belief that they, as bearers of an established socio-cultural authority, were *naturally* fitted to be the spokesmen for their community. Seeking to empower themselves by even the slightest influence over the perception of reality in the

67 Ageron, *Algériens musulmans*, 1182–3.
68 Hafnawi, 'Ṣāliḥ al-Sharīf', 230.
69 *Die Woche – Bilder vom Tage* 3 (1916), quoted in Heine, 'Salih ash-Sharif', 92.
70 See Carlier, 'Culture politique', for an analysis and critique.

spheres of power, these marginal voices at the edges of the world political stage are early illustrations of a pattern that other self-constituting representatives would follow in different ways.

Messali, after all, whose fifteen-minute speech at the Communist International's Brussels Congress is taken as a founding text, and the Emir Khaled, grandson of the famous 'Abd al-Qādir,[71] whose 1919 letter to Woodrow Wilson, requesting the representation of Algeria at Versailles with a view to the Algerian question being placed before the League of Nations, has led to the reinscription of this retired captain of the French army as 'the first Algerian nationalist',[72] are, in a sense, barely less marginal voices. They too spoke on the fringes of circles of power seen as determining the future of their fragmented world. Like those of the earlier generation of exiles, their interventions sought to find space for the representation of the colonised in the arenas of world power. The difference is not in the substance of their speech but in that, in different ways, Messali and Khaled were to some extent able to achieve their aim of representation – by creating the groups they claimed to represent. Khaled's list won the Muslim vote in the Algiers municipal elections in 1919.[73] Messali, after a long struggle, would implant his movement in Algeria in 1936. This success was due, ironically, to the new disorder's successful integration of *them* in its own networks of communication. Khaled and Messali's attempts to raise colonised voices were more successful, in terms of their impact on Algerians in Algeria, because they had integrated the norms of a newly fashioned international

[71] The emir 'Abd al-Qādir ibn Muḥyī al-Dīn (1807–83), son of the local head of the Qādiriyya *ṭarīqa*, was the principal leader of Algerian resistance to the conquest in the west and centre of the country in 1831–4, 1835–7 and 1839–47 (concluding treaty relations with the French and attempting the consolidation of a state in the intervals between fighting). Imprisoned in France 1848–52, he settled thereafter in Damascus on a French pension and became one of the greatest Sufi thinkers and spiritual figures of the nineteenth century.

[72] On Khaled, see Ageron, *Algériens musulmans*, 1050–2; Ageron, *Historie de l'Algérie contemporaine*, vol. II, 282–93; Kaddache, *Emir Khaled*; Koulakssis and Meynier, *Emir Khaled*. Khaled and the émigrés in Switzerland were mutually unaware of their parallel depositions in 1919 – unsurprisingly so, since during the war Khaled had served on the French side of the trenches harangued by Salih al-Sharif. Khaled's letter to Wilson was talked about immediately after his death in Algeria but long unsubstantiated, leading to dispute over his nationalist credentials. The letter was rediscovered in the archives by Claude Paillat, and published in an Algiers weekly by Ageron ('Vérités sur l'Emir Khaled', *Algérie-Actualité*, 6–12 March 1980), thereby revising the opinion of 'Khaled-the-loyalist' which he had previously held against Kaddache and Sa'adallah. ('L'Emir Khaled fut-il le premier nationaliste algérien?'). A concise discussion is Koulakssis and Meynier, *Emir Khaled*, 8–9.

[73] Kaddache, *Vie politique*, 41–2. The administration promptly declared the vote invalid.

politics[74] – the League of Nations and international socialism – and were firmly implanted in colonial relations of movement and exchange. The Emir Khaled was a graduate of St-Cyr and a decorated officer of the French army who was elected, via a highly discriminatory French voting law, to a French legislature. Messali's path to Brussels led through military service and labour migration to Paris, to the PCF, and to a French wife.

The trajectories of al-Sharif and Boyrâz, on the other hand, were made in a logic of continuity with the same forms of resistance that had led their grandparents and parents out of Algeria in the 1830s and 1870s. Displaced by conquest and inheriting an unbroken tradition of religiously imagined resistance, exiles considering themselves 'natural' leaders of the community could find voice only in the conjunctural space of wartime alliances against France, and, as it turned out, at the price of further dislocation and disconnection from the Maghrib and its people, on whom their pronouncements had virtually no impact. The few Maghribis directly reached were those prisoners of war harangued and ministered to by Salih al-Sharif – and many of them were highly unreceptive to his version of their duty.[75] His stand was made in the terms of an already-vanished world. For all his reception into Ottoman service, his agenda was not that of the new rulers of Turkey. Enver et al. were not much interested in the caliphate, and, as al-Madani would later discover, his successors in shaping post-war Turkey considered that they 'had no business interfering in the affairs of French Muslim colonies'.[76]

[74] In this respect the Lausanne committee's 1919 declaration, with its appeal to 'universal conscience', the logic of national independence for every 'people with its language, its traditions, its history' (perhaps the contributions of the French-trained lawyer Bash Hamba), is a belated attempt to play by new rules.

[75] Some did sign up for the Ottoman army; one Algerian 'deserter', lieutenant Rabah Bu Kabuya, wrote pro-Ottoman tracts, signed 'Lt. el Hadj Abdallah', which were shipped as far as Singapore (Dejeau de la Batie, Chargé d'Affaires, Bangkok, to Briand, 23 Dec. 1915 no. 81, ISHMN/MAE/Guerre 14–18/P76/1655/1). Ageron reports forced recruitment at the Halbmondlager (*Algériens musulmans*, 1178, n. 5); Heine found no evidence of this but cites 'reports of those willing to fight on the Turkish side . . . angry about the delay of their departure', but then feeling 'badly treated after their arrival in Istanbul' ('Salih ash-Sharif', 94, n. 12). A French escapee told how Maghribi POWs at Hamlin, similarly approached, consented to be sent to another camp 'to consult their leaders, the qa'ids, as to what they ought to do, for the poor fellows were much perplexed' (Report by Sgt-Major Darches, Cabinet Militaire, Government-General, Algiers, 27 June 1916 no. 3157, AGGA/9H10).

[76] Al-Madani, admiring the exploits of Mustafa Kemal's war of independence, wrote in 1921 to the secretary of the Permanent Bureau of the Turkish Congress – in Lausanne, where Salih al-Sharif had died the year before – 'enclosing his photograph . . . and expressing his admiration for the resistance of Turkey and the example it set to Tunisian patriots eager for independence'. The rebuff of the Turkish representative came directly to the notice of the French embassy (Embassy, Berne, to MAE, 22 Dec. 1921 no. 520, ISHMN/MAE/Tunisie 1917–1940/623/319/1).

On the other hand, there would be an enduring significance to the experience of exile in its numerous forms. Self-exile through *hijra*, a form of resistance subsisting until 1911, would be replaced, as a mark of refusal, after the entry of French troops to Fez in 1912,[77] the fall of the Ottoman state in 1918, and the extension of colonial rule to Syria in 1920, by the experience of directly coerced movement in the forms of internment and deportation. Those individuals who, having made themselves sufficiently troublesome, were privileged to be subject to such highly controlled movement, could thereby gain a considerably potent capital of prestige among sympathisers for whom they were thus instituted as iconic leaders. The political trajectories of Messali, Bourguiba and Sultan Muḥammad ben Yūsuf (later Muhammad V) of Morocco are strongly, indeed constitutively, marked by such experiences.[78]

Khaled's career was also a series of exilic movements, from his birth into a third generation of family exile in Damascus, to his death there, via St-Cyr and the French cavalry, Algiers (itself an exile, or a profoundly strange 'homecoming', for a man who had grown up as an Ottoman Syrian notable?), France and Egypt. The idiom of *hijra* could still express resistance in speaking of him when, in 1923, he arrived in Alexandria, following his discreetly coerced departure from Algiers. Denying French press reports that his withdrawal from the imminent elections to the Algerian *Délégations financières* (the colony's representative assembly) and sudden move to Egypt were due to ill health, a Constantine paper insisted: 'His defence of the interests of the Muslims who suffer under the yoke of the colonisers [is] the cause of his emigration from his homeland, [and of his going,] with his noble family, to seek refuge under the protection of God.'[79] Egypt, of course, was rather under the occupation of the British, but this does not appear to have lessened the force of the image of a coerced emigration, east to an at least nominally independent Muslim country, as an act of sacrifice and resistance.

The all-but-forgotten Algero-Tunisian exiles in Europe left their mark, too, at least in some memories. Al-Madani, in his memoirs, recalls his uncle Muhammad Boyrâz as 'one of the vanguard' ('min al-ra'īl

[77] Fez had been the major centre in the west for Algerian *muhājirīn*.

[78] Exile is one of the most visible ways in which the system affirms its own enemies as icons; this is particularly patent in the case of the Moroccan monarchy. In Tunisia, 'Abd al-'Aziz al-Tha'alibi's story is different because his (prolonged) years of exile (July 1923–July 1937) happened to coincide with rapid and critical changes in the internal politics of Tunisian nationalism; and because he belonged already to an older generation. On his return to Tunis, he was in his sixties.

[79] *Al-Najāḥ* 130, 19 Oct. 1923, tr. extr., Governor General, Algiers to Prefect, Constantine, 30 Jan. 1924 no. 1842, ADC B3/286/7.

al-awwal').[80] Shortly after the death of Salih al-Sharif, an article appeared in a Tunis newspaper, in 'mourning for those who have died far from their homeland and families, [– we] salute their noble souls'.[81] A Residency official, at least, saw a clear reference to 'Alī Bash Ḥamba, Isma'il al-Safa'ihi and Salih al-Sharif.[82] All three, along with Muḥammad Bash Ḥamba (younger brother of 'Ali[83]), had gone into exile and had died in Europe or the East; 'Ali Bash Hamba and al-Safa'ihi in Istanbul in 1918, Salih al-Sharif and Muhammad Bash Hamba in Switzerland in 1920. These dates thus mark a watershed not only in the circles of international geopolitics, but in these smaller circles of voices on their edges, too.

Transgressive itineraries (iii): the *riḥla* of Sidi Lakhdar Ben Husayn

Others would continue their travels, in part connecting, by their further itineraries, these earlier histories with much later ones. In 1919–20,[84] Sidi Muhammad Lakhdar (al-Khidr) Ben Husayn left Europe and moved to Egypt, where he began teaching at al-Azhar, the great mosque and university of Cairo. In 1930, he would be the founding director of the review *Nūr al-Islām*, which in 1936 became the *Majallat al-Azhar.* At the cessation of hostilities in 1918, Tawfiq al-Madani left the prison in Tunis where had been detained since January 1915.[85] He would study at the Zaytuna and the Khalduniyya, and be involved in the beginnings of the Destour. At the end of 1919, 'Abd al-'Aziz al-Tha'alibi published, through an editor in the intellectual centre of Paris,[86] a book that would establish him as the figurehead of Tunisian nationalism: *La Tunisie*

[80] *HK*, I, 64.

[81] *Al-Ṣawāb*, 16 April 1920, quoted in Resident General, Tunis, to Millerand, 2 April 1920 no. 468, ISHMN/MAE/Tunisie1917–1940/622/317/106.

[82] In fact Safa'ihi's family was with him in Istanbul, where they remained after his death. Salih al-Sharif's brother, in ill health, remained in Tunis.

[83] The Bash Hamba (Bāsh Ḥāniba) brothers – 'Ali, 1876–1918, and Muhammad, 1881–1920 – both studied at Sadiqi College in Tunis and then read law in Paris. Leading Young Tunisians, they set up the newspaper *Le Tunisien* in 1907 and were involved in the constitutive moments of Tunisian nationalism: the Zaytuna students' strike of 1910; the protest over the land-registration of the Jellaz cemetery in 1911; the tramway boycott in 1912. 'Ali was expelled to France in 1912, and thence left for Istanbul. Muhammad went to Switzerland where he ran the *Revue du Maghreb* during the war.

[84] Sayadi, *Jam'īya al-Khaldūniyya*, 206, says he left Damascus for Egypt in 1919. It seems more likely that he was still between Lausanne and Berlin at this date – in any event he signed, or agreed to have his name affixed to, the Algero-Tunisian declaration of 1919, and was in Berlin in July 1920.

[85] *HK*, I, 98–147.

[86] Jouve & Co., whose offices were at 15 rue Racine in the sixth arrondissement, a short walk from the Senate, the Panthéon, the Sorbonne and the Collège de France.

martyre, ses revendications. He was arrested in Paris in July and transferred, in August, to the military prison in Tunis.

There are telling ironies in this changing of the guard. The alliance of wartime exiles including Muhammad Bash Hamba, the francophone Young Tunisian who carried on an important correspondence with al-Tha'alibi, creates a curious link between the latter and the conservative *'ulamā*, al-Sharif and al-Safa'ihi – Bash Hamba's colleagues, but representatives of the group most vociferously opposed to al-Tha'alibi's outspoken *salafī*-reformist leanings, in their attempts to maintain dominance in the Tunisian religious field. Al-Safa'ihi, as Hanafi *qāḍī* of Tunis, had himself authorised the deposition for blasphemy against al-Tha'alibi which had led to the latter's trial in July 1904.[87] (It is worthwhile noting, too, in this context, that al-Tha'alibi was yet another descendant of Algerian emigrants.[88]) Al-Madani's uncle Boyrâz, the devotee of Afghani, would be similarly at odds, at least in this respect, with Salih al-Sharif, the Rifa'i and critic of 'Abduh. Whatever their doctrinal differences, their position as members of an established notability-in-exile made them collaborators in their self-assertion as spokesmen for the Islamic Maghrib.

A further development of this history is provided by the presence in their group, and continued activity long after 1920, of shaykh Muhammad Lakhdar Ben Husayn. His was a very distinguished saintly family: his maternal grandfather was Sidi Muṣṭafa Ben 'Azzūz, eminent shaykh of the Rahmaniyya order, who in 1844 had migrated from Algeria to the Jerid in south-western Tunisia, and settled in Nefta.[89] Muhammad Lakhdar completed his Zaytuna studies in 1906, and edited, while still a student there, an important, moderately reformist literary journal, *al-Sa'āda 'l-'uẓmā*, Tunisia's first Arabic periodical review[90] and 'a focus of intellectual activity reaching all who were concerned about Arabic culture and accommodating both opposed groups [i.e. reformists and

87 Green, *Tunisian 'Ulamā*, 185.

88 Berque (*Intérieur du Maghreb*, 210) has the Tunisian branch of the family emigrating from the area of Bejaïa before the nineteenth century, but a long and detailed biographical note established by the Residency says that his family, 'of Algerian origin and highly regarded . . . established themselves in Tunisia at the time of the conquest of Algeria': Residence General, Tunis, 31 Oct. 1923 (13), pp., ISHMN/Résidence/R464/2224/1/154–166; publ. *Wathā'iq* (Tunis) 19 (1993): 52–64.

89 According to Muwā'ada, *Muḥammad al-Khiḍr*, 22, his paternal grandfather, shaykh 'Ali ben 'Umar, also an *'ālim*, was from the oasis of Tolga, another important Rahmaniyya centre in southern Algeria. Sidi Mustafa's story, before and after his *hijra*, is told in Clancy-Smith, *Rebel and Saint*, especially ch. 5.

90 Published twice per *hijri* month. Sayadi, *Jam'īya al-Khaldūniyya*, 205; Muwa'ada, *Muḥammad al-Khiḍr*, 137.

conservatives], while retaining mutual respect, politeness and integrity'.[91] The journal was produced in twenty-one editions between March 1904 and February 1905 before being closed down under pressure from the conservative Zaytuni *nuẓẓār* (senior *'ulamā*) – insisting as always on their monopoly over religious knowledge and its legitimate enunciation.

'Balanced, calm, sincere, brilliant, and a great writer' according to the reformist Fāḍil Ben 'Ashūr,[92] Sidi Lakhdar taught Arabic composition at the Zaytuna and at the Sadiqi College, the modernist secondary school founded by the reforming minister Khayr al-Dīn in 1875. Some time before the war,[93] he left Tunis, and like Salih al-Sharif taught at the Umayyad Mosque in Damascus before becoming involved in the German–Ottoman anti-colonial propaganda effort. His photograph appeared, shortly after the 1916 meeting at the Esplanade Hotel, on the front page of a Berlin newspaper, along with the other shaykhs who had 'gone to Berlin to demand the liberation of Algeria and Tunisia'.[94] After the war he remained in contact with activist circles, notably in Berlin, where his presence was noted in July 1920.[95] He became more notable, though, for his intellectual success in Egypt, where he took part in the controversies around the works of 'Ali 'Abd al-Rāziq and Taha Ḥusayn, and, in 1928, founded the religious association al-Hidāya 'l-islāmiyya and the periodical of the same name. He ended a distinguished career as rector of al-Azhar, a post he held from 1952 until his death.

In May 1915, it was popularly known in Tunis that he had left Damascus with Salih al-Sharif for a mission to Berlin. The exiles' movements were, then, known to at least some in Tunis. In 1928, Sidi

91 Ben Achour, *Mouvement littéraire et intellectuel*, 65.

92 *Ibid.*

93 Sayadi, *Jam'īya al-Khaldūniyya*, 205, writes that he emigrated to Istanbul in 1911. Green, *Tunisian 'Ulamā*, 251, has 1914. Ben Achour, *Mouvement littéraire*, 113, refers to his self-exile in the context of the 'oppressive life imposed by the state of siege [March 1912] and the years of the Great War'. Muwa'ada, *Muḥammad al-Khiḍr*, 60–1, quoting the shaykh's own account in 'Khilāṣat al-riḥla 'l-sharqiyya' (serialised in *al-Zuhara*, (Tunis), March–April 1913, repr. in Muwa'ada, *Muḥammad al-Khiḍr*, 251–329), has him leaving Tunis for Alexandria on 18 July 1912, whence he went to Cairo and then via Palestine to Syria.

94 *Berliner Lokal-Anzeiger*, 11 Jan. 1916. Note, 'Sidi Lakhdar ben el Haoussine', Secretary-General, Government of Tunisia, 17 March 1919; Resident General, Tunis (Saint) to Governor-General, Algiers, 6 March 1926, AGGA/25H32/3/139–147.

95 MAE to Laurent, Ambassador in Berlin, 10 July 1920, AGGA/29H35/31. A 'Congress of Muslims of all Nationalities', seemingly mainly Turkish nationalists but also including Syrians and Tunisians, passed a series of resolutions in Berlin on 21 May 1920, asserting among other things the rights 'of all peoples to independence' and of 'oppressed peoples to armed resistance in defence of their liberty'. MAE to Governor-General, Algiers, 3 July 1920 no. 139, AGGA/29H35/32.

Lakhdar was approached by the Destour, who wrote to him for guidance about the methods of instruction in Arabic in use in Egypt, so that they could be published in Tunisian newspapers and applied at the Zaytuna.[96] Most notably, though, and in a remarkable logic of continuity with his participation in the 1919 Algero-Tunisian committee (itself a reinvention of the Ottoman Jamʿīyat istiqlāl Tūnis wa-'l-Jazā'ir) he was to reappear in 1945 at the head of a 'Front for the Defence of North Africa', apparently founded in Cairo in February 1945,[97] with the aim of rallying international, and especially the Arab states', support for Maghribi independence. Sidi Lakhdar, the French Interior Minister warned, 'entertains relations with the Secretary General of the Arab League which may be damaging to our interests'.[98] In something of a replay of the 1919 message to Wilson at Versailles, the Front sent a dispatch to US President Truman, published also in a Cairo newspaper, entreating the president 'to protect the principles of liberty and human rights in the cases of Tunisia, Algeria and Morocco, for the safeguarding of a durable peace and in view of the realisation of the aims for which the United States has fought'.[99]

This language is thoroughly the legitimate speech of the world political system. One of shaykh Muhammad Lakhdar's associates in this group, the emir Mukhṭār ibn ʿAbd al-Qādir al-Jazā'irī[100] had, in 1944 – not inappropriately on Bastille Day – addressed from Cairo, in the name of the 'Executive Committee of the High Assembly for the Defence of Arab Algeria', a long appeal for Algerian independence to none other than Charles de Gaulle, in his capacity as president of the CFLN, shortly to become the new Provisional Government of the French Republic. De Gaulle himself was then in Algiers, whence he would leave for France in August (to demand from Eisenhower the immediate liberation of Paris). The text began:

On this historic day when our brothers of the Algerian and Moroccan contingents seal with their blood, alongside the liberating Allied armies, their adhesion

96 Note, Direction de la Sûreté publique, Tunis, 24 Jan. 1928 no. 89D, ISHMN/Résidence/R485/2242/1/423.
97 But a 'committee' for Algeria existed at least from the summer of 1944. The 'Front' was probably merely the latest umbrella grouping of exiled activists in Cairo, gathered especially around the Rifi emir Muḥammad ibn ʿAbd al-Krīm al-Khaṭṭābī.
98 Minister of the Interior, Paris, to Governor-General, Algiers, 31 Oct. 1945 no. AlgI246/2004, ADA/4I/28/5.
99 *Al-Baṣīr* 26 August 1945, tr. extr. with *ibid.*
100 Other descendants of ʿAbd al-Qadir had also been involved in the activities of the Berlin–Lausanne group during the First World War, of whom at least one – ʿAli Pasha, son of ʿAbd al-Qadir and vice-president of the Ottoman parliament – was on the payroll of the *teşkilāt-ı mahsuse* (Lüdke, 'Jihad made in Germany', 101).

to the principles in defence of which this gargantuan struggle was begun, we believe that the moment has come to recall to your attention, in all sincerity and liberty [of speech], to you who embody the spirit of resistance for the deliverance of your subjugated homeland, that Algeria and her heroic sons are waiting, too, for the hour of liberty and independence to strike for them.[101]

The strategy of negotiation with global power, harking back to 1916, had now internalised the legitimate language of the system, but their demand remained that of independence. (A more complex dynamic had meanwhile occurred within Algeria, as we shall see in the next chapter.) Sidi Lakhdar's 'Front' subsumed, it seems, this 'Assembly' in a 'Higher Committee for the Defence of Algeria', whose members included Sidi Lakhdar himself, the emir al-Mukhtar, and a prominent *salafī*-reformist recently arrived from Algeria, where he was established as a senior figure in the Association of Algerian Muslim *'ulamā*, shaykh Faḍīl al- Wartilānī. Al-Wartilani, with Sidi Lakhdar and two others, was charged with representing the Front to the Arab League.[102] The AUMA president, shaykh Bashīr al-Ibrāhīmī, would later, in 1952, himself arrive in Cairo, perhaps to link up with this existing network in hopes of establishing the reformist *'ulamā* as the dominant representatives of Algeria in the Middle East. By the time Tawfiq al-Madani arrived in April 1956, it was to join the FLN's diplomatic offensive.

The 'Committee for the Defence of Algeria' issued a long tract at the end of December 1944. Signed by Mukhtar al-Jaza'iri and al-Wartilani and diffused in Cairo, it may have reached at least some *'ulamā* circles in Algeria. Entitled 'Declaration of the Higher Committee for the Defence of Algeria to the Algerian nation, in particular, and to the sons of North Africa, in general',[103] it proclaimed the end of imperialism, and, referring both to the Atlantic Charter and to the 'Manifesto of the Algerian People',[104] fixed as the people's objectives: 'the independence of Algeria

[101] Translation of Arabic text, dated Cairo, 14 July 1944 (4 pp.), CIE, Algiers. AGGA/29H35/2.

[102] The Front also apparently included Egyptians as well as Moroccans, Tunisians and Algerians in exile. It appears to have been organised largely around al-Azhar, but may also have had connections to the Muslim Brothers, with whom both Sidi Lakhdar and al-Wartilani were said to be associated.

[103] French tr., Director, Service des Affaires musulmanes, Delegation in North Africa, GPRF, to Director, CIE, Algiers, 7 Feb. 1945 no. 2402 DGF/AM, ADA/4I/28/6. What appear to be partially reproduced MS copies of the Arabic original are in AWC/al-Ghassiri papers (Shaykh Muhammad al-Ghassiri taught at the reformist Madrasat al-tarbiya wa-'l-ta'līm in Constantine).

[104] Elaborated by the liberal Algerian deputies led by Ferhat Abbas, and addressed initially to the Allied 'responsible authorities' (20 December 1942) and in its final, much longer, form to the governor-general (Peyrouton) on 31 March 1943, the *Manifeste* was the major platform around which Algerian politics would revolve from 1942 to the early 1950s.

under the aegis of its [own] nationality; the realisation of the unity of the Maghrib; adhesion to the Arab League; the immediate release of [political] prisoners and internees, and the repatriation of deportees'. With the imminent end of the war, the text asserted, 'the form that will be given to the world . . . will last for centuries . . . Today is the day long awaited when we must loudly declare our mind as to nationality and the independence of the homeland, as a corollary of our faith in the oneness of God, and an obligation of life itself.' At the same time, the *'ulamā* proclaimed that 'the French people, the free and the pure (not those who have [changed their original nationality to] become French, nor the egoists) is itself our great support for the realisation of these objectives'.[105] The strategy of self-assertion through negotiation with global power, as far as possible in the terms of its legitimate language, and the enunciation of these demands at critical junctures of time and space, in moments of the decisive refashioning of the world, marks a continuation of the paths pursued by Sidi Lakhdar, Salih al-Sharif and Muhammad Boyrâz, twenty-five years previously.

In the first half of the twentieth century, then, complex movements of individuals and ideas occurred that both retraced and extended the painful exodus from Algeria begun in the 1830s, renewing connections between the refigured, war-torn and colonised spaces of Algeria, Tunisia, Europe and the Mashriq, and establishing in the process new locations and new media of expression – from the literary review and the Paris-published manifesto to the subversive, smuggled pamphlet, or the petition submitted to the American president and the 'international community' – by marginalised voices seeking space to speak.

The itinerary of Sidi Lakhdar appears in continuity with that of his grandfather,[106] of Muhammad ibn Ahmad al-Madani, Muhammad Boyrâz or Salih al-Sharif, but also expresses a series of important shifts; from a vanished, Ottoman and pre-colonial world to a new one of reimagined unity, of brother Arab nations in a relegitimised new world order. As the descendant of an important Algerian saintly family who became one of the first *'ulamā* in Tunisia to articulate reformist ideas, he also demonstrates an important transition in forms of religious

[105] On the role of this conception of the ideal France, see below, ch. 3.

[106] For Sidi Mustafa's activities in exile, see Clancy-Smith, *Rebel and Saint*, ch. 5. Sidi Lakhdar's maternal uncle, Si al-Mekki ben 'Azzuz, mufti of Nefta and *muqaddam* of the Rahmaniyya *zāwiya* there, had also emigrated to Istanbul c. 1899. Note, a/s 'Sidi Lakhdar ben el Haoussine' (note 94 above); Clancy-Smith, *Rebel and Saint*, 315, n. 49.

expression and notions of legitimate knowledge and authority.[107] While Salih al-Sharif attacked 'Abduh as a 'Wahhabi', Sidi Lakhdar founded *al-Sa'āda 'l-'uẓmā*, if not quite 'to create a reformist religious organ as shaykh Muhhamad 'Abduh . . . had done with *al-Manār*',[108] at least to promote 'a rapprochement between traditionalist and modernist shaykhs on the basis of a reform programme which was at once temperate and within an Islamic context'.[109] His continued activity up to the mid-1940s creates a link between the first generation of resistance through religiously imagined exile, that of his grandparents, and the reformulated language of an Arab-Islamic Algerian nationalism emanating from the reformist *'ulamā* a century later.

Sidi Lakhdar had previously, in 1903 and 1904, travelled to Algeria, the country of his forebears. He wrote an account of his journeys, 'comprehensively describing the itineraries and monuments, citing with interest the scholars and men of letters whom he met, the discussions he had with them, the remarks and ideas that came to him'.[110] The account was serialised in *al-Sa'āda 'l-'uẓmā*, and was considered a 'summit of perfection'[111] in the distinguished prose genre of *riḥla* (travelogue). His later travels in Europe and the Mashriq as scholar, activist, religious notable and would-be representative voice of the Maghrib might be seen as a continuous effort to seek purchase on the fragmented world, a trail of attempted speech acts from the oasis *zāwiya* to the Arab League, via Tunis, Damascus, Berlin and Lausanne, telling part of a larger story of resistance, illustrating through a complex series of displacements – of physical location and of forms of language – a continuity of struggle for representation and authority across a century of domination.

[107] The frequently reiterated opposition of a 'passive', fatalistic Islam of the brotherhoods with an active, resistant nationalist reformism is too simple. The example of Sidi Lakhdar is one among several of saintly families undergoing a shift towards accommodation or engagement with *salafī* reformism around, and after, 1900. Other instances include the Ben Shaykh Ḥuṣayn (Bencheikh Hocine) family of the *zāwiya* of Sidi Khalifa at Mila, near Constantine (Rouadjia, *Frères et la mosquée*, 59–61), a family near Aïn-Temouchent in the Oranais (discussed in Launay, *Paysans algériens*) and the Derdur family of the Aurès (Colonna, 'Transformation of a saintly lineage'). Anti-reformist brotherhood members like Salih al-Sharif could also be far from fatalistic collaborators.

[108] 'Rapport sur la presse indigène en Tunisie depuis les origines jusqu'au 20 septembre 1906', Secretariat General of the Government of Tunisia (12 pp.), ISHMN/MAE/ns Tunisie 1882–1917/P18/ns 26/2/17–32, p. 7.

[109] Green, *'Tunisian 'Ulamā*, 188.

[110] Ben Achour, *Mouvement littéraire*, 77–8. The *riḥla*s are reproduced in Muwa'ada, *Muḥammad al-Khiḍr*, 233–50.

[111] Ben Achour, *Mouvement littéraire*, 77–8.

Perpetual exile

On the evening of the twenty-seventh day of Ramadan (a Wednesday, 1 December) 1937, thirty young students of an independent Islamic school in Constantine, the provincial capital of eastern Algeria, gave a theatrical performance at the town's *Université populaire* to an audience of about eight hundred. The play, by shaykh Muḥammad ibn al-'Abīd al- Jalāli, began with a song, sung by the boy and girl pupils and extolling education for both sexes. The first scene told the story of children sent abroad 'to learn the ways of other peoples and to improve themselves'. In the second, an actor appeared on stage and recounted to the audience the event of the children's return from Egypt and Syria. In a third scene, the students reappeared, and recited their thanks in verse to the benefactors who had made possible their enlightenment and improvement in the cultural and spiritual centres of the east. After an interval, the scene changed; the audience was now shown a sketch in which impoverished Algerian children, victims of the evils of (their parents'?) gambling, are arrested and appear before a court, which nonetheless acquits them on the grounds that they 'had acted without discernment'.[112] At the end of the performance, the patron of their school, shaykh 'Abd al-Hamid Ben Badis, thanked the audience and exhorted them to provide for the education of their children, that they might give back prosperity to Algeria.

It is unsurprising that the ideal of educational and moral improvement envisioned by shaykh al-Jalali involved a *riḥla fi ṭalab al-'ilm* (a journey in quest of knowledge) to the Mashriq. Such travels had been an integral part of Maghribis' spiritual and intellectual life for centuries. Ben Badis himself had travelled to the Hijaz some years before; al-Ṭayyib al-'Uqbī, the leading spokesman of *iṣlāḥ* in Algiers, had spent much of his youth in Medina, and Bashir al-Ibrahimi, another leading reformist *'ālim* and Ben Badis's successor as leader of the Association of *'ulamā*, had studied in Syria. It would later become a priority of the AUMA to finance further study for the graduates of their schools, initially at the Zaytuna, or the Qarawiyyīn in Fez, and later at al-Azhar and in Damascus, Baghdad and Kuwait. In the absence of a great seat of higher Islamic learning in Algeria – one of the most cherished plans of the reformists was to establish their own Islamic university[113] – the Zaytuna and its Mashriqi

[112] Account of the event, held by the Madrasat al-tarbiya wa-'l-ta'līm, in Report, SD, Constantine, 2 Dec. 1937 no. 4030, ADC/B3/274/6, and attached leaflet in Arabic and French.

[113] The Emir 'Abd al-Qadir University of Islamic Sciences would eventually be inaugurated in Constantine in 1984.

counterparts held an important place in the development of the Algerian *salafiyya* movement.

In comparison with the disastrous, expropriated and miserable condition of what Tawfiq al-Madani called 'the very many children who live, ignorant and abandoned of all morality, in the streets'[114] of the cities of French Algeria, the notional east of *'urūba* (Arabism), *'arabiyya* (the Arabic language) and original Islam was a place of escape, of morality and improvement, of purity and purification. When Algerian emigrants, performing *hijra* out of the conquered land of illegitimate rule in 1861, reached the Tunisian frontier, they reportedly burned their tent-poles, divorced their wives and only after three days of fasting, prayer and ritual ablutions, remarried and entered the territory of the *beylik.*[115] Seventy years later much had changed, but al-Jalali's play could still look east for social and spiritual salvation. Moreover, the sacrifice and difficulty of emigration was looked to as an empowering process. If the migrant labourers of the French factories sent back vital remittances to their families in the impoverished mountains of Kabylia, and returned themselves with radical ideas and forms of radical political organisation, the students of the *'ulamā* in Tunis were, as Ben Badis wrote in a book published by the Algerian Zaytunis on the subject of *hijra*, those 'who take flight voluntarily from your country, to suffer, and to return thereafter to deliver [your homeland]'.[116]

Other forms of communication, sometimes across surprising distances, persisted in spite of Algeria's relative isolation. Arabic-language newspapers entered Algeria, and circulated, if ephemerally, from as far afield as São Paulo and Buenos Aires.[117] A large stock of lithograph prints of Muḥammad ibn 'Abd al-Krīm al-Khaṭṭābī, hero of the Rif war, depicted as conqueror of the Spanish army, was seized in Algiers in 1928. The prints had initially been reported on the Moroccan border,

[114] In a speech at the prize-giving of the Algiers madrasat al-shabība 'l-islāmiyya, held at the Cercle du Progrès, 30 August 1931. Report, Chief, SD, Algiers, 2 Sept. 1931 no. 3140, ADA/2I/32/8.

[115] Pélissier, letter to Napoleon III, 28 December 1861, quoted in Ageron, 'L'émigration des musulmans algériens', 1051.

[116] *Al-Thamra 'l-ūlā*, publ. by *Jam'īyat al-ṭalaba 'l-jazā'iriyyīn al-zaytūniyyīn*, Tunis, Maṭba'at al-shabāb, 1936–7 (and banned in Algeria). tr. extr., n.p., n.d. [CIE, Algiers, 1937], ADA/4I/69/5.

[117] *Al-Qalam al-ḥadīdī*, published in São Paulo, was banned in Algeria (11 September 1928), as were at least four publications from Argentina and four from the USA, in addition to those emanating from the Mashriq, Libya, and Tunis. 'Etat des publications en langue arabe dont la circulation est interdite en Algérie' (5 pp.), CIE, Algiers, 29 March 1938 no. 421, ADA/4I/178/6; correspondence in ADC/B3/285/7 (1928). On the circulation of books and reviews in rural Algeria in the 1930s, see Mostefa Lacheraf's recollections of his childhood in the Hodna (*Des noms et des lieux*, 26–7).

Figure 3. Muhammad ibn ‘Abd al-Krim al-Khattabi, hero of the Rif war, routs the Spanish army. Print seized in Algiers in 1928. (CAOM.)

being sold at Oujda, but 1,622 copies were found in an Algiers print shop, and seizure orders eventually went out as far as Constantine. The prints had been made in Algiers, from an illustration executed in Cairo, on a plate manufactured in Dresden.[118] Other leading icons of the 1920s, from the other end of the Mediterranean – Sa‘d Zaghlūl, hero of the Egyptian revolution of 1919, Egypt’s King Fārūq (not yet unpopular), and Mustafa Kemal Pasha (not yet Atatürk), along with his colleagues in the insurgent Turkish nationalist army, still at this time set alongside the Ottoman caliph, Abdülmecit – were illustrated in popular portraits, some of which were produced in Tunisia and diffused in Constantine and Algiers among tobacconists and newspaper-sellers,

[118] Governor-General, Algiers, to Minister of the Interior, 28 July 1928 no. 18756B, AGGA/29H35/37; Governor-General, Algiers, to Prefect, Constantine, 5 July 1928 no. 17871B, and seizure orders, Constantine, 7 July 1928, with copies of the print, ADC/B3/285/7.

before passing from the major cities to towns like Blida. Some of these images endured in circulation into the late 1930s.[119]

It was thus hardly true that Algerians existed only in the isolation of a jealous French embrace. On the other hand, the tracing and policing of colonial boundaries, and their ever-wider extension through the destruction of surviving 'legitimate' rule and the colonisation of spaces of sanctuary (Tunisia, Morocco, the Levant), had, by the interwar years, produced a profoundly and irreversibly altered world. Throughout much of Africa and Asia, new political and cultural imaginaries had to be crafted, and had to find space to express themselves, within the geographical and institutional frames established by colonial states and colonial histories. The process of reconceptualising an intensively colonised, expropriated and redistributed, remapped and rebuilt space as the national homeland of Arab-Muslim Algeria was not the simple one of 'reawakening' to a primordial sacred landscape, unchanged in its 'essence' by all those soldiers, farms and perpendicular towns. The mythically purifying journey east in search of redeeming sacred knowledge and moral strength had become, by the 1930s, a metaphor for the uncrossable distance separating Algerians, not from their Arab and Muslim 'brothers' in the Mashriq, but from their dreamed-of, precataclysmic past. If the kind of radical social and spiritual reform created in the maraboutic revolution of the Maghribi sixteenth century, and the Wahhabi campaigns of the Arabian eighteenth, operated in a world under the sovereign sign of a continuously present Islamic history untroubled by invasive Europe, the Algerians of the 1930s were forever exiled from that world. There could never be any return to the past before the world was fragmented, and reunited in its strange new order. The imaginary, vanished world of authenticity-before-conquest had to be painstakingly recreated, rewoven in among the very fabric of *Algérie française*. The spokesmen for liberation had to rename the spaces of colonialism, from their margins and interstices, in languages that could restore to the land of the ancestors something of the imagined perfection of its untainted, original, *'salafī'* self. And the words they would use were not recovered echoes of the unsundered world before empire, but neologisms coined in the fires of the conquest and its tortuous, century-long aftermath.

independence is not a rebirth but a result of colonialism

119 Report, SD, Algiers, 20 March 1923 no. 702, ADA/2I/27/1 (portraits on sale in Blida, with enquiry on their origin and distribution); Report, Police spéciale, Algiers, 29 August 1938, no. 6105 ADA/2I/32/2 (photographs on sale in Algiers).

2 The conquest conquered? Natural and unnatural histories of Algeria

> Where there is power, there is resistance . . . Just as the exercise of power is heterogeneous, so is resistance; 'there is no single locus of great Refusal, no soul of revolt, source of all rebellions, or pure law of the revolutionary.' Resistance does not operate outside power, nor is it necessarily produced oppositionally: it is imbricated within it.
>
> Robert Young[1]

> Algeria has been transformed by the forcible harnessing together of Frenchmen and Algerians. By force of circumstance, this transformation has necessarily been a common effort.
>
> Ferhat Abbas[2]

Negotiations of rule in a time of triumphalism

In October 1937, the European population and officials of Constantine prepared to celebrate the centenary of the arrival of modern civilisation in the ancient capital of Numidia. The Age of Reason had arrived, a century earlier, in the person of General Valée, an artillery engineer considered 'the finest technician in the French army'.[3] Valée's cannon breached the walls of Constantine, the unconquerable City of the Air,[4] and after a bitter house-to-house street battle, the fall of the janissary barracks signalled the end of the Ottoman *beylik*. Some of the city's defenders tried to escape by clambering down the sheer rockface that falls away from Constantine on three sides, or by letting themselves down on ropes, which broke, hurling them down to death in the Rhummel valley below. The governor, Aḥmad Bey, withdrew with his remaining

[1] Young, *White Mythologies*, 86–7.
[2] Abbas, *Autopsie d'une guerre*, 10.
[3] Julien, *Histoire de l'Algérie contemporaine*, 141.
[4] Constantine, in local parlance *bled al-hawā*, sits atop the inclined plane of a massive rock outcrop, dominating the plains to the north and cut off to the east and south by the deep gorge of the river Rhummel. Not only is the location breathtakingly spectacular, it afforded the city a virtual invulnerability since Antiquity.

3 CONSTANTINE. – Vue Générale prise de la Route de Sétif. – LL.

Figure 4. Constantine from the south-west, early 1900s. (Postcard, author's collection.)

troops southwards to the Aurès mountains, where he led a sporadic resistance until 1848. The town was pillaged.

A century later, 4,000 copies of a pamphlet in Arabic, entitled *Appeal to the Muslim Population of Constantine* and signed by ʻAbd al-Hamid Ben Badis, were circulated in the city. The text was an appeal for a boycott of the celebrations, due to include, like the year-long centenary of colonial Algeria seven years previously, military parades in commemoration of the triumph of French arms. Self-evidently, for the strictly demarcated 'European' and 'native' populations of colonial Algeria the fact of conquest was encoded in memory in very different ways. But it was not the *fact* of the conquest that provoked the protest of shaykh Ben Badis; he castigated, rather, the unwillingness or inability of the colonial population to put the history of the conquest in its proper place – in the past – and decried the planned celebrations as an attack on the dignity of Constantine's Muslims, and on that of their forebears.

My brothers of Constantine – a century ago, in this same season, your glorious ancestors, fighting in defence of their homes, and the French soldiers of the conquest, fell together on the field of honour, achieving equal glory. A page of history, telling of the valour and bravery of each, was thus turned. A century separates us today from this tragedy whose memory, fading with the passing days, ought to have been effaced from the recollection of men. A century should have sufficed for the healing of wounds, [time enough] closely to unite the different peoples of a country from which the traces of such events would have vanished.

Today, men without consideration seek to reawaken these distant memories and resurrect hate and rancour by celebrating the anniversary of the fall of Constantine. These military marches, and all the vain parades in which their conquerors' pride finds satisfaction, are a supreme assault on our dignity and an insult to the memory of our glorious forefathers, ruining the efforts of our ceaseless striving for racial fraternity. This indecency reaches its height when such celebrations occur at a time when the demands of the Muslims of Algeria are yet unrealised, their natural rights remain unrecognised, and special repressive legislation hangs in perpetual menace over their heads.[5]

A number of readings of such a text are, of course, possible, and due caution should be exercised in the absence of the original Arabic. Several observations can, however, be made with some safety, all relating to the overriding concern of the text, which seems to be, not a riposte to colonial triumphalism in the evocation of heroic resistance, but rather a preoccupation with equality of dignity. 'Our glorious fathers' are aligned not against but alongside the French casualties in the ranks of the meritorious dead of the costly battle – the 'combat of giants' as the official commemorative plaque would put it – for Constantine. (It is perfectly possible, too, that the shaykh was aware of the fact that the first troops through Valée's breach on 13 October 1837 were not French regulars at all, but *zouave*s recruited in Kabylia.[6] The French had begun to enlist men from among the renowned fighting tribes of the *zwāwa* as early as 1831, twenty years before Kabylia itself was 'pacified'.) Those on both sides did their duty, both achieved equal shares of glory, and thus 'the page is turned', 'li fât mât' – 'the past is dead'.[7] The memory of 'this tragedy' should give way to unity in equal partnership, with equal dignity for all Algeria's inhabitants in its new order.

Yet at the same time that he conjures away the divisive and hateful spectre of past tragedy, the writer must, too, in speaking of it, affirm the solidarity-in-repression of his own generation with its 'glorious forebears' – equally disdained, insulted and *re-conquered* in the costumed, mass-ceremonial simulacra of the triumphalist 1930s, the apparent

[5] French tr. of pamphlet, CIE, Algiers, 6 Oct. 1937, ADA/4I/13/4 (2G).

[6] Julien, *Historie de l'Algérie contemporaine*, 141. Lamoricière's *zouave*s at this early period would have been local recruits, drawn from groups that had customarily furnished troops to the Ottoman *beylik*. After 1841, with the creation of new colonial regiments, the 'Zouaves' became an exclusively French corps.

[7] The formula used by Boumédienne to Giscard d' Estaing on the occasion of the first visit to independent Algeria by a French head of state, in 1975 (Etienne, *Algérie, cultures et révolution*, 28).

ICI COMMENCA
LE 13 OCTOBRE 1837
LE COMBAT DE GEANTS
QUI DONNA
CONSTANTINE À LA FRANCE
PORTE ET CORPS DE GARDE TURC
DE BAB-EL-DJEDID
DEMOLIS EN 1925

Figure 5. Plaque laid in Constantine, October 1937, in commemoration of the city's conquest a century earlier. *(Constantine, son passé, son centenaire (1837–1937), Recueil des notices et mémoires de la Société archéologique de Constantine*, vol. 54, published in Constantine in 1937. Middle East Centre library, St Antony's College, Oxford.)

apogee of French Algeria. The memory that he wishes away is also one that he cannot do without. Dignity must mean respect for oneself *and* for one's history, one's ancestors. Both, in Constantine in 1937, were seen not as respected equals but as the conquered native. It is the inability of the coloniser, and the colonial system, to move from a principle of conquest to one of partnership that Ben Badis laments. This inability is neatly symbolised in the irreconcilability, which his text so significantly *attempts to overcome*, of histories of victory and defeat. No single memory of equal dignity in this shared past has been created, and neither has the page been turned. The past is not dead, but lives on in the daily injustice of conqueror to conquered, and in the self-recognition of the colonised in his forebears' defeat.[8]

[8] Lakhdar Bentobbal doubtless speaks for other nationalist militants in recalling the 'discovery' of his colonised condition through primary school history classes, which taught Algerian children that, from Poitiers in 732 to Isly in 1844, 'the French presence in their land was the outcome of a long series of battles lost by their ancestors'. (Djerbal, 'Mémoire des acteurs', 23–4). Bentobbal joined the PPA and was an ALN chief in the

In the previous chapter we saw how, in the wake of the earthquake of conquest, religious notables struggled to establish discursive and physical spaces for the representation of colonised populations for whom they claimed a right to speak. We saw how their strategies, improvised in the conjunctural circumstances of exile, war and revolution, adapted to the shifting currents of world events, from alliance with the German and Ottoman empires to depositions before Wilson, Truman and de Gaulle. I emphasised how, across a century of displacement and disruption, they located themselves within a remarkably varied series of institutions of authority, from the Zaytuna to the Ottoman secret service, from the Sufi *zāwiya* of Nefta to the Arab League in Cairo. We saw, most significantly, how these voices at the margins of world power, and beyond the confining space of the colony itself, though constituting important linkages across time and space between successive forms of resistance, were unable to achieve their representative aim. I indicated that the recognised 'founding fathers' of nationalism in Algeria, Messali and Khaled, were able to establish themselves as legitimate representatives at least in part because of their position within what had become recognised frames of movement, between colony and metropole, and means of expression, through elections and internationalist anti-colonialism. At the end of the chapter I returned to Algeria, to begin asking what kinds of dynamics were occurring within the space of the colony itself. Ben Badis's pamphlet of October 1937 gives an important indication of this.

What is so extraordinary about Ben Badis's text, and the attitude it seems to express, is the endurance and perseverance of Algerians in seeking to find some means of accommodation with the inflexible autism of the colonial system. The protest over the Constantine celebrations cannot be read simply as an assertion of *autonomy*, contesting the fact and finality of the conquest, a statement of refusal. It is much more the expression of a desire for *recognition*, a continuing effort to live with the fact of French rule, and to find a workable partnership with the colonial state through which its apparently invincible domination might be negotiated. Such was the stated programme of the movement at its inception: the slogan of Ben Badis's *al-Muntaqid*, Algeria's first *salafī* newspaper, in 1925 was 'li-sa'ādat al-umma 'l-jazā'iriyya bi-musā'adat al-firansā 'l-dīmūqrāṭiyya', 'For the welfare of the Algerian nation with the aid of democratic France'. Defending itself against colonialist detractors (but also to the Algerian population, since the tract was produced in Arabic as

north Constantinois (*wilaya* II) early in the revolution, before becoming one of the dominant figures in the ALN/FLN.

well as in an abridged French version) shortly before being closed down by the administration, the journal elaborated on this formula:

We work, and that with nothing but truthfulness, sincerity and rigour, for the welfare of the Algerian nation – there can be no [such] welfare for it except through the reform of its religious and mundane life – through the aid of democratic France, the nation whose awakening has been the foundation of every [other] awakening to this day ('al-umma allatī kānat nahḍatuhā asāsan li-kull nahḍa ilā 'l-yawm') and who was able, through her policy and power, to assemble the whole civilised world around her and to come out victorious from the greatest war history has known, with the strongest army in the world; who counts Algeria part of herself and as a pupil, such that this Algeria has become a measure to the world of the power of France in civilisation and the development of nations.[9]

There is no need to suppose from these texts that Ben Badis had in any respect 'accepted' the colonial discourse of France's civilisational mission, but rather that he appreciated its potential value as a terrain of contest on which Algerians, too, could stake claims. These texts seek, not the reversal of conquest in a dream of independence, but the recognition in the world *after* conquest of 'natural rights' to dignity, decency and an equitable system of justice. This strategy of negotiation, rather than simple 'refusal' – and certainly not revolution – remained the guiding principle of the *'ulamā* into the 1950s. With this went a determination to establish themselves as the leading, if not the only, legitimate representatives of Muslim Algeria: its legitimate guides, leaders and spokesmen; eventually, its legitimate interlocutors with the colonial government; and, above all, the legitimate speakers of its truth. When this was clearly no longer possible (as of the spring of 1956), they remained determined to survive as an independent centre of authority. This determination would be ended, perhaps forcibly, only in the autumn of 1957.[10]

The *'ulamā* were, however, only one group of voices among many engaged in the negotiation, inflection and contest of colonial domination within the colonised space of France's Algerian *départements*, in the period from the end of the First World War to the mid-1950s. Through these crucial years, a vast number of spatial and symbolic sites of physical and discursive contest emerged: books and newsprint; music played by ambulant singers or recorded, for the first time, on vinyl and played over

[9] 'Wa-'llatī ta'uddu 'l-jazā'ir juz'an minhā wa-talmīdhatan lahā ḥattā ṣārat hādhihi 'l-jazā'ir 'ind al-nās miqyāsan li-maqdarat firansā 'alā tamdīn wa tarqiyat al-umam'. (*al-Muntaqid* no. 14, 1 Oct. 1925/14 rabī' al-awwal 1344, BnF).

[10] See below, ch. 3, 'The death of the *'ulamā*' (pp. 137–43).

the radio; schools, theatres, mosques and *zawāyā*; boxing and football matches; cultural and political circles (most notably the Nādī al-taraqqī, or Cercle du progrès, shaykh al-'Uqbi's 'Progress club' on the place du Gouvernement in the centre of Algiers); the urban and suburban spaces of Paris, Lyon, Marseille, Algiers, Oran and Constantine. . . This chapter concentrates on two related areas in which Algerians sought to negotiate with colonialism in its most strident moment of triumph: the meaning of Algerian history as it was fought over, in speeches and in print, through the 1920s and 1930s between proponents of dramatically different visions of the Algerian past and future; and the legal-discursive constitution of 'Algerian Muslim identity' itself, invested in the key symbolic space of the *statut personnel musulman* (Muslim – standing effectively for 'native' – personal status), a creation of colonial legislation translated in Arabic as *shakhṣiyatunā 'l-islāmiyya*, 'our Islamic personality'.

Within these contested spaces, the symbolic resources of community and culture, the construction of authority over the meaning of the past and the direction of the present and future, were struggled over by competing dissident voices, each articulating distinct projects and demands, each seeking to constitute itself as the natural representative voice of 'Algeria'. Seeking to establish a viable 'community of discourse', in Wuthnow's phrase,[11] each voice that dared to speak out in the name of 'Algeria' produced a competing version of the meaning of that name, while at the same time seeking to negotiate an ever-elusive unity of action with its rivals.

It was into this complex situation that Tawfiq al-Madani arrived, at a quarter past nine on the evening of 8 June 1925, at the railway station in Constantine.

His brothers' 'awakener'

On arrival in Constantine in his twenty-sixth year, al-Madani already had a substantial career of which to boast. He had been a precocious politician and journalist, writing his first articles for the Algiers newspaper *al-Fārūq* in 1914. Imprisoned in 1915 for the duration of hostilities for what seems to have been a wildly ill-conceived attempt to

[11] Since this period is not one of linear 'national renewal', but rather a moment of 'relatively abrupt, episodic ideological innovations [in which] the conjuncture of changing resources and shifting institutional contexts can be seen clearly', and through which significant 'cultural change comes about' (Wuthnow, *Communities of Discourse*, 548).

organise an anti-colonial revolt in the Tunisian south, after his release in 1918 he became one of Tunisia's most prominent activist-intellectuals. From 1920, he was heavily involved in the Destour, becoming secretary of its central committee and considered by the protectorate's police as the party's 'propaganda agent'.[12] A journalist, he became director of the review *Ifriqiya* and editor of the major Tunis newspaper *al-Zuhara* (which had been considered as safely pro-French[13]) and published widely both in the press and in pamphlet form on international affairs, particularly the independence struggle in Ireland and the question of the status of Tunisia.[14] He would later be – or consider himself – the acknowledged authority on domestic and international politics among the Algerian reformists, and wrote on these subjects in Ben Badis's flagship review, *al-Shihāb*.[15] He began, in 1922, to produce a nominally annual illustrated review, *Taqwīm al-Manṣūr*, which in fact appeared in five editions between 1922–3 and 1929–30,[16] and which covered everything from poetry to the explanation of electricity and wireless telegraphy; from the agricultural calendar to the rise of Ibn Sa'ud in the Nejd and the progress of the Rif war; from the history of Tunisia under the

[12] Report, Commissariat spécial, Tunis, 9 June 1922, ANT/AGGT/MN5/3/17.

[13] Founded in 1890, *al-Zuhara* was run by yet another Algerian émigré. Identified with opposition to the protectorate, it was banned in May 1904 but later 'considered semi-official'. When the Arabic-language press was suspended in 1911, *al-Zuhara* was the only title allowed to continue publication. Others were readmitted only in January–February 1920. ('La presse indigène de Tunisie . . . jusqu'au 20 septembre 1906', report to Secretary-General of the Tunisian Government (12 pp.), ISHMN/MAE/nsTunisie 1882–1917/P18/ns26/2/17–32; 'Note: Ahmed Tewfiq el Madani', n.d, n.p. [Tunis, Residence, June 1925], AGGA/25H/32/2/120–124; notes on the press, ANT/AGGT/MN5/1). After al-Madani's assumption of the editorship, however, it was reported that *al-Zuhara* 'show[ed] itself clearly favourable to anti-French, nationalist ideas' (Note, n. p. [Sûreté publique?, Tunis], 4 Oct. 1924, ISHMN/Résidence/R94/1700/1/318–319).

[14] *Al-Ḥurriya thamarat al-jihād aw niḍāl irlandā ḍidd sayṭarat al-inkilīz*, Tunis, 1923; *La Tunisie devant la Société des Nations/Tūnis wa jam'īyat al-umam*, Tunis, 1923. The latter seems to have been an appeal, like Khaled's to Wilson four years earlier, for the League of Nations to consider the status of the protectorate, with a view to the international recognition of Tunisia as 'a sovereign state with an independent nationality' and the admission of the Regency to the League ('Note: Ahmed Tewfiq el Madani', in note 13 above). He was also the author, in March 1943, of a long memorandum on the Tunisian question addressed via the American occupation authorities in Algiers to President Truman, a would-be parallel text to the much better-known *Manifeste du peuple algérien* (Copy in French, dated Algiers, 7 March 1943, in AGGA/25H/32/10/838–842, with note, CIE, Algiers, 3 May 1943, AGGA/25H/32/10/837).

[15] *HK*, II, 61. A series of these articles is in *HK*, II, 275–330. Among the pieces claimed for al-Madani's authorship is the famous *kalima ṣarīḥa* of April 1936, otherwise universally attributed to the pen of Ben Badis.

[16] Al-Manṣūr was his journalistic pseudonym. The subsequent editions appeared in 1924, 1925, 1926 and 1929–30.

ninth-century Aghlabid dynasty and the Muslim conquest of Sicily to the biographies of Mustafa Kemal Atatürk and ‘Abd al-‘Aziz al-Tha‘alibi.

As secretary of the Tunisian Committee of the Caliphate, al-Madani corresponded with the last caliph of the Ottoman dynasty, Abdülmecit, and attempted to promote, in the storm over the caliphate's abolition, the safeguarding of the caliphal institution, separated from a secular Turkish state, as the seat of a spiritual power reasserted throughout the Muslim world.[17] In November–December 1924, he was part of the third Destour delegation to Paris. By this date he was also a member of a Tunisian ‘Scientific Association’, secretary of the ‘League of the Pen’, and president of one of Tunis's theatrical groups, al-Sa‘āda. In 1925, he became a member of the governing committee of Tunis's principal modernist-intellectual institution, the Khalduniyya Society,[18] in whose rooms on the suq al-Attarin, opposite the Zaytuna, Muhammad ‘Abduh had lectured in 1903. By this time he was considered ‘the passionate . . . soul of the Destour’, of its leaders ‘certainly the most active . . . and one whose personal activities must be considered extremely dangerous’.[19]

Of all these, it was the portrayal of Maghribi history in the theatre that provided the immediate pretext for al-Madani's removal from Tunis. Following close on the heels of an article[20] in support of ‘Abd al-Krim's ongoing struggle in the Rif war, al-Madani's company, al-Sa‘ada, prepared a production of the play *Ṭāriq ibn Ziyād*, portraying the eighth-century conquest of Andalusia by the Arab-Berber armies of North Africa, in which the conquering heroes were costumed as contemporary Rifis. The allusion was hardly subtle, and the play was banned by the Residency. Al-Madani was formally expelled from Tunisia on 6 June 1925.[21]

The form of colonial power exercised in Algeria, and the social forms and possibilities produced by it, differed considerably from those existing at the same time in Tunisia. The social, political and cultural situation al-Madani found on arrival in the land of his forebears was very different to that he had left behind, and the difference is well illustrated by the group we find on the platform at Constantine station, waiting for

[17] *HK*, I, 324–8.

[18] Note, Sûreté publique, Tunis, 16 April 1925, ISHMN/Résidence/R97/1704/1/147–8.

[19] Report on Destour, n.p, n.d. [Tunis, after Nov. 1923], (16 pp.), ISHMN/Résidence/R97/1704/1/71–86, pp. 10, 13.

[20] ‘The truth about events in the Rif. Long live the Rif, free and independent!’, *Ifriqiya*, 25 May 1925, MS note, Residence, Tunis, 27 June 1925 (ISHMN/Residence/R97/1704/1/156). French tr. publ. in *Renseignements coloniaux* (*BCAF* monthly supplement), no. 6 *bis* (June 1925): 230–2. *Ifriqiya* was banned shortly afterwards.

[21] The expulsion order was rescinded on 28 November 1933, but he never returned to live permanently in Tunisia.

the evening train to Algiers five days after al-Madani left Tunis. He was met on arrival in Constantine by Smaïl Māmī, director of the Constantine newspaper *al-Najāḥ*, Algeria's sole *grand journal d'information* in Arabic, and the only Arabic newspaper of the colonial period to achieve daily publication,[22] and his associate 'Abd al-Hāfiẓ Belḥāchemi. The following day he met 'Abd al-Hamid Ben Badis and Mubarak al-Mili, whom al-Madani had known while he was studying at the Zaytuna, and who was then teaching in the reformist *kuttāb* (Qur'anic school) established by Ben Badis in the rue Alexis-Lambert. Leaving the city after his two-day stay, he was escorted to the station by al-Mili, Mami, Belhachemi, two other acquaintances and five student well-wishers from the Constantine *médersa*, the official, bilingual school where aspirants to the Muslim civic judiciary were trained.[23] At the station, Mami introduced him to Si Muḥammad Ben Muṣṭafa Ben Bādīs, father of 'Abd al-Hamid, and his second son, Mouloud 'Zoubir'.[24] The father was on his way to Algiers to participate in a session of the colony's highest assembly, the budget-voting *Délégations financières*, accompanied by his son, a *bachelier* and lawyer.[25]

[22] Founded by Mami, a Zaytuna graduate, in August 1920, *al-Najāḥ* survived until September 1956. Briefly achieving daily publication in 1930, it thereafter produced three editions per week, and had the highest circulation of any Arabic paper in Algeria (*c.* 6,000 copies of each edition. But N.B. the late-1930s circulation of the leftist *Alger républicain*, 50,000; the conservative *Echo d'Alger* reached 80,000). Cool towards the *salafiyya*, whom Mami criticised for breaking Maliki orthodoxy, it advocated emancipation through economic self-empowerment. Celebrated in 1930 by al-Madani *(Taqwīm al-Manṣūr* no. 5, 246–7) and *al-Shihāb* ('one of the greatest achievements of the Arabic press', *al-Shihāb*, Feb. 1930, 59–60, quoted in Merad, 'Formation de la presse', 21), its later open conflict with the AUMA would see it branded 'a government paper in Arabic' (*al-Baṣā'ir*, 20 May 1938, tr. extr., ADA/4I/13/3) by Ben Badis, himself an occasional contributor to *al-Najāḥ* in its first years of publication. Mami now attacked the *'ulamā* for their 'corrupting and dangerous teaching' (*al-Najāḥ*, 4 May 1938, ADA/4I/13/3). (See 'Notice sur le journal "En Nadjah"', Prefecture, Constantine, 19 Feb. 1925, ADC/B3/286/7; 'La Presse indigène en Algérie', May 1936 (11 pp.), ADA/4I/178/1; 'Journaux indigènes paraissant en langue arabe en Algérie', CIE, Algiers, 31 Dec. 1937, ADA/4I/178/1; Merad, *Ibn Badis*, 33–4; Nasir, *al-Ṣuḥuf al-'arabiyya 'l-jazā'iriyya*, 43–5.)

[23] There were three such schools: in Tlemcen, Algiers (the Tha'ālibiyya, above the Marengo gardens on the north side of the Casbah) and Constantine (at the foot of the rue Nationale, later rue Clemenceau, on the edge of the Rhummel gorge). A second school, the Madrasa al-Kettāniyya, was opened later in Constantine, on the suq al-'Asr, with support from the administration but not as an official adjunct to the existing *médersa*, in part to counteract the success of the reformists' schools; Houari Boumédienne was among its students, as were a large number of future officers of the Constantinois ALN.

[24] Ben Badis senior had four sons: 'Abd al-Hamid was the eldest, followed by Mouloud, al-'Arabi (Larbi) and Salim (Gouvion and Gouvion, *Kitāb Aāyane al-Marhariba*, 64).

[25] Note, SD, Constantine, 9 June 1925 no. 758, 'arrivée à Constantine du nommé Toufik Ahmed Ben el Madani'; copy of telegram, Governor-General, Algiers, to Prefect,

Al-Madani's Constantinois acquaintances thus included the two most formidable intellects of the Algerian *salafī* movement, the two most durably successful men in Arabic-language Algerian journalism, and two of the most prominent figures of the urban patriciate whose standing had been preserved through all the vicissitudes of the previous century. 'Abd al-Hamid Ben Badis and Mubarak al-Mili produced the most substantial written corpus of Algerian reformism, Ben Badis in his *tafsīr* (Qur'anic exegesis), published in serial form in *al-Shihāb* (and posthumously in a single work), and al-Mili in his attack on anthropolatry, *Risālat al-shirk wa-maẓāhirihi* ('Treatise on Polytheism and its Manifestations'). Ben Badis's father and brother represent the urban and urbane class of notables who retained land and prestige; who, liberally sprinkled with *légions d'honneur*, had found a certain space in the workings of the administration or the higher echelons of the Muslim judiciary, and had invested in their children's futures both with the traditional cultural capital of *'ilm* acquired in Tunis and the Mashriq, and with the newer forms of advancement in the French university and the professions to which it gave access, especially law and medicine. All of these personalities were in some way engaged in strategies enabling them to 'work the system to their least disadvantage', leading to very different outcomes and alliances for each of them. Mubarak al-Mili and 'Abd al-Hamid Ben Badis, determined to reshape in their own way the cultural world of Algeria, according to their passionately held convictions regarding the true character of Islam and of an Algerian community – defined, for them, above all in religious terms – would be drawn into conflict with the colonial order while seeking an accommodation with it. Smaïl Mami and 'Abd al-Hafiz Belhachemi, from being suspect 'agitators',[26] may have achieved their ambitions as directors of Algeria's most successful Arabic newspaper at the price of a certain cooption.[27] Si

Constantine, n.d.; Note, SD, Constantine, 12 June 1925 no. 793; report, n.p., n.d. [SD, Constantine, 12 June 1925], 'Séjour du nommé Toufik Ahmed à Constantine', ADC/B3/170/2.

[26] Mami, engaged in frequent trips to Tunisia to promote *al-Najāḥ*, was in touch with Tunisian associative groups and was 'said to be the liaison agent between Algerian agitators and the "Young Tunisians"' (Commissariat spécial, Tunis, 4 April 1921 no. 358, ANT/MN16/1/44; Controleur civil, Souk el Arba, to Delegate Resident General, Tunis, 1 Oct. 1924 no. 61, ISHMN/Résidence/R94/1700/1/313). Belhachemi was identified as one of the suppliers of the 'subversive' nationalist iconography (portraits of Mustafa Kemal et al.) mentioned in the previous chapter.

[27] It remains uncertain whether Mami actually took instructions from the administration. *Al-Najāḥ*'s articles were carefully scrutinised by the government-general, and on occasion it was threatened with closure (Governor-General, Algiers, to Prefect, Constantine, 30 Jan. 1924 no. 1842, ADC/B3/286/7). It was also read in Morocco and Tunisia, and was reported as having subscribers in Syria.

Muhammad Mustafa Ben Badis, faced with an eldest son not only labelled as a dangerous propagandist, but espousing positions directly opposed to his own family's local political standing, broke with him in October 1933. In letters to Jean Mirante, the director of *Affaires indigènes* in Algiers, Ben Badis senior lamented his son's support for the independently minded Constantinois *élus* (Muslim elected representatives) led by Dr Mohamed-Salah Bendjelloul, 'the enemies of his father and brother, [who] do nothing but criticise them and who have attacked nothing [so much as] the name of Ben Badis'.[28] 'Abd al-Hamid was forced, on 5 November, to quit a building owned by his father, where he had established a school with sixty pupils, and where he himself taught. Si Muhammad Mustafa, approached by friends of 'Abd al-Hamid, remained 'unshakeable' towards his eldest son, 'whose present conduct aims to ruin his [father's] influence and attack his politics', and the son, faced with the choice, chose his convictions over his father.[29] The second son, Mouloud, a member of the Constantine *Conseil général* who also ran a newspaper, *L'Echo indigène*,[30] was, in his father's words, 'yet more furious than I against his brother, all the more so since he [i.e. Mouloud] spends all his efforts in fighting that vile association,[31] [trying] to reduce its action and destroy its influence . . . [He] refuses to meet 'Abd al-Hamid and will not speak to him.'[32]

In Tunisia, perhaps all of these men would have gravitated to the Destour, or in Morocco, to the Istiqlāl. But however coercive the French occupations of Algeria's neighbours, however determined the intention of a 'perennial' French presence in the Mornag vineyards near Tunis or the plains of *Maroc utile* ('usable Morocco'), Algeria's situation was different – not only in degree, but in kind. Conquered by firepower and immigration, 'by the sword and the plough' in the notorious phrase of Marshal Bugeaud, the ruthless victor over 'Abd al-Qadir in the 1840s,

[28] MS letters in Arabic with French *précis*, Muhammad Mustafa Ben Badis to Mirante, 14, 24 Oct. 1933, AGGA/15H/21/1.

[29] Prefect, Constantine, to Governor-General, Algiers, 6 Nov. 1933 no. 21756, AGGA/15H/21/1. I have been unable to determine whether they were later reconciled; it remains public knowledge in Constantine that relations between 'Abd al-Hamid and his family were cool at best, although they also, it seems, protected him against overly intrusive harassment.

[30] Published in Constantine in 1933–4 (Merad, *Ibn Badis*, 24, n. 2).

[31] That is, the Fédération des *élus* of the *département* of Constantine, founded in June 1930, an offshoot of the Fédération des *élus* musulmans created in September 1927. A bitter rivalry opposed Ben Badis senior and Dr Bendjelloul, leader of the Constantinois *élus* from 1933 and 'Abd al-Hamid's colleague in the establishment of the first Muslim Congress in 1936, at least since Bendjelloul's victory over Ben Badis in the Constantine *Conseil général* elections of 1931.

[32] Muḥammad b. Mustafa Ben Badis to Mirante, 14 Oct. 1933 (note 28 above).

but also by a vicious mortality in the seventy years following the seizure of Algiers, by systematic expropriation and pauperisation, and by the modern power of the legal text, the administrative clerk, the map, the census, the school, the police and the prison, Algeria, defined as 'an integral part of French territory', was more than physically conquered and legally bound – as by a treaty of protectorate or an international mandate – to the metropole.

It is now usual to speak of 'the myth of *Algérie française*', but the term is rarely given its full force. Cartographically mapped and juridically inscribed into the body of the French Republic, the 'myth of *Algérie française*' was a massive edifice of the modern inscription of will into fact. This myth was no mere *untruth*; it was, on the contrary, a brutal operation of the power of modernity to reorder the world, to produce new truths of its own volition. In the consciousnesses and practices of colonising and colonised subjects, in law, in material facts on, and in, the ground, 'Algeria' really *was* 'France', just as, conversely (and as historians of France have increasingly demonstrated), the reality of colonial rule was an integral part of the metropole itself. It is impossible to understand the war that would be fought against the Algerian revolution if this is not appreciated, just as it must be understood that the revolution did not merely 'reveal the (underlying) truth' of Algeria – it too created, by its own wilful violence, a new truth of Algeria.

The redefinition *en masse* as 'French' of Algeria's Jewish population is the most striking example of this extraordinary force of colonial power to refashion the world,[33] as was the geographical redefinition of Algeria described in the previous chapter. But it was not only geography and its toponyms, or even confessional populations, that were colonised by linguistic and judicial, as well as material, means. The introduction of the *état civil* (civil register) in 1882 compelled all Algerians to record themselves under a patronym recognisable as such to the French authorities. This bureaucratic power over the very proper names of persons, that is, over the most basic social means of individual self-definition, survives in the abusive denomination 'SNP' (*sans nom patronymique*, 'without a surname') of persons in the colonial archives, as in the reverse order of personal names frequent in North (and West) Africa; one reads 'Kateb

[33] The Jewish population obtained full French citizenship *en masse* through the Crémieux decree of 1870, and although this was rescinded under the fascist legislation enacted by Vichy, by the outbreak of the revolution most Algerian Jews of indigenous descent were considered just as 'French' as were settlers of French, Maltese or Spanish origin. They were thus massively 'repatriated' between 1960 and 1962 to a territory which had never in any sense been their home.

Yacine', not Yasīn Kātib, the writer preferring to have his name printed as it was fixed for him in the register of the colonial school.

From the wording of legal codes and the lines and colours across the surface of maps, through the dividing up and classification of populations, to the physical implantation in the earth of rows of stocky vine-stumps and the long, shaded avenues of colonial-agricultural villages, carving out a rural landscape of vineyards and red-tiled roofs, and an urban fabric of vaulted façades, shuttered windows and wrought iron-work, line by line of legal text, block by block of masonry, colonialism reordered the space and the face of the land. All this awe-inspiring power went under the enchanting names of 'progress', 'modernity', 'civilisation': the colonial order in Africa was constructed as much by the words that spun significance into law, land, and labour as by the practices of administration, agriculture and architecture themselves. The new (dis) order which reshaped the world beyond the colony's frontiers also shaped the physical world of colonial Algeria itself, and created the language with which this world was given meaning. It was within this system of meaning that the 'civilising' subjectivity of the French colonial citizen was framed. This same refigured reality was the world out of which a language seeking to represent the Algeria of the colonised, its past and future, would have to be fashioned. Such were the conditions under which al-Madani's companions on that summer evening in 1925 had to make their history, and under which new versions of Algeria's past had to be elaborated.

The difficulties of negotiating with colonialist triumphalism, with a France which now believed itself perfectly 'at home' in the land that Si Muhammad ibn Ahmad al-Madani, Sidi Mustafa Ben 'Azzuz and shaykh al-'Arabi al-Sharif had long since quit, may have appeared a deeply unsatisfying form of politics to the ambitious young nationalist from Tunis. In July 1938, a report made to the Algiers political police reported that al-Madani had

> long since ceased to engage directly in politics because there are not, in Algeria, men capable of true political action . . . 'Since I cannot find the [sort of] faithful men required, I serve the people by my pen and make a school of my thought. [Such] men will come out of it . . . I hope that God may come to my aid, to put an end to the sleep of my Algerian brothers.'[34]

Having settled in Algiers in 1925, the young intellectual turned his hand to a longer-term project of cultural production and education – the composition of treatises on history and geography, to journalism and

[34] Note, CIE, Algiers, 22 July 1938, 'a/s Tewfik el Madani', ADA/4I/13/5(2E).

various works of social improvement, in his self-appointed role as 'awakener of the people'. His Algerian brothers, of course, had never been 'asleep'. On the contrary, the exigencies of their daily survival for over a century had demanded that they struggle by every means at their disposal. In doing so, they had begun already to articulate their own languages of Algeria's past, present and future, in what al-Madani would call 'an anarchy of speech'.

'An anarchy of speech'

In seeking to negotiate, to inflect and attenuate the coercion of colonial order, other Algerian spokesmen had developed a sophisticated language articulating the recognised, 'legitimate' vocabulary of the system itself. The so-called 'assimilationist' movement of French-schooled, republican professionals and intellectuals, labelled 'nationalists' by their contemporary colonialist detractors, but dismissed as bourgeois *aliénés*, if not 'collaborators', by the radical nationalists of Messali's movement, before becoming nationalists again in a misleading retrospective unity after 1962, are probably better understood, in the idiom of an Algerian folklore they might themselves have recognised, as the jackal who has to deal with a lion.[35] Seeking to establish themselves as spokesmen for the disenfranchised Algeria upon whose subjection the colonial *chef d'œuvre* was founded, the 'Young Algerians' – the mainly pre-1914, enthusiastically francophile 'first generation' of Dr Benthami Ould Hamida and Chérif Benhabylès, and, with a more pronounced Islamic overtone, from 1919–23, the Emir Khaled; then, in the 1930s, the 'second generation' of Dr Bendjelloul, Ferhat Abbas, Ahmed Boumendjel and Ahmed Francis – all sought to achieve, through their journalism and politics, the equality of standing, the partnership in dignity evoked by Ben Badis in the text with which I began.[36] Trained as schoolteachers, in pharmacy, medicine or the law, they sought to extend the emancipation already accorded Algeria's Jews to the whole of the colony.

As Abdelkader Djeghloul writes, their strategy was one not of conflict, but of 'resistance-through-dialogue'[37] with the colonial state, predicated

[35] Yacine-Titouh, *Chacal*.

[36] Ageron writes that the Jeunes Algériens (an originally laconic title echoing Mashriqi Young Turks and Egyptians, but adopted by them, as in the title of Ferhat Abbas's collection of articles of 1931) consisted of 'personalities, groups, a loosely structured political movement which was quite representative of the modernised and *francisé* elite which the Europeans [of Algeria] called the "*évolués*" and who were known to the metropolitans as "*assimilés*."' (*Histoire de l'Algérie contemporaine*, 313).

[37] Djeghloul, 'Formation des intellectuels', 654.

on the eminently reasonable supposition, in the face of the might of the system, that the only imaginable future lay in the conquest for Algerians of the civic sphere in equality, the conquest of that same power that had transformed the world in which they lived. The nature of Algeria was irrevocably remade, and in this new world, the only possible future lay in emancipation *through* the awesome power of colonial modernity. As Ferhat Abbas declared:

An immense hope is born in our hearts. *Already the griefs of the conquest are being effaced in our memories. Tomorrow, it will be forgotten*. And this land, fallen, through the defeats inflicted on Islam, into a terrible anarchy, will see the qualities of its race reborn in the living breath of French thought. All is not lost, the roots are not dead, while a few branches flourish. Tomorrow, by the labour of all, the tree will recover its past splendour . . . We glimpse a day close at hand when, thanks to a better policy, our mountains will be covered by white houses, by metalled roads, by fountains running clear water. The *gourbi* ['native hut'] will fall into ruin, never to rise again.

In the distant *douars* [villages], in the centre of the village of mud, a stone is laid. The edifice arises. The houses multiply. The school, the municipal *djemaa* [council], the hospital, the post office, the police station. Here there is hygiene, medical assistance, security. The natives rush in, congregate, settle. The Algerian village is created. The plough is forged, the mind is cultivated and disciplined, the hand becomes dexterous. And under the golden sun of Africa, the cult of Labour and Peace enters every heart. That durable, humanitarian work, the glory of strong peoples, is accomplished.[38]

Such visions, perfectly integrating both the register of ideal colonial progress (civilisation, labour and discipline) and the image of its realisation in the ideal colonial settlement (the rationally planned village of whitewashed stone, complete with the apparatus of the rational state) occur frequently in the formulations of Algerian demands and visions of the future from the years preceding the First World War to the end of the 1930s. It is noteworthy that Abbas here expresses precisely the same desire in regard to the past of the conquest that we encountered earlier under Ben Badis's pen in 1937. The passage just quoted is from the conclusion to his collection of articles, first published in 1931. It is worth returning, in this regard, to the preface to the same work:

Many brochures and books have been printed, many speeches made, on the occasion of the celebrations of the centenary of the conquest of Algeria . . .[It] is inappropriate, to my mind, to draw up balance sheets on such an occasion, to light Venetian lamps on tombs. 1930 belongs to the dead, to those whom 1830 and the fifty years of Conquest buried in the apotheosis of victory and the mourning of defeat. Let us not insult them in commercialising their sacrifice.

[38] Abbas, *Le Jeune Algérien*, 165–6, emphasis added.

Let us not disturb their rest with dancing and the simulacra of battle . . . The century which passes away has been a century of tears and blood. And it is above all we, the *indigènes*, who have wept, who have bled. We bury this century, then, without regret and without joy, with a last prayer to God and to men that these dark days should not return, but also with the timid hope that they might have served to prepare for us better days to come.

Fraternity, of late, has been much spoken of. It is the one word we should hold onto. The centenary celebrations are nothing but a clumsy reminder of a painful history, an exhibition of the wealth of some before the poverty of others. Fraternity, on the contrary, is a programme. It is the future.[39]

Abbas would later explain this strategy – for him, a passionate conviction – as 'recourse to liberal and republican France against colonialist and tyrannical France'.[40] The invocation of *la France démocratique*, the ideal France of France's own ideal self-image, against the manifest injustice of French imperial reality, was a key theme of 'Young Algerian' discourse just as it was a key preoccupation of liberal French historiography. It also underpinned the approach of the *'ulamā*, who sought, in their self-appointed task of resurrecting Muslim Algeria from 'decadence' and defeat, a partnership with that idealised 'France', whose immense power and resources were to be employed for the 'improvement' of Algerians. It was, one imagines, with perfect conviction that shaykh Tayyib al-'Uqbi proclaimed, to an enthusiastic crowd of some three thousand gathered on Algiers' place du Gouvernement from the balcony of the Cercle du progrès, on the return of the delegation of the Algerian Muslim Congress from Paris in 1936, that 'the *indigènes* will henceforth be treated on the same equal basis as their French brothers in the metropole, for they are, without distinction, sons of the one *patrie* which is France'.[41] (But Charles de Gaulle would say something very similar from a different balcony not far away – twenty-two years later, and in the midst of a war. . .)

These were, of course, not the only voices to be heard. In Paris, the ENA had adopted a programme which called explicitly for Algerian independence, and this movement would gain ground rapidly in the 1940s. But we ought not to be misled into supposing that the discourse painstakingly fashioned and passionately articulated by Abbas and others was simply the superficial daydream of élites disconnected from, and unrelated to, the people they claimed the right to represent, that 'their ideas never enjoyed mass appeal'.[42] The personal prestige of

[39] *Ibid.*, 29–30. [40] Abbas, *Nuit coloniale*, 110.
[41] Comm. div., SD, to Prefect, Algiers, 20 July 1936 no. 4670, ADA/2I/32/3.
[42] Michel Le Gall, 'The historical context', ch.1 in Habeeb and Zartmann (eds.), *Polity and Society*, 13. Abbas's post-1945 party, the UDMA, may have been 'a general staff

Bendjelloul (to whom popular songs were dedicated in the 1930s) and Abbas was very considerable, and popular memory, in Kabylia but also elsewhere, retained as late as the 1970s a recognition of Abbas as having been 'a man who spoke for Algerians'.[43] Nor did such conceptions of a history overcome – of the conquest conquered – of a genuine partnership in fraternity, equality and democracy, vanish in a supposed radicalisation of Algerian politics in the wake of the final defeat of the Blum–Viollette project in 1938,[44] or even after the collapse of the Third Republic in May 1940 and the seismic shifts of global power-structure brought about by the Second World War. In 1946 Abbas could still write as his credo:

> 'Neither assimilation, nor new masters, nor separatism. A young people pursuing its democratic and social education, developing its scientific and industrial capacity, advancing its intellectual and moral renewal, associated with a great liberal nation; a nascent democracy guided by the great French democracy; such is the clearest image of our movement of Algerian renewal'.[45]

A recreation of Algeria, and simultaneously a recreation of France, realised in its own ideal image, Abbas's dream was nothing less than to transcend colonial reality, the reality of 'French Algeria' and of imperial France, through the transformative power of colonial modernity itself. Thus the colonial town plan – the neat white houses, the central square with its municipal buildings, its school and hospital, its well-maintained roads – became the ideal Algerian village. The colonial ideologies of industriousness, discipline and hygiene were adopted as watchwords for the renewal of Algerian society, the colonial prerogatives of liberalism and democracy adopted as if they really meant what they purported to declare – that all men were created equal, and France came bearing the Rights of Man.

without troops' by the late 1940s, but only in the context of a reciprocal dynamic of violent radicalisation engaged by the revolutionary voluntarism of the PPA and the administration's growing and suicidal obsession with 'security' through repression. The situation had, in any case, been irrevocably changed by the massacres of May 1945.

43 Personal communication. The university in Abbas's home town, Sétif, now carries his name.

44 The Blum–Viollette bill, introduced in 1936 by the Popular Front, was an attempt to reform the system by extending citizenship to a larger number of Algerians, in essentials a more generous version of the 1919 Jonnart reforms, and in no way a project for majority rule. Vitriolically attacked by the colonial lobby and buried by them in the National Assembly, it was also always opposed by the Messalists, who were themselves hardly radicalised by its entirely predictable defeat. For the liberal French historians, it nonetheless represented the greatest of several 'lost opportunities' for salvaging Algeria.

45 'Appel à la jeunesse algérienne', 1 May 1946, in Ageron, 'Un manuscrit inédit', 186–7. This text would be considered by the PPA as 'proof of Abbas' treason to the national cause'.

Ferhat Abbas was to remain, as late as the end of the 1940s, the leading voice among those who continued to seek a resolution of Algeria's unbearable oppression by some means other than armed secession. His visions of the possible political future of Algeria ranged from the French 'province' of *Le jeune Algérien* in 1931 to the autonomous-but-associated republic with its own parliament and constitution of the *Manifeste* in 1943 and the statutes of the AML in 1944. For him, it remained 'work and science which give liberty to people'; in the wake of the massacres of 1945, he remained convinced that 'the use of violence is a crime against the people', and that fraternity, as equal citizenship achieved through negotiation, was the only possible way forward.[46] Once the revolution was unstoppably underway, however (and after his own nephew was killed by the FLN, a 'mistake' for which the Front later apologised, but doubtless also an effective demonstration), he would serve as the first president of the FLN's provisional government, alongside Tawfiq al-Madani, who was the sole representative of the AUMA in that cabinet and also served as translator for Abbas's historic declaration of support for the FLN, made in Cairo in the spring of 1956. In the 1920s and 1930s, however, that lay in an as-yet-undetermined future. It still seemed possible – indeed, it seemed the only imaginable possibility – that the conquest could be conquered, the conquerors made to live up to the tantalising promises of 'loyal collaboration' that their mendaciously generous self-image constantly reiterated.

It is in this light that we need to read the various visions of Algerian history articulated by another group of writers, would-be representatives of their community who followed very different itineraries to that eventually traced out by Abbas. Si Amar Boulifa, Chérif Benhabylès, Hocine Hesnay-Lahmek and others also sought to give a new meaning to Algeria's history, and to read from the past a way forward for the future. Their visions, too, demanded that the history of conquest should be transcended in a fraternal future of emancipatory civilisation.

Si Amar Saïd Boulifa was born (according to different sources) in 1861 or 1865, at Adeni, near Larba'a N'Aït Iraten (colonial Fort National), and died in Algiers in the year of the centenary, on 8 June 1931.[47] One of the first generation of Kabyles to receive a French education, he became a teacher of Berber language, composing a Tamazight grammar, a collection of Kabyle poetry, and a noted work on the status of women

[46] *Mon testament politique* (1946), in Ageron 'Un Manuscrit inédit', 195, 190–2. His later memoirs, especially *Autopsie d'une guerre*, restate the same convictions.

[47] Yacine-Titouh, *Chacal*, 177–91, and her *Les Voleurs de feu* ch. 2; preface by R. Aït-Said to the 1999 edition of Boulifa, *Le Djurdjura*.

in Kabyle society as well as his historical essay, *Le Djurdjura à travers l'histoire*, which was published in Algiers in 1925 with the help of a subvention from the government general and the regional educational authority, the Algiers Académie.[48] An account of 'the struggles of the Zawawa in defence of their social and political liberties . . . the principal historical facts relative to Kabyle independence, which has always been animated and sustained by a democratic ideal',[49] the book relates an unending Berber defence of liberty in the mountains of Kabylia, which, throughout history, 'no invader had conquered', until the arrival of the French and their subjection of the region in 1857. Since that time, Boulifa says,

> this Djurdjura, endowed with the most remarkable qualities, can no longer live its life of bygone times . . . Today, as in earlier times, it is not indifferent to the benefits of civilisation. Engaged in this path [of progress], Kabylia, conscious of the strength of its wings, avid for space and liberty, can, in perfect safety, quit its centuries-old cage and take flight to better horizons. Its innate love of freedom, its struggles for independence, its aptitude for work and order . . . permit us to predict for [this country], in its rapid and certain evolution, a brilliant future. Civilisation, which smiles upon it and attracts it [to her], will soon bestow upon it her [abundant] benefits.[50]

Arabs are all but invisible in Boulifa's narrative. The principal antithesis to his free and democratic Kabyle is the Ottoman Turk, the traces of whose 'debauchery and depredation are still easily observed in the loose morality of the lower regions of Kabylia'.[51] The internalisation and redeployment of colonial Orientalism's categories of 'native' is patent: Boulifa's historical Kabyle is the same austere, primitively democratic peasant that the creators of the 'Kabyle myth' had believed they saw in the berberophone mountains; his 'Turk' is the same lascivious Oriental despot they saw in their late nineteenth-century erotic novels.[52] Boulifa himself may or may not have really shared these perceptions; what is significant is the way in which the images are made to serve an Algerian's vision of his own community's dignified past and liberated future. The text is a plea for a loyal partnership of coloniser and colonised in which the potential of each might be realised. The conquest, for Boulifa, was a new dawn of opportunity for the enfranchisement of Africa in a radiant future of modernity and progress:

[48] Among the personalities thanked in the preface is Mirante, the Director of *Affaires indigènes*.
[49] Boulifa, *Le Djurdjura*, 'Avertissement', iii.
[50] *Ibid.*, vii.
[51] *Ibid.*, 262.
[52] On the colonial construction of Berber identity and the 'Kabyle myth', see ch. 5 below.

It is . . . our conviction that brave and loyal Kabylia, tended and supported by a grateful France,[53] will soon recover all its vigour, and that, in a near future filled with promise, it will attain a moral and material prosperity worthy of its intelligence and industriousness. . . . The future is full of promise, if one remembers that Barbary has forever been the cradle of regeneration for the civilisations of the past. With Europe exhausted, and the home of enlightenment displaced, the future remains for Africa, where a future United States will not be slow to emerge. North Africa, reservoir of energy and intelligence, can, in this future, play a glorious part. The Berber, supported, guided, following the traditional spirit of his race, will carry high and far the banner of progress and civilisation, as for the glory of humanity.[54]

There is an echo here of the 'Latin Africa' literature of colonial ideologues such as Louis Bertrand, for whom colonial Africa was the cradle of a Latin revival in the face of European decadence and exhaustion.[55] Boulifa, however (entirely unlike Bertrand and his colleagues, for whom the Africans themselves were racially unfit to play any part in this grand scheme), recuperates the colonial myths of regeneration and civilisation for a 'true' emancipation of (at least some of) the colonised. His history writes into the text of Europe's advancing 'glory of humanity' an ideal of North African liberty, formed through the ages to reach its apotheosis in the light of progress borne by France. If this entailed a rejection of the Arab, and even the Islamic, components of the Maghrib's heritage, so be it.[56]

Chérif Benhabylès' account, published eleven years earlier, was considerably more sympathetic to the Arab and Islamic past, although it certainly internalised an Orientalist conception of Islamic civilisation as a thing *of* the past. A *fils de grande tente* (a son of the Ottoman-era Arab aristocracy), Benhabylès attended the administration's Constantine *madrasa* and became a *qāḍī* (judge), took a doctorate in law and was naturalised as a French citizen, thus giving up the jurisdiction of 'Islamic law' in civil matters without, in his own eyes, ever ceasing to be a believing Muslim. As *délégué financier* for Dra el-Mizan, a commune on the south-western edge of Kabylia, in 1943, he signed the platform of demands advanced by Abbas and his colleagues as the *Manifeste du peuple algérien*. A major restatement of the moderates' position, the

[53] Grateful, that is, for the 'glorious' participation of Kabylia in the 'deliverance' of France in 1914–18, its 'bloody and cruel losses which France cannot forget' (*Ibid.*, 266).

[54] *Ibid.*, 266–8.

[55] See Lorcin, *Imperial Identities*, 196–213, on Bertrand.

[56] This has been a tendency not entirely absent from more recent 'Berberist' conceptions – on the great poet and linguist Mouloud Mammeri's rejection of Arabic, see Colonna, 'The nation's "Unknowing Other"', 165.

Manifesto marked a significant moment in the history of Algerian nationalism, setting forth as it did the demand for an autonomous state, 'associated' with France,[57] of which all Algerians, whether of European or indigenous origin, would be equal citizens. He later became a member of the Conseil de la République at the establishment of the Fourth Republic, and, in May 1959, a senator of the Fifth.[58]

His *L'Algérie française vue par un indigène* (1914) was an exposé of Algeria's recent history and current situation as he saw it. The book also included translations of a series of lectures given at the Constantine notables' intellectual club, the Cercle Salah Bey, by the mufti of that city, shaykh Mūlūd Ben Mūhūb, under the title 'War on Ignorance',[59] as well as the text of the Young Algerians' first major declaration, their manifesto of June 1912.[60] The book is thus a remarkable compendium of social and political reformist thought as it was emerging in circles of both 'lay' and religious Algerian notables in the years before the First World War. His book concluded in a strikingly similar fashion to that of Boulifa:

> We must recognise that Muslim civilisation, whose existence cannot be justly denied, illuminated this land for some moments, and if those who inhabit it now lag several centuries behind their neighbours, we must not forget that they are the descendants of a race whose letters, arts, sciences, and all their historical past, attest to sophistication and good taste. The Algerian Berbers are, to speak plainly, neither better nor worse than their African brothers, they have the faults of some and the qualities of others; it is a question of guiding them, little by little, of making them understand through reason, and of making them appreciate in their hearts, the beauty and grandeur of the work to which France calls them!
>
> Led by a firm, but well-intentioned and gentle, hand, drawn by the splendours of a brilliant civilisation, and by the 'magnet of interest' also, they will then trace their path towards France . . . whose glorious mission has been to carry, through the whole universe and the different ages of its history, the resplendent banner of civilisation![61]

It must, of course, be emphasised that these texts were addressed primarily to a French, not an Algerian, readership, and it is partly in this that they differ crucially from the works that would shortly be

[57] The term 'federation', which occurs in the statutes of the AML, the organisation set up to press for the Manifesto's implementation, probably suggests a closer constitutional union that Abbas actually had in mind: see Ageron, 'Ferḥat 'Abbās et l'évolution politique', 133 n. 31, 142.

[58] Ruedy, 'Chérif Benhabylès'.

[59] Benhabylès, *L'Algérie française*, 143–93.

[60] *Ibid.*, 117–21. The 1912 declaration proposed a series of reforms in return for the mooted conscription of Algerians.

[61] *Ibid.*, 138–9.

produced by the reformist *'ulamā* writing principally in Arabic. For Abbas, Boulifa and Benhabylès, the crucial power of decision regarding the future of Algeria lay in France, and it was thus in French that they formulated their representations. In their reading of the irreversibility of colonialism, however, and their adoption of a strategy to deal with it in its own terms, they have much in common with what Ben Badis in 1937 was to call his own 'ceaseless striving for racial fraternity'.

These writers also, nonetheless, differed profoundly from the *salafīs*. Enthusiastic admirers of French modernity, it seemed clear to some of them, as for many of their contemporaries in the Mashriq, that the importance of Islam lay only in the past. While the *'ulamā*, like the francophones, sought a partnership for emancipation with the temporal authorities under whom they were obliged to live, the former insisted on retaining a socio-cultural authority within the state which the more radical francophiles found frankly oppressive. Among the most outspoken of them, Rabah Zenati, editor of the secularist and assimilationist *La Voix indigène*, hoped that 'the Muslims will gradually free themselves from the medieval grip of Algerian clericalism [whose] pontiffs, imprisoned in the cage of theology, entrench themselves in a furious intransigence so as not to have to admit their inferiority'.[62]

Another outspoken rejectionist of Algeria's Arabic and Islamic past was Hocine Hesnay-Lahmek. A more obscure figure than those already mentioned, Hesnay-Lahmek was a Kabyle who, like Benhabylès, was naturalised as a French citizen. His book *Lettres algériennes* was completed in May 1930, at the height of the centenary celebrations, and published a year later. Expressed in the form of an exchange of letters

[62] *La Voix indigène*, 3–10 Jan. 1936, 'Analyse de la presse indigène', 1er quinzaine de janvier, 1936, AGGA/15H/1. Zenati (1877–1952) was the author of *Le Problème algérien vu par un indigène* (Paris, Comité de l'Afrique française, 1938); despite his volume's being published by the colonial lobby in Paris, he ought not to be seen simply as a stooge. On the contrary, and even if one considers that he believed too much of colonialism's own mythology, he belongs with the other 'negotiators' for Algerian emancipation. Vatin writes of him, along with Mohamed el Azziz Kessous (*La Vérité sur le malaise algérien*, preface by Dr Bendjelloul, Bône, n.d. [1935]), and S. Faci (*L'Algérie sous l'égide de la France contre la féodalité algérienne*, pref. by Maurice Viollette, Toulouse, 1936), that 'while paying tribute to the coloniser and placing themselves deliberately in his wake, [they] propose modifications, suggest transformations and reforms, which imply a critique of the *status quo*' (Vatin, 'Conditions et formes', 897). Saïd Faci, a schoolteacher born in Kabylia in 1880, naturalised French in 1906 and militant in the Ligue des droits de l'homme, was a founder of *La Voix des humbles*, the journal of the Association des instituteurs d'origine indigène published from 1922 to 1939 (Colonna, *Instituteurs*, 187–95). A 'periodical journal of social education' with a circulation of around 3,000, its credo was 'the emancipation of the natives through French culture'.

between friends, the book offers a vision of Algeria's history, its present condition and its future, in which the author hopes for the peaceful and egalitarian union of all Algeria's inhabitants. The book's first part, entitled 'The Past', is a refutation of 'Arab-Muslim' Algeria and a defence of North African history and its people as purely Berber and Mediterranean. The volume concludes with a reference, in the voice of a French correspondent, to a lecture given in the presence of the president of the Republic, during the celebrations of the 1930 centenary:

> The brilliant speaker . . . said: 'Oh, we are not loved, but we are admirably tolerated, by the natives' . . . I am sure that, having heard him, the Head of State must have asked himself, what is the cause of this deaf hatred that prevents the French and the Berber populations from being as one? . . . It is, my dear friend, in our singular and deplorable error of having wished to annex Algeria without applying to it those great principles . . . that presided over the formation and development of France . . . It is in certain of these Algerian laws . . . 'juridical monstrosities', [which] will disappear because they constitute an obstacle to an indispensable union and a flagrant attack on Berber honour and French idealism.[63]

The end of oppression and the future of a Mediterranean Algeria in unity with the power of Europe are here, again, advanced as achievable through the transcendence of 'real', imperialist and tyrannical France by her progressive and just *alter ego*. But in *Lettres algériennes* (much more strongly than in the work of Boulifa or Benhabylès) this vision was set against a background of historical justification that excised Arabic and Islam from the Algerian past and from the 'true character' of the land and its people.

Hesnay-Lahmek's book provoked an outcry, and was attacked in a series of five newspaper articles by the leading *salafī* reformist al-Amīn al-'Amūdī (Lamine Lamoudi). Lamoudi was a founder and leading member of the AUMA, its secretary-general for five years (1931–5), and editor of *La Défense*, the reformists' weekly French-language mouthpiece.[64] In the Young Algerian paper *L'Ikdam*, Lamoudi published a withering critique of Hesnay-Lahmek's conception of Algerian history as

> a tissue of errors, untruths, contradictions, and gross insults addressed to the Arab race and the Muslim religion to which your ancestors, the Berbers, and so many other peoples – I might even say the whole of Humanity – are indebted for countless things of beauty and worth. I am an Arab of pure blood and am proud to be so; what is more, I am a fervent Muslim, of which I am also proud. And it is

[63] Hesnay-Lahmek, *Lettres algériennes*, 176–9.
[64] Published at Saint-Eugène (Algiers) from 1934 to 1939 (Merad, *Réformisme*, 110–11).

as both an Arab and a Muslim that I have a duty to denounce and attack your theories, as ridiculous as they are dangerous.[65]

Lamoudi's attack, through a paper not directly attached to the *'ulamā* but directed by the liberal 'second-generation' *jeunes Algériens* Mohamed-Salah Bendjelloul and Sadek Denden, indicated already, in 1931, the limits of acceptable discourse. In many respects, the AUMA's concerns were similar to those of the authors of these 'pro-French' texts. They would – as we shall see in the next chapter – have had no argument with the epigram, carried on the flyleaf of Benhabylès' work, by the author's mentor, shaykh Ben Muhub: 'Muslims, you must without delay put yourselves to work! By divine Truth, we have reached the lowest, the most vile degree of decadence!' But it was specifically *as* Muslims and Arabs that, for the *'ulamā* (who would later, as we shall also see shortly, develop quarrels with both Dr Bendjelloul and shaykh al-Muhub), Algerians were to put themselves to work, to harness the power of modernity for their own emancipation. It was in this respect that the truth of the Algerian past became an important battleground.

It is in this light, therefore, that we also need to read Ferhat Abbas's famous, or notorious, article of 1936, 'La France c'est moi!', which he was never afterwards allowed to forget,[66] and which is often cited as the classic example of the liberal élite's self-mystification, in contradistinction to the equally famous riposte of Ben Badis's *al-Shihāb* two months later, the 'clear statement' (*kalima ṣarīḥa*) of an Algerian national reality. Refuting the libellous label of 'nationalist' affixed to him by his colonialist enemies,[67] Abbas had written:

If I had discovered the 'Algerian nation', I would be a nationalist and I would not blush at that as if it were a crime. Men who have died for the national ideal are daily honoured and respected. My life is not worth more than theirs. But I will not make this sacrifice. The Algerian *patrie* is a myth. I have not found it. I have questioned history, I have questioned the living and the dead, I have visited the cemeteries – no-one has spoken to me of it. Of course, I have found 'the Arab empire', 'the Muslim empire', which do honour to Islam and to our race, but these empires are extinguished . . . Should a Muslim Algerian seriously dream of

[65] 'Une réplique nécessaire au jeune et présomptueux Hesnay-Lahmek', *L'Ikdam* (n.s.) no. 10, 15 Sept. 1931. An abridged Arabic translation appeared in *al-Najāḥ*. Further instalments appeared in *L'Ikdam*, 1 Oct. (part II), 1 Nov. (part IV) and 15 Nov. (part V) (BnF; no. 12, which presumably carried part III of the article, missing).

[66] In 1960, composing the first part of his memoirs, he defended his position as 'a policy which, at least, had the merit of *addressing reality*. The Algerian people existed . . . But was it necessary, first, to demand for it a juridical status according to the national norm, *or to try to save it, by the means at hand*, from the physical and moral collapse into which it was falling?' (Abbas, *Nuit coloniale*, 129, emphasis added).

[67] On this occasion, an article in *Le Temps*.

building his future with the dust of the past? Don Quixote is not a man of our times. One does not build on the wind. We have brushed aside once and for all [such] daydreams and illusions to tie our future definitively to that of the work of France in this land . . . Behind this word ['nationalism'], some seek to oppose our economic and political emancipation. And we want this double emancipation, with all the force of our will and our social idealism. Six million Muslims live in this land which has been French for a hundred years, living in shacks, barefoot, without clothing and without bread. Of this famished multitude, we want to make a modern society through the school, the defence of [the rights of] man, that this society should be French . . . Without the emancipation of the *indigènes*, French Algeria cannot endure. *La France, c'est moi* because I am the multitude, the soldier, the worker, the artisan, the consumer. To refuse my cooperation, my welfare and my contribution to the common effort is a gross heresy.[68]

In response, the *'ulamā* declared:

For our part, we have consulted the pages of history, and we have consulted present circumstances, and we have found the Algerian Muslim nation (*al-umma 'l-jazā'iriyya 'l-muslima*) existing just as the other nations of the world have been formed and exist. This nation has its history, filled with great deeds, it has its religious and linguistic unity, its particular culture, its customs, its moral character, with its part of the good and the shameful, just as does every other nation of the world.

Furthermore, this Algerian Muslim nation is not France. It cannot become France. It does not want to become France. It could not become France even if it wanted to. On the contrary, this nation is distanced in every respect from France, in its language, its moral character and its religion. It desires no assimilation, and has its own homeland, namely the Algerian homeland with its own borders as they are now established and well known.[69]

Nowhere could the distinction between a 'natural', 'authentic', and an 'unnatural', 'alienated' history of Algeria be more clearly located – or so

[68] *L'Entente franco-musulmane*, 27 Feb. 1936, reprinted in *La Défense*, 28 Feb. under the same title 'En marge du nationalisme. La France, c'est moi!' (quote from *L'Entente*, AWC). Extracts in 'Analyse de la presse indigène, 2ème quinzaine', Feb. 1936, p. 2, AGGA/15H/1 refer to both editions. Abbas wrote a defence of his position, published in *La Voix des humbles* (no. 167, April 1936, pp. 2–3), insisting that his statement was 'an act of faith' (Merad, *Réformisme*, 398 n. 1). Koulakssis and Meynier, referring to the version printed in *La Défense*, point out that, in this text, the phrase 'Et cependant je ne ferai pas ce sacrifi[c]e' occurs as 'Et cependant je ne mourrai pas pour **la patrie algérienne** parce que cette patrie n'existe pas?' The emphasis and punctuation, they claim, 'entirely change the sense of the formulation' (*Emir Khaled*, 7). The revision is surely untenable; the formulation appearing in *L'Entente* is different, and what appears to be a printing or editing error in a single phrase of the second version can hardly transform the meaning of the entire article.

[69] '*Kalima ṣarīḥa*', *al-Shihāb*, April 1936: 42–5, AWC. Original copies of this much-quoted text are surprisingly rare. Merad, who worked from a complete, private collection, gives a partial translation (*Réformisme*, 398–9), and the Arabic is also given by al-Madani, *HK*, II, 63–5. On the text's authorship, see pp. 228–9 below (note 8).

most commentators on this exchange have supposed. In a more sophisticated reading, Djeghloul suggests that 'in its essentials, the famous polemic of 1936 . . . is a polemic without object. It masks more than it clarifies the problem of the definition of the nation as a concept capable of expressing multiple and contradictory meanings.'[70] The point at issue in determining the meaning of the Algerian past was appropriately, at the time, passed over – for Abbas, there was never any question of abandoning Islam, and he hastened to explain as much to the reformists. In essentials – the need to grasp the power of modernity, to reach an accommodation with France in a language the French could, or claimed to, understand – Abbas and the *'ulamā* were agreed. What is more noteworthy is that the quarrel is explicitly over the legitimate representation of the community. The opening of the *al-Shihāb* article is less frequently quoted than the famous phrases cited above, but is, perhaps, more crucial:

> In truth, we live in a society where chaos reigns on every side – anarchy rules in religion, in morality, in the economic life [of our people]. And to all this we have today added a new chaos, perhaps the most dangerous and the most significant for the life of the nation, that of *an anarchy of speech in the name of the nation (fauḍā al-takallum bi-'sm al-umma)*. Today, any orator who rises to speak, on whatever occasion, takes himself to be speaking for the whole Islamic community in this country, and takes the words that he speaks on his own account for the true speech of the nation, whose word is decisive . . . No, gentlemen! *We speak in the name of a great part of the nation. Indeed, we claim to speak in the name of the majority of the nation.*[71]

Al-Shihāb's heated defence of 'the Algerian Muslim people' was an indication of rather more profound conflicts over those 'multiple and contradictory meanings' concealed behind the apparently singular (whether denied or affirmed) 'Algerian nation'. What was really at issue was the very name of the people, and the question of who had the right to speak it.

The name of the people

> When an Algerian described himself as an Arab, the French lawyers told him: 'No, you are French.' When he demanded that he be given the rights of the French, the same lawyers told him: 'No, you are an Arab.' Ferhat Abbas[72]

[70] Djeghloul, 'Formation des intellectuels', 662.
[71] '*Kalima ṣarīḥa*', emphasis added.
[72] Abbas, *Nuit coloniale*, 110.

My point is not merely that the abusively simple categorisations of 'nationalist' and 'collaborationist' are inadequate for a grasp of these histories. It is that the struggle in colonial Algeria was a conflict over the very meaning of 'Algeria' itself. The *kalima ṣarīḥa* of 1936, more than any other text, is routinely cited to prove the nationalist credentials of the reformist *'ulamā*. Opposed to Abbas's myopia, their 'clear-sightedness' *(baṣā'ir)* is seen in this 'most complete and explicit affirmation of the constitutive characteristics of the Algerian personality', 'the deep reality of the Algerian Muslim people . . . its true identity, at once intangible and indestructible'.[73] But this discourse on the 'reality' of Algeria has its own genealogy, not in some pre-existing 'deep reality', nor in 'the pages of history' – although they had certainly been written by this time, and doubtless it was the texts of al-Mili and al-Madani that were meant – but in the categories of colonial legislation.

The argument into which these texts spoke was concerned with a very specific, real and pressing problem: that of the colonial order, which had maintained the masses of the Algerian population outside the blessed realm of citizenship, in the perpetual subject status of the conquered. The small but ancient indigenous Algerian Jewish population had, of course, been conquered too, between 1830 and 1870, but had a very different juridical fate to that of their Muslim neighbours, much of whose language and culture they had nonetheless largely shared for centuries. This anomaly points to what should be an obvious fact. As Balibar insists:

> We must . . . observe that the exteriority of the 'native' populations in colonisation, or rather the representation of that state as racial exteriority . . . is by no means a given state of affairs. *It was in fact produced and reproduced within the very space constituted by conquest and colonisation* with its concrete structures . . . and therefore on the basis of a certain *interiority*.[74]

As historians of colonialism have realised,[75] it is not (and never was) adequate to conceive of colonial encounters in terms of a clash of pre-existing bounded entities, 'colonised' and 'coloniser', 'Algeria' and 'France'. As Fred Cooper and Ann Stoler point out, 'the otherness of colonised persons was neither inherent nor stable: his or her difference had to be defined and maintained'.[76] The struggles of colonial legislators, administrators and opinion-formers, and of all those seeking to

[73] Merad, *Réformisme*, 397.
[74] Balibar, 'Racism and nationalism', 42–3, emphasis added.
[75] Cooper and Stoler (eds.), *Tensions of Empire*; Stoler, 'Rethinking colonial categories'.
[76] Cooper and Stoler (eds.), *Tensions of Empire*, 7; Wolfe, 'Land, labor, and difference'.

establish themselves as spokesmen of the colonised, were in large part articulated around the legitimate naming of colonial populations.

None of the three answers offered in 1936 to the apparently crucial question of whether or not 'the Algerian nation' existed – Abbas's, that it did not; *al-Shihāb*'s, that it did; and the PPA's, that even if it hadn't (an inadmissable proposition), it would if Algerians wished it[77] – can be regarded as having been 'correct'. The dispute is a 'polemic without an object', a struggle over a symbol whose *only* reality is in its invocation, whether in denial, affirmation, or projection. 'Nation', I argued earlier, is located not in objective social structures (and even less in 'the consciousness of identity located in the *nafs*, the *genius* of the . . . people'[78]), but in the contest over the meanings with which social structures are endowed. The key symbol identifying 'Algerians' in the colonial period was not some metaphysical essence of resistance transmitted across the generations and impervious to colonial power. It lay in a specific structure of social relations set up by the operation of colonial power itself and which enframed and identified Algerians as colonised subjects. Into this conceptual space, confining and defining several million human lives, was condensed a range of meanings extending from the purely juridical (and supposedly transitory) status of non-citizen to the most potent racial fantasies of sexual threat and subhuman terror. The symbolic site of 'Algerian' identity (not, of course, labelled as such but as 'native') was a repressive invention of colonial jurisprudence, the *statut personnel musulman*.

The *statut personnel* has been a perpetual stumbling-block of Algerian historiography – unsurprisingly so, given its centrality to colonial politics. The problem of reforming the status of Algerians in the interwar period was articulated around the question of the right to full citizenship, and whether this citizenship could be accorded to a person of Muslim 'personal status', *i.e.* subject to the Islamic civil law dispensed by the Muslim branch of the official colonial judiciary.[79] Most Muslim Algerians could

[77] The French-language PPA mouthpiece had riposted: 'Our national conception is clear and even supposing the inadmissible, that is that no Algerian *patrie* ever existed, are not five million people capable of working to create it?' (*El Ouma*, March–April 1936, quoted in Kaddache, *Nationalisme algérien*, 422). The actual primacy of populist voluntarism is clear in this neat statement. For the PPA, history is unimportant, what matters is the future; but history is already being assumed, in the background, as *doctrine*, in which 'the inadmissible' is already an operative category.

[78] Or 'the trans-class, trans-segmentary national invariant', a 'national sedimentation' of selfhood (Koulakssis and Meynier, *Emir Khaled*, 9, 13–16, 19). The resort to metaphysics or geological metaphor is merely another restatement of what ought to be investigated.

[79] Christelow, *Muslim Law Courts*, details the system's development in the nineteenth century.

not accede to citizenship – electoral enfranchisement, civic rights and escape from the repressive special legislation of the *indigénat*[80] – except by abandoning their 'Muslim personal status', something the vast majority would never do.[81]

On 13 March 1936, shortly after Ferhat Abbas published his editorial in *L'Entente* and before the reply of *al-Shihāb*, Lamine Lamoudi –the reformist whom we met earlier in connection with his attack on Hesnay-Lahmek's *Lettres algériennes*, and editor of *La Défense*, the publication which had reprinted Abbas's declaration of faith in the future of a French Algeria – gave a lecture in Algiers entitled 'La qualité de français dans le statut des indigènes' ('French nationality under native status'). The lecture is a neat illustration of the way the dilemma of the *statut personnel,* and the problem of reform, were viewed by the Algerian *salafīs*.

Our status as French is recognised by legislative decree but refused to us in practice. This is the cause of every dispute and misunderstanding. The remedies applied to this problem have been uniformly insufficient and ineffective . . . The senatus-consulte of 1865[82] attributes to us, as of right, the status of French national. Why then [are we obliged to go through] the process of naturalisation, which ought to apply, in law, exclusively to foreigners desiring to change their national status, and not to we who *are* French? . . . The native Muslims have remained 'honorary Frenchmen', and on occasion 'serving Frenchmen' – when, for example, it is a question of going off to war. Natives of different social classes are [all] in a position of inferiority, because we are not French. Regarding the *statut personnel,* sometimes cherished, sometimes criticised, we have been promised that it will be respected. In this, France has kept her word. We, for our part, have accepted every law which has been imposed on us; we have given proof

[80] On the *indigénat,* instituted in 1881, and surviving in various forms until 1944, see Collot, *Institutions*.

[81] Shaykh al-'Uqbi, giving his personal *fatwa,* declared that 'whoever admits the substitution of a single principle of a non-religious law or regulation for any principle of Islamic law, is an apostate' (*al-Baṣā'ir,* 30 July 1937, quoted in unsigned report, [CIE] Algiers, 6 Aug. 1937, ADA/2I/39/4). Al-'Uqbi accepted the *tawba* (recantation) of a naturalised Muslim. It was expected by the colonial authorities at this time that Ben Badis would be more severe, declaring such *tawba* inadmissible even *in extremis* (*ibid.*). In fact, the 'official' AUMA line, as expressed by al-Mili, was more nuanced: 'If a *naturalisé* does not repent, he will be condemned on the Day of Judgement . . . If he believes, he should be glad to be informed on so important a question. If he does not believe, the Muslims consider him an apostate, even if he is not naturalised . . . Our judgement [in this matter] is not a declaration of hostility against those who have been naturalised . . . The safeguard of Islam should not be a cause of strife among men' (*al-Baṣā'ir,* 18 Feb. 1938, tr. extr., ADA/4I/13/3(2F)). Ageron evaluates the number of naturalisations at around forty per year on average during the 1920s, 157 per year in the 1930s (*Histoire de l'Algérie contemporaine*, 316).

[82] The decree (senatus-consulte) of 18 July 1865 established the 'Muslim native' as 'French', but as governed by Islamic civil law and thus as excluded from French citizenship (Brett, 'Legislating for Inequality').

at every moment of our prudence and loyalty, but what recompense have we had? And yet the French Muslims are men, faithful co-workers with the good Frenchman.[83]

The principal obstacle to the accession of Algerians to citizenship, *via* the 'naturalisation' proposed by the system, as Lamoudi explained, was the *statut personnel*: 'It represents our traditions, our customs and our beliefs. This regards three principal issues: marriage, divorce, and inheritance.' And he called, 'in the interest of peace and pacification', for the suppression of the *statut*'s role as an obstacle to citizenship. Not, it must be noted, for the suppression of the *statut* itself, which 'represents our traditions, our customs and our beliefs', but for the removal of the bar to citizenship which it was held to constitute for those 'non-French Frenchmen' who lived in what was, apparently unalterably, French territory, but who, as Muslims, considered Islamic civil law as a fundamental and irrevocable part of their lives.

Initially, at least, this crucial space of conflict lay on purely religious ground – the Algerian Muslim community, *al-umma 'l-jazā'iriyya 'l-muslima*, was a community defined by its faith. Algerian Muslims had lived for centuries (if, admittedly, not always easily) alongside their Jewish neighbours, sharing language and numerous aspects of culture, and defining themselves through religious belief and practice. This situation was transformed by colonialism. In its historically specific form of conceptualising the world and ordering society, *inter alia* through the textual power of legal ordinance, French colonial modernity reconstituted *al-umma 'l-jazā'iriyya 'l-muslima* as a carefully objectified category, 'French' by nationality – since 'Algeria' was simply another part of France – but, since governed by a special civil code, un-French in civic status. The *exceptions* made to this 'un-Frenchness', as well as the specific 'privileges' (in the strict sense of the word) applied through it, illustrate the way the *statut* had come to operate by the time of the First World War. On the one hand, these 'un-French French' were eligible for conscription, for the duty of male citizens to offer themselves up as cannon-fodder in defence of the republic. On the other, they were also subject to a massive system of special repressive legislation, the *indigénat*, which criminalised a potentially limitless series of activities not considered infractions of the French penal code and applying only to 'natives'. On the clearly defined and easily policed category of *indigène musulman* was founded every procedure of discrimination, from inequality of salary to exclusion from the franchise and susceptibility to draconian *lois*

[83] SD, report to Prefect, Algiers, 13 March 1936 no. 1483, ADA/2I/32/3.

d'exception, from which Algerians suffered and which constituted their experience as colonised subjects, excluded, by a subtly half-measured 'inclusion', from *la cité française*. Thus, after the failed attempts at the physical *cantonnement* – restriction to reservations – of the indigenous population in the nineteenth century, the repressive device of the *statut personnel* served as an effective means of judicial *cantonnement* through the first half of the twentieth.

The *statut personnel* was thus the site in which the colonial oppression of Algerian Muslims was organised and exercised. *At the same time*, it was the key symbolic space which 'represents our traditions, our customs and our beliefs', 'part of our ancestral patrimony'[84] – a strictly sacred space whose limits, for most Algerians, marked the boundary between apostasy and belief. Although probably never intended as so diabolical a device, the 'native status' of oppression in Algeria was legislated into existence in the very space from which Algerians not only could not, but for the most part *would not*, escape. This doubling of the category at the heart of colonial politics is the key to the dynamics of resistance-through-dialogue, and its failure, throughout the interwar period. The *statut* was the key pretext for the exclusion of the majority population from the social and political 'emancipation' that France claimed to bring, but resolutely refused to deliver, and which Algerian spokesmen up to the mid-1940s continued to demand.[85] Both Abbas and shaykh al-'Uqbi, faced with the system's intractability, had envisaged 'mass naturalisation' by decree. Both were ardent partisans 'of French education, reaching into all *milieux*, into every class of society'. The dearest wish of both was

> that Muslims and Frenchmen should not only maintain good neighbourly relations but should constitute a single family . . . The Algerians must become one single people, whether they are French or Muslim; each will retain, in this [single] people, the beliefs of his forefathers . . .. If tomorrow the naturalisation *en masse* of the Algerian *indigènes* was decreed by the French government, the Algerians, obliged to respect French law, would remain Muslims, *de facto* and *de*

[83] *L'Entente franco-musulmane*, 27 Feb. 1936, 'Analyse de la presse indigène', 2ème quinzaine, Feb. 1936, p. 7, AGGA/15H/1.

[85] The Jonnart law of 1919 enlarged the Muslim constituency eligible for citizenship, but in fact, as Nouschi notes (*Naissance du nationalisme*, 54), the criteria for eligibility acted as 'so many filters', limiting its impact. The 1947 statute of Algeria transformed matters, giving citizenship of the French Union to all Algerians, but minority rule was preserved by the *cantonnement* of the 'Muslim vote' in a second college, where 1,300,000 electors, voting on behalf of a population of 8 million, voted for the same number (60) of Algerian representatives as the 532,000 voters of the first (almost entirely European) college. (Vatin, *Algérie politique*, 260–1).

iure . . . The Muslims could then benefit [from citizenship] without being considered as having abjured Islam.[86]

What al-'Uqbi, and the other *'ulamā*, opposed most vigorously was *individual* naturalisation, considered a voluntary renunciation of Islamic law and a debilitating division of the community. Abbas and Bendjelloul similarly told Minister of the Interior Marcel Régnier, in 1935, that in the absence of a measure giving full citizenship 'dans le statut' (without abolition of Islamic civil law), Algerians would accept an *en masse* decree of citizenship in whatever terms it might be imposed upon them.[87] Of course, such an emancipatory imposition was the last thing the colonial lobby wanted.

In the face of this intractability, this central *illogic*, of the system, then, a reversal in the *statut*'s meaning occurred by the mid-1940s. The parallel, radical discourse of the revolutionary-populists always insisted that no emancipation was possible without a completely sovereign Algerian state, conceived as the political expression of *al-umma 'l-jazā'iriyya 'l-muslima*, now understood to mean 'the Algerian (Arab-)Muslim nation'. The question of the European and Jewish minorities' possible status remained undecided, despite the FLN's eventual official policy of equal citizenship for all Algerians, of whatever origin, who would opt for *Algerian* nationality – a neat reversal of colonialism's posited assimilation.[88] From serving as the key site of exclusion from French citizenship, the 'Muslim personality' of Algerians became the key space in which an alternative, Algerian citizenship would be created. De Gaulle's speech in Constantine of 12 December 1943, and the ordinance of 7 March 1944, offering Algerians French citizenship *dans le statut* (but, for the majority, not yet. . .) were not only too little, too late. A whole alternative discourse had been created. Slogans on the walls of Algiers, Sétif and Constantine proclaimed: 'Citoyens français? Non! Citoyens algériens, oui!' and 'A bas la citoyenneté française! Vive la citoyenneté algérienne pour tous!'[89]

Unable to escape from their subject status, then, some Algerians appropriated it for themselves, infused it with their own meanings. The colonial creation and maintenance of the judicial/religious/ethnic difference of the colonised population in the *statut* had produced a

[86] Al-'Uqbi, interviewed by Robert Randau, in Randau and Fikri, *Les Compagnons du jardin*, 180–2.

[87] Daoud and Stora, *Ferhat Abbas*, 70–1.

[87] *Tous Algériens*, GPRA Ministry of Information brochure, Tunis, March 1961, 111 pp. (BNT). Carlier, however, describes how the problem was already in the late 1940s conceived by leaders of the OS, as among the colonialist ultras, in terms of bloody rupture and separation (*Entre nation et jihad*, 27–8).

[89] Ageron, *Histoire de l'Algérie contemporaine*, 567.

crucial discursive site of contest, invoked and mobilised first by colonial administrators and the settler lobby, seeking to eternalise the subject status of Algerians, but subsequently by Algerians themselves for whom the *statut personnel musulman*, translated into Arabic as *shakhṣiyyatunā 'l-islāmiyya*, 'our Islamic personality', came to signify something the colonial system, *having created it as such*, could not admit – the definition of specifically 'Muslim Algeria' as a political community.

This is not to say (absurdly) that Algerians identified themselves 'as Muslims' because the French colonial state did so. The point is rather that the political centrality of 'Arab-Muslim identity', as the definition of the boundary of community, was not a necessary, pre-existing or 'revealed' fact, but a contingent and constructed one, in the development of Algerian nationalism. In the Mashriq, where indigenous Christian populations were not juridically removed from the 'national' community, and where larger, more diverse constituencies articulated their demands in Arabic, other, more explicitly secular, definitions of 'Arab' nationalism emerged. In Morocco, both Islam and the nation were crystallised around the monarchy. It is the particular configuration of institutions and resources (the particular 'political economy of meaning') obtaining in each case that largely accounts for each outcome. In Algeria, it was not *as* Muslims, *because* they were Muslims, that Algerians became nationalists – the projects of the FLN and its predecessors were not determined by a 'Muslim consciousness'. Their project of national salvation was decidedly this-worldly. But they would, nonetheless, ultimately abide by the primacy of Islam as the central defining factor of what 'Algerian' should actually mean. Already, in November 1919, the dissident, anti-naturalisation faction of the Jeunes Algériens led by the Emir Khaled had crushed the other remnants of the 'first generation' Young Algerians, led by Dr Benthami, in the Algiers municipal elections, standing on a platform of defence of the 'Muslim personality' against the gradual, individual naturalisation supported by Benthami. This victory indicated the powerful social sanction attached to the *tabu* key-symbol of 'personal status'/Islamic identity.[90] The full mobilisation of an irreducible 'Arab-Muslim Algerian identity' in this same site was developed, especially from the mid-1930s, by the reformist *'ulamā*. Their concern with it, however, derived not from primarily political concerns but from their preoccupation with cultural and religious authority.[91]

[90] Kaddache, *Vie politique*, 41–3, 65–76.

[91] It is important, in his context, to remember the very specific formulation given to this notion by Ben Badis himself, who identified *shakhṣiyyatunā 'l-islāmiyya* as Algeria's true *jinsiyya qawmiyya*, 'ethnic', or perhaps 'foundational' nationality, an invariant

It was particularly the reformist *'ulamā* who were in a position to invest in and colonise this space of self-definition, infused with a very specific cultural meaning of Arab-Islamic 'authenticity'. In so doing, they refigured the repressive, confining category of colonial legislation as the *nafs*, the inviolable 'genius' of Arab-Muslim Algeria, 'that which we hold most dear'[92] – the Algerian community's very 'self'. This language of pristine selfhood effectively became the central domain of their socio-cultural authority. In al-Mili's words, 'we do not hesitate to declare publicly that we are the guardians of Islam and of Arabism'.[93] But the significance of this, while implicitly and ultimately political, was first of all conceived by the reformists themselves as a question of *religious* authority. 'The Islamic personality' of Algeria thus conceived condensed into one symbolic site the religio-cultural heterogeneity of Algerian society, bringing the affective and practical diversity of belief, ritual and law into *one* space of authoritative enunciation. The recuperation and reformulation of the *statut personnel* as the key signifier of 'Algerian-ness' thus constituted a kind of discursive *tawḥīd*: the multiplicity of Algerian religious and cultural realities were thereby reduced to a single sign of 'authentic' selfhood, whose enunciation was appropriated by the reformists. This does not simply mean, as Merad has it, that the reformists 'contributed powerfully to the restitution of a sense of national dignity to their community, *revealing to it its history, its cultural values,* inspiring it with the pride of belonging to the great Arab-Islamic nation',[94] as if 'it' did not know, had never had, autonomous histories, other values. It does mean that, in seeking to establish themselves as legitimate spokesmen for 'Algeria', its 'deep reality' and truth as they saw it, they created in turn a particular confining category, a particular formulation of a prescribed, predestined 'identity', a self to which it was the duty of Algerians to be true.

substance. He distinguished this from a *jinsiyya siyāsiyya*, the purely 'political nationality' of juridical categories which might, and indeed did, change with the vicissitudes of history – one day Ottoman, the next French (*al-Shihāb*, February 1937: 504–6, quoted in Merad, *Réformisme*, 397). If he thought the two should ideally converge, there is no suggestion that he believed they necessarily must; in explicitly theorising the *separation* of the cultural from the political as an acceptable state of affairs – provided that there be 'equality and loyalty' between all groups involved – Ben Badis is the antithesis of Gellner's minimal definition of a nationalist, i.e. one who holds that the cultural and political must be congruent.

92 Ben Badis, 'Appeal to the Algerian People and its Elected Representatives', Aug. 1937 (in Arabic and French), ADC/B3/274/1.

93 *Al-Baṣā'ir*, 18 Feb. 1938, tr. extr., ADA/4I/13/3(2F).

94 Merad, *Réformisme*, 427, emphasis added.

Such was the import of the long text, already referred to in the previous chapter, printed in Cairo at the end of December 1944, by Sidi Lakhdar Ben Husayn and shaykh Fadil al- Wartilani:

> To the Algerian nation, in particular, and to the sons of North Africa, in general; sons of the Arabs, resisters of oppression, sons of Muhammad, adepts of the Truth and of a firm faith; grandsons of the builders of the glory of the civilisation of al-Andalus, who eliminated despotism and destroyed its empire; descendants of those who blazed light over Europe after such long, dark nights, who emancipated the Reason of the West from its servitude and returned to it its liberty in matters secular and religious, after it had been the prisoner of its king and the slave of its priests. It is time that you recall this precious heritage . . . Your nationality is one and the same – you are either Arabs, or naturalised as Arabs; your religion is one . . . your *madhhab* one . . . your habits and traditions, your customs are the same . . . At this time, we have to choose between two things: either a noble life, worthy of being lived, or an atrocious death, with no resurrection, if we accept the transformation that the French would impose upon us. You should know that all life in the bosom of another – however happy or brilliant it may appear – is worse than death. If . . . we are incorporated into France, it would be as if we had entered the stomach of a lion . . . We would be like the beasts one leads to labour and even to death, as if we were a vile and despicable race . . . [The] French pretend to offer us Fraternity, Equality and Equity, if only we renounce our personality. But what value has an individual who renounces his origin, to become another person? He will have an existence between heaven and earth, but one that is neither life nor death.[95]

Here, the circle is complete – the French idiom of 'naturalisation' is appropriated and applied to the Arabisation of pre-Islamic, Berber North Africa; the trope of civilisation is remobilised against Europe in the evocation of the enlightening brilliance of the Islamic golden age, which, long before 1789, 'emancipated the Reason of the West' from the bonds of clericalism and despotism. The glorious history of the Arab-Muslim Maghrib shows Algerians who they truly are, and must be. Any other way lies a destruction worse than death itself. The 'natural' history of Algeria is revealed in its unitary 'Islamic personality', and the foreign presence of the Other (in dialogue with whom, and out of whose own discourse, all of this is created) is set up as its absolutely unnatural antithesis. *Tajnīs*, changing one's nationality, accepting the citizenship of the occupier, is not simply a question of switching juridical categories, and is certainly not a means to emancipation – it is an atrocious death from which no-one can return.

[95] Director, Service des Affaires musulmanes, Delegation in North Africa, GPRF, to Director, CIE, Algiers, 7 Feb. 1945 no. 2402, DGF/AM, ADA/4I/28/6; partial MS copy in AWC/Ghassiri papers.

For some, negotiating the rule of colonialism meant conceiving of Algerian histories and futures that would later appear deeply unnatural, ('collaborationist', 'treacherous'). And yet this was precisely the point; the *nature* of the world was changed, and a way had to be found to live with it. In the struggle to produce the dominant representation of 'Algeria', though, it turned out that no status for the colonised could be accepted by the coloniser save that of defeated native, son of a defeated native. Nothing demonstrated that better than the centenaries of 1930 and 1937. In fixing Algerians in this inflexible space of oppression, however, colonialism also turned out to have created a space that a particular group of Algerians, the *'ulamā*, were themselves ideally placed to colonise – a space they could appropriate, refigure, and make their own. This category, defining Algerians and an Algerian 'self', against and apart from the colonising 'others' and *out of* the very discursive confinement in which the system sought to fix them, would later serve to identify a space of resistance to a murderous colonial war, and the defence of a dream of liberty. It was also, though, serving already to construct new claims to unitary, sacred authority, an exclusive conception of national community reduced to a unitary and unanimist 'essence'. In the very same space in which colonialism's device of repression was transformed into an active, auto-emancipatory subjectivity, its twin, subjection, also re-emerged. For 'liberation', it seemed, could only occur as the work of the people's awakeners – those able to remedy the masses' mortal ignorance:

> The Arab sons of Algeria are totally ignorant of everything regarding the Algerian nation. They are ignorant of its history, its natural character, its organisation and laws, the races of its inhabitants, the state of its culture and power of its economy. It is as if they lived in houses not their own, on land that did not give birth to their fathers and grandfathers; as if they were created in a land severed from its roots and ignorant of ancestry . . . But they do not live, who live ignorant of their nation.[96]

If this is a general lament of all nationalists, it was a view particularly propounded by those intellectuals and activists who would congregate in the *salafiyya* movement – Algerians, struggling with colonial domination, could not save themselves.[97] They would have to be taught to live; in order to be free, they would have to be taught how to know themselves. They were to be 'a Muslim nation'; but what did 'Muslim' mean?

[96] Al-Madani, *Kitāb al-Jazā'ir*, 2.

[97] The same assumption has sometimes been made by historians; cf. Merad's judgment quoted on p. 29 above.

3 The doctors of new religion

> We have come to teach you your religion, which you have begun to lose.
>
> shaykh Muḥammad Khayr al-Dīn to people of al-Kantara (Aurès), December 1937[1]

> To make people understand . . . to teach them to know themselves . . .
>
> Si 'Amor Derdūr, reformist *'ālim*, Aurès[2]

> Algerian, your country is dead, what means will you employ to revive it? It is by your religion that you may revive your land . . . Every evil to which you have been subject – disdain, indigence, privation of the good things of this world – has as its cause the abandonment of your religion . . .
>
> *al-Iṣlāḥ*, reformist newspaper published in Algiers, 19 September 1929[3]

The preceding chapter offered a sketch of the competitive field and the political conditions within which the *salafī* vision of Algerian nationhood was produced. This chapter explores how the *'ulamā* articulated their claim to unitary, sacred socio-cultural authority in the key physical and discursive spaces of Algerians' communal life: education, ritual, the form and meaning of religious culture itself. In particular, I will focus on a series of small – indeed peripheral, but for that very reason illustrative – events that took place in the watershed year of 1936, in the provincial capital of eastern Algeria, Constantine, and its environs. This narrow chronological and geographical focus throws into bolder relief the small details of the plays of power involved. 1936 saw a conjuncture of persons, time and place, symbolic resources and institutional context, which produced telling events whose close analysis reveals much about the changes taking place in the structures of influence and authority

[1] Quoted in Caïd, *douar* al-Kantara, to Administrator, CM Aïn Touta, 14 Dec. 1937, ADC/B3/274/3. The Aurès is the great mountainous massif, whose inhabitants are principally berberophone, in the south-eastern corner of northern Algeria, separating the hinterland of Constantine to the north from the Ziban oases and the Sahara to the south.

[2] Quoted in interview, Colonna, *Versets de l'invincibilité*, 330.

[3] Quoted in Kaddache, *Nationalisme algérien*, 224.

within Algerian society. It marks a moment five years into the life of the *salafī* movement as an institutionalised organisation, when its influence, in many ways centred on the city of Constantine, was beginning to be felt throughout the country, and four years before the death of its founder. It was the year of the victory of the left-wing, anti-fascist Popular Front in France and of the creation of the first Algerian Muslim Congress, whose delegation to Paris included both the liberal-'assimilationist' *élus* and leading *'ulamā*. It was the year in which that delegation's programme was dramatically upstaged, at the municipal stadium in Algiers, by the unscheduled appearance and incendiary speech of Messali Hadj[4] – the event that marks the implantation of the revolutionary nationalist movement in Algeria. Throughout the Mediterranean, 1936 was more generally a year of possibility and danger, of effervescent expectation – of the outbreak of civil war in Spain, of disturbances that led to new, more liberal colonial dispensations in Egypt and Syria, and of a revolt that did not in Palestine. In examining this particular moment, however, I also seek to show how things had changed over a longer *durée*, and so we begin with earlier expressions of the relationship of Algerians to their history, and with the different meanings of divergent responses to the experience of conquest.

From a victory of God to a culture of shame

> Evil, surely, was too ferocious in the world for it not to imply some eschatological meaning! This end of the world into which the Maghrib was falling could not, to the eyes of many, but announce the parousia that would re-establish legitimate rule. For the effervescent mentalities that abound at this time . . . if there is no alternative but to lay down one's arms in recognition of an undeniable military inferiority, this can only be by divine decree . . . It will be enough to wait until God changes his mind.
>
> Jacques Berque[5]

[4] The delegation of the Algerian Muslim Congress (which had not included Messali or a representative of the ENA, but whose leaders had had a stormy interview with Messali in Paris) held a public meeting on its return from France at the stadium in Algiers on 2 August. Messali's 'irruption' into this meeting and his address, which departed radically from the accommodationist tone of the other speakers (notably Bendjelloul), was a watershed event for the populist movement. The ENA, hitherto an exclusively *emigré* organisation, would have thirty cells already established, and another thirty-one in the process of constitution, by the time Messali returned to France in November. For the populist leader, 'this meeting at the municipal stadium, and [my] propaganda tour through the country [which followed it], marked the first beginning of Algerian nationalism, and the first stirrings of national consciousness' (*Le Cri du peuple algérien*, no. 6, quoted in Stora, *Messali Hadj*, 149). Accounts of the meeting in reports and press clips (esp. *Echo d'Alger*), AGGA/9H/46/1; Kaddache, *Vie politique*, 302–3.

[5] Berque, *Intérieur du Maghreb*, 410–11.

Around 1852, a religious notable of Constantine composed a history of the city, from its ancient foundation through the reigns of the eighteenth-century beys, up to the death of the most celebrated among them, Ṣālaḥ Bey, in 1792. Si al-Ḥāj Aḥmad ibn Muḥammad al-Mubārak, the son of a religious and merchant family, was educated at the family *zāwiya* at Mila, some fifty kilometres north-west of Constantine, then at Constantine itself and, intermittently, during commercial visits to Tunis where he dealt in perfumes and silk, at the Zaytuna. He was affiliated to a small local *ṭarīqa*, the Ḥanṣaliyya, and had close personal ties to the shaykh of the order; he became a Hansali *muqaddam*, as did his son and grandson after him, and he composed a treatise on the life of the venerated sufi Sidi Aḥmad al-Zwāwī, who had become the leading figure of the Hansaliyya in the mid-eighteenth century and whose *zāwiya* at Rouffach, near Constantine, was the most important centre of the order in Algeria. Al-Haj Mubarak was later considered largely responsible for the flourishing of the Algerian Hansaliyya in the early 1800s. In the 1840s, he was *khaṭīb* (preacher) at Constantine's Great Mosque and occupied a seat on the colonial administration's Muslim Judicial Appeal Council, until he was removed from his official posts when it was discovered that he had maintained secret relations with Ahmad Bey, still resisting the conquest in the south Constantinois.[6] Si al-Mubarak's manuscript, *Kitāb ta'rīkh Qusanṭīna*, not published until 1913, accorded particular emphasis to the multisecular vitality of his city, relating the many sieges laid against Constantine, each of which failed to break the 'tenacity born of a symbiosis between the inhabitants and their town of rock'.[7] Constantine, perched atop its dizzy precipice, was a city that 'no enemy ever penetrated by force': 'None ever entered into Constantine, and all who tried to take her were always thrown back – until the day when God decreed the entry of the French soldiers into the city in 1253 [1837]. Authority belongs to God, the Only, the Powerful.'[8]

And the author gives a curious reflection on the meaning of this epochal, world-ending event, which he himself had very probably witnessed:

> The first *'ulamā* of Constantine were well-versed in the arts of the talisman and practised astrology. They placed, near Bāb al-Wād, a talisman whose virtue was to prevent any enemy from penetrating the city. I have read in one book: 'Constantine was assailed eighty times, but never could an enemy enter . . . such

[6] Dournon, 'Kitāb tarīkh Qosantīna', 266–8; al-Ḥafnāwī, *Ta'rīf al-khalaf bi-rijāl al-salaf*, II, 78; Gouvion and Gouvion, *Kitāb Aāyane al-Marhariba*, 135–6; Grangaud, *Ville imprenable*, 321–2; s.v. 'Ḥanṣaliyya', *EI*[2].
[7] Grangaud, *Ville imprenable*, 330.
[8] Dournon, 'Kitāb tarīkh Qosantīna', 285.

was the power of the talisman that the learned men set up.' Perhaps this talisman was nothing but the rampart that used to be situated inside Bab al-Wad, which Ben 'Isa had destroyed on the orders of Ahmad Bey . . . when God decreed the entry of the French to Constantine, on their second expedition [against the city].[9] Everyone knows this rampart – it was destroyed some fifteen years ago.[10]

Mystical immunity is lost, vanishing in the face of modernity's fire-power. It is instructive to compare this account with another, by a contemporary, Muḥammad Ṣāliḥ Ben al-'Antarī, who, like al-Mubarak, died in 1870.

Born between 1790 and 1800, he was the son of a secretary to Ahmad Bey, last Ottoman governor of Constantine. His father was killed in 1837, the year of the city's fall, on the orders of the bey, who suspected him of treason. Ben al-'Antari later became a principal secretary to the directorate of the Constantinois *Bureaux arabes*,[11] following, as Grangaud observes, a logic of 'continuity in family prerogatives' – a family that made its living and earned its social standing from serving the state had no reason not to continue to do so; or at least, so it must have seemed. At the request of his superior in the *Bureau arabe*, Captain Boissonnet, Ben al-'Antari composed a history of the Ottoman *beylik*. Published in 1846, his *Kitāb al-akhbār al-mubayyina li-'stilā' al-Turk 'alā Qusanṭīna*[12] carried a dedication to the Duc d'Aumale, younger son of King Louis-Philippe and governor of the province of Constantine,[13] and concluded with the narration of the arrival of the prince to take up his position as new ruler of the city. In presenting this event, the writer portrays the French governor as a new legitimate sovereign:

In his description of the arrival of the Duke at Constantine, he shows how the latter begins [his rule] with a meeting of the religious *diwan* (council), to hear the grievances of his subjects – 'in the same fashion as the former rulers', he expressly notes. Al-'Antari sees, in the acts of this son of a king, a continuity of the forms and customs of sovereignty that legitimates his own choice of adherence to the new régime.[14]

These two witnesses to the fall of Constantine indicate in different ways the same need to live with the conquest. Where Si al-Mubarak

[9] A first, abortive, expedition against Constantine was attempted in 1836.
[10] 'Kitāb tarīkh Qosantīna', 272.
[11] Military offices which, from 1844 to 1871, managed rural administration and intelligence-gathering.
[12] 'The clear history of the rule of the Turks over Constantine', Constantine, Félix Guende, 1846 (St-Calbre, 'Constantine', 73–6).
[13] It would not become a *département* until the reorganisation that accompanied the revolution two years later.
[14] Grangaud, *Ville imprenable*, 331.

evokes the lost assurance of a magical token that was, perhaps, after all, merely a bit of wall, Ben al-'Antari looks for a new order of legitimate governance after the pattern of the old. Both, in their different ways, look to a transcendent, divine order for reassurance. It is only God who is able to decree the entry of an enemy into Constantine, so the conquest, even if – as for Si al-Mubarak – signalling a disastrous end to an era of unassailable integrity, must nonetheless be, in some sense, a victory of God. *Lā ghālib illa 'llāh* – there is no Victor but God.

This is not to suggest that these authors, or other Algerians who might well have invoked this formula in the face of the calamitous events of the 1830s, were simply fatalistic, holding up their hands to heaven in passive incomprehension. Such would, indeed, be a later interpretation of their responses to the conquest, among those who, like al-Madani's uncle, lamented the 'passive inertia that shackled the hands of the Muslims' and concluded that 'the Islamic lands had been emptied of their true guides'.[15] Perhaps, instead, we should see their historiographical attempts to place the conquest, and the new régime resulting from it, within the frame of a known, ultimately legitimate and total cosmic Order, as indicating one among several possible strategies of reconciling the 'world-as-it-is', in the new disorder of colonial fragmentation and the loss of sacred assurance, with the 'world-as-it-should-be' – and, on a higher level, is *known* to be – within the logic of a sophisticated and centuries-deep cultural frame of reference supplying the means of comprehending the world and one's position in it.[16]

Such expressions of the experience of colonisation through the explanatory frame of existing narratives of divine order are referred to by Georges Balandier, in the context of sub-Saharan African societies, as a type of mythology capable of emplotting, and hence of coping with, colonialism in recognised terms. Among the Fang in Gabon, for example, the 'legend of Nsas', in the version attested during the last decade of the nineteenth century,

> ties the poverty of the black and the wealth of the white to an actual divine decision . . . At a certain point, God (Nzamö) addresses both black and white and tells them: 'You, Black, get up and go find your wives; people the earth. You will remain always naked. You, White, you will be rich, richer yet than you have

[15] *HK*, I, 22.

[16] Cf. Gilsenan's observation on the appeal of Islamic organisations in mid-twentieth-century Egypt, which provided 'an integrating and transcendent meaning in terms drawing legitimacy from the ultimate order, but presented as having immediate relevance to the present spiritual and material realities . . . Such movements resolved, or pointed to the apparent resolution of, an increasingly obvious disjunction between the world order as it was and as it should be' (*Saint and Sufi*, 205).

dreamed.' The intention is barely disguised: on one side, accumulation of merely demographic capital, on the other, the capitalisation of all material goods.[17]

Joseph Desparmet, an astute observer of Algerian popular culture and a distinguished dialectologist and folklorist (at a time, before 1914, when such disciplines went unrecognised in the colonial academy), noted similar rationalisations of catastrophe in the oral literature of the Algerian peasantry, where, for example, Husayn Dey, ruler of Algiers in 1830, is said to have 'sold' Algeria to the French, or is punished for his tyranny by a local saint, and revealed to have been secretly a Jew or a Christian.[18] Another example of such a strategy in Algerian oral literature is the '*Dīwān* of the Saints', a cycle of 101 tales collected by Desparmet in Blida in 1908,[19] which relate the deliberations of a council of saints, held in Algiers under the presidency of the great sufi master Sidi 'Abd al-Qādir al-Jīlānī of Baghdad, on the eve of the conquest. The saints decry the corrupt and murderous rule of the *beylik* and discuss who shall reign in its place, conferring about both the benefits and the oppression that French domination will bring.

Our Constantinois authors, like these other tellers of tales, exemplify the first of a number of divergent responses to the events through which they lived. This type of response, sublimating the immediately real in a kind of higher, 'ultimately real' (the conquest of the *rūmiyyīn*, European Christians, can only 'truly' be part of the all-conquering design of God), overlaps in time with other means of reconciling the legitimate with the manifestly illegitimate divisions of the world, as well as prefiguring and offering an instructive contrast to still other, later interpretations of the conquest's meaning and the action required to remedy its shattering impact.

Beginning very shortly after the conquest and persisting in similar form up to at least 1908, the date of the saints' *dīwān*, these narratives, seeking to naturalise the sudden fragmentation of the world, could be considered as forerunners of some of the historical visions considered in the previous chapter. Whether in popular, oral form or in the literary compositions (first in Arabic and then in French[20]) of intellectuals, framed either in terms of an Islamic cosmology of divine sovereignty and saintly intercession (Mubarak, the *dīwān*) or of universal rational

[17] Balandier, 'Mythes politiques', 89–90.

[18] Desparmet, 'La Conquête racontée par les indigènes'.

[19] Desparmet, 'L'Oeuvre de la France en Algérie'; Christelow, 'Oral, manuscript, and printed expressions'.

[20] Among the later writers, only Benhabylès was, apparently, literate in Arabic – though this cannot be taken simply as an index of progressive cultural 'alienation'. Boulifa was a pioneer of the study and promotion of his maternal tongue, Tamazight.

civilisation and progress (Benhabylès, Boulifa), such narratives attempted to inscribe a lived reality of disruption into a grander scheme of reassuring, legitimate order. It might not be an exaggeration to see Ferhat Abbas as the last notable exponent of such a response to the colonial situation.

Also shortly after the conquest, and continuing in mitigated form into the 1950s, there emerged a second type of response, equally grounded in cultural logic and equally seeking to reconcile the incomprehensible transformation of the visible world with a known, ultimate reality. Prophetic and mahdist rumours and annunciations, which up to the early 1880s at least gave rise to sporadic rural revolts, and which persisted long thereafter, were 'framed by the conviction of an ultimate crisis of the community, an ultimate crisis of the end of time, beyond everyday time, just as action to confront it would transcend everyday action and its rationalities'.[21] Informed by long-standing notions of eschatology encoded in local forms of knowledge about social and spiritual authority, apocalyptic movements such as the Dahra insurrection of 1845, or Bū Ziyān's rising in the Ziban (1849), sought to sublimate the illegitimate disorder of the mundane in the ecstatic anticipation of a realm of justice ushered in by radical, divinely inspired human agency.

For the cultural and economic ecological infrastructure, principally the southern *zawāyā* and oases, where such movements concentrated their energy, these efforts were enormously costly. Julia Clancy-Smith has presented a strong case for a revision of the conventional periodisation of the nineteenth century (which sees 'primary resistance' coming to an end in 1870 with Moqrani's rising in Kabylia), suggesting instead that we should see a growing trend towards strategies of accommodation on the part of religious notables from the moment of the destruction of Bu Ziyan's stronghold, Za'atsha, by the French in 1849.[22] From this moment on, Muslim notables, seeing themselves charged with the maintenance of whatever authority they could muster, and having responsibility for 'cultural survival', engaged in implicit pacts with the

[21] Gilsenan, *Recognising Islam*, 143; von Sivers, 'Realm of justice'; Clancy-Smith, *Rebel and Saint*, chs. 4, 6. The Bu 'Amāma revolt in the west began in 1881. Harbi recalls the circulation of prophetic rumours, in the rural north Constantinois, at moments of expectation and crisis as late as 1947–8 and again in 1952 (*Une vie debout*, 94).

[22] Clancy-Smith, *Rebel and Saint*, ch. 7, esp. pp. 214–15, and her conclusion: 'After the 1849 repression, [religious] notables either withdrew from rebellious activity, concluding implicit pacts with the colonial regime . . . or emigrated.' As she also shows, 'withdrawal, *hijra* and retreat were, in and of themselves, politically charged actions which ultimately bore cultural fruits with immense ramifications after the turn of the century' (p. 260) – as we also saw in chapter 1. Von Sivers ('Realm of Justice') situates the last 'apocalyptic revolt' in 1879.

colonial administration in order to ensure their ability to sustain this role. Simultaneously, another alternative, that of *hijra* to the unconquered *dār al-islām*, was being pursued by substantial numbers of Algerians, among them the families discussed in chapter 1. Rather than occurring as a sequence of responses in descending order from primary revolt to quietism, 'preparing the way' for ultimate revolution, these were multiple, overlapping possibilities of thought and action pursued in varying ecological contexts by different social groups at different moments. Each displays a different approach, rooted in specific, culturally grounded logics, to the problem of living with defeat.

We can also trace some of the major shifts and reformulations in these strategies up through the First World War and beyond. The prophetic tradition, for example, while no longer feeding into a dynamic of apocalyptic revolution, continued in various forms to provide means of reconciling the world's manifest disturbance with ultimate truths of the sovereignty of God and his inviolable order. In March 1913, a prophetic text contained in an almanac, printed in Egypt and circulated in Tunisia, was picked up by the French authorities and transmitted to the prefects in Algeria, with instructions to maintain careful surveillance of the circulation of such texts, predictions from the east being considered dangerously subversive.[23] Entitled *The Revelation of Secrets*, the text contained a series of predictions for the year 1331 (1913):

> The dignity of the *umma* will be revived, its sultan rendered more powerful, its armies will be victorious! The hearts of the Muslims will go to the caliph of God, the Sultan, the Imam, as the peoples go on pilgrimage to the sacred house of God; Islam will recover its vigour, its force, its brilliance . . . The state of the Sudan will change, troubles will break out on the frontiers and the people will rise in revolt. The war of Young Tunisia[24] will spread and reach Algeria, and by their revolt these lands will rid themselves of French dominion. In Morocco, agitation against the French will continue, calamities will strike them in great number and France will be powerless to stem the advance of the war of Young Tunisia in revolt. France will treat harshly the princes of Tunis and the sultans of Morocco, if they submit to her. The tie that binds the inhabitants of the city of Tunis to the sublime nation[25] will become tighter, for the latter will take back Tunis; the strength of the Moroccans will increase and they will vanquish France.[26]

A more local expression of the prophetic idiom was turned up by the colonial authorities in the vicinity of Mascara in 1917. *Akhbār dhāt ta'sīs*

[23] Governor-General to Prefect, Constantine, 26 March 1913 no. 110, ADC/B3/285/13.
[24] Tunis had seen the Zaytuna students' strike in 1910, the riots over the Jellaz cemetery in 1911, and the 1912 tramway boycott.
[25] That is, the Ottoman state, or the *umma islāmiyya* generally?
[26] French tr. (no Arabic) in ADC/B3/285/13.

fī mā yaqa' bayna 'l-muslimīn wa 'l-firansīs ('Well-Founded News Concerning What Shall Occur Between the Muslims and the French'),[27] supposedly composed by a well-known eighteenth-century Oranais scholar, Muḥammad Abū Ra's al-Nāṣirī, begins by predicting the 1830 conquest, the divisions among the Algerians and the failure of 'Abd al-Qadir, who is castigated for killing 'religious scholars and leaders of the Arabs because of his poor judgment and his attachment to the weak-minded'.[28] Subsequently, 'the Algerians would eventually take up French ways, bringing corruption of morals – alcohol, prostitution, cheating and lying. The Muslims' world would be turned upside down to punish them for their weakness of faith, with drought in the rainy season and floods in the dry season, women turning against their men, and slaves being set free.'[29]

These disorders of the natural and social world are an eloquent expression of the unnatural new order of things, an encoding of the meaning of conquest in suitably apocalyptic terms. Whereas in the Egyptian text, the Islamic world is renascent and triumphant, this vision, which, as Christelow suggests, appears considerably older, both sets the cataclysm in terms of an assumed religious code and explains it in terms of Algerians' supposed deviation from this code. In a sense, this anticipates the *salafī* view of things that would arise somewhat later.

Another example of the prophetic idiom can be drawn, again, from popular oral literature. Although it has not been generally considered as such, it does not seem inappropriate to see the subversive popular poetry in celebration of the (supposedly converted) German emperor Wilhelm II in the guise of *El Hāj Giyūm* ('Guillaume'), which circulated in Algeria during the First World War, as a refiguration of much older visions of inexorable, avenging justice in the person of the *mahdī*, or 'lord of the hour' (*mawl al-sā'a*):

> Russia is dead
> Germany has stripped her bones!
> France takes mourning and weeps.
> . . . Hail *Giyūm*
> Who rises in an aeroplane, does battle with the stars.[30]

[27] Found by Christelow in AGGA/9H/16, and quoted in 'Oral, manuscript and printed expressions', 266–8. A similar text had been reported in the same area in 1914, during anti-conscription protests, and the prophecy was thought to have been circulating in the region since around 1870.
[28] *Ibid.*, 267.
[29] *Ibid.*
[30] Ageron, *Algériens musulmans*, 1176 n.4; Ageron, *Histoire de l'Algérie contemporaine*, 265.

Another version has:

> *Hāj Giyūm!* See his star arise!
> Ay, ay, what can be done against him?[31]

In these texts, a number of important shifts are visible. The Egyptian almanac's predictions for 1913 echo a new pan-Islamic discourse encouraged by the state ideology of Abdülhamid II,[32] reflecting a widespread contemporary view of the Ottoman state and caliphate as the hope of Islam and Muslims everywhere from Zanzibar and India to Algeria and Morocco. There is a similarity here with the themes that would shortly afterwards be developed in the writings of Salih al-Sharif and his associates. The popular refrains to the glory of 'El Haj Giyum' similarly reformulate nineteenth-century expectations of deliverance in terms of current world politics – strikingly, in this case, the *mawl al-sāʿa* of apocalyptic tradition, rising in the west[33] with the 'secret signs' of prophetic authority, is replaced by the German emperor rising to the stars in that symbol of modern power, the aeroplane. Languages of authority and salvation were undergoing rapid and substantial change. The *salafiyya* movement's assumption of religio-cultural authority in the first half of the twentieth century had a substantial impact on this process, and set in motion a different, and distinctively new, approach to the problem of reconciling the reality of the colonial world with the higher reality of the world as it ought to be.

In May 1955, the French authorities in Algiers noted the circulation in the city of several thousand printed copies of an old prophetic text, known as 'the prophecy of shaykh Aḥmad'. Purportedly originating with the guardian of the tomb of the Prophet in Medina, the text was known to have circulated in Algeria in 1875, 1880, 1881, and again shortly after the end of the Second World War. In the nineteenth century it had been considered part of the subversive chain of prophetic rumour of which the French had learned to be duly suspicious, although the document contained no explicitly anti-colonial message, consisting merely of a call 'for Muslims to observe their religion', and promising salvation to the recipient of the text who would copy and further circulate it. A handful of occasional customers of an Algiers printer, having received the text in manuscript, probably from Egypt (it had apparently recently

31 Ageron, *Algériens musulmans*, 1177 n.1.

32 An ideology revived by the Committee of Union and Progress, particularly after 1913 (Kayali, *Arabs and Young Turks*, 187).

33 Traditionally, in the symbolically dense *seqiya 'l-ḥamra* (Western Sahara), birthplace of the 'maraboutic revolution' in the sixteenth century.

circulated in Cairo), had decided to have the printed version made in order to diffuse it more widely. According to the French report, this was the first time that this text had been circulated in print in Algeria.[34]

This incident attests to the continuance of very old forms of popular religious activity, as well as to their transformation – the sacred text is no longer an individual artefact, a kind of amulet produced in manuscript by a religious specialist and laboriously passed from hand to hand through the community, but is transmitted as a mechanically mass-produced pamphlet, vying for attention in a standardised typeface (shared, perhaps, with commercial advertisers and the Communist Party). It is also at least conceivable that, in the early summer of 1955, such texts acquired – at least for some readers[35] – a significance beyond their ostensible content. While probably having nothing to do with the FLN in its origins, this text may nonetheless have been interpreted by some as a call not so much to strictly religious observance as to the 'duty' invoked by another printed proclamation: that diffused in Algiers by the nascent FLN seven months earlier. Even were this not the case, the text may be taken as a further late development of the prophetic idiom, establishing a certain community of discourse along the path of its face-to-face/hand-to-hand transmission and carrying with it the promise of ultimate reassurance for this world and the next.

Such means of expression of religion and community, though, now had a powerful rival bent on their suppression. The 6 May 1955 edition of *al-Baṣā'ir*, the official paper of the AUMA edited by Tawfiq al-Madani, carried a scathing attack on 'the prophecy of shaykh Ahmad' from the pen of shaykh Aḥmad Saḥnūn, a reformist preacher at St-Eugène in Algiers,[36] who, quoting Mālik ibn Anas and a Prophetic *ḥadīth*, denounced the apocryphal character of the text as well as suggesting that it was 'a message inspired by the colonialists, aiming to provoke a diversion in the minds [of the Muslims] from the political questions which so keenly preoccupy opinion . . . Independently of their profoundly puerile character, the meaningless so-called revelations of this false prophet constitute an unforgivable act of impiety.'[37]

34 Note on the Algerian press, May 1955: ADA/4I/10/2.

35 If they were linked in popular imagination with subversion and insurrection, as they were in that of the authorities, which is of course by no means certain.

36 Sahnun, a respected poet and imam, survived the revolution to become a vocal spokesman for a moderate, non-violent Islamist politics in independent Algeria. He would be a driving force behind Rābiṭat al-da'wa, the first loose coalition of Islamist groups to emerge in late 1988 following the October riots, before the emergence of the FIS (Willis, *Islamist Challenge*, 117). Attacked in Islamist circles in the 1990s, he was the target of an assassination attempt in 1996, and died, aged ninety-six, in December 2003.

37 *Al-Baṣā'ir*, no. 317, 6 May 1955, tr. extr., ADA/4I/10/2.

Figure 6. Leading *'ulamā* at the founding of the AUMA in Algiers, 1931. Facing the camera at the top of the picture, right to left: Mubarak al-Mili, 'Abd al-Qadir Ben Ziyan, Larbi Tebessi, Lamine Lamoudi, 'Abd al-Hamid Ben Badis, Tayyib al-'Uqbi, Muhammad Sa'id Ait Jarr, Muhammad Khayr al-Din (CANA.)

The same edition of *al-Baṣā'ir*, celebrating the twenty-fifth anniversary of the Association's foundation, gave its view of the conditions in which the *salafī*-reformist project had been born:

> The religious anarchy brought about and perpetuated by the intransigent and frequently unorthodox rigorism of a retrograde religious tendency, entrenched by the guilty indifference of a religious notability turned in upon itself . . . eventually provoked . . . the founding of an organisation of religious purification. But it required the ostentatious celebration of a painfully outrageous centenary to make this project a living reality. The blind will eventually see, the deaf hear, the unthinking realise that a century of humiliation and slavery has passed . . . and that another will succeed it. God, says the Prophet, will raise up at the dusk of each century one from the community who will renew its religion. Indeed, a man arose . . . and on 17 *Dhū 'l-Ḥijja* 1349 [5 May 1931] an association of religious reform was created: the Association of Algerian Muslim *'ulamā*.

For the reformists, the Islam – the multiple, adaptable, coherent and locally grounded systems of belief and practice – through which Algerians had sought for a century to comprehend the world and their position in it was nothing but anarchy and impiety. The impasse in which Algerians' social and political life was trapped by the suffocating repression of triumphant high colonialism could now be explained only by the supposition that the community of believers had somehow fallen into 'decadence', had become blind, deaf and unthinking – that their belief was not 'true', that they had 'begun to lose' their religion, as one of the reformist leaders, Muhammad Khayr al-Din, told the assembled people of the rural town of al-Kantara in 1937. According to another salafī, Muḥammad al-Ghassīrī, Algerian society had 'fallen into mediocrity and debauchery, [had] become contemptible . . . Such was life in Algeria before the appearance of the Association of *'ulamā*.'[38] *Al-Shihāb* railed against 'the indifference of so many young people who no longer recognise Algeria as a Muslim land';[39] *al-Baṣā'ir* lamented the young Muslim 'who has forgotten [his] glorious past and prepares nothing for the future, choosing contemptible debasement after having known greatness'.[40]

The proponents of the *salafiyya* saw themselves as the one remedy to this state of affairs, Ben Badis as the *mujaddid* (renovator) raised up after a century of domination to arouse the people from their 'sleep': 'a bright torch shining upon the people, awakening it from its long slumber . . . a wave that reaches into the distance and washes away the [people's] impurity'.[41] Ahmad Sahnun, the critic in 1955 of apocryphal prophecy, declared in 1937: 'If they had been united in Islam, the [Algerian] Muslims would have long ago obtained their rights. Nonetheless, Algeria shall live and recover its past splendour thanks to this shining star, the Association of *'ulamā*.'[42] The Mzabi newspaper *al-Umma*[43] similarly hailed the AUMA as 'the dawn of a new day for the Muslims'.[44] For Mubarak al-Mili, the Algerians were 'a sick man to whom the *'ulamā* attend. This people remains attached to the old principles of the *zawāyā* and the brotherhoods: this is a grave disease . . . The *'ulamā* aim for the

[38] Colonna, *Versets de l'invincibilité* 329, quoting 'Progress of reformism in the Aurès' by al-Ghassiri, AWC/Ghassiri papers.
[39] *Al-Shihāb*, March 1936, Analyse de la presse indigène, 1ère quinzaine, March 1936, AGGA/15H/1.
[40] *Al-Baṣā'ir*, 10 Jan. 1936, Analyse de la presse indigène, 1ère quinzaine, Jan. 1936, AGGA/15H/1.
[41] Speech by Ṣa'īd Ṣāliḥī at the Cercle du progrès, Algiers, 26 Sept. 1937. Report, Comm. div., SD to Prefect, Algiers, 27 Sept. 1937 no. 6564, ADA/2I/39/3.
[42] *Ibid.* Another speaker at the same meeting had insisted that 'we are not like those who demand independence, but we do demand liberty and equality'.
[43] Not to be confused with French-language ENA paper of the same title.
[44] *Al-Umma*, Jan. 1936, Analyse de la presse indigène, 2e quinzaine de janvier, 1936, AGGA/15H/1.

moral and social improvement of the Muslims. The union of all believers is indispensable for the attainment of this end.'[45]

What the cultural life of Algeria consisted of, the means by which its people understood the world and their place in it, was to the reformists nothing more or less than a culture of shame. It was, in their eyes, to this 'debasement', more than to the pitiless forces of colonial capital and racist social order – and certainly not to an all-conquering design of God – that the conquest and seemingly irremediable oppression of Algerians must be due. The people, deprived of their true guides, had lost their true religion and hence had lost themselves; they would have to be taught to know themselves, in order to become who they 'truly' were.

Writing of the reformists' impact on Algerian culture, Berque spoke of 'Islam jacobin',[46] a phrase upon which he did not expand but which is suggestive both of a furiously proselytising rationalism and of an obsessively centralising claim to unity. It is worthwhile exploring the reformists' project, and its implications, with these two aspects in mind.

Jacobin Islam (i): a resurrection of learning

Society, in the *salafī* vision of things, was formed of only two classes: the learned and the ignorant, a rearticulation of the old categorical division of *khāṣṣa* (the notability) from *ʿāmma* (the common masses).[47] The crucial task of the reformist *ʿulamā*, the self-appointed 'leaders of Islam'[48] who, it was said, 'guide the people with clear vision',[49] was self-consciously conceived of as a work of enlightening the 'ignorant'. 'Every people', Ben Badis told 400 of the Association's members assembled in Algiers in September 1937, 'has its leaders, just as the shepherd is responsible for his flock. We, as *ʿulamā*, have the task of bringing light to our brothers.' He compared the Muslim masses to 'plants watered by the learned, [who] maintain them and allow them to grow', and insisted that the Association's efforts be redoubled 'to lead the ignorant out of obscurantism': 'We *ʿulamā*', he concluded, 'have as our duty to enlighten and educate, as the Prophet commanded us.'[50]

looking down upon the "ignorant" peasant

45 Report, Comm. div., SD to Prefect, Algiers, 25 Sept. 1937 no. 6559, quoting a speech made by al-Mili at the AUMA general assembly at the Majestic cinema in Algiers.
46 *Maghreb entre deux guerres*, 67–72.
47 'The classes of the people', *al-Shihāb*, 8 March 1928, tr. extr., AGGA/15H/21/1.
48 *Al-Baṣā'ir*, Jan. 1936, Analyse de la presse indigène, 2e quinzaine, Jan. 1936, AGGA/15H/1.
49 *Al-Umma* (M'zabi), 21–28 Jan. 1936, in *ibid.*
50 Quoted in Comm. div., SD to Prefect, Algiers, 24 Sept. 1937 no. 6520 (3 pp.), ADA/2I/39/3.

This is precisely the mission invoked by the reformists who were active in rural Algeria in the 1930s. Quoting her interviews with a leading Aurassi *'ālim*, Si 'Amor Derdur, Fanny Colonna notes that the *salafī* project was

explicitly a *revolution* (*thawra*), not against colonial authority but against *ignorance* (*thawra ḍidd al-jāhel*). This firm distinction between political agitation or insurrection and 'cultural revolution' is essential . . . Above all, it marks a desire [on the part of the reformists] to avoid being confounded with [the political action of the populist PPA/MTLD], and claims for them a character which is *other*, different – a vocation above all of *educators*: 'To make people understand . . . to teach them to know themselves, through a "general [or 'total'] education" (*tarbiya 'āmma*), to become a Muslim nation.'[51]

And this salutary, civilising mission was required because Algerians had fallen into ignorance (*jāhiliyya*), of which Colonna identifies three aspects in her informant's perception of the society he set out to save:

a biological discontinuity in the generations of the doctors of religion; [the] state of ignorance of the peasants regarding their duties *and* their rights; finally, the *illicit* character of their [cultural] practices, including religion, and the *backward* character of their knowledge: 'In history, there are moments when men of culture are present, then at other times these men die, and *ignorance returns*. Then it happens that one knows nothing any more of Islamic duties, *salat*, *zakat*, etc.'[52]

What Colonna aptly calls the reformists' 'invention of ignorance', the conviction that Algeria – and particularly rural Algeria – was characterised by a state of 'religious anarchy', of illicit practice and backward belief, recast the lived culture of the people as 'uncivilised' as well as illegitimate.[53] This transformation in worldview, far from being an entirely internal matter of the 'recovery' of a true and prior Islam, was a function of the brutal exposure of Algeria to colonial forms of order and knowledge, and, as we shall see below, to the curious gaze of the colonial observer of 'native customs'. The reformists' own view of Algerian religious culture, and their castigation of its locally rooted forms as pre-Islamic 'ignorance' (*jāhiliyya*) were profoundly marked by the disruptive innovations of colonialism, to which they were far from impervious. Take, for example, the reformists' view of the rural *kuttāb* (Qur'anic school), as 'a place of disorder and noise, [an image] which was to become the norm . . . how can one not see what this [vision] owes to

[51] Colonna, *Versets de l' invincibilité*, 330, original emphasis.
[52] *Ibid.*, 331, original emphasis.
[53] *Ibid.*, 328.

the irruption of a new [type of] school, in which one sits quietly on one's bench, before one's desk?'[54] This latter would be precisely the model of the reformists' schools. Al-Madani's *Taqwīm al-Manṣūr* for 1929–30 gives a revealing iconography of reformist education in the class photographs taken at al-Tayyib al-'Uqbi's Madrasat al-shabība 'l-islāmīyya in Algiers, which show girls in neat, knee-length white dresses, their hands folded in their laps, and rows of boys in jackets and fez, flanked by their teachers (all in European dress, sometimes with a *burnūs* over the jacket), sitting upon benches and with a blackboard in the background. The school as disciplinary institution was remoulded by the *salafīs* on a European model, replacing the internal rhythms of Qur'anic prosody and the sacred art of calligraphy, scratched onto the *lawḥa* (wooden writing-tablet) by the pupil and inscribed onto the amulet by the master, with a standardised timetable, a grid-plan of writing-in-order dividing up the day into a rationally devised scheme of bodies of knowledge, constituted into discrete subjects each with its allotted hours, to be studied via standardised, printed textbooks produced mainly in the Mashriq.[55] The form and order of the school itself, and the arrangement of bodies within it, the very notion of how knowledge should be constituted and transmitted, and even the technique of producing and enframing the Arabic script – of which, too, the reformists not unnaturally considered themselves the guardians[56] – were transformed in this 'resurrection' of learning.

No aspect of Islam, in fact, was impervious to the newly scientific and rational ordering of things. Tayyib al-'Uqbi's lectures, given each Sunday afternoon in the early 1930s at the Algiers Nadi al-taraqqi, are an instructive source of examples. Before an audience of some seven hundred, on one occasion, he gave a novel explanation of the meaning of *ramaḍān*:

> *Ramaḍān* signifies, etymologically, 'rain' [*sic*]; thus fasting washes and cleans the body of all material and moral impurities. The Prophet Muhammad said: 'The fast is the purifier of the heart.' Besides being an obligatory ordinance of God, the fast of Ramadan presents, from the practical point of view, an undeniable

[54] *Ibid.*, 333. Compare the sympathetic description of the rural *ṭāleb* and *kuttāb* given by Lacheraf, *Des noms et des lieux*, 26–33, and cf. Colonna, 'Invisibles défenses' and 'Saints furieux'. The emergence and significance of reformism in the Maghrib seems to me indissociable from its colonial context, in contrast (again) to earlier 'reforms', e.g. Wahhabism in the eighteenth-century Nejd.

[55] AUMA school timetable, Arabic MS and French tr., with Note, SLNA, Algiers, 27 Dec. 1948 no. 1216 SLNA, ADA/4I/13/2(2C).

[56] In the same, 1929–30, edition of *Taqwīm al-Manṣūr*, several articles addressed the reform of Arabic orthography, and castigated the Kemalist language reforms in Turkey.

advantage: it rests the body and purifies circulation, eliminating toxins from the bloodstream.[57]

A month earlier, he had commented on the value of prayer: '[Shaykh al-'Uqbi] demonstrated how, in meeting together frequently in holy places, Muslims learn to know and love one another better. From a practical point of view, [he] presented prayer, with its ritual movements, as a kind of beneficial sport. His demonstration led him to give a brief anatomical description of the human body.'[58]

If the reformists saw themselves as the bearers of true Islam, of water and light, sight and hearing, an awakening torch, a purifying wave, to a world slipped back into ignorance, blindness and impurity, their perceptions both of themselves and of the society they wished to transform arose in, and out of, the colonial disarticulation and reordering of the world. It is noteworthy that reformism as 'renovation' (*tajdīd*) was seen to arise at the dusk of Algeria's *colonial* century, in a calendar fixed by the conquest. The reformists' Islam was a thoroughly new kind of response, seeking to integrate the transformative power of modernity – science, the school – with an essential and changeless conception of the community's 'personality' in a language of enlightenment as progress *and* self-rediscovery, which the *'ulamā* alone were fit to enunciate as the true leaders of the community.

This implied a considerable shift in the Algerian religious field. While previous religiously grounded responses to the fact of conquest and defeat, as illustrated by the two Constantinois historians with whom I began, had sought to reconcile the conflicting realities of the world in codes that presumed the permanence and ultimate inviolability of Algerians' trust in, and knowledge of, God and His Revelation,[59] the reformists in effect stripped them of all such dignity. As Colonna concludes: 'it becomes progressively clearer [as we investigate the question] that what the reformists call ignorance covers more or less [everything

[57] Report, SD Algiers, 17 Oct. 1931 no. 3775, ADA/2I/32/8. It seems odd that the learned al-'Uqbi should have so radically misconstrued or reinvented the etymology of *ramaḍān* (whose literal meaning is the 'scorching heat' of midsummer); the general sense of the exposition still holds, however, if the initial point has been misunderstood by the informer, or lost in the policeman's translation.

[58] Report, SD Algiers, 8 Sept. 1931 no. 3198, ADA/2I/32/8.

[59] In her work on rural Islam, Colonna refers to this as the 'mental foundation' of Algerian society in the colonial period ('Invisibles défenses'). Even the Mascaran 'predictions' ascribed to al-Nasiri, while decrying Algerians' religious laxity as having brought catastrophe upon them, implicitly supposed the recognition by its audience of the religious idiom in which it spoke – the people are assumed to know what is the religion from which they have slipped. The reformists, by contrast, credit Algeria's masses with nothing but ignorance.

concerning] the ordinary religion and way of life of [Algerian] peasants at this time. They protest, not a few juvenile disorders, a few excesses in the harvest season, but *the very means of celebrating life and death.*'[60]

The recitation of the *burda* (an epic poem in honour of the Prophet) at burials, the practice of public food distribution celebrated as a communal feast (*zarda*), music at weddings, ritual visits to the tombs or the sanctuaries of long-dead or living saints (*ziyāra*) and the cultural logics underlying such expressions of faith all were *jāhil.* The means of rationalising, and thus of living with and through, conquest and defeat discussed above were forgotten, condemned as 'fatalism' (or else, much later, appropriated as unyielding national resistance for the great epic of 1954). New kinds of ritual, and new understandings of the past and present, were to replace them.

Up to a point, in this regard, the *salafīs* were thus in strange agreement with their most virulent opponents, the fringe of francophile secularists such as Zenati and Hesnay-Lahmek who also saw everyday Islam, the 'ordinary religion' of their community, as a hopelessly failed archaism. The point of contention was not the goal pursued – the conquest of modernity as emancipation – but the cultural terms in which this aim was to be expressed, the *meaning* of 'the nation' to be enfranchised. For the *'ulamā*, this meaning was certainly not to be found in the Catholic-and-secular creeds of the French Republic. Nor, however, was it to be creatively produced through the multiple expressions of Algerians' diverse, and historically shifting, self-perceptions. The multiplicity of 'Algeria', in locally rooted 'backward' language and culture as well as in 'alienating' accretions introduced from Europe, was what they saw as 'anarchy' (*fauḍā*). Such anarchy was to be remedied by societal unity under a reformed and purified Islam.

If the *muṣliḥīn* were labelled 'Wahhabis' by French commentators (as by Berque in my opening epigraph), as well as by their opponents in the brotherhoods and official Muslim judiciary, there was at least one respect in which the term was justified: their obsession with unity (*tawḥīd*[61]) as a theological principle to be rigorously applied to social life. If for 'Abd al-'Aziz Al-Sa'ud in Arabia this notion was first of all doctrinal, and consequently territorial and political, for Ben Badis et al. it was doctrinal, and consequently social and cultural.[62] 'Algeria' was to

[60] Colonna, *Versets de l' invincibilité*, 333.
[61] 'Unicity', used of the absolute oneness of God.
[62] The direct doctrinal influence of Ibn 'Abd al-Wahhab seems to be slight. Merad notes that the Algerian reformists' sympathy for Wahhabism was 'no doubt motivated by political and sentimental considerations rather than doctrinal attachment, (*Réformisme*,

be a unity, one single Muslim nation 'taught to know itself' by those properly equipped to know its Truth. Only thus, and thereafter, in their view of things, could there be freedom.

It was with this aim that the reformists struck out at the sufi brotherhoods, the multiple *buyūt al-ʿilm* (houses of sacred knowledge), each with its own specific, localised modalities of access to the truth, as purveyors not of religion but of *taʿaṣṣub* (factionalism) and *tafrīq* (division). Hence their assault on the figure of an older Islamic authority – the itinerant lettered *ṭālib* of the countryside who had assured the survival of literacy and the presence of the sacred text in rural Algeria[63] – as a charlatan, a purveyor not of Islam but of magic. He now seemed a hopelessly archaic and irrational figure, as through the eyes of a Kabyle poet:

He has learned the Qur'an and *gone mad with it*,
Entered into trance and with a chaplet on his knee
From dawn to dusk, he sits writing talismans
Interfering in the plans of God.

Compare this with other lines by the same writer:

Now come the reformers
The mosques are open
To instruction and the Qur'an . . .
I asked him, he is an *amuslih*[64]

219); it was Ibn Saʿud's status as independent sovereign that most attracted their attention. Even al-Mili's *Risālat al-shirk* was composed on the whole without reference to Ibn 'Abd al-Wahhab, who does not figure in his list of sources. Al-Mili mentions the *Fatḥ al-mubīd bi-sharḥ kitāb al-tawḥīd*, sent to him from Jeddah just before his book went to press, and of which he was able to take some account, but overall he insists on the originality of his own work (*Risālat al-shirk*, 15, *pace* Merad, *Réformisme*, 217 n.4).

63 At least until the early 1900s, despite the effects of colonisation. In 1877, there were still at least eighty-one such teachers to be found in one commune of western Algeria, some of whom were locals but others from Tangier, Fez and elsewhere. Most were itinerant, engaged by the local community for one year. In the Oranais in 1903, there were 90 schools with around 1,270 pupils officially authorised, but more than 640 schools, with a total of over 5,000 pupils, were found to be in existence without authorisation, which in some cases had been requested but never received. A 1907 report lists 350 established schools in the *département*, providing instruction in reading, writing and the Qur'an, with some also teaching elements of grammar and *fiqh* (Sidi Khalīl's *Mukhtaṣar*). Some of these schools claimed to have been in existence for centuries, but many had been founded after 1900. Most received between twelve and thirty pupils, although some had fewer than five. (Comm. civil, CM Aïn Temouchent, to Prefect, Oran, 24 Aug. 1877 no. 750, 'Etat des tholbas marocains ou autres installés dans la commune en qualité d'instituteurs', MS, 10 pp.; 'Enseignement privé des indigènes', Sec. Gen. Affaires indigènes, Prefecture, Oran, 5 Aug. 1903, MS, 16 pp.; 'Statistique des écoles privées musulmanes', Inspecteur de l'Académie d'Alger, Oran, 3 Oct. 1907, MS, 28 pp. AWO/I/18(4064)).

64 Kabyle form of Arabic *muṣliḥ*, 'reformer'.

Wearing neither turban nor chaplet
But only trousers and a shirt.[65]

The unification of the religious field under the social authority of the reformists as a necessary aspect of the spread of 'civilisation' to the masses, recreating the community and leading it to 'improvement', were the goals of the Algerian *salafiyya*. Hence their eagerness to reach an accommodation with the Ibadi community in the Mzab,[66] as well as their particular efforts at implantation in the rural, berberophone Aurès and Kabylia. From this point of view, the 'dissipation of [the reformists'] efforts' in the activities Merad calls 'politics', and which he considers as having been 'not without its damaging effects for the spiritual and doctrinal work', by which he means sustained works of exegesis and doctrinal elaboration, 'which was apparently their fundamental ambition'[67] may not appear as the failing that he considered it. Properly doctrinal elaboration and disputation may have appeared at the time as a less pressing goal, in the service of the *salafī* vision of national revival, than did the reduction of heterogeneous centres of religious authority by a single, dominant movement of reform. If the reformists effected a 'resurrection' of learning in a new kind of Islamic pedagogy, one imbued with the rational force of modernity and intended to remedy the ignorance of Algeria, bringing its divided and backward populations together into one purely Muslim nation, there remained a number of rival voices articulating 'Islamic' meanings, and they would have to be dealt with.

Jacobin Islam (ii): the meaning of religion

Shaykh Mubarak al-Mili, having left the reformist school in Constantine where he was visited by Tawfiq al-Madani in 1925, settled for a while in Laghouat (al-Aghwāṭ), the 'gate of Africa', a yellow and orange garrison town overlooking a green oasis on the southern threshold of the Saharan Atlas. There he opened a new school and composed his *Ta'rīkh al-Jazā'ir fi'l-qadīm wa-'l-ḥadīth*. On the foundation of the AUMA in 1931, he became the Association's treasurer, and would remain a senior figure in the movement until his early death in 1945. When, after seven years, he quit Laghouat, he stayed briefly in Bou Sa'ada, on the high plateaux further north, before returning, in September, 1933, to Mila, the ancient north Constantinois town where he had first been instructed

[65] Quoted in Colonna, *Versets de l' invincibilité*, 358–9 (original emphasis), from Yacine, *Poésie berbère et identité* (Paris, Maison des Sciences de l'Homme, 1987), 12, 20, 23.
[66] A compromise with 'heresy' inconceivable to a doctrinally rigorous Wahhabi.
[67] Merad, *Réformisme*, 432, 436–7.

as an adolescent at the *zāwiya* of Sidi Muḥammad ibn Manṣūr, a saintly *murābiṭ* highly regarded throughout the area.

Mila had changed greatly since Ahmad al-Mubarak, witness to the conquest and author of the *Kitāb ta'rīkh Qusanṭīna*, had himself been schooled there as a boy, a century before. Beyond the walls of the old town there had grown up 'the new village', a colonial adjunct to the city, towards which 'the centre of gravity of prestige and power had now shifted',[68] and around which had sprung up new peripheral quarters, le Kouf and Senaoua, whose inhabitants – in part, families who had lost land in the massive sequestrations of 1871, and who held low-status occupations (butchers, masons, livestock traders) – were all considered 'newcomers' by the established families of the town. Ostracised by the latter (who for a long time refused their daughters in marriage to 'newcomers'), it was nevertheless inhabitants of le Kouf 'who were the first to build permanent, modern houses, and to send their children to [the French] school'.[69] It was, equally, inhabitants of this quarter who would first join the PPA and later the FLN. And it was in the 'new village', not within the walls of the old town, that al-Mili, aided by local notables and the European mayor, set up a reformist Qur'anic school and *nādī* (club, circle). By the summer of 1936, the reformist organisation in Mila had acquired two contiguous properties, on the first of which a mosque and a private house were being built, while on the second, another house was being transformed into a school. The whole enterprise was run under the supervision of al-Mili, by the *nādī islāmī* of Mila, whose president was a schoolteacher (and, hence, French civil servant), Ben Amira. The Association's 'honorary president' was the mayor of the town, Monsieur Giuli. It was anticipated that the following year, Ben Amira, who was due to retire from the *école communale*, would take up a teaching post at the new reformist *madrasa*, situated just across the street.[70] The symbolic transformations taking place in this provincial urban space could hardly be more dramatic. Shortly before these developments were reported by the local military commander, an apparently trivial incident occurred that illustrates the depth of the socio-cultural transformation affecting this small corner of Algerian society, and the struggle for mastery of this process.

[68] In the words of Si Lakhdar Bentobbal, who grew up in Mila in the 1930s and 1940s, quoted by Djerbal, 'La Guerre d'Algérie', 541.
[69] *Ibid.*
[70] 'Situation politico-religieuse dans la commune de Mila', report, Commandant du détachement de Senégalais, Mila, 10 June 1936 no. 170/PS (11 pp.), ADC/B3/273/13.

On 19 May 1936, the Constantine prefecture received a letter from Si Ḥānī Ben Shaykh Zwāwī, head of the Hansaliyya *ṭarīqa* and shaykh of the order's principal *zāwiya* at Rouffach, the spiritual centre in whose rise to prominence in the early nineteenth century Si al-Haj Ahmad al-Mubarak, as *muqaddam* of the order, had played an important role. The saintly shaykh informed the prefect that, on the morning of 15 May, a Friday, a number of Hansali *ikhwān* (brothers) had been returning to their homes in the commune of Fedj Mzala from a pilgrimage to Rouffach when, passing through Mila,

in the village itself, they were attacked, grossly insulted and beaten by several Muslims. Their provisions were even stolen, as were the clothes they were carrying with them. The most serious and regrettable things occurred . . . highly offensive insults were uttered against the revered *murābiṭ*, shaykh Ahmad Zwawi – all of this in broad daylight, in the middle of the village and before the eyes of both Europeans and natives of the place.[71]

On the same day that the outraged shaykh's grievances were received at the Prefecture, mayor Giuli reported the same episode:

On Friday the fifteenth of this month, at about 9.30 a.m., some twenty natives, returning from an organised pilgrimage to shaykh Zwawi at Rouffach, passed through Mila, dancing and singing religious airs. On their way [through the town], a few young louts (*voyous*) who happened to be about set to following [the pilgrims] and began shouting to try to cover their [singing] voices. Monsieur Brot, a municipal councillor, having intervened, the singing stopped, but one of the natives from the group of pilgrims, having turned back [and become separated from the others], was pulled aside and pushed about by the young louts. They even indulged in some pranks, in rather bad taste, at his expense. ['Ils se livrèrent même sur lui à des plaisanteries de mauvais goût.'] This incident, which, to my mind, was nothing but a minor street disturbance ['une manifestation de la rue'], has been considerably amplified by the partisans of shakyh Zwawi.[72]

While downplaying the incident's importance, and perhaps seeking to keep his protégé al-Mili out of the affair by attributing the scuffle to 'a few young louts', the mayor nonetheless tellingly observed that 'without exaggerating the import of these occurrences, it is nonetheless prudent not to ignore their significance, since this took place between adepts of considerably different religious sentiments, and it is to be feared that, were they to be repeated, public order might be disturbed'.[73]

71 Letter in ADC/B3/273/1.
72 Mayor, CPE Mila to Prefect, Constantine, 19 May 1936 no. 375, ADC/B3/273/1.
73 *Ibid.*

A third report, this time from the district administrator, expands on the identity of the mayor's 'young louts' and is the first account of the affair to mention al-Mili explicitly:

At about ten o'clock, [the pilgrims] came through Mila, singing the ritual songs of their brotherhood. When these pilgrims arrived outside the 'Cercle islamique' [i.e. *nādī islāmī*], which has its premises in rue Nationale at Mila, they were accosted by young followers of shaykh Mubarak al-Mili . . . [these latter] set after [the pilgrims] a hostile crowd of Muslim children who shouted at them and threw stones. One old man was reportedly even pulled from the mule that he was riding and abused ['aurait été l'objet de sévices'] by these young tearaways . . . While this incident itself, considering only its immediate consequences, is apparently insignificant, it seems to me, nonetheless, that one ought not to underestimate the repercussions it may have on the Muslim milieux of the area.[74]

Five days later, the (false) rumour ran through Constantine that shaykh al-Mili had been arrested by the justice of the peace at Mila 'for having incited his partisans to mistreat a group of *ikhwān* belonging to the brotherhood of Ben Shaykh Zwawi',[75] and that Ben Badis himself had rushed to Mila to aid his friend and colleague.[76] Both al-Mili and shaykh Zwawi were summoned, separately, to the district administrator's office and invited to ensure by 'personal and energetic intervention in respect of their followers'[77] that the trouble should go no further. They both, having 'by turns attempted to prove that responsibility for the incident could not be imputed to their respective adepts', nonetheless 'formally engaged themselves to employ all their authority in order to avoid any dangerous consequences that might arise from the incident, and to prevent their recurrence'.[78]

When Sidi Sa'īd ibn Yūsuf al-Ḥansalī, the founder of the order,[79] received his spiritual mission, while prostrated in the mosque of Sidi Abū 'l-'Abbās al-Marsī in Damietta, on his return from the Hijaz via Egypt, it came in the form of a whip, handed to him by the angel Gabriel

[74] Administrateur adjoint détaché, Canton de Mila, to Prefect, Constantine, 20 May 1936 no. 151, ADC/B3/273/1.

[75] Chief, SD Constantine to Governor-General, Algiers and Prefect, Constantine, 25 May 1936 no. 2110, ADC/B3/273/1.

[76] In fact, Ben Badis and al-Mili met on 24 May at Chateaudun-du-Rhummel (Administrateur adjoint détaché, Mila, to Prefect, Constantine, 25 May 1936 no. 155, ADC/B3/273/1).

[77] Secretary-General, Prefecture, Constantine, to Governor-General, Algiers, 23 May 1936 no. 20027, ADC/B3/273/1.

[78] MS, Administrateur adjoint détaché, Mila, to Prefect, Constantine, 4 June 1936 no. 162, ADC/B3/273/1.

[79] Born Shawwāl 1052/1643, near Fez, a descendant of the original founder of a *zāwiya* in Morocco.

himself. From among the assembled company of Mashriqi saints, Sidi 'Abd al-Qadir al-Jilani was heard to say: 'Take this whip, which will serve to bring back to the straight path all deviators whom you meet, and which will heal any sick person whom you strike with it. Go, and return to the land where the sun takes its rest.'[80] The reformists claimed no such mystical investiture, but while their conviction of their canonical mission to bring deviators back to the straight path replicates exactly the charge given the saint, it would appear that the symbolic means of violence conferred upon the mystic – significantly doubled, in his case, with the power of healing – sometimes found its expression, among the *salafi*s, in less subtly encoded forms of coercion. This is visible in incidents such as the affair of the *ikhwān* at Mila, and also in small symbolic spectacles that occurred elsewhere at around the same time, marking acts of adherence to, or defiance of, the new cultural orthodoxy.

Shortly after the trouble with the Hansali adepts, al-Mili undertook a tour of Lesser Kabylia, stopping briefly in his birthplace at el-Milia. There he constituted a reformist group and, apparently, initiated a 'war of ideas' that shortly afterwards gave the local administrator the impression of a suddenly increased solidarity, formed about his office by the notables of the area and by 'those who consider themselves true believers (de véritables moumenines) [who] are hostile to the new ideas purveyed by the *'ulamā* and their followers'.[81] On the other hand, at least one member of a family affiliated to a sufi brotherhood in el-Milia, Aḥmad Ben Rabaḥ Gherbī, a landowner and heir to generations of *muqaddam*s of a *ṭarīqa*, reportedly made his profession of 'return' to the reformists' straight path by publicly burning 'all the sacred books which he had inherited from his father and grandfather'.[82] In Mila itself, sometimes very subtle plays of power occurred over the capital of religious expression and distinction. One Si Yūsuf Bū 'Arūj, a wholesale merchant, refusing to join the reformists' circle, reportedly saw his business boycotted by al-Mili's supporters, but, being of substantial means with established trading activity well beyond the town itself, was able to withstand the pressure. Having accomplished the pilgrimage to Mecca with his brother, he received, on his return, the customary visits of friends and relatives at his house, furnishing a special reception room for the purpose. Shaykh al-Mili himself went to see him, and tried to persuade him to come to the mosque at the *nādī islāmī* to give a public

[80] Gouvion and Gouvion, *Kitāb Aāyane al-Marhariba*, 133–4.
[81] Administrator, CM El-Milia, to Prefect, Constantine, 15 Oct. 1936 no. 6288, ADC/B3/273/13.
[82] *Ibid.*

account of his pilgrimage and the spiritual benefits he had gained from it. Bu ʻAruj refused, saying that his friends could come freely to see him at his own house.[83]

The details of shaykh al-Mili's activities, and the conflicts in which they became involved, demonstrate the complex nature of *salafī* reform in its relationships to existing cultural practices, the transformation of the social and physical landscape, and forms of power and authority. The reformists' attacks on the brotherhoods, on 'illicit' practice and 'backward' forms of knowledge and belief, were not simply theological polemics in the press and the pulpit, but gave rise – whether intentionally or not – to verbal and physical violence in the streets of provincial Algerian towns and on occasion around and within the sanctuaries of *zawāyā* themselves. A month after the incident in Mila, on 1 June 1936, the day of the *mawlid al-nabī*, the Prophet's birthday, a group of adepts of the ʻIsāwiyya order in Constantine were insulted and ridiculed outside their *zāwiya* by three young men. The sufis, 'outraged', registered a complaint with the police. On the same day, a group belonging to a different *ṭarīqa* in Constantine were gathered for their ritual when four Algerians, reportedly 'in a state of inebriation', burst in upon them, one of them making 'a gesture judged obscene in such a place'. According to the police, the *muqaddam* of the order prevented the scene degenerating into a fight.[84] The 'war of ideas' at Mila, Lakhdar Bentobbal remembers, 'threw minds into conflict and set the members of families against each other'.[85] The existing rigid hierarchies of provincial urban society could not stand the pressure: 'The barriers which had until then been maintained between young and old, between elder and younger sons, began to collapse.'[86]

Coming in the wake of the colonial refiguring of space and its significance – the reduction of the old town, assured behind its walls, to a periphery of the new, extra-mural settlement with its displaced and more dynamic population – the reformist implantation of cultural circle, school and mosque outside the ancient centre marked a sharp break with 'backwardness', and a challenge for control over, as well as a necessary coexistence in, the spaces of modernity established by the European mayor and the European school. Alarmed by the assault on his disciples,

[83] 'Situation politico-religieuse' (note 70 above), p. 8.
[84] Chief, SD to Prefect, Constantine, 4 June 1936 no. 2586, ADC/B3/273/2.
[85] Djerbal, 'La Guerre d'Algérie', 542.
[86] *Ibid.* On this generational tension, see also the account in Harbi, *Vie debout*, chs. 1–3. Harbi grew up in the same region, in el-Arrouch, north-east of Mila, between Constantine and Philippeville (Skikda).

the shaykh of the Hansaliyya order, from his *zāwiya* at Rouffach, requested that the administrator at Mila close down the small Hansali mosque in that town, to spare it from possible attack. The mosque in question was situated behind the ancient walls of the old city.[87] The crisis of the established hierarchy of symbolic, spatial and cultural order before the onslaught of the Islam preached in the new town – in the rue Nationale – could not be more neatly expressed than in this transformation in relations of power between such spaces, as in the spectacle of boys, encouraged by young adepts of the *muṣliḥīn*, dragging an old sufi brother from his mule, and turning his ritual sacred utterances to ridicule with shouts of mockery.

These small moments of symbolic and physical violence – the burning of books, the stoning of pilgrims – that show up as disturbances of the peace in the reports of colonial administrators, indicate a much more portentous, and largely invisible, struggle over symbolic authority, imbricated in the broader violence of the colonial transformation of Algerian society, its structures and spaces, and implicating not only the outward forms of cultural practice and the places of their articulation, but the very meaning of religion itself. The *ḥajjī* who chose to stay at home to receive his friends, as 'custom' dictated he should, was resisting not simply involvement in a cultural movement with which he happened to disagree, but the transformation of his personal religious experience of pilgrimage into an exemplary public lesson, the *appropriation* of 'his' Islam, as personally lived in the accomplishment of his devotions, by a movement claiming the right to speak for 'the' Islam of all Algerians.

A very similar incident had occurred on a larger scale a few months earlier. On 31 March, three of the Algerian municipal councillors for Constantine, at the behest of shaykh Ben Badis, had sought an interview with Dupré, the secretary-general at the city's Prefecture. They requested permission for a ceremony to be held, under the auspices of Ben Badis's Constantinois educational society, the Jam'īyat al-tarbīya wa 'l-ta'līm al-islāmiyya, at the Great Mosque, on the following Friday, 3 April, in honour of the pilgrims due to return from the Hijaz. Believing the necessary permission obtained – or perhaps considering it inconceivable that the administration would deny Constantine's Muslims the use of their own principal mosque for such an event – Ben Badis issued invitations, in the form of pamphlets addressed to the whole populace, for the meeting the following day, and departed for the port of Bône (Annaba) to meet the pilgrims who were due to disembark there.

[87] Administrator, Mila, to Prefect, Constantine, 20 May 1936 no. 151, ADC/B3/ 273/1.

Figure 7. The Great Mosque, Constantine. (Postcard, author's collection.)

Dupré, meanwhile, had telephoned Algiers, whence came the opinion 'that it would be best if monsieur Ben Badis were forbidden to carry out his project'.[88] Fearing that 'a religious building [for which he was responsible] should become the theatre of an innovation created for political ends',[89] Dupré duly refused the reformists the use of the mosque. Ben Badis, notified of this decision by the sub-prefect in Bône, telegraphed his dismay to Constantine: 'Great surprise see this meeting refused after distribution invitations in town . . . Respectfully but energetically protest this refusal without grounds dare believe will be possible you reconsider your second decision in order avoid any unfortunate interpretation on part Muslims sincere respects Benbadis president Ettarbia Assoc'.[90] The refusal stood, of course, but at around 3.30 p. m. on the Friday, Ben Badis went to the Great Mosque anyway, accompanied by ten or a dozen of the returned pilgrims, to announce the cancellation of the meeting to a crowd of some one and a half thousand. Lamenting 'with all his heart the actions of ill-intentioned persons whose conduct had led to such a regrettable state of affairs', the shaykh 'prayed that God might guide them back into the straight path', thanked the assembled crowd and recommended that each of them, too, should undertake the pilgrimage. The meeting was over in a quarter of an hour and broke up with reformist supporters grumbling at the behaviour of the Prefecture.[91]

Aside from illustrating the ways in which the colonial administration, sensitive and suspicious as it was, could mishandle such minor affairs so as to create accomplished works of oppression from the most unpromising materials, the affair of the returning pilgrims throws into relief a number of aspects of a significant social power struggle that found expression in such apparently trivial confrontations. The power of speech, particularly speech in sacred space, and power over that space itself, were both directly involved, as, in a more generally significant way, was the question of the ownership of the symbolic goods of religion. According to the prefect,

> the conduct of monsieur Ben Badis demonstrates a double failing. *He summoned* the Muslim [population] to an official mosque[92] without the sanction of the

[88] Prefect, Constantine, to Governor-General, Algiers, 24 April 1938 no. 15393, ADC/B3/273/9.

[89] *Ibid.*

[90] Telegram, Ben Badis, Bône, to Prefect, Constantine, ADC/B3/273/9.

[91] Prefect to Governor-General, 24 April no. 15393 (note 88 above); Report, SD, Constantine, 3 April 1936 no. 1262, ADC/B3/273/9.

[92] 'Une mosquée classée', i.e. technically maintained by *ḥubūs* (*waqf*) endowments which had been confiscated by the colonial public domain, and for which the state was

Administration or the responsible Muslim religious officials; *he spoke* in this same mosque in violation of our instructions and after he had been duly notified of the refusal of his request. I should add that his initiative has been the subject of numerous [adverse] comments in the town, and has provoked angry protests on the part of certain pilgrims' families.[93]

In fact, the press of Smaïl Mami's *al-Najāḥ* issued a counter-pamphlet[94] to the invitation printed by the Jam'īyat al-tarbīya, contesting the reformists' celebration of the pilgrims' return, and insisting that they wished to receive visitors at their homes. The *'ulamā* called, in their printed announcement, for an end to the costly private receptions held at pilgrims' houses, and took it upon themselves to organise a single, public reception at which the pilgrims would be honoured and their edifying example simultaneously promoted to their fellow Muslims in a unifying expression of community under the single banner of one, true Islam. The families of the pilgrims for whom *al-Najāḥ*'s pamphlet claimed to speak, on the other hand, may indeed (like Yusuf Bu 'Aruj at Mila) have wished to preserve what they considered a practice 'in pursuance of the tradition of the Prophet and the pious ancestors as followed in all the Islamic lands',[95] which was, perhaps, how they saw their own means of celebrating one of the great expressions of their religion. The ostensible conflict over the physical space of the mosque was also a struggle over the symbolic spaces of the experience of Islam itself, over the meaning of one of the faith's central duties and the way it was to be celebrated.

For his part, the city's leading official Muslim jurist, the mufti Mulud Ben al-Muhub, who had been a student of 'Abd al-Qādir al-Majjāwī, 'the earliest exponent of Islamic modernism in Algeria',[96] and was

therefore responsible; although by this time the state's responsibility was supposedly delegated to voluntarily constituted 'assocations cultuelles'. It was in these mosques that the reformists had been forbidden to speak by the 'Michel circular' of 2 March 1933. Privately built reformist mosques such as that of the *nādī islāmī* in Mila were not under the state's jurisdiction.

93 Prefect to Governor-General, 24 April no. 15393 (note 88 above), emphasis added.

94 If this was inspired by the Prefecture, no indication survives in the files. The example of the recalcitrant *ḥajjī* at Mila suggests genuinely grounded local opposition to the reformists' hegemonic aspirations; nor is this the only instance of such opposition in Constantine.

95 Printed Arabic leaflet with French tr., ADC/B3/273/9.

96 Christelow, *Muslim Law Courts*: 279. Al-Majjawi (d. 1913), a prominent religious educator of Tlemceni origin who set up an independent school in Constantine before being appointed to the official *médersa*, was the author of a text, printed in Cairo in 1877, which already 'decried the intellectual and cultural inferiority of Algeria vis-à-vis both Europe and the Middle East', and 'proposed as a remedy an educational curriculum, based on modern teaching methods already in use in Egypt, which concentrated on both religion and science' (*Ibid.*, 230–1). He thus anticipated the reformists' programme by forty years. Christelow identifies al-Majjawi, well before 'Abduh's visit to Algeria

himself, as we saw, the mentor of the leading 'Young Algerian' Chérif Benhabylès, was adamant:

What. . . Ben Badis proposes [i.e. the meeting at the Grand Mosque] is contrary to religion. These ceremonies have never been prescribed by Islam, and, as regards Constantine, have never taken place in a mosque in this city. The tradition is the following: on their return, the pilgrims remain at home for at least three consecutive days in the course of which they receive their relatives and friends. They are nonetheless free, during this time, to go individually to whichever mosque they may choose in order to pray . . . The projected ceremony is not of a religious nature and would have no other effect but to assemble at the mosque a rag-tag crowd, composed mainly of the partisans of Ben Badis . . . This innovation of assembling the pilgrims on their return from Mecca dates from last year and is due to Ben Badis. Last year's meeting, the first of its kind, was held at the *nadi al-taraqqi* and presided by Dr Bendjelloul.[97]

Ben Muhub, himself among 'the most staunchly puritanical of reformists'[98] who, in light of his own intellectual trajectory and his own declarations of 'war on ignorance' can hardly be labelled an ossified traditionalist, must have been rattled by the AUMA's attempted encroachment into *his* space of authority. The fact that this authority was invested by the colonial state (he would later be named mufti of the new Paris mosque, symbol of 'la France islamique'[99]) had not necessarily diminished it – Ben Muhub had been a tireless campaigner for Algerian social and spiritual reform, as his pre-1914 lectures, delivered at Constantine's nādī Salah Bey, show, and he clearly considered himself sufficiently possessed of a knowledge of Islam adequately to fulfil his functions without the aid of Ben Badis *et al.*[100] He was also not the only reformist to resist the hegemonic aims of the AUMA, especially in its later, more politically engaged phases – Tayyib al-'Uqbi, while never failing vigorously to pursue his *salafī* mission as he saw it, continued, after his break with the Association in 1938, to preach an apolitical *iṣlāḥ* on his own authority. He was criticised by the AUMA, not for 'selling out' to the administration, but for his stubborn independence from the unifying movement that the association incarnated.[101] While the *'ulamā*,

in 1903, as the initiator of a Constantinois 'local *islah*'. Ben Muhub (1863–193?) became a professor of *fiqh* at the *médersa* in 1895, and mufti in 1908.

97 'Declaration of M. Benmouhoub, Mufti', Prefecture, Constantine, 1 April 1936, ADC/B3/273/9.

98 Christelow, *Muslim Law Courts*, 251.

99 *Ibid.*, 269.

100 According to Christelow (*ibid.*, 279) he had also been personally at odds with 'Abd al-Hamid Ben Badis, his former student (Cheurfi, *Ecrivains*, 80) since 1912.

101 Reports (1945) in ADA/4I/14/9 (criticism, by Muhammad Khayr al-Din and Larbi Tebessi, of al-'Uqbi's 'inaction' and failure to reassociate himself with the policies

too, were seeking above all a workable, negotiated solution, it was not 'collaboration' they objected to, but resistance to their drive for singular authority.

At the same time, the leaders of the brotherhoods were making their own stand, insisting that they, too, *knew their religion* and that the reformists' unifying mission was in fact an illegitimate and unacceptable arrogance. A month after the Hansaliyya brothers were turned upon at Mila, nine leaders of the principal sufi orders in Constantine petitioned the prefect in the city, in his capacity as representative of the state and as *ḥākim* (governor), to intervene to put a stop to the reformists' activities. The reformists, 'creators of corruption and disturbance among the Muslim community',[102] appeared to the established representatives of religious authority as so many dangerous and ill-mannered upstarts, their activities affronts to the position of the shaykhs and to the cultural patrimony they incarnated.

Members of the saintly notability who had traded apocalyptic resistance for accommodation with the establishment in the mid-nineteenth century had made 'implicit pacts' with the newly unconquerable order of things, pacts whereby their socio-spiritual capital would be employed to keep the oppressive peace rather than in suicidal attempts to break it, in return for which the colonial régime would allow them to maintain their role as custodians of an Algerian religio-cultural patrimony and as legitimate spokesmen for their community and its interests.[103] The *salafī* attack on them, their belief and its expression, threatened to disturb this managed imbalance of power. The situation, the petitioners warned, 'may have a deleterious effect on our integral connection to our French state' – the customary language of loyal devotion carries a reminder bordering on a threat, that the stress under which the *mrabṭīn* find themselves may sever the bonds that tie them to France (*rābiṭatanā*), unless the *ḥākim* fulfils his side of the bargain. The reformists, to the brotherhoods' *muqaddam*s, are dangerous impostors: 'this little gang, which has given itself, in distorting affectation, the title "Association of

advanced by the AUMA). A reading of al-'Uqbi's mission is McDougall, '*Shabiba Islamiyya* of Algiers'.

102 'Hā'ulā'i 'l-mushawwishīn al-mufsidīn baynanā ma'āshir al-muslimīn' Petition, Arabic MS with French *précis*, 11 June 1936, ADC/B3/273/2.

103 Clancy-Smith, *Rebel and Saint*. This is not to deny that, for some *mrabṭīn*, as for other Algerian élites, colonial accommodation meant protection for exploitative positions (Lacheraf, 'Colonialisme et féodalités; for a critique of this terminology, von Sivers, 'Capitalisme fiscal'). But the generalised stereotype of the marabout as collaborator and charlatan, preying on the ignorant masses and guarded from attempts at redress by the colonial administrator, cannot be taken at face value.

Algerian Muslim *'ulamā'*', and which, since its foundation, has spread its sinister Wahhabi propaganda and its noxious communist ideas'. This, they insist, is not religion – their doctrine is proclaimed 'in the name of religion, which [however] has no part in it'. They have no right, it follows, to speak for Islam, and are explicitly declared illegitimate in their claim to be the guides (*murshidīn*) of the community: on the contrary, they are 'these iniquitous tyrants whom we did not elect . . . Or do we need them to be our guides, for lack of someone to guide us? We have no need in any respect for those most rebellious among us.'

As for the 'corruption and disturbances' with which the reformists are charged – an exactly symmetrical accusation to those of *jāhiliyya* (ignorance) and *bid'a* (illicit innovation) levelled at the brotherhoods by the AUMA – they threaten the very bases of spiritual and social order. The reformists, the petitioners complain, attack, through their *durūs* (preaching and study) and in the associations they patronise, 'most particularly those who hold fast to the values of the masters, the spiritual shaykhs, to such an extent that this has led to disputes between fathers and sons, between a man and his brother, between men related to one another by marriage'. Thus the most fundamental relationships of societal solidarity, in the eyes of the shaykhs – those of each crucial type between men: filial, fraternal, marital – have been thrown into crisis, as has the overarching spiritual hierarchy of disciples and masters. As Lakhdar Bentobbal remarked of Mila, the hierarchical structures of the old order were beginning to collapse under the strain.

The petition of the sufi notables is a last gasp of part of this old order. Appealing to the prefect as *ḥākim* to defend their established prerogatives, they were clinging to pacts that had ensured their survival in the late nineteenth century but which now afforded no protection from a dynamic, rival group of would-be spokesmen whose grip on the means of salvation, previously the assured property of the brotherhoods, was becoming ever firmer. The colonial state could (or, besides lending some support to alternative centres of authority,[104] would) do little to protect one Islam from another. The pacts of cultural survival on which the

[104] The rival, anti-reformist Jam'īyat 'ulamā al-sunna al-jazā'iriyyīn founded in September 1932, and the Constantinois Jam'īyat al-salām, and the journals *al-Ikhlāṣ* (1932–3) and *al-Balāgh al-jazā'irī*. The latter was run from Mostaghanem by the remarkable 'modernist mystic' shaykh Ben 'Aliwa, who founded a successful new *ṭarīqa* as late as 1920, and who, while fiercely opposed to Ben Badis et al., took a similar line to the reformists on a number of issues (notably individual naturalisation), such that he too might, according to Berque, be classed 'among the neo-Wahhabis'. He died in 1933–4, 'surrounded by a formidable *baraka*' (Berque, 'Ça et là dans les débuts du réformisme', 491–2).

mrabṭīn had, since 1849, increasingly staked their social existence were, by 1936, as good as expired. The notables' rehearsed overtures of loyalty could now only serve to open them to charges of collaboration (in the pejorative sense), and to later discredit.[105] Commenting on the petition of the Constantine *muqaddams*, the governor-general wrote to the prefect: 'I can do nothing more than leave you the charge of taking all measures you might judge prudent for the avoidance of any undesirable incident.'[106] The fate of the appeal is probably indicated in another letter, sent to Algiers two days after the sufi notables composed their *doléances*. On 13 June, the prefect replied to the governor regarding an earlier petition, from another group of Constantinois notables, which had protested at the 'fiscal' pressures of the reformists on local families. Declaring himself incompetent to interfere in the affairs evoked by the petitioners, he advised that 'I can propose nothing but the pure and simple filing of the complaint which you were so good as to forward to me.'[107]

This did not, however, mean that the war was over. The purveyors of 'old' religion would continue to assert themselves as best they could against the self-appointed doctors of the 'new', and they could still, for a while, find allies in the struggles being played out for dominance of the spaces of Algerian cultural expression. The reformists' control of the sites and symbols of religion and culture was not yet by any means total. A few months later, in October 1936, the AUMA clashed again with rival spokesmen for the good of the Algerian people, again over both physical and symbolic space in which the reformists considered themselves the only people fit to speak.

The momentary and, at best, partial unity of would-be Algerian representatives achieved by the first Algerian Muslim Congress in June 1936 had already vanished by August. Dr Mohamed-Salah Bendjelloul, leader of the Constantine Fédération des *élus* and first president of the Congress (which he had hoped to dominate[108]), caused outrage with an interview published by the newspaper *Marseille-Matin* on 13 August, in which, commenting on the events in Algiers of a fortnight previously – the dissident speech by Messali at the stadium meeting on 2 August, in which the populist leader had rejected the basic premises of the Congress,[109] and the murder of the mufti of Algiers, Ben Dali 'al-Kaḥḥūl' the

[105] It is noteworthy that the very similar expressions of loyalism produced by the AUMA are always considered in a more nuanced fashion in the literature.
[106] Governor-General to Prefect, Constantine, 7 July 1936 no. 4082, ADC/B3/273/2.
[107] Prefect, Constantine, to Governor-General, 13 June 1936 no. 22561, ADC/B3/273/2.
[108] Ageron, *Histoire de l'Algérie contemporaine*, 437, 445.
[109] I.e. partnership with France and political development within the French state. The Charter of Demands adopted by the Congress called for the administrative

same day – he declared, 'C'est une guerre de religion qui commence.'[110] If this was intended as a despairing comment on his compatriots' fractiousness, he was nonetheless about to be implicated in precisely such a struggle himself.

On 4 October 1936, an article appeared in Constantine's leading French-language newspaper on the subject of a public event due to occur the following weekend:

To judge by the encouragements which the organising committee has received from all sides . . . the *zarda* of the tenth and eleventh of October will be a great success. This ancient tradition which the *Comité des meskines* has revived has brought joy to the hearts and the faces of the Muslims; the news has spread like wildfire in town and throughout the region, and everywhere preparations are underway to come to attend this great festival of the Muslim family, where, in sharing bread and salt around a communal couscous, we forget the rancour of division and reaffirm the ties of friendship and the love of one's fellows.[111]

The *zarda* was a public distribution of food to the poor, celebrated as a two-day festival of social solidarity and religious community, on a sacred site – the city's cemetery – which symbolically connected the living and the dead of all social ranks in the sharing of bread, meat and the word of God. A multifaceted expression of the bonds of community, the ritual of *zarda* connected the honour due to the dead with the care owed to the poor and reaffirmed, in its setting and the practices that unfolded there – communal eating, *dhikr* (the repetition of sufi formulae) and the recitation of the Qur'an (in its entirety) – the reality and legitimacy of social order under God. Such festivals, according to the same article, had traditionally been celebrated by the people of Constantine on the *coudiat* Sidi Aty, a bluff to the southwest of the old city, just outside the walls, named for a saint who had long ago been buried there. The cemetery on the *coudiat* had existed in the Ottoman period, and the *zarda* celebrated there was held, first, in honour of Sidi Aty himself, and by association 'in honour, equally, of all the dead buried there'.[112] As the city expanded after the French conquest, a new cemetery was

incorporation (*rattachement*) of Algeria within the metropole (hence suppression of the Délégations financières, the Government General and separate 'native' legislation), a single electoral college and juridical regime for all, a single educational system, etc. (Kaddache, *Vie politique*, 299 n.12).

110 Ageron, *Historie de l'Algérie contemporaine*, 441. Although the true circumstances of the 'Kahhul affair' remain obscure, it seems most likely that the murder itself, and certainly the implication in it of Tayyib al-'Uqbi (who was eventually acquitted, but not until the business had mostly ruined his public life), was contrived by the colonial police.

111 *Dépêche de Constantine*, 4 Oct. 1936, ADC/B3/273/11.

112 *Ibid.*

established further out, beyond the *coudiat*, and the celebration of the *zarda* was moved to the new site. The association with the *wali* was nonetheless preserved in the name given to the festival, the '*zarda* of the *coudiat* Sidi Aty', 'although the event is held in honour of all our dead. This is what gives the *zarda* its character of a religious festival, from which is proscribed everything that might bring harm to our religion, to morality and to the respect due to the dead.'[113] Such harmony was not to be. The original *coudiat* Sidi Aty had been the site chosen, in 1837, by technician–General Valée for his siege artillery. Almost a century later, the *zarda* named for the saint's little hill was, in turn, to be a battleground.

The importance of the event planned in 1936 was increased by the neglect from which the festival had apparently suffered in recent years, and by the severity of the suffering inflicted on Muslim Algeria by the world economic crisis, which had struck hard at an already impoverished population. A sign of recovery from these hard times as well as an affirmation of the truths of community and religion in a period of political and social turbulence, the *zarda* seemed an especially blessed prospect:

> The *zarda* is so popular and esteemed a tradition among the Muslims that it lifts the spirits of all, great and small, rich and poor, of all social ranks; in families that are sometimes divided, discord often vanishes on such an occasion. Non-Muslims themselves, respecting the habits and customs of their Muslim brothers, consider the *zarda* a grand event, worthy of encouragement; they never fail to contribute their assistance to the organisers of this festival . . . The festival of the [first] evening consists in the recitation of the whole of the Qur'an, of sacred books, of religious chants, and of poetry in honour of the Prophet. The moral precepts of religion spread their beneficent balm in the souls and the hearts of good Muslims. This is Islam: simple, benevolent, and democratic, as it can be seen in this great feast of the Muslim family. This is the secret of the success of the *zarda*, and that which we celebrate on Saturday and Sunday next will enjoy, in this respect, the greatest such success.[114]

The article concluded with thanks to those who had already made donations towards the cost of the event, and gave the address to which further donations should be sent: the Comité des meskines ('Committee for the Poor'), whose address at 8, rue Chabron, Constantine, was also that of the Constantinois Fédération des *élus*. The Committee was chaired by Dr Bendjelloul, and it was he who, on 30 September, had requested the authorisation of the festival from the city's mayor. On the previous day, 29 September, Bendjelloul had met with his local political

[113] *Ibid.* [114] *Ibid.*

allies and the heads of the Constantine sufi *ṭarīqa*s to organise the *zarda*. Given the political conjuncture – Bendjelloul's recent newspaper interviews, which were unfavourably commented upon by much of Algerian opinion, including that of his erstwhile Congress allies the Badisiyya *'ulamā* – the timing of the festival, of which he was visibly the patron, was perhaps not innocent, and certainly not insignificant.

The reformists, in fact, responded furiously. On the evening of the same day that the *Dépêche de Constantine* announced the *zarda* in such glowing terms, Ben Badis and some 150 of his colleagues held their own council. The AUMA president's fears, as reportedly expressed at this meeting, are highly instructive:

> Our currently elected representatives have sided entirely with the members of the brotherhoods and wish to revive the maraboutic customs which we fight against. Already they intend to give a *zarda*. In the course of this ceremony, cinematographers will come to film the great flock of [Muslims] present, and, in the towns where these films will be shown, they will [be exploited to] demonstrate our physical and intellectual inferiority, our attachment to archaic ways. The government, seeing such a return to old customs, will refuse us the satisfaction of the demands presented by us in Paris . . . they will lose all interest, believing us still fixed in medieval backwardness. Moreover, the [Muslims] will derive no comfort from this festival of charity and will remain in their miserable condition. Dr Bendjelloul is about to ruin our dearest aspirations. We must unite and oppose, with all our strength, such lamentable deviations. We must rely on the Government to forbid this event.[115]

Over the next several days, the reformists in Constantine circulated a demand for the revocation of the permission given by the mayor for the *zarda*, arguing that 'the Muslim cemetery is a sacred place and may not be profaned by acts of rejoicing, [particularly those] of an overtly political character'.[116] The proscription of celebrations of all kinds in relation to death, the dead, tombs and cemeteries is a constant feature of *salafī* doctrine, and one aspect of the reformists' opposition to the *zarda* was clearly the illicit nature, in their eyes, of such an event. More important, though, it seems, was the meaning of this festival itself as an expression of Algerian religious culture. In part, the issue was political – to the reformists, the *zarda* was religious practice used as a vehicle for political aims, an intolerable effrontery on the part of Bendjelloul and an offence against those solely competent to speak for Islam, i.e. the reformist *'ulamā* themselves. At Batna, in the Aurès, Bendjelloul was denounced

[115] Chief, SD, Constantine, to Governor-General, Algiers, and Prefect, Constantine, 5 Oct. 1936 no. 4182, ADC/B3/273/11.
[116] Chief, SD to Prefect, Constantine, 6 Oct. 1936 no. 4181, ADC/B3/273/11.

by the local reformists and their supporters for adopting an 'anti-Islamic' political stance, for selling out to the government and abandoning the policy of the Congress, and for omitting to consult the reformists on the question of the *zarda*, which concerned the religious sphere 'in which they consider themselves exclusively qualified to make judgements of Qur'anic principle'.[117]

But more than this, the *zarda* appeared to the reformists as an exemplary expression, not of benevolent, democratic and egalitarian Islam, but of that shameful culture of backwardness and inferiority of whose appearance to European eyes they were perfectly terrified. Not only was such an event doctrinally reprehensible, it threatened to become a ludic spectacle of difference, of archaic 'native customs' and inferior mentality, which would be set up on display for the curious European population and, worse still, captured on film to be shown to the amusement and condescension of Europe and its rulers. The dignity of Algerians and of Islam, at the very moment when they demanded its recognition, seemed to them to be at stake. In printed proclamations distributed on the first day of the festival, the reformists warned:

> Today a trap has been laid for the people: a scrap of meat has been laid upon it and the whole covered with the name of 'great *zarda*' and 'popular feast'. The meat which you will eat at this *zarda* is illicit, for it is not given in honour of God. You are being mocked, and your religion is mocked in the eyes of foreigners. *The photographic apparatus is ready! The trap is laid!* . . . Distance yourselves from the *zarda* and draw near to God.[118]

The reformists attacked Bendjelloul's *zarda*, on the one hand, as no more than a political gimmick to curry favour with the populace, and yet simultaneously as a gross impiety and a mortal danger:

> Has our people, known for its valorous traditions, lost the consciousness of its dignity and honour to the extent that we should exchange our conscience for a plate of couscous? No and no again! The Muslim is not some wild beast that can be captured with bait . . . The organisers [of the *zarda*] hope to . . . discredit our religion by covering in its name practices worthy only of the age of paganism; to ruin the credit of its people in political terms by showing us to be backward and superstitious; to show before [the eyes of] our detractors that barbarism is an inherent flaw of our race and our religion . . .[119]

On the first day of the *zarda*, Ben Badis published an open letter to the prefect in the *Dépêche de Constantine*:

[117] Commissaire de Police to Sub-Prefect, Batna, 11 Oct. 1936 no. 6353, ADC/B3/273/11.
[118] Printed notices in Arabic and French, ADC/B3/273/13, emphasis added.
[119] *Ibid.*

> Sir, We have the honour of drawing your attention to the grave consequences that may result on the occasion of the *zarda*, to be given by the *Comité des meskines* . . . The cemetery is a sacred place of prayer and contemplation, which must not be turned into a place of celebrations that are not in conformity with the Muslim religion. The *zarda* will, without doubt, provoke an influx of young persons who, mostly non-practising, will enter the cemetery in a state of inebriation and may profane the tombs and commit the most regrettable acts . . . We must object at the fact that, in the case of such an event . . . the *'ulamā*, who alone are qualified in questions touching the religious sphere, were not consulted as to their point of view.[120]

If the official language of protest concerns strictly the question of religious propriety, and the pretension of the AUMA to exclusive jurisdiction over such questions, the concerns underlying their stand were more complex. The reformists were not only doctrinally opposed to the event as an illicit practice, but appalled by the prospect of Algerian culture that it seemed, *in their eyes*, to offer to the gaze of Europeans. To its defenders, the *zarda* was a celebration of community in honour of the dead and for the well-being of the living, and a demonstration of the democratic and egalitarian nature of Islam. For its opponents, it was a mockery of religion, an illicit practice from a pagan era of ignorant superstition, a return of the enslavement to magic that the modern world disavowed – an embarrassment of Algerians before Europeans' eyes. For neither side was the event conceived without a primary reference to a Eurocentric norm of 'modern' social behaviour.

In the cemetery where the feast took place, Bendjelloul had electric light installed, and thousands of Algerians, from across the eastern part of the country, passed along the road illuminated by garlands of red, white, and blue electric bulbs that led to the site itself. Constantine's notable sufi families were present, including most of the signatories to the petition against the AUMA that had been sent to the prefect four months earlier: Sidi Hani Ben Shaykh Zwawi, of the Hansali *zāwiya* at Rouffach, donated five of the fattest head of cattle received; Sidi Aḥmad al-Tījānī gave a thousand francs.[121] The success of the feast exceeded all expectations. The donations received were reported as totalling 29,510 francs in cash; forty head of cattle were slaughtered; twenty thousand kilograms of bread and thirty-five 'enormous jars' of couscous were prepared. The police estimated the attendance at twenty-five thousand and noted that, when all expenses were paid, Dr Bendjelloul's committee reported a sum of 29,000 francs remaining for distribution to the poor.

[120] 'Tribune publique', *Dépêche de Constantine*, 10 Oct. 1936, ADC/B3/273/11.
[121] *Dépêche de Constantine*, 9 Oct. 1936, ADC/B3/273/11.

It was reported that no untoward incident occurred and that the occasion was perfectly orderly.[122] The prefect wrote to the governor-general that the protests of the AUMA, 'who presented [the *zarda*] as contrary to true Islamic principles and damaging to the dignity of the Muslims, as potentially harmful to [the realisation of] their political demands, [. . .] appear to have been without significant effect'.[123] The local *sûreté* chief reported that the 'spectacle' had attracted over two thousand curious European observers.

The *zarda*, like the affair of the pilgrims and the local cultural politics of Mila, crystallised multiple social conflicts in spaces and through languages of authority whose structures were undergoing rapid and substantial transformation. It is in these conjunctures of struggle over discursive resources – of doctrine and ritual, community and history – that the changing self-perception of Algerians becomes visible. The *salafī* vision of Algerian community emerged in significant tension with existing alternatives, both in the discourses of other groups and individuals and in the actual cultural practices of Algeria's richly creative and diverse population. The examples of the Constantine *zarda* and the other events of 1936 demonstrate the intensity of the conflicts occurring, as well as the limits of the reformists' dominance of religious culture at this time.

In the next few years, however, their grip on the legitimate enunciation of Islam would grow steadily firmer, as earlier forms of reconciling the contradictions of reality – God and conquest – became ever more untenable. Taking change into their own hands, rural families sent their sons to reformist mosques in Constantine, or to Tunis, for their religious education, instead of to the old centres of spiritual authority in the *zawāyā* of the steppe or pre-Sahara.

Simultaneously, their claimed authority as spokesmen of/for the Algerian community as nation became more visibly political. At the end of the 1930s, and again in the mid-1940s, after the Anglo-American occupation of North Africa and the fall of the Vichy régime, Algerians of all political tendencies sought new possibilities of unifying their diverse efforts in a single representative grouping. The reformists would come to consider themselves uniquely qualified, as the speakers of Algeria's true 'self', for the leadership and the definition of their community. Initially standing aside from – or, rather, *above* – politics, they came, after the death of Ben Badis in 1940, to appreciate the inherently

[122] Chief, SD to Prefect, Constantine, 12 Oct. 1936 no. 4279, ADC/B3/273/11.
[123] Prefect, Constantine, to Governor-General, Algiers, 12 Oct. 1936 no. 36597, ADC/B3/273/11.

political nature of their self-appointed task of 'resurrecting' Muslim Algeria and placing it, revitalised and equipped for a negotiated emancipation, under their divinely sanctioned guardianship. They thus came to conceive of themselves as encompassing the more explicitly political groups which emerged from the struggles of the interwar period. For the *'ulamā*, the unity of these movements could only reside in their own leadership: 'We must have a single party, one which can encompass those of Messali and of Ferhat Abbas – this must be the party of the *'ulamā*.'[124] Such was the view expressed at a meeting of the senior reformists in Algiers in July 1944. The Association's vice-president, al-'Arabī al-Tebessī (Larbi Tebessi), reportedly affirmed: 'No political party can survive without the *'ulamā*, and we ourselves need all men of integrity and sincerity – any leader, be he Messali or Ferhat Abbas, must consult the *'ulamā* who alone are qualified to guide the people, for we have the key of religion.'[125]

To the extent that the *'ulamā* had, by now, successfully established their claim to dominant authority in the enunciation of Islam and 'the Algerian personality', all the political actors of Muslim Algeria, moderate notables and radical populists alike, would indeed have to submit to the terms of their requirements in the cultural domain. The PPA, scorned by the reformists and established notability as a 'band of beggars',[126] a disreputable party of illiterates led by 'stray sheep' and a 'turbulent demagogue' whose revolutionary programme for independence they had dismissed as 'fantasy' and 'noxious propaganda',[127] would soon count in its ranks young men of the generation of Lakhdar Bentobbal, whose socialisation had been significantly marked by the destabilising and recreating effects of the reformists' own civilising mission. The revolutionary voluntarism of the men who would launch their war on 1 November 1954 was brought into being under specific historical conditions not of their own making, and 'the tradition of all

124 Intelligence note, CIE, Algiers, 13 July 1944 no. 684CIE, ADA/4I/14/9.
125 *Ibid.*
126 In fact, the social base of the PPA was founded on a lower middle class of small proprietors, traders and artisans: café owners, tailors, bakers, jewellers, shopkeepers, as well as skilled and semi-skilled workers. In the towns, it was the dynamic and upwardly mobile sector of the population who formed the nuclei of PPA/MTLD cells; cf. Lakhdar Bentobbal's reminiscences of Mila, above – his own family owned land and had commercial interests.
127 In speeches made at the AUMA congress, Algiers, 22–26 Sept. 1937 (reports in ADA/2I/39/3), and to the émigré workers at the reformists' *nādī al-tahdhīb* (educational circle) in Paris (Report, SAINA, Paris, 5 July 1937, 'Le Cercle de l'éducation', (8 pp.), ADA/4I/13/3(2F); Note, SAINA to Minister of the Interior, Paris, 28 Sept. 1937, ADA/4I/13/3(2F)).

the dead generations', as well as the socialisation gained in the radical workers' movement, the French army, and clandestine political action, formed a part – a conditioning part, rather than a causal one – of that universe. Such 'tradition' was now most vocally spoken of and for by the reformist *'ulamā*. But this did not mean that the single representative voice of *al-umma 'l-jazā'iriyya 'l-muslima* would be theirs. A quite different 'sole guide of the people' would shortly emerge – one that might, in the domain of 'national culture', submit to the reformists' requirements, but that would also quite definitively subordinate their voice to its own.

The death of the *'ulamā*

'The abrupt passage to direct action on the part of the extremist separatists, on 1 November 1954, surprised the *'ulamā*, who, their excesses of language notwithstanding, had not seriously envisaged the hypothesis of a recourse to the use of violence and disorder, and thereafter found themselves unexpectedly faced with a situation they had not foreseen.'[128] Thus did the government-general's police see the situation of the AUMA almost a year after the outbreak of the FLN's revolutionary war. The *'ulamā* had, indeed, played no part in the resort to armed struggle, although as the nation's self-appointed spokesmen some of them lost little time in attempting to define it, and the enemy it was supposed to destroy, in their own terms. The revolutionaries were quickly identified as 'soldiers of Islam' by reformist preachers, and Muhammad Khayr al-Din, who had been active in the Mashriq and now found himself in Switzerland, reportedly declared to a Swiss journalist: 'We are the enemies of colonialism – colonialism is represented [in Algeria] by France, which keeps our language and religion in a state of oppression . . . Algeria must be fully sovereign, *since the Algerian nation . . . is now conscious of its personality*.'[129] In the week after the revolution's first anniversary, the *khuṭba* at Friday prayer in the Sidi M'hamed mosque of the popular quarter of Belcourt insisted that it was a form of jihad to provide aid to the families of those who fought 'for the good of Islam'.[130]

In the immediate aftermath of the insurrection, the reformists still hoped that their movement might be seen as what they claimed it was,

128 Direction de la Sûreté nationale en Algérie, Synthèse des Renseignements généraux, 'L'Association des oulama d'Algérie', Algiers, Oct. 1955 no. 6442SNA/RG3 (43 pp. plus appendices), p. 25, ADA/4I/14/1.

129 *Ibid.*, p. 30, emphasis added.

130 Renseignement, PRG Algiers, 15 Nov. 1955 no. 9751, ADA/4I/14/2.

'the true guide of the Algerian people',[131] and that the armed action of the FLN, which they (in common with almost everyone else) expected to be of limited scope and short duration, might be used as a catalyst to precipitate the change of regime in Algeria that they had been demanding, in one form or another, since the 1930s. On 29 December 1954, Tawfiq al-Madani briefed a small gathering of his colleagues, at the AUMA offices in rue Pompée in central Algiers, on the Association's own strategy for Algerian independence: the struggle, he reportedly explained, was to be construed as a triangle, each of whose sides constituted a step in the process. The first was the independence of education and Islamic endowments (*habous*); the second, built upon the means gained in the first, would be 'the education of the masses with the aim of cultivating the desire for independence'; the third, eventual, aim was to be the establishment of an independent, sovereign Arab government. This lengthy procedure was still, at this late date, envisaged as achievable through legal means – if a majority could not be obtained in the Algerian Assembly,[132] it would be necessary, with the support of the Arab states, to have recourse to the international community, which would have to accede to the demonstrated unanimous desire of the people for independence.[133]

If this approach was a logical continuation of the strategies followed by the shaykhs in exile whose stories were told earlier, it also fits the preoccupations and expectations that the *'ulamā* had displayed since the mid-1940s. As their community's 'natural leadership', they still envisaged a negotiation of rule, although from 1945 onwards it became increasingly clear that, rather than the partnership with the colonial state that Ben Badis had sought, the transfer of power to a sovereign Algerian state would be necessary. As they were still primarily concerned with their own, cultural-religious domain of sovereignty, it was the issues of freedom of education in Arabic, freedom to preach and organise, and freedom – above all – to speak in the name of Islam without the illegitimate competition of government-appointed Islamic functionaries, that

[131] *Al-Baṣā'ir* (n.d. [Dec. 1954?]), quoted in 'L'Association des oulama d'Algérie' (note 128 above), p. 26.

[132] Established by the Statute of 1947, the Assembly replaced the *Délégations financières* that had been in existence since 1898. The Assembly, as well as having the budgetary autonomy of its predecessor, was mandated to examine and modify, in certain respects, metropolitan law and was charged with the application of the provisions of the Statute itself, which were subject to an unachievable two-thirds majority vote and therefore never implemented.

[133] PE, Maison-Carré to Prefect, Algiers, 31 Dec. 1954 no. 99/S, ADA/4I/14/2.

most exercised the reformists.[134] It was not until 16 June 1954 that the AUMA, frustrated in its repeated attempts to force meaningful concessions on the question of religious authority, issued a declaration to the effect that 'the religious question cannot find any logical resolution save within the framework of an overall solution to the Algerian problem, which is an indivisible whole'.[135] The particular priorities of the *'ulamā* were thenceforward publicly linked to the question of national independence, but a year later, a meeting of the Association's central committee was still apparently hearing, from al-Madani, an exposé on the question of Islam's separation from the state, the official recognition of the Arabic language, and the local difficulties of certain reformist schools.[136] The immediate approach was still one of negotiation; it was decided to make fresh depositions to the governor-general, the president of the Algerian Assembly and certain metropolitan politicians and – most extraordinarily – to request that the administration itself employ the reformists' graduates from the Ben Badis Institute and the Zaytuna as teaching personnel within the official educational establishment. If this was envisaged as a means of 'infiltrating' the system, and – more crucially – of relieving the pressure on the Association of a numerous body of employees whom it could not afford to pay decently, it nonetheless suggests that the reformists' belief in a non-violent, negotiated solution possessed a remarkable resilience.[137]

134 These issues came together in the question of the status of *habous* properties, pious endowments made over for the maintenance of religious institutions, which had been confiscated in 1839, with the state assuming the responsibility for paying and maintaining the religious infrastructure thus despoiled of its livelihood. The state's (mis) management of this sphere was, to the reformists, among colonialism's most intolerable abuses, and the primary concern of the AUMA from the moment of its reconstitution after the Second World War was to gain control of a budget, in lieu of the confiscated *habous*, by means of which the Association's role as provider and arbiter of Islam for Algerians might be assured. This imperative was all the more important since the Association, as a whole, appears to have suffered from more or less constant financial difficulties in the 1940s and early 1950s.

135 'L'Association des oulama d'Algérie' (note 128 above), p. 16.

136 The law of 1905 on the separation of church and state was never effectively applied in Algeria. A decree of 1907 modified the existing arrangements (Christelow, 'Time of transition', 128), providing for the establishment of 'associations cultuelles', but these were not autonomous of the administration. The 1947 Statute promised separation (art. 56), as well as the teaching of Arabic at all levels in schools, but this was never ratified by the Algerian Assembly, which set up a commission to examine the practicalities of separation only in November 1951. The total separation of Islamic affairs from the purview of the colonial government remained a basic demand of the AUMA up until 1954.

137 Renseignement, PRG Algiers, 13 June 1955 no. 4832, ADA/4I/14/2. The Ben Badis Institute was an upper-level school, established in 1947 in Constantine to further the

In pursuit of this strategy of garnering international support for a negotiated independence under their own auspices, the *'ulamā* had invested significant efforts in a diplomatic offensive with the aim of establishing themselves as the recognised spokesmen for Algeria in the brother countries of the Middle East. Fadil al-Wartilani travelled to Egypt and Lebanon, and published articles in the Lebanese and Syrian press emphasising the reformists' role as leaders of the Algerian nation and awakeners of its self-consciousness. Bashir al-Ibrahimi, since 1942 the *de facto*, and since the congress of June 1946 the elected, president of the Association, went to Cairo in March 1952, perhaps for the same purpose, and remained there through the revolution. It would be as diplomats and spokesmen that the reformists who eventually joined the FLN – notably al-Madani, Si 'Amor Derdur, Muhammad Khayr al-Din, and Abbas Ben Shaykh Husayn - would make themselves useful and prominent. Their services, however, were only given over to the FLN's revolution once it was made very clear – by the inability of the French government to respond to the situation by any means other than escalating repression, and by the FLN itself – that this was the only option remaining open.

Although the *'ulamā* are generally considered to have 'rallied' to the Front with their declaration of 7 January 1956, penned by al-Madani in his capacity as the Association's secretary-general, the AUMA did not thereby announce its dissolution, as Ferhat Abbas's party, the UDMA, did, and as the FLN had insisted, in its self-proclamation of 1 November, that all other would-be representative Algerian groups must. On the contrary, addressing the congress that decided upon the announcement of public support for those 'legitimately engaged in the effort of struggle', al-Madani reportedly declared:

> We are the guides of the people and we have our place at the head of the delegation that will surely, very shortly, be called to negotiate with the French government. I think it urgent that we draw up a proclamation, stating our position in favour of the constitution of a democratic Algerian government, around which all communities, minorities and majority, would assemble. We cannot stand aside from the discussions *that must be held to put an end to this violence which our religious convictions reprove, since on both sides it is the innocent who are its victims.*[138]

education of promising students from the Association's *madrasas*, and to prepare them for higher study at the Zaytuna, the Qarawiyyin, or in the Mashriq.

[138] Intelligence note, Comm. div., PRG, Algiers, 9 Jan. 1956 no. 241, ADA/4I/14/2, emphasis added.

The declaration was to be made public and delivered to both 'French and Muslim political authorities', as well as to the United Nations. Whatever the text was, it was not a statement of the AUMA's self-effacement in favour of the unifying FLN. The manifesto does not announce the dissolution of the Association, but calls for 'loyal negotiations with the authentic representatives of the Algerian people legitimately engaged in the effort of struggle' – if this is a reference to the FLN, it seems more than likely that the reformists included themselves alongside, or rather 'at the head of' the Front, rather than behind its banner. The same text offers no indication (however veiled) of exhortation to armed struggle, but rather 'calls upon the people to remain in the straight path, to keep its patience, to persevere in good works, to unite and forget past divisions', and when speaking of the revolution itself, refers to the resort to violence as a 'gesture of despair', warning that any cynical ploy of partial reform of the colonial order can now only lead 'the despair of the Algerian people to its most terrible paroxysm'.[139]

The issues most discussed at the reformists' congress of January 1956 were reportedly the same agenda that had so preoccupied them over the past decade: the Association's financial difficulties, the problems of ensuring the continuation of its pedagogic programme, and of gaining control of the management of *habous* revenues. There was thus no brutal change of direction brought on by the unfolding crisis, but rather an attempted continuation of business as usual. The AUMA's own internal politics were probably instrumental in al-Madani's own decision, shortly afterwards, to throw in his lot with the FLN's External Delegation in Cairo. Bashir al-Ibrahimi, surprised in Cairo by the events of 1 November, had meanwhile been attempting to forge an alternative union of Algerian political groupings, working alongside Ahmed Mezerna, an ally of Messali Hadj in the now hopelessly factionalised and schismatic PPA/MTLD. Their efforts came to naught – Mezerna was incarcerated by the Egyptian secret services at the behest of his FLN opponents and al-Ibrahimi, who, like Messali, refused to recognise the FLN's monopoly of power, was sidelined for the rest of the war.[140]

139 'Résolution de l'Assemblée générale de l'Association des oulamas musulmans d'Algérie', French text, supplement to *al-Baṣā'ir* no. 350, 20 Jan. 1956 (Arabic text in no. 349), ADA/4I/14/2; Harbi (ed.), *Archives*, 109–10.

140 Mezerna attempted to renegotiate the FLN's very existence as a plural 'front' of multiple groups, of which Messali's MNA and other parties (UDMA and AUMA) would be constituents, but this failed to gain anyone's support. Mezerna was arrested at Cairo airport on 11 July 1955. The FLN attempted to assassinate Messali in September 1959; he eventually died in exile in France in 1974.

In Algiers, the Association continued to operate and to collect funds on its own account, and as late as the winter of 1956, with the Battle of Algiers in full flame, the colonial police entertained plans to bring the reformists back 'on side'.[141] In November 1956, the movement's leadership in the capital tried to breathe new life into their failing independence, lamenting that 'it appears that our Association, which had succeeded in taking a preponderant place among the movements of liberation, is now absolutely overwhelmed by events . . . It is urgent that an end be made of this state of affairs.'[142] But their days were numbered. In March 1957, the FLN instructed all AUMA members not already actively employed in the Association's *madrasas* to join the Front in Tunisia. The AUMA leadership in Algiers, apparently trying to preserve its independence of action and its own base of militants, however, immediately ordered all its members, instead, to report to the director of the nearest *madrasa*, and to establish themselves in any village without a school.[143] Two weeks later, on 8 April, the acting (and, in the absence of al-Ibrahimi, *de facto*) president of the AUMA, Larbi Tebessi, who had been the first reformist leader to broker an agreement with the FLN, disappeared. It has been alleged both that he was abducted and murdered by the French special services and by the *jaysh* (the ALN).[144] Whatever the truth, his removal decapitated the movement. The AUMA in Algiers continued, in April, to collect funds for the upkeep of its schools, but in May, the FLN demanded that the sums collected be handed over to the Front, declaring: 'It is no longer possible for us, in the present circumstances, to permit your adherents to collect funds in

[141] Note, 'Sur la possibilité de reprendre en mains l'Association des Oulama', SLNA Algiers, n.d. (after Oct. 1956, before April 1957), ADA/4I/14/2. The numbers of grassroots *'ulamā* interned, fled, or having joined the FLN by this point, however, would have made any such initiative fruitless.

[142] Intelligence note, PRG Algiers, 30 Nov. 1956 no. 14135, ADA/4I/14/2.

[143] Intelligence notes, PRG Algiers, 14 March 1957 no. 3198; 22 March 1957 no. 3510, ADA 4I/14/2.

[144] Meynier, *Histoire intérieure du FLN*, 190 n.192, reports 'unverifiable speculation' by French agencies that Tebessi may have been assassinated by the FLN. Roberts, 'North African Islamism', 20, sees the AUMA under Tebessi as fully integrated with the FLN by this date and argues strongly for French responsibility in Tebessi's murder. Rumours persisted in the Aurès, Tebessi's home region, to the effect that he was eliminated by the *jaysh* as being too independently minded (personal communication); responsibility has in some accounts been laid (along with much else) at the door of Abbane Ramdane, then the interior FLN's chief strategist, himself murdered by his comrades in December 1957. The officer who commanded the French army's torture and death squad in Algiers at this time, and who was responsible for the murders (on 6 March) of Larbi Ben M'hidi and (on 23 March) of Ali Boumendjel, does not mention Tebessi in his notorious memoir (Aussaresses, *Services spéciaux*).

Algiers for the exclusive benefit of your Association.'[145] The *coup de grâce* came that September: all AUMA members of age and ability to participate actively in the struggle for liberation were instructed by the Front to proceed to join the *jaysh* in Tunisia or Morocco via the maquis. Those who must remain in Algeria were instructed to cease all activity until further notice – they would be paid monthly, in the meantime, from the war chests of the revolution.[146]

By this time the leading *salafī*s were working for the FLN in the Arab east, were in exile in Morocco, had been sidelined or had otherwise disappeared. The leadership of the AUMA, generally committed to non-violence and hoping to preserve its independence, was effectively eliminated in the infernal machine of the FLN's brutal and fratricidal emancipatory war, and France's brutal and fratricidal colonial war against it. As nationalists, spokesmen and militants for the nation and its sovereign state, some of them, like al-Madani, survived. As *'ulamā*, independent arbiters of good and ill, censors of society and the state, they did not. They had, nonetheless, created a domain of their own sovereignty over which they might expect to rule at least in part. Obliged by the force of terrible circumstance to choose their camp, the *salafī*s would thenceforward be integrated into the retrospectively unified-and-glorious national movement, whose own history as the latest and ultimate incarnation of Algeria's perennial history of patriotic struggle they would happily go on to write, and into which they would (re-)write themselves. That history would now be part of a *national* story – and once 'the nation' was freed, its meaning would remain to be fought over.

[145] Intelligence note, PRG Algiers, 6 May 1957 no. 5296, ADA 4I/14/2.
[146] Comm. div., PRG, to Prefect, Algiers, 20 Sept. 1957, no. 10332, ADA/4I/14/2.

4 Saint cults and ancestors

> . . .'heritage', and 'ancestry'. . . 'rootedness', all signifiers of the imaginary face-to-face relation between man and his origins.
>
> Etienne Balibar[1]

The ashes of Sidi 'Abd al-Raḥmān al-Tha'ālibī

In 1770, a Danish fleet bombarded Algiers. The conflict would later be numbered among the many victories won by the Regency's then-governor, Baba Mehmet Osman Pasha, in his lifelong commitment to jihad against Christian crusader-imperialism and in defence of the integrity of Muslim Algeria, the caliph's 'front line' with European aggression in the west.[2] A popular song apparently composed at the time, however, attributed the invincibility of *al-Jazā'ir al-maḥrūsa*, Algiers the Well-Guarded, to an agency at once more and less substantial than that of the Ottoman janissary-king:

> How can it come into the minds of the unbelievers that they should attack Algiers,
> Proud Queen of towns and cities, Algiers which possesses so many saints,
> Solely concerned with deflecting disaster from her?. . .
> The first among these protectors is Sidi 'Abd al-Rahman al-Tha'alibi, Sword and Rampart of the city;
> Ocean of learning, vicar of the Prophet, possessor of the treasures of blessing,
> His sacred writings dissipate my ills and worries; they are to me as a garden of flowers, reviving the eyes and pleasing in scent.
> All my ambition is to walk in the footsteps of this prince of the pious and mystic.

[1] Balibar, 'Racism and nationalism', 57.

[2] This is the version in al-Madani, *Muḥammad 'Uthmān Basha*; for the war with Denmark, pp. 97–8.

Figure 8. 'Algiers the Well-Guarded'. (Seventeenth-century engraving, from G. Fisher, *Barbary Legend: War, Trade and Piracy in North Africa, 1450–1830.* Oxford, Oxford University Press, 1957. By permission of Oxford University Press.)

Algiers under his protection will enjoy undisturbed repose, and glory in constancy; let us not be troubled.
This master of divine perfection will never forget us.[3]

Sidi 'Abd al-Rahman, Algiers' foremost patron saint, 'this formidable erudite, conscientious exegete. . . vivid dreamer',[4] was born in 1384[5] into the Tha'āliba nobility who had dominated Algiers and the Mitidja (the city's hinterland) in the second/eighth century. He established a *zāwiya* in the flourishing Hafsid city of Bejaïa (Bougie), and studied in Tunis, Cairo and the *ḥaramayn*, returning to the Maghrib in 1416, where he died in 873/1468–9. The saint's renowned mystical accomplishments,

[3] French tr. attributed to Edmond Fagnan, 'Les saints d'El Djezaïr', *RA* 1894 (possibly from the account by Venture de Paradis, first published by Fagnan as *Alger au XVIIIème siècle* (Algiers, Jourdan, 1898), in Kaddache, *L'Algérie durant la période ottomane*, 202.
[4] Berque, *Intérieur du Maghreb*, 49.
[5] *Ibid.*; G. Marçais, 'Sidi 'Abd er-Rahmane', 155 has '*circa* 1383', and another source (in Klein *et al, Feuillets d'El-Djezaïr*, 12), 1387.

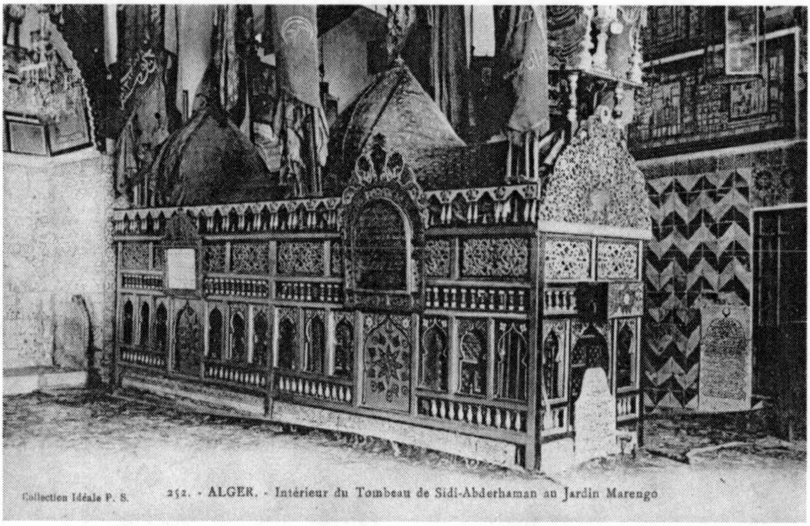

Figure 9. The tomb of Sidi 'Abd al-Rahman al-Tha'alibi. (Postcard, author's collection.)

particularly his extraordinary visions, 'his passionate asceticism, his faith and learning, conserved for him a place of choice in Algerian hagiography'.[6] Among other fabulous exploits, he was said to be given to meditation while floating on his prayer mat over the sea. Another story tells how he was once visited by the renowned Oranais saint, Sidi Mhammad Ben 'Aouda, who tamed lions and rode about on their backs. The visitor remained overnight, leaving his lion in the stable with Sidi 'Abd al-Rahman's cow, who was found in the morning to have devoured the lion.[7] The moral – humility – was one of the *walī*'s particular virtues. Over his mortal remains was placed a splendid sanctuary, begun in 1611 and remodelled as a mosque in 1696,[8] set upon the heights of Algiers, on the northern edge of the old city and originally outside the ramparts of the town. The mausoleum became a site of particular veneration, coveted as a final resting place by the capital's foremost citizens for three centuries: within its precincts, where the remains of Sidi 'Abd al-Rahman lay in the prayer hall itself, 'below a magnificent reliquary of sculpted

[6] Berque, *Ecrits sur l'Algérie*, 214.

[7] Dermenghem, *Culte des saints*, 12; Marçais, 'Sidi 'Abd er-Rahmane', 156. The same story is attributed to a local Kabyle *murābiṭ* in Djaout, *Chercheurs d'os*, 59–60.

[8] Berque, *Intérieur du Maghreb*, 209.

and gilded wood, surrounded by silken banners',[9] were also laid to rest the legendary saints Wali Dada (d. 1541) and Sidi Mansur (d. 1644), Dey Mustapha Pasha (r. 1798–1825), and his son, Dey Omar Pasha (r. 1825–27), Haj Ahmad Bey of Constantine, and Professor Mohammed Bencheneb, the extraordinary Algerian scholar who succeeded in the colonial academy, and who died in 1929.[10]

In a memoir written by a prominent notable of Algiers at the end of the nineteenth century and published, after independence, by Tawfiq al-Madani,[11] Sidi 'Abd al-Rahman's mausoleum is the setting for a highly instructive story. In 1830, with the city about to fall under the French cannonade which reduced the landward defences at Fort l'Empereur, the sanctuary became a refuge for women of the city's noble families, who fled there with their valuables. These were, as it turned out, unprotected by the site's sanctity from the clutches of the occupying soldiery – but the saint himself remained impervious to the coloniser's possession of the city, the mosque, and everything else found there. The ashes of Sidi 'Abd al-Rahman, it was said, had vanished from his tomb, and nothing was found in the reliquary but sand.

Commenting on this legend, Berque writes: 'A fine symbol, surely, of the disproportion that exalts a sign, and above all the religious sign, according to the very evanescence of its material carrier.'[12] More immediately, though, the story is an eloquent illustration of the means by which conquest and dispossession were imagined, narrated and lived with by Algerians in the later nineteenth century. Read together with the popular celebration of Sidi 'Abd al-Rahman, the saint-protector who, only sixty years before his dramatic disappearance, was promised 'never [to] forget us', the story of the vanishing ashes in the mosque dramatically expresses a consciousness of the familiar world's having abruptly come to an end.

There are at least two possible readings of the significance of this story. On the one hand, there is the reading made by Berque, that of the metaphysical imperviousness of the *genius loci*; the saint who, more than

[9] Klein et al, *Feuillets d'El-Djezaïr*, 13.

[10] Berque, *Intérieur du Maghreb*, 208–9.

[11] The account is in *Mudhakkirāt al-ḥāj Aḥmad al-Sharīf al-Zahhār*, edited by al-Madani, (Algiers, 1976) 181, and quoted in Berque, *Intérieur du Maghreb*, 209. The memoirs of al-Zahhar (1781–1872), who became *naqīb al-ashrāf* of Algiers before the conquest, was exiled in 1832, serving both Ahmad Bey and 'Abd al-Qadir until 1847, when he retired to Fez, before returning to Algiers where he resumed his former position, are the basis for Berque's *Intérieur du Maghreb*, ch. 12, and al-Madani's *Muḥammad 'Uthmān Basha*, Part 2.

[12] Berque, *Intérieur du Maghreb*, 209.

any other, embodies the 'soul' of the place and is himself the symbol of its inviolability, remains impervious to conquest. The conquering army, taking possession of Algiers, its land, buildings, people and goods – and eventually of the whole territory marked out by colonisation and by the symbolism woven into the name *Algérie* and everything connected with it – was, from the first, incapable of capturing the deeper 'spirit' of the land and people as expressed in the religious symbol of saintly power. The story thus expresses a defiance of the reality of the historical catastrophe that has befallen the city of the saint. For Berque, as for nationalism, the symbol of the vanishing ashes is powerfully indicative of a deeper, metaphysical 'self' of the people (located, significantly, in religion), which the coloniser is unable to penetrate, dominate and possess.

This reading posits precisely that changeless self, awaiting the moment of its re-possession, that I have argued is a retrospective fabrication of the nationalist imagination. Read backwards from the revolution, in an attempt to make all of Algerian history into a cohesive narrative of the nation's self-manifestation (or in an attempt to explain the terrible war of decolonisation and its ineluctability), the legend appears as a neat illustration of the ultimate inviolability of the *nafs* of Algeria, the 'national spirit' that would eventually reappear on the 'long-awaited day' in the guise of the FLN. This has been a recurrent mode of emplotting such motifs in the colonial history of Algeria. But once we dispense with *Geist* and 'self' as explanatory categories, taking them instead as figures of representation embedded in discourses that must themselves be objects of investigation, another reading becomes visible.

In this other reading, the story is a dramatic recognition of catastrophe, symbolising in the disappearance of the saint's physical remains the collapse of the divinely guaranteed age of impervious glory of which he was the pillar. With the fall of the city, the sacred assurance embodied in the protecting saint (*walī*) of Algiers, like that symbolised by the 'talisman' of the early *'ulamā* at Constantine's Bāb al-wād,[13] has ended. No longer able to fulfil the role *vis-à-vis* the population that his presence in the topography of the town and in the religious imaginary of its people prescribed, the saint vanishes – leaving behind not only a synechdochic handful of sand for the coloniser to appropriate, but all the rest of the land as well. The saint can no longer fulfil the pact in terms of which he exists (in virtue of which he is credited with sanctity) – if he is, himself, by virtue of his exalted nature, inviolable, he can remain so now only in absence from the place whose own inviolability his presence was

[13] See pp. 99–100 above.

heretofore held to ensure. The narrative of the ashes symbolises the devastating, unprecedented force of the catastrophic irruption of modernity into a world of divine order, emphasising the total dispossession of a place and people even whose revered dead have been taken from them, whose sacred order of things has been shattered beyond redemption. The saint himself, to be sure, is inviolable, but neither living people nor their places of habitation can ever, save in the consoling imaginary of religion and nationalism, pretend to such security.

This chapter, as a parallel to the previous one, examines the process by which pre-colonial notions of inviolability, the assurance of order, and the normative values of collective self-identification, clustered around the figures of saintly intercessors, expressed in their hagiographies and in the ritual practices of veneration of which they were the objects, gave way in the colonial period to a new kind of 'sanctity' – that is, a new articulation, through new kinds of iconic individuals, of the 'forces of ideological cohesion'[14] through which the community was (re-)imagined. Who, for a nationalist conception of history and community, were Algeria's legitimate, 'totemic' ancestors, and how were they understood?

It is important, again, to emphasise that the process of identifying these ancestors was a work of creative imagination, not of 'recovered memory'. The 'pious ancestors' (*salaf al-ṣāliḥ*) of the reformists' national culture (and of nationalist hero-worship) were not the bearers of some immaculate selfhood, 'the vital forces of the nation. . . this will-to-be rooted in the depths of time'[15] – irrepressibly resurgent bearers of an ineluctably triumphant mission.[16] The 'message of Jugurtha'[17] – Africa to the Africans, struggle until freedom – did not echo down the ages, passed on in memory (and even less in genetic makeup). The war of 'Abd al-Qadir did not leave 'an indelible mark in the psyche of the Algerian people'[18] – at least, not in the homogeneous, exalted way imagined in such formulations. Jugurtha, like the other Berber monarchs of antiquity, was barely memorialised at all in the berberophone cultural tradition of the Islamic period, and only returned to Maghribi historical imaginations in the twentieth century, when French classicists brought

[14] Sebti, 'Sharifisme, charisme et historiographie', 441.
[15] Berque, *Intérieur du Maghreb*, 430.
[16] As Boumédienne, speaking in 1976, would have it: 'This generation has not only fought colonialism, but has known the signal honour of achieving victory. *There resides the difference between ourselves and our ancestors*' (quoted in Remaoun, 'Pratiques historiographiques', 317, emphasis added).
[17] Sahli, *Message de Yougourtha*.
[18] *Pace* Danziger, *Abd al Qadir and the Algerians*, xii.

him into the Kabyle schoolroom.[19] ʻAbd al-Qadir, though doubtless thought of as a great spiritual figure and leader of jihad, could be remembered in other ways too; if the Emir Khaled could, in 1919, draw mass support in Algiers from his grandfather's name, the prophetic text discussed earlier, found in 1917 in ʻAbd al-Qadir's own home region of Mascara, criticised his failures and accused him of causing the deaths of 'religious scholars and leaders of the Arabs because of his poor judgment and his attachment to the weak-minded'. It was perhaps not forgotten in Constantine that it had been the emir's peace agreement with the French in 1837 that had given the invader time and resources to lay his successful second siege against Ahmad Bey, nor that the two leaders had been virtually at war with one another over their respective zones of influence in the pre-Saharan south.[20] These figures neither lived nor entered history in the pristine state of iconic heroism; they *were* not, but only *became*, through particular narratives of their lives, the 'prominent heroes of anti-colonialism' that later historiography (mis)recognises in them.[21] They had to be produced as such, imagined in new historical discourses whose creation was itself part of a complex project of producing new kinds of meaning with which to endow the social world, new ways of conceiving its past truth, present nature and future destiny.

Saints, according to Mohammed Kerrou, are 'these exceptional persons [who] are constructed, at particular moments, according to variable cultural referents that lend them weight as bearers of [particular] messages'.[22] Saints and *mahdīs* (properly so called[23]), at one time, and

[19] A cursory examination of the most accessible recensions of nineteenth-century Berber literature (those of Mouloud Mammeri and Tassadit Yacine) gives no indication of any memory of the ancient dynasties. According to Salem Chaker (personal communication), some fragmentary references can be found here and there in the tradition, but essentially the Kabyles who today identify Tacfarinas (the anti-Roman rebel, now the stage-name of a popular Kabyle singer), Jugurtha and Massinissa as national heroes owe what they know about these historical figures to their reintroduction in the French colonial school, and their subsequent reappropriation by nationalism. Sahli, whose *Message de Yougourtha* helped establish the modern nationalist cult of Jugurtha, was a student at the Ecole Normale at Bouzaréah. (Massinissa, a popular name for male children among berberophone communities, has become even more emblematic since the martyrdom of the first victim of the 'Black Spring' in April 2001, Massinissa Guermah).

[20] The Treaty of Tafna was agreed on 30 May 1837. For the latter point, Clancy-Smith, *Rebel and Saint*, 72–3, 75–8.

[21] Touati, 'Algerian historiography', 92.

[22] Kerrou (ed.), *Autorité des saints*, 13.

[23] Brett, 'Le Mahdi dans le Maghreb médiéval', argues that both the Saadians in sixteenth-century Morocco and ʻAbd al-Qadir in nineteenth-century Algeria were late examples of the specifically mahdist idiom of leadership, which, in the twentieth century, 'has been overtaken by nationalism as an effective political force'.

national ancestor heroes or 'men of the hour' at another, are all iconic individuals invested with the admiration or adulation of those who see in them the embodiment of values through which the community at a particular time identifies itself, in whom it sees its protectors, its 'salvation'. Saints and heroes 'incarnate. . . the principle of the constitution of the group',[24] representing to the community its own ideal of itself – or that ideal which is set up for people's consumption, and on which they are enjoined to model themselves.

One does not become a saint except from the moment when there exists a social and historical demand for spiritual power that can be deployed both on the level of *mentalités* and on that of reality, such that the emergence of a [saintly] personality forms an adequate framework for the collective existence of the group. . . [It is] social demand [and not spontaneous individual 'extraordinariness'] that imposes an individual model capable of incarnating a collective will in its personal qualities.[25]

This 'socio-anthropological' perspective on the social production and reproduction of saints, understood as iconic authority figures, in whose ideal personalities the community embodies its own normative values, enables an analytic approach to the historical transformations in the 'modalities of saint-making' which occur in nationalism. Understanding the role of sanctity in these terms, it becomes possible to see the cultural system advanced, in part, by *salafī*-reformism as in fact, and despite itself, a reinvention of the social function of the saint, rather than as a Weberian–rational attempt to abolish it (as Gellner influentially suggested). The *salafiyya* movement as a whole, of course, had a particular construction of ancestral purity – that supposedly located in the first Muslim generation, now reimagined in modernist terms – as its foundational reference.[26] And, as we have seen, in their modernising and rationalising zeal for the reform of religion and the re-establishment of learning, its proponents attacked with particular vehemence all instances of what, to their modernist eyes, now appeared to depart from that

[24] Kerrou (ed.), *Autorité des Saints*, 13.
[25] *Ibid.*, 12–13.
[26] Here again, the *salafiyya* of the late nineteenth- and early twentieth-century reformists is radically different from that of the Wahhabis (of the eighteenth century or the twenty-first), not in terms of their foundational reference, but in its meaning. A striking formulation occurs in Tha'alibi, where he defends the abolition of the veil as returning the Muslims to the condition of society 'as it was at the time of the Prophet and his Companions, which is to say, like [contemporary] European society' (*Esprit libéral*, 12–13). This is not, of course, unqualified – what is meant is an idealised European society embodying the modernist principles of science, rationality, emancipation and liberalism already perfectly enshrined, for Tha'alibi, in the Qur'an.

reimagined originary ideal and was condemned as magic, superstition, ignorance. If the *zarda* and *ziyāra, dhikr* and astrological prophecy, were to be swept from the house of religion, so too were the intercessory authority-figures whose rich inheritance of symbolically dense narratives, expressions of locally rooted and widely interconnected communities and their worldviews, were now to be read as so many idle tales of charlatans. The reformists' modernism thus radically delegitimised the religious underpinnings of the social authority of saintly lineages and their role as articulating nodal points of the community.

In fact, however, the reformists did not durably efface the beliefs and rituals of 'ordinary religion'[27] from Maghribi Islam – intercessory saints and ecstatic practices survive today in North Africa, and in the Maghribi diaspora – although they did, to a large extent, delegitimise them, covering them with a sense of 'shame' internalised to some degree by their adepts.[28] Instead of abolishing the idiom of sainthood, the reformists recreated it, investing it, particularly through the medium of historiography, with the new legitimate language of civilisation, science, rationality and the nation. The normative values of the community were restructured, and new figures of ancestral authority were found to carry them and their message. In this way, the *salafī* cultural project sought to reconstitute the inviolable, sacred order in which a 'purified' Algeria might be located, an Algeria that would be of the reformists' own making, one they could re-possess, whose whole and unsullied self they could define as the eternal and recovered meaning of the nation.

In this effort, too, they met as much as with failure as with success. No generalised rediscovery of ancestral greatness can be traced to the reformists' Arabic historiography – in fact, al-Madani's inventive mythmaking would go largely unnoticed. His texts, however, do give early expression to a broader shift in dominant structures of historical imagination and cultural authority. Some of the figures encountered in this historiography – and more particularly the values embodied in them – would, with others produced in the more directly political arena of revolutionary action,[29] become new symbols of the community-as-nation in the institutionalised hagiography of independent Algeria. Others, while never achieving widespread iconic status, nonetheless clearly illustrate the dynamics of

[27] I borrow this term from Kerrou (*Autorité des saints*, 12; See also Colonna, *Versets de l'invincibilité*, 63ff.).

[28] Eickelman, *Moroccan Islam*, 'Introduction'; Andezian, 'Mysticisme extatique'; Andezian, *Expériences du divin*; Colonna, *Versets de l'invincibilité*, chs. 3, 4.

[29] The personal following of Messali (attacked in the 1940s precisely for practising a 'political maraboutism') before 1954; the status of the FLN heroes Mourad Didouche, Larbi Ben Mhidi, Mustafa Ben Boulaid, Zighout Youssef, thereafter.

the new kind of 'saint-making' in which *salafī* historiography, while railing against 'saints', itself abundantly engaged.

Exemplary ancestors (i): discovery, progress and the conquests of civilisation

From the shores of Lebanon, the Phoenicians sailed west. The 'Arab sons of Canaan' traded, settled and mixed with the peoples of North Africa and Sicily,

> and there was no conflict between these peoples and the principles of the eastern maritime civilisation of Phoenicia of the *banī Kanʿān,* who in those days crossed the seas and founded commercial cities on their shores, by which means the light of eastern civilisation was spread, brightly radiating into the darkness of western barbarism. Through commerce they developed harmonious acquaintance, based on the interaction of the interests of each – this was the finest means by which to bind peoples together, creating fraternity between them, in the cause of human progress. What a contrast between this, and the resort to aggression with fire and steel, subjugating weak peoples to the guns of imperialism![30]

The greatness of Phoenician civilisation, emblematic for al-Madani of the superiority of the east over the west and foundation of a multi-millenary Arab *grandeur,* is a recurrent theme in his histories.[31] It is the distant 'Arab' ancestors of the present-day Levantines and North Africans who hold the key, in al-Madani's reconstruction of a master-narrative of the progress of human civilisation, to the greatest achievements of antiquity. Their loss, and the loss of the memory of their exploits, can be remedied in the writing of the true history of this age, recovered by the historian's science from the silence of the elapsed ages and the misrepresentations of dominant European knowledge.

> In all the ancient world there was no civilisation that had a greater influence on the course of world events than did that of the Phoenicians; theirs it was that spread light into the dark places of the earth. Their civilisation travelled through the world in all directions, carrying with it the most advanced inventions that the genius of mind and of workmanship could produce in Phoenicia, Egypt, or

[30] Al-Madani, *Muslimūn fī jazīrat Ṣiqiliyya*, 20.

[31] Note that Lebanese Maronite nationalist history made precisely the opposite argument. For Pierre Gemayel, the Phoenicians/Lebanese 'contributed to the blossoming of Mediterranean civilisation . . . Western humanism, a tributary of Rome and of Athens, owes to them [i.e. the Phoenicians/Lebanese] its first foundations' ('6000 years in the service of humanity' (1955), quoted in Gordon, *Self-Determination and History*, 103). This 'authentic past', of a Maronite-dominated Lebanon at a time of pan-Arab assertiveness, roots (Christian) Lebanon in the 'humanist' West, implicitly opposed to the (Islamic) East of which, to al-Madani, his proclaimed forebears were the first great emissaries.

Greece . . . They were the first to build ships and to travel adventurously by sea. Thus they brought the furthest extremities of the earth into contact with one another. . . They were the great agents of the spread of civilisation, for the acquaintance of the nations of the world one with another; they were emissaries of peace, civility and culture.[32]

In the same text from which this passage is taken, published in his *Taqwīm al-Manṣūr* in 1929/30, al-Madani adduced a mysterious Brazilian inscription as 'proof' of the initial Arabisation of North Africa by the 'Phoenician Arabs' in the depths of antiquity. This ethnolinguistic origin of the Phoenicians, and their role as ancient vanguard not only of the Arab migrations of a much later age but of the linguistic politics of a still later one, are, however, only part of the secret revealed in this extraordinary document. Even more remarkable than what can be read from its form ('proof' that the Punic language was an Arabic dialect remarkably close to that spoken in the twentieth-century Tunisian sahel) is the story that the inscription itself tells, or is made to tell, as to its own origin.[33]

In introducing this story, al-Madani takes his reader back to the golden age of Carthage:

[The city] was like New York or London [are] in our modern age, with its large population and abundant public works. The Carthaginians, at that time, after the destruction of their original homeland in Phoenicia, did not content themselves with the territorial possessions that lay before them. They founded their national republic on the soil of Africa, the first ordered republic to be founded anywhere in the world; they endowed it with a constitution, the first to be seen on the face of the earth. [They sent sailors in all directions to discover new lands and found new cities], and thus their ships reached the islands of the English in the north, and the land of Cameroon in the south. The famous travels of Hanno[34] have come down to us as testimony to this greatness, and to these dazzling achievements.[35]

What would the world of today have been like, he asks, had Carthage been allowed to continue its peaceful mission of civilising the earth? When 'a craving for empire and covetous greed led [Rome] to perpetrate

[32] *Taqwīm al-Manṣūr* no. 5, 71.

[33] The inscription was discovered in 1872. Published by Ladislau Netto, the director of Brazil's National Museum, it caused some controversy and was declared a fake by Renan. Cyrus Gordon, an expert on Ugaritic texts, offered a rehabilitation, dating the voyage recorded (by a crew from Sidon, leaving the Red Sea and rounding the Cape of Good Hope) to 534–531 BCE. His translation is markedly different from that proposed by al-Madani (Gordon, *Before Columbus*, 119–27).

[34] The *periplos* of Hanno records a voyage through the pillars of Hercules (Gibraltar) to uncharted lands in West Africa.

[35] *Taqwīm al-Manṣūr* no. 5, 74–5.

its barbarous crime, the wrecking and destruction of Carthage', humanity and human progress lost 'one of the most advanced civilisations in the world'. This ancestral Maghribi grandeur – imagined as such here almost certainly for the first time – is illustrated by al-Madani in a truly remarkable story: 'The Carthaginians, in their last days, had discovered the continent of America.'

It is the strange inscription that these explorers left 'in that same land they had discovered'[36] that furnishes the memorial of this forgotten exploit. By comparing different Phoenician and Carthaginian scripts, al-Madani suggests, 'it can be seen that this inscription dates from shortly before the destruction of Carthage'.[37] Deciphering the text, the modern Maghribi historian reconstructs the story of its presumed author, his unknown, long-lost ancestor-hero.

Al-Madani understands the inscription to be the final testimony of a landing-party, left on the shores of Brazil by the commander (*malik*) of an ancient expedition, who has returned to Carthage with news of their discovery, promising to return as soon as possible. But they remained alone, enduring for almost ten years before 'desperation and despondency overcame them'; most of their number died, leaving only six individuals alive before their leader, too, succumbed. At last, the heroes see that their admiral has turned his back on them, and so one of them, in the last agonies of abandonment, writes an indictment against him, as a witness to their exploit and their suffering. Far away, though, in the Mediterranean, Carthage is about to fall, and it is this that has sealed their fate:

> Perhaps the Carthaginians had prepared their ships, had decided upon the voyage to the [newly] discovered country – but the Roman fleet destroyed these ships. Or the commander and his crew may have returned to find Carthage in mortal danger, and thought only of defending their nation, until the city died and they with it. Perhaps they never even returned to Carthage, but were drowned in storms on the return journey, or were sunk by the Roman navy . . . And when the story of Carthage was ended, and no stone remained standing on another, its survivors sold in the slave markets, not one of those who remained revealed the secret of this discovery to the Romans. And even supposing that they had known of it, obsessed as they were with murderous wars and with the spread of their domination throughout the whole of the ancient world, they would hardly have troubled themselves with the discovery of new continents. And thus, the Roman policy of conquest was the cause of leaving the continent of America unknown for another sixteen centuries.[38]

[36] *Ibid.*, 78. [37] *Ibid.*, 80. [38] *Ibid.*, 83.

There is no reason to suppose that this extraordinary story gained much credence in North Africa when al-Madani published it in 1930. Very few, if any, young Algerians, future militants of nationalism and the revolution, were likely to be found in the centenary year of colonisation imbibing with astonishment and indignation the news that it was Arabs (and Maghribi Arabs at that) who had first discovered America 1,600 years before Columbus. The socialisation of future *mujāhidīn* is unlikely to have included animated debates about the destructive consequences for human advancement wrought on history by the barbarism of Rome. There was quite enough motivation nearer to hand in the cities and countryside of Algeria, and in the living memories of its inhabitants, for dissent and revolt. The effective causes of revolution are hardly to be found in such texts, and it would be pointless to look for them there.

That, in any event, is not the purpose here. It was no part of the reformist programme to contribute to the empowerment of an armed struggle that they did not know was coming, whose actual advent they feared and whose violence they opposed, until they had no option but to throw in their lot with it. This is not evidence of 'national awakening'. The value of such texts lies not in the extent to which they can be made to fit a nationalist teleology but in the insights they can provide into the particular kind of historical imagination which the reformists' self-knowledge, inventing pious ancestors of a wholly new kind, was engaged. In this heroic tragedy, an exemplary tale of the epic of universal human progress, the lost Arab discoverers of the New World are presented as forgotten and rediscovered ancestral heroes to their ethnic and spiritual descendants, still suffering, almost two-and-a-half millennia later, from dispossession and enslavement at the hands of European empire. In no respect is al-Madani here *re*asserting a purely indigenous past suppressed by colonialism and recovered, simply 'revealing [to Algeria] its history'.[39] The wholly new interpretation of Maghribi greatness given here would surely have been strictly unimaginable to North Africans a generation previously. This was no suppressed truth that had lain immune to change and preserved from violation, like the signs on a rock in the Brazilian jungle, awaiting the moment of its opportune discovery. Rather, the narrative of progress and civilisation instantiated in this story is the product of a profoundly new way of imagining the world, the past and the community. The 'ideological cohesion' of this new form of community is expressed through entirely new iconic ancestors, defined not by religion and Arabic as its language, but by a racial

[39] Merad, *Réformisme*, 427.

and civilisational 'genius', and Arabic as *its* language, preceding Islam (but, as we shall see in the following chapter, crowned and perfected in Islam) and rooting the 'nation' in time properly 'immemorial' – that is, time before revelation.

The unidentified heroes lost on the distant shores of Brazil represent something that is, perhaps, quite new at this time in Maghribi historiography. Nameless, unknown, their words dragged back to some semblance of life from a pre-Islamic proto-history that, to be situated at all in conceivable time, must be located in the European (Christian) calendar, they are nonetheless presented as members of *the same community* as the Algerians grouped around the coffee-tables of Constantine over two thousand years after their deaths. Their sacrifice in the cause of civilisation and their suffering at the hands of imperial Europe are presented as part of a total, coherent Maghribi past, in which North African Arabs distinguish themselves by heroic achievement and see their world of peace, prosperity and progress ruined by the violence of imperialism. The lost discoverers of the New World and the readers of *Taqwīm al-Manṣūr*[40] are brought together by their identification in a common community, whose ties of 'belonging together' are spun across a vast tract of space and time by the constitution of this narrative as national history, their shared story.

Of course, it is impossible to say whether this would have been the message which al-Madani's readers would have taken from the text, but it is surely a message that he intended to send. The story, alongside and interwoven with its scientific credentials as the foundation of its claim to truth, is an engaging, heroic tragedy; this history works both by its assumption of a scientific register and in its eliciting of empathy. Moreover, the ironies of the story play expertly on the colonial obsessions of civilisation, backwardness and barbarism, and in so doing, of course, the text is equally caught up in those same obsessions, which it reproduces in its own dissonant key. The polemic against Rome is aimed less at historical Rome itself than at modern Europe in general as Rome's heir,

[40] This readership is difficult to assess, although it was clearly limited. Al-Madani's periodicals, like his books and the reformist press, were produced and circulated on individual subscription. The authorities decided against banning *Kitāb al-Jazā'ir* partly because its circulation might only be increased by the publicity (Note, Mirante to Sec. Gen., Algiers, 9 June 1932 no. 5454, ASSA/9H/46/6). But circulation numbers (a few thousand at most) are of course misleading – one copy might circulate among a whole community, and its few literate members would read aloud to the rest. These texts also reached peripheral areas: *Taqwīm al-Manṣūr* was seized in a rural commune of the Aurès in 1926 (Administrator, CM la Meskiana, to Prefect, Constantine, 15 Sept. 1926; Chief, Brigade mobile, Tebessa, to Prefect, Constantine, 3 Oct. 1926 no. 761 (7 pp.), ADC/B3/170/2).

and France-in-Algeria, in particular, as the self-proclaimed bearer of a renewed mission of civilisation in 'Latin Africa'. The narrative's overarching principle, history as the advance of civilisation in conflict with barbarism, is a leitmotiv of al-Madani's work.[41] The colonial obsession with a civilising mission pursued in the tracks of Rome is inverted by al-Madani's version, which overturns the balance, installs Carthage as the civilisational apogee of antiquity and casts Rome as its barbarian destroyer. Phoenician, Canaanite Carthage, in an inversion of colonial geography, is the bearer of a civilising force from the East, bringing light to the dark places of the West.

This inverted (but structurally unchallenged, and hence only ambivalently subverted) colonial paradigm is perhaps the closest that al-Madani's discourse comes to being the perfect negative of colonial knowledge that it is sometimes supposed to be. As Partha Chatterjee has shown for the Indian case, the logical structure of 'civilising' colonial reason is transferred intact into nationalist thought, where it finds new ways of expressing and furthering the claims to power of those who can manipulate it. Al-Madani appropriated the governing categories of a European historical discourse, its universality and orientation towards a single, global goal of progress, represented in this text by Western modernity's own symbol of founding achievement, the discovery of the New World. Only the location of universal progressive agency is removed, from the northern and western to the southern and eastern shores of the Mediterranean. The opposed centres of gravity of world history as seen from Europe are preserved (are, perhaps, introduced for the first time in this sense into a Maghribi historical vision[42]); only their polarities are switched.

[41] The medieval period's statebuilders – Rustamids, Almoravids, Almohads, Hammadids and 'Abd al-Wadids – are also evoked as having produced outstanding achievements of art, learning and letters. Unusually, perhaps because of his Tunisian upbringing and Turkish family connections, al-Madani also showed a particular interest in the otherwise much-neglected (and, as in the Mashriq, generally maligned) Ottoman period.

[42] If the Mashriq was, before the nineteenth century, a revered place of origins and knowledge, it was not always the fixed centre of civilisational gravity that it became under *salafī* and Ba'thist/pan-Arab influence (on this, Lacheraf, *Des noms et des lieux*, *passim*). In Maghribi hagiography, from the sixteenth to the nineteenth centuries, regionally recognised spiritual authority was predominantly located in the far *west*, in the *seqiya 'l-ḥamra*. Among the principal Egyptian spiritual masters, al-Badawī (d. 1276) of Tanta and al-Shādhilī (d. 1258) were of Maghribi origin – and Cairo, after all, was founded by the Fatimids from the west. If the principal text of legal scholarship in North Africa was for centuries the *Mukhtaṣar* of Sidi Khalīl (d. c.1374), an Egyptian, it was a Tlemceni scholar who brought it to the Maghrib (in around 1402: Berque, *Intérieur du Maghreb*, 49), and an eighteenth-century Moroccan scholar could lecture on that text in Medina, and comment thereafter of Imām Mālik's own city that 'the country . . . is

This does not, however, tell the whole story. In producing their nationalist discourse of the past as a new kind of 'authentic' culture, anchorage for a newly reimagined Algerian community, the reformists themselves were not working in a cultural vacuum. Certainly, they were not 'revealing' Algerian culture; they were proceeding to the destruction and recreation of much of what had constituted Algerian culture. But this does not mean that they imported, wholesale, an entirely new system – Western nationalism as a total model, universal and substantially homogeneous – and imposed it on Algerian society. The conceits of colonial historiography are not merely turned on their head here; rather, a distinct, hybridised language of history is produced. As such, it is the persistence and transformation of endogenous elements in the discourse, just as much as the appropriation and ambivalent subversion of exogenous ones, that require analysis.

Al-Madani's narration of the nation's glorious ancestry occurs through the deployment, and transformation, of a specific cultural idiom – this is, after all, a properly *salafī* history. The radically innovative treatment of its totemic ancestor-figures is a reformulation of an older historiographical form, one that can be traced to Qur'anic discourse: that of the 'edification and fashioning of "normative models"'.[43] Such models had previously been socially embodied predominantly in the cult of saints and saintly ('maraboutic') lineages. The substitution effected in *salafī* history of distant – including pre-Islamic – racial, ethnolinguistic and civilisational ancestors for considerably nearer (and, frequently, living) spiritual models must be seen, not as a triumph of disenchanted historicity recognising 'the sheer reality, or "positivism", of events',[44] but as the eviction of one kind of sacred ancestor in favour of another. This reinvention of established cultural form is perhaps nowhere more clearly visible than in the presentation of the significance of the Islamic conquest of North Africa, in which *al-fatḥ al-islāmī* becomes *la mission civilisatrice*.

The expansion of Islam in its first century provided Muslim societies with a rich source of narrative structures, personalities and motifs to draw

devoid of well-grounded scholars, particularly in Malikism' (Abū Sālim al-'Ayyāshī, *al-Riḥla 'l-'Ayyashiyya* (Fez, 1898–9), I, 276, quoted in El Mansour, 'Maghribis in the Mashriq', 86).

43 Touati, 'Algerian historiography', 84. The Qur'an's own model individuals are sketchily drawn (e.g. Abraham: Q 3.95; cf. Q 3.67, Q 4.125, Q 6.161, Q 16.120–3). Formulaic figures with a reiterated role, such as the 'warners' (to whom Touati is referring – the prophets Ḥūd, Ṣāliḥ and Shu'ayb, sent to their different peoples with the injunction to worship only God), are for that very reason efficient bearers of the text's message.

44 Touati, 'Algerian historiography', 90.

upon in their later historical literature. *Fatḥ*-histories (conquest narratives), notably the *Futūḥ al-buldān* of al-Balādhuri[45] (and, for Egypt, the Maghrib and Andalus, the *Futūḥ Miṣr* of Ibn 'Abd al-Hakam[46]) had their canonical place in the classical tradition, and local variants, both oral and written, of conquest-accounts flourished up to the beginning of the twentieth century, alongside and intermingled with epics of martial deeds whose generic style goes back to the pre-Islamic *maghāzī* ('raids') literature of the *ayyām al-'arab* ('days of the Arabs'), the model for early histories of the Prophet's own campaigns in the Arabian peninsula. Desparmet's recension of popular epic tales circulating in the Mitidja before the First World War, which he supplemented with printed texts produced in Tunis and evidently available in Algeria, includes poems relating the conquests of Syria, Yemen, Ifriqiya (i.e. the north-eastern Maghrib), and of cities as far apart as Tlemcen in Algeria and Kufa in Iraq.[47] Rather than reflecting a preoccupation with the historical Islamisation of these territories themselves, such texts express very local and contemporary historical memories and anxieties, as Desparmet himself was quick to realise.

The motif of *fatḥ* ('opening' to Islam; conquest, victory) is not merely a formulaic liturgical device, or a marker of purely chronological historical periodisation. In Islamic cultures generally, it functions as a key symbol condensing the historical epic of the first/seventh century with a conception of intemporal divine presence and sovereignty and a guarantee of the inviolable possession of human time and space – Berque glosses the term as 'the opening into space that certain victories give the conqueror, figuratively, access to the open'.[48] The narrative structure of *fatḥ*-histories not only recalls the glories of the first age of the faith; it places the tribulations of a world without legitimate rule in a universal moral scheme, gives assurance of aid and succour in such a present, and promises the coherent and divinely guaranteed order and meaning of all things at their end. This rich complex of meaning condensed into one verbal sign, imbued with the sacred quality of God's own speech, is perhaps what accounts for the power of the phrases recited three times over a child on his first entry to a Qur'anic school in the countryside of Algeria in the early 1900s: 'Qul: bi-'smi 'llāhi 'l-raḥmāni 'l-raḥīm. In tastaftiḥū fa-qad jā'akumu 'l-fatḥu. Innā fataḥnā

[45] Aḥmad ibn Yaḥyā (d. 892).
[46] 'Abd al-Raḥmān Abū 'l-Qāsim ibn 'Abd Allāh (d. 871).
[47] Desparmet, 'Chansons de geste dans la Mitidja'.
[48] Jacques Berque, *Le Coran* (Paris, Sindbad, 1990), 554, quoted in Colonna, *Versets de l'invincibilité*, 9.

laka fatḥan mubīna. Wa-ukhrā tuḥibbūnahā naṣrun mina 'l-llāhi wa-fatḥun qarībun wa-bashshiri 'l-mu'minīna': 'Say: in the name of God, the Compassionate, the Merciful . . . If you seek victory, victory has already come upon you [Q 8.19] . . . Indeed, we have won for you an undoubted victory [Q 48.1] . . . And other things which you desire [will He bestow on you], victory from God and a speedy conquest – bear news of it to the faithful [Q 61.13].'[49]

In post-conquest Algeria, old-established idioms of *fatḥ*-literature served to represent the horrific catastrophe that had been experienced, especially in the countryside, while simultaneously reassuring their audiences of the ultimate inviolability of the divine order that had been overturned. One of the texts discussed by Desparmet, *Futūḥ al-Yaman al-ma'rūf bi-ra's al-ghūl* ('The Tale of the Conquest of Yemen, or the Ogre's-Head') recounts 'the conquest of Yemen' as a mythical war of good and evil, in which the historic space of Christian and pagan south Arabia becomes the paradigmatic kingdom of monstrous, godless tyranny, presided over by the Ogre of the title. This figure, well known in vernacular Arabic literature,[50] is presented in *Futūḥ al-Yaman* as 'a Christian by birth, who, on ascending the throne, has an idol of green emerald made, with rubies for eyes, before which he prostrated himself with his people and from within which the devil spoke his predictions and commands, always in accordance with the ogre's own passions and desires'.[51] The Prophet and his Companions are apprised of the ogre's depredations by an old woman, who is sent to Muhammad by the ogre's own lieutenant, as a witness to his deeds:

She drew aside her veil. . . and appeared covered in blood. 'Go', she said to the assembled Companions, 'See my camel, which is tethered at the door, and your eyes will show you what I have to tell.' 'Alī ibn Abī Ṭālib went out, and saw the severed heads of twelve young men suspended as a necklace across the animal's withers.

These turn out to be the heads of the woman's own sons. Who could have committed such a crime? asks the Prophet.

'Mukharriq,[52] also called the Ogre's-Head. He heard that we had testified to the Lord of the Heavens and the Earth, whose Apostle you are. He sent his *wazīr*, with a great army that took us all prisoner, whether nomads in tents or settled folk in houses. He massacred, pillaged, took away women and children, and the

[49] Desparmet, *Coutumes, institutions, croyances*, 90; Colonna, *Versets de l'invincibilité*, 9–10.
[50] Joseph Desparmet, *Contes populaire sur les ogres* (Paris, Leroux, 1909–10, 2 vols.), for Algerian examples.
[51] Desparmet, 'Chansons de geste dans la Mitidja', 215.
[52] 'One who tears apart', violates, exceeds all normal bounds.

Figure 10. Sacred liberation – Ra's al-Ghul slain by 'Ali ibn Abi Talib. (Print, early 1900s, published in Desparmet, 'Les Chansons de geste dans la Mitidja'.)

lands of our tribe remained as desert, abandoned to wild beasts and birds of prey.'[53]

The ogre-king's lands are eventually conquered, the tyrant himself slain by 'Ali, the churches demolished and mosques raised in their place. The ogre's *wazīr*, having previously converted in secret and assisted the Muslims, is taught the doctrines of Islam by the Prophet himself, and named governor of the country.

Stories like this mobilised existing cultural resources to emplot – and thus, to some degree, to cope with – what can only be understood as the traumatic wars of the nineteenth century within recognisable frames of historical–religious understanding. Bugeaud's flying columns, which finally forced 'Abd al-Qadir's surrender in 1847, and the systematic destruction wreaked on insurrectionary Kabylia in 1870–1, found their mythical embodiment in the ogre, 'strong and gigantic, terrifyingly ugly – not stupid, since he has the power of sorcery, but bestial and

[53] Desparmet, 'Chansons de geste dans la Mitidja', 214.

cannibalistic . . . unbelieving and immoral, he violates all the principles of Islam'.[54] Well into the 1930s, this image was widespread among the Algerian rural population – Saïd Boulifa, whose historical vision of the conquest and its significance was, as we saw, quite different, apparently used to observe that 'trusting collaboration would be established between the two races who inhabit Algeria if only the French would stop teaching their children that the natives are savages, and if the latter would stop teaching theirs that the French are *ghūls*'. Mohamed Harbi, born in 1933 in the rural north Constantinois, recalls how, in his childhood, his mother would send him to bed with the warning: '"Go to sleep, or I'll call *Bijou* to come and eat you up!" – "Bijou" was Bugeaud, who thus assumed the face of an ogre.'[55]

The reformist *'ulamā* would seem to have little enough in common with Boulifa, and his vision of universal liberty and progress borne by France, but (*pace* Desparmet, who saw the popular tales and the message of the *salafiyya* as different moments in the same, essentially unalterable, native xenophobia) they shared more with him than they did with this kind of narrative tradition, an everyday, 'ordinary' culture that they would certainly have considered mere *khurāfāt* (superstitious fairytales). In al-Madani's histories, the theme of *fatḥ* is certainly central, but it does not have the stature of a closed and self-sufficient event within which, as in the tale of *ra's al-ghūl*, a total historical vision is encapsulated. The *futūḥ*, reduced to the historical events of the seventh-century conquests, are rather subsumed into a larger, broader story within which they do (as we shall see in the next chapter) hold a pivotal place, but in which their meaning also undergoes an important transformation.

Al-Madani's total history is not that of the progressive revelation of God – it does not begin with Creation, nor in the Hijaz, and does not end with the universal triumph of Islam in the *Futūḥ al-buldān*. God is certainly present, and the coming of Islam *is* related as the crucial, climactic event in North Africa's history, but it is not so in and of itself. Rather, the Islamisation of the Maghrib is understood as one episode in the longer general advance, not of the Truth, but of 'true civilisation' – as its culminating point, indeed, but, as such, as only one point on a much longer road. The merit of the Muslims of the great age of conquest is not as messengers of God alone, but as the bringers of *civilisation*, which the revelation of Islam has finally crowned. The *fatḥ* is a final, glorious moment in a centuries-old mission of civilisational advancement and

[54] *Ibid.*, 213.
[55] *Ibid.*, 213–14; Harbi, *Vie debout*, 10.

discovery begun by the Arabs long before they were Muslims, in the ancestral greatness of Phoenicia and Carthage.

In describing the *fatḥ*, al-Madani does refer, of course, to the specifically religious aspects of morality (*akhlāq*) and the will of God, to the canonical division of Good from Ill (*al-maʿrūf* from *al-munkar*), and the duty of guidance in the straight path (*ṣirāṭ mustaqīm*) and way prescribed by the Prophet (*ʿalā ghirār sunna istannahā lahum*'[56]). On the other hand, the criteria of true belief (the observance of prayer and the giving of alms) most insistently referred to in the Qur'an itself as evidence of the efficacy of *fatḥ* are noticeably absent. Instead, al-Madani foregrounds other, political, characteristics of the community born of conquest; the *fatḥ*, he says, occurred 'to bring them out of the shadows of tyranny and oppression, into the light of justice and freedom'.[57] This is not, as in the story of *ra's al-ghūl*, simply because the reign of Islam brings righteous government, legitimate because divinely sanctioned; rather, the legitimacy of the rule of Islam is itself equated with, and elided into, its perfect fulfilment of 'true civilisation' (*al-madaniyya al-ḥaqqa*), a notion that seems clearly closer to late nineteenth-century racial and evolutionary European conceptions like those of Gustave le Bon than to older Arabic concepts of 'civilisation' such as *ʿumrān* or *ḥaḍāra*.[58] Rather than societal perfection proceeding from Islam *per se*, Islam is itself reimagined as the crowning perfection of 'civilisation', understood as the racial genius of the Arabs, as their achievement in the world, inaugurated since deep antiquity. Civilisation and its attributes – liberty, equality and fraternity; moral and material progress; technical and scientific achievement; the discovery and unification of the world – are taken over from European constructions of the worldwide progress of history, and the long-established narrative topos of the *fatḥ* is reimagined in this image. The conquest of Sicily, for example, is celebrated as

> a page of nobility and pride from among all those of a history abounding in glory. This is the page that our most noble forebears wrote with their pure blood upon the surface of the Sicilian earth, recording it by their great deeds in the book of

56 Al-Madani, *Muslimūn fī jazīrat Ṣiqiliyya*, 21.

57 Al-Madani, *Kitāb al-Jazā'ir*, 21.

58 Le Bon's *Civilisation des Arabes* (1884) was highly influential on intellectuals of al-Madani's generation. Al-Madani's *madaniyya* is a quite different idea to Ibn Khaldun's *ʿumrān,* around which most of the *Muqaddima* revolves. The internalisation of European ideas of civilisation had played a crucial role since the mid-nineteenth century. Hourani notes that Guizot's organising category of 'civilisation' is a key theme for al-Afghani (*Arabic Thought*, 114–15). François Georgeon locates the appearance of *medeniyet* in the Turkish political lexicon at the moment of the *tanẓīmāt* ('Manifeste de l'occidentalisation', 44).

discovery, rushing boldly through it. . . into the gates of immortality. What memories it arouses in our souls, this purifying story, these pages that tell of the struggle of our forefathers *in the cause of Islamic conquest, in the cause of culture and progress, of the spread of knowledge and true civilisation*. Indeed, the memories of the noble, righteous forebears have bequeathed to us a lofty stature in the annals of history, and in east and west a noble remembrance – for they were a people who conquered, *in the cause of God and civilisation*, the proud ones of the earth.[59]

The Arab *mission civilisatrice* begun by Carthage, and most strikingly illustrated in that paradigmatic exploit of Western imagination, the discovery of the New World, is consummated in Islam, the 'moral civilisation' (*madaniyya akhlāqiyya*) brought to the Maghrib by those conquerors, who, unlike others before and after them, 'came not as colonisers seeking land, but with a Call, bringing right guidance . . . In Islam were realised liberty and independence!'[60] The Berbers 'saw that, in bringing them religion, the Arabs had come as their equals, not as masters or rulers'.[61] Islam, then, rather than being complete-in-itself, rather *completes* a process begun long before. Islam is the crowning glory of civilisation, not the whole edifice. In it (as we shall see in the next chapter) the fatal flaws of Carthage are remedied, and the missing factors of societal advancement in the Maghrib supplied. The Berbers, we are told, had achieved 'total independence' at the end of the Byzantine era,[62] but it is only with the arrival of Islam that they became capable of both independence and unity. If this unity is, initially, achieved *against* the Arabs under the leadership of the Berber chief Kusayla and the legendary Kāhina[63] – by the miscalculation of the Arab general 'Uqba ibn Nāfi' – the ultimate triumph of Islam and Arabic signals the Maghrib's achievement of complete spiritual and civilisational grandeur. The supreme glory of Islam, the conquest and flourishing of al-Andalus, is the work of 'the North African nation' in which Arab and Berber are united by their common racial origin, their common character and the light of the new faith.[64] Moreover, within this history, Algeria is quickly set on the road to sovereign statehood. The first Islamic state to achieve its own independent governance within

[59] Al-Madani, *Muslimūn fī jazīrat Ṣiqiliyya*, 3, emphases added.
[60] Al-Madani, *Hādhihi hiya 'l-Jazā'ir*, 55.
[61] Al-Madani, *Qarṭājanna fī arba'at 'uṣūr*, 160.
[62] *Ibid*., 145.
[63] On the Kāhina, the legendary Berber (and sometimes Jewish) sorceress-queen, see the work of Abdelmajid Hannoum.
[64] Al-Madani, *Qarṭājanna fī arba'at 'uṣūr*, 159; al-Madani, *Kitāb al-Jazā'ir*, 75; al-Madani, *Hādhihi hiya 'l-Jazā'ir*, 55.

the empire of the caliphs, says al-Madani, was that created at Tahert (Tiaret) under the Rustamids (in 161/778): Algeria was thus 'the first nation to realise its independence within the orbit (*dā'ira*) of Islam, the first independent Islamic kingdom, and with that, the Algerians preceded, in founding their own state, both the Egyptians and Moroccans'.[65] The appropriation of a Khārijī (hence, conventionally, 'heretical') dynasty, founded by a Persian,[66] as the first national state of 'Algerians' is another radical departure from earlier, local self-conceptions of Sunni (Māliki), Arab/Berber Maghribi communities.

As we saw earlier, Islam itself was reimagined in *salafī* thought and practice. Just as Tayyib al-'Uqbi's demonstration of the value of prayer was an extraordinary refiguration of the crucial centrepiece of Islamic practice in terms of new normative ideas of science and individual well-being, so al-Madani's retelling of the conquest, the pivotal moment of Algerian history, recast the meaning of that event, and of the past of which it was part, as a new narrative of the universal progress of civilisation, liberty and justice. The acts of God no longer so much determine the march of history as fall in with it:

> The Byzantine era was one of tyranny piled on tyranny, of ignorance and corruption, until their iniquities multiplied and their evils became so great that the Berbers rebelled against them from every direction, for they wanted independence and sought their freedom, and God, at the same time, desired to bring the world out of its ages of darkness and into ages of light; He sent His Apostle with Guidance and the Religion of Truth.[67]

The significance of *fatḥ* is now embodied in, and measured by, the new normative values it is made to carry: 'The Muslims came to this land wishing to bring it out of the shadows and into the light. . . The Berbers saw before them a new, spiritual kind of conquest; the Arabs came with a just constitution in their hands, a constitution from which they never wavered in their judgments – the Book of God.'[68] Similarly, much effort is expended in establishing the ancient racial and linguistic affinity of Arab and Berber, and in presenting Punic influence as having 'paved the way for the supremacy of the Arabic language in these regions'.[69] The success of Arabisation and Islamisation must be explained, it seems, in 'scientific' – racial, linguistic and cultural – terms,

[65] Al-Madani, *Hādhihi hiya 'l-Jazā'ir*, 56.
[66] 'Abd al-Raḥmān ibn Rustam (d. c.788).
[67] Al-Madani, *Kitāb al-Jazā'ir*, 74.
[68] *Ibid.*, 75.
[69] Al-Madani, *Qarṭājanna fī arba'at 'uṣūr*, 35. Writing elsewhere of the Maltese vernacular, he asserts that:

and in terms of the political values that privilege constitutional government and the rule of (equitable, fraternal) law. 'True civilisation', in fact, is that same 'civilisation' that the French claim to bring, but that al-Madani contrives to find historically embodied, and truly held to, in the Arabs. It is difficult to read 'al-fatḥ al-rūḥī' or 'madaniyya akhlāqiyya' without resonances of 'conquête morale' or 'rayonnement civilisationnel', not to see the depiction of Arab–Berber unity in true liberty, equality and fraternity, the government by a just constitution from which they do not depart, as an image thrown back at the colonial discourse of a wished-for 'loyal collaboration' that the colonial system itself ensured could never emerge. I am not suggesting that al-Madani consciously constructed a counter-image of the colonial present dressed up in historical guise – there is no reason to suppose that he did not believe himself simply to be writing true history. There is every reason, however, to think that in doing so he was, consciously or not, caught up in the structures of meaning and expression with which the colonial world he inhabited was suffused, and that, *nolens volens*, he contributed to their reproduction in the very language and idiom – of Arabic and Islam – that he believed himself to be protecting from – indeed, asserting against – them.

Exemplary ancestors (ii): struggle and sacrifice, unity and strength

Our spirits are for the homeland, our hearts for the nation and our arms for vengeance. We were created free; we shall not accept servitude. We have lived as our fathers lived before us, as our own masters; we shall not consent to live after them as despised slaves. Tawfiq al-Madani[70]

An adequate discussion of the themes of struggle, resistance, sacrifice and martyrdom in contemporary Algerian culture would require an

> the people of Malta are a remnant of the pure Phoenician race; their Arabic speech remained pure for centuries and they did not acquire it, as some think, during the Arab occupation of Malta. On the contrary, it was the language of their forefathers since the Phoenicians settled that island, and they never at any time exchanged it for another – as, indeed, nothing has ever influenced any people who trace their origins to the Arabic root to exchange their Arabic tongue for another. (*Taqwīm al-Manṣūr* no. 5, 73)

The insistence on Punic antecedence here adopts, and inverts, the Maltese belief that their vernacular was not introduced by the Arabs and is *not* Arabic; for al-Madani, Punic antecedence *is* Arabic! The same story is told of Sicily, where 'there remains a community of whose Canaanite origin there can be no doubt – they speak their language, a corrupted Arabic' (*Muslimūn fī jazīrat Ṣiqiliyya*, 16).

70 Al-Madani, *Ḥanbaʿl*, 34.

entire, and careful, study in its own right. It would be necessary to consider primary schooling, civic institutions, newspaper reports, the novel[71] . . . The presence of the revolution, not only as celebratory epic but as massive, physical and mental trauma, is immense, so immense to anyone considering such questions from this side of the rupture of decolonisation that it is difficult to situate oneself in the undetermined world before 1954, when there was no certainty, in the eyes of anyone save the militants of the PPA/MTLD, that there would be a revolution, much less that it would become a seven-year war, and would be successful. It is nonetheless with this lack of certainty in mind, rather than in constant anticipation of the great *telos* of 1 November that this issue in particular must be approached.

I insist on this point because it is important not to read the valorisation of armed struggle and the cult of martyrdom, which are consistently present in al-Madani's historical writing, beginning in the 1920s, simply through the lens of 1954. It would be unfounded (and to subscribe once more to uncritical teleology) to seek revolutionary causation in the normative values of *salafī* historiography; again, this cultural work is not an inspirational 'awakening of consciousness'. The influence, and effective force, of this discourse is to be found rather in the subsequent representation of the revolution, in the officialised national culture of independent Algeria, than in the making of the revolution itself. Indeed, the most significant effect of the reformist imagination of historical struggle, resistance and sacrifice is to be found in the constitution of the idealised, normative, historical selfhood of the *salafī* intellectual himself – in his fashioning of his own history, and of his place in history, rather than in his *making* of history. The instantiations of these values as they occur in the exemplary heroes of al-Madani's narratives are examined here, then, with a view to elucidating not a primary doctrine of revolution, but what it is that they reveal about the structuring practice of *salafī* discourse, about the manner of construction of a worldview that, in a world transformed by the massive upheavals of revolution and the war waged against it, would play a significant part in the shaping of the past as it would be viewed from that new reality.

[71] On schooling, see Ghalem & Remaoun, *Comment on enseigne l'histoire en Algérie;* Remaoun, 'Enseignement de l'histoire et conscience nationale'; Laamirie et al., *La Guerre d'Algérie*. Institutions of state: particularly the 'revolutionary family' – the ONM (Organisation nationale des anciens Mujahidin), ONEM (Organisation nationale des Enfants de Mujahidin) and ONEC (Organisation nationale des Enfants de Chouhada) (*chouhada/shuhadā'* – 'martyrs'). Literature: Tahar Ouettar, *Les Martyrs reviennent cette semaine* (tr. Marcel Bois, Algiers, ENAP, 1981); Djaout, *Chercheurs d'os*.

The exaltation of uncompromising resistance to uncompromising aggression is a constant feature of al-Madani's historiography. Writing, under the title 'The Spirit of Struggle', of the colonial period, he declared in 1956 that

> the history of the Algerian nation was, from that calamitous day [5 July 1830], a history of heroism the like of which the world has, in truth, never seen. It was a history of long struggle, of continuous sacrifice and tenacious resistance that never abated for an hour of the day; sometimes by relentless war. . . with blood, destruction and fire, at other times by political means. Thus the struggle of proud Algeria continued, for one hundred and thirty years.[72]

Algeria, from 1830 to the 'long-awaited day' of 1 November, endured 'the desperate attempts of imperialism to destroy her'.[73] True to its unalterable Arab-Islamic *kiyān* (existential essence), the eternal Algerian nation 'never ceased to astonish the world by its deeds, never ceased to write with its blood pages of magnificence and greatness in the field of heroism on the noble Algerian soil, soaked from generations of old with the blood of heroes on the ground of struggle and combat'.[74] This same image of a land marked since ancient times by the blood of martyrdom is invoked, too, at the close of the first volume of al-Madani's memoirs, in the narration of his exilic return to Algiers:

> In the path of sacrifice and jihad. . . I settled in the city of my forefathers, the cradle of heroism and of struggle, the city whose nourishment is sacrifice and martyrdom. I took up the struggle again with temerity, revolt in my soul, there where the image rose before me of those forefathers who have marked this pure earth with their blood, where I could almost sense in the air the perfume of their souls that they employed in the service of God and the homeland, for the good of Islam and of the Muslims.[75]

These later texts (published in 1956 and 1977 respectively) do more than fall in with the revolutionary 'legitimate language' dominant at the moment of their composition. They themselves contribute to that language and to the framing of Algerian history in its terms, but not only that – they also constitute instances of a larger discourse. They must be situated in the context of a continuous cultural production which began at least as early as 1927, with the publication of al-Madani's first sustained work of history, *Qarṭājanna fī arbaʿat ʿuṣūr*,[76] in which these same images are consistently central. The persistence of these normative

[72] Al-Madani, *Hādhihi hiya 'l-Jazā'ir*, 83. [73] *Ibid.*
[74] *Ibid.* [75] *HK*, I, 340.
[76] And perhaps before then; I have been unable to locate his earlier *al-Ḥurriya thamarat al-jihād, aw niḍāl Irlandā ḍidd sayṭarat al-inkilīz.*

values throughout this corpus, and the retrospective valorisation of the *salafī*s' vision of national culture in the state establishment after independence (in the fields of religious affairs, culture and education, where former members of, or sympathisers with, the AUMA lodged themselves in considerable strength), correlative with the equally retrospective exaltation of the reformists as saviours of the national soul, 'revealers of its truth',[77] further suggest that the *salafī* language of history, and the values embedded in its principal figures, played a significant role in the formulation of this 'legitimate language'. Uncompromising struggle and sacrifice, stainless honour and inviolable sovereignty, martyrdom rather than submission, are key themes in al-Madani's texts, clearly legible in the structures of his narratives and boldly embodied in their principal characters. All of North Africa's inhabitants, indeed, since ancient times, are supposed to incarnate these same values:

> The Berbers excelled from the earliest times by their sacrifice and desperate striving in the path of freedom, and by their passionate love of independence. They never submitted to a conqueror, nor ever turned to resignation, and if [ever] they yielded for a time under the rule of force, [it was only until] a propitious opportunity seemed good to them for the destruction of their enemies. . . They have lived under the occupation of different nations for some three thousand years, and have not ceased to uphold all of the excellent qualities inherent to them.[78]

This redeployment of the same notion of 'Berber independence' that informed the quite different history of Boulifa provides a grounding, in the posited 'innate character' of Algeria's people, for a totalising depiction of 'Algeria in arms' that is further idolised in *salafī* history's positive heroes. Just as 'the people' is constituted as a single, unitary category, hypostatised in the figure of the resisting fighter for independence, so the outstanding heroes of the narrative – Hannibal, Massinissa, Jugurtha in Antiquity; 'Uqba ibn Nāfi', the *mahdī* Ibn Tumert and his general 'Abd al-Mu'min in the medieval period; Salah Bey of Constantine, Mehmed Osman Pasha of Algiers, the emir 'Abd al-Qadir in modern times – are exemplary figures.

[77] Qasim, 'Inniya wa-aṣāla'; Zakarya, Ilyādhat al-Jazā'ir; al-Ṭammār, *Ta'rīkh al-adab al-jazā'irī*; Sa'adallah, 'Rise of Algerian nationalism'; Sa'adallah, *Abḥāth wa-'ārā fī ta'rikh al-jazā'ir*; Kaddache's evaluation of the *'ulamā* (*Nationalisme algérien*, 220–7); and (critically) Haddab, 'Intellectuels et le statut des langues'; Deheuvels, *Islam et pensée contemporaine*; Chachoua, *Islam kabyle*, 255–60. Chachoua remarks that it is principally reformists or their sympathisers who, up to the end of the 1980s, 'represent the legitimate national, and nationalist, "social science"' (*Islam kabyle*, 260). In the 1970s, al-Madani himself was for a time editor-in-chief of the official *Majallat al-Ta'rīkh*, review of the National Centre for Historical Studies in Algiers.

[78] Al-Madani, *Qarṭājanna fī arba'at 'uṣūr*, 18.

Figure 11. The nation liberates herself – Algeria in arms. (Cover of al-Madani's *Hādhihi hiya'l-Jaza'ir*, 1956. Middle East Centre library, St Antony's College, Oxford.)

A particular concern of al-Madani's historiography, and one to which he would devote most of his efforts after independence, was the rehabilitation of the Ottoman period of Algerian history. There is, to be sure, an immediately political dimension to this preoccupation. The dominant characterisation of Ottoman Algiers as 'a nest of pirates', a despotic realm of bloodletting, lust and tyranny (vividly painted, of course, by early Orientalism, but readily reproduced in the accounts of Benhabylès and Boulifa, who also tapped into widespread popular memories of at least some pre-colonial rulers[79]) was a major historiographic justification for the conquest. This aspect of al-Madani's work was not, however, merely determined by a purely negative relation to colonialist history. His youthful infatuation with the Turkish nationalist struggle, his activism on behalf of the caliphate in the early 1920s, and his autobiographical identification, later, with the last Maghribi efforts, including those of his own uncle, to reconnect North Africa to Istanbul, reflect the same concern. After independence, he would continue his self-appointed (and rather lonely) task of retrieving Algeria's Ottoman past, travelling to Istanbul to catalogue the correspondence with the Regency held in the archives.[80] This was a genuine commitment to a vision of history in which the pre-colonial imperial relationship held an important place.

Writing in the 1930s, he declared: 'I know of no period in the history of any place on earth so ill-used, so maligned, of which such slander is heard and whose honour is so degraded, as that of the history of the rule of the Ottoman Turks in Algeria.'[81] The particular virtues of the Ottoman period are carefully distinguished from those of earlier times. He does not mean to suggest, he explains, that this era was one of perfectly good governance, nor one of civilisation, comfort and justice, greater than others; nor can it rival, in the efflorescence of learning and letters, the ages of the Rustamids (second–third/eighth–tenth centuries), Hammadids (fifth–sixth/eleventh–twelfth centuries) or Ziyanids (seventh–tenth/thirteenth–sixteenth centuries). The Ottomans excelled, rather, in the achievement of the unity and strength of an Algerian state able to withstand the intensified assaults of European expansion. Having established the territorial unity of Algeria 'under one central authority from the Tunisian frontier to the borders of Marrakesh, from the Mediterranean to beyond the Ziban', this government 'preserved the country from falling to sack at the hands of the Spaniards, after the light of Islam had gone out of al-Andalus'. Furthermore, its important link to the Porte notwithstanding, Algeria enjoyed great independence at this time, one 'much wider than that enjoyed today by the English "dominion" lands such as Canada and Australia'. Thus organised and unified, Algeria as a sovereign state 'gained worldwide renown,

[79] The Constantinois beys' extension of their effective rule southwards (to the Ziban and Suf) in the late eighteenth and early nineteenth centuries becomes a positive act of 'national unification' in al-Madani's accounts (and, later, in the work of Kaddache, for example); it is doubtful whether their expeditions were so happily received by pre-Saharan populations at the time (cf. Clancy-Smith, *Rebel and Saint*, 74).

[80] Several of these documents were published during the 1970s in *Majallat al-Ta'rīkh*.

[81] Al-Madani, *Muḥammad 'Uthmān Basha*, 7.

engaged in foreign wars and emerged successful and victorious from them'.[82]

If the Ottoman period was not one of great civilisational advances, of the progress in science and letters that al-Madani chronicles for the ancient and medieval periods,

> this was only because the Muslims' greatest concern had become their struggle against Christian Europe – this since the time of the murderous, barbarous Crusades, and since Europe had begun to look upon the lands of Islam with greedy, covetous eyes. There were few Islamic territories, from the heart of Asia to the shores of the Atlantic, that were not caught up in murderous and deadly battle with the vanguards of European Christianity and European imperialism.[83]

Among the paragons of this age was Muḥammad 'Uthmān Pasha (Mehmed Osman, dey of Algiers 1766–91), 'one of the finest ruling personalities of the Turkish period'.[84] He and his predecessors are worthy forebears: 'The pious ancestors (*al-salaf al-ṣāliḥ*), in the days of this Pasha and before him, had a great appetite for jihad, and they travelled by sea aboard vessels of war, raiding and rivalling each other in vaunting their prowess in these exploits'; 'Among his pious deeds in the service of God and exemplary actions was the fact that he had a love of jihad and stood always prepared for war.'[85] Muhammad 'Uthman himself was the first to build a new kind of warship, which he used against the Spanish. During his reign, the number of privateers engaged in corsairing against the European powers increased: he fought successfully against Denmark, and triumphed in three wars against Spain. Alongside his other good works – the building and embellishment of mosques, the extension of irrigation works – the dey appears as a kind of warrior-ascetic. The description of his character, selectively excerpted from the contemporary account by the late eighteenth-century French traveller and diplomat Jean-Michel Venture de Paradis, highlights his personal moral rectitude, frugality ('the dey has, for sole personal income, the pay of a common soldier'[86]), parsimony, refusal of special favours, and unflinching devotion to duty ('the interests of the state have always been sacred to him, and he has never allowed laxity in this respect in favour of anyone'[87]).

Alongside his perpetual zeal for war, this depiction of the Ottoman ruler is remarkably close to the image that Berque gives as the original meaning of *murābiṭ*, the term describing those 'who withdraw from the world and devote themselves to holy war'.[88] Originating in the medieval

[82] *Ibid.*, 8–9. [83] *Ibid.*, 11. [84] *Ibid.*, 133.
[85] *Ibid.*, 97. [86] *Ibid.*, 163. [87] *Ibid.*, 164.
[88] Berque, *Intérieur du Maghreb*, 53.

institution of *ribāṭ al-jihād* (approximately, a 'monastery-fortress'), this meaning was still current, according to Berque, in the late fifteenth century, in the face of Spanish incursions on the coasts of the western and central Maghrib. The Spaniards had held Oran from 1509 to 1708; having retaken the city in 1732, they were finally ousted in 1791 – the last year of the reign of al-Madani's hero. If, as Berque suggests, this meaning of *murābiṭ* was also still 'lively' for the emir 'Abd al-Qadir, the social position, and cultural meaning, of 'marabout' was quite differently viewed, at least by the reformists, and by those who had come to accept them as the spokesmen of Islam, by the time al-Madani's book on Muhammad 'Uthman was published, in 1938. The presentation of the Ottoman dey in this idiom (or, rather, with this idiom perhaps in the subconscious background) is another new refiguration of an older meaning. While the contemporary bearers of inherited 'maraboutic' dignity were evicted by the reformists from their places of honour, the role they had filled was refashioned in the guise of 'national hero'.

At the other extreme of chronology, Hannibal, in particular, seems to have been a favourite hero for al-Madani. After the Second World War, when the cult of Jugurtha as national hero had already begun in Algeria, he chose to illustrate the perfect exemplar, in a tragedy for the theatre, through Hannibal. His name is even explained as 'a pure and obvious Arabic name',[89] underlining again, and by means of 'science' (etymology), the 'authentic' Middle Eastern and Arabic origin of the positive heroes of the story. 'The world's greatest general'[90] is a model of patriotic zeal and duty: 'He took the attributes of his father [the Carthaginian general Hamilcar] and his morals when only a boy, and did not aspire to anything but war and struggle [. . . vowing] to work for Rome's everlasting overthrow. . . The boy took this historic, extraordinary oath with great zeal, when he was no more than nine years of age.'[91] This perfect re-inscription of the ancient Roman historians' myth of Hannibal – the diabolical, vowed enemy, destined from his earliest youth to inflict on Rome the most terrible defeats it had yet known[92] – as a national hero of North Africa's unending struggle against European imperialism, is a neat example of how historical meanings are displaced and replaced in the construction of nationalist histories.

[89] Al-Madani, *Qarṭājanna fī arba'at 'uṣūr*, 49.
[90] *Ibid.*
[91] *Ibid.*
[92] Lake Trasimene, 217 BCE, and Cannae, 216 BCE.

Al-Madani's *Hannibal*, which was first performed at the Algiers Opéra on 9 April 1948, during the theatre's annual Arabic season,[93] provoked grave disquiet at the nearby Government-General, although it might reasonably be wondered how much of the classical dialogue was understood by the 'very numerous spectators of the proletarian classes'[94] who reportedly saw the piece. Mahieddine Bachetarzi, in his memoirs on the early years of the Algerian theatre, emphasises this problem, and al-Madani, preoccupied as he was with the 'cultural level' of the Algerian masses and experienced in theatrical productions since the early 1920s in Tunis (where modern Arabic-language theatre first arrived in North Africa from Egypt), cannot have ignored it.[95] The scheme of the drama is clear enough, as it moves through the stages of Hannibal's personal struggle against Roman imperialism. He is accompanied in his heroic exile by a resolute band of followers, notably the princess Sappho and her suitor Matabal, the couple whose story is really the main focus of the play. They are married towards the play's end by Hannibal, with his dying breath: 'Be happy in sacrifice and jihad; live a noble life or else die the death of heroes in the field of struggle.'[96] The ponderous phrases of the rhetoric were perhaps clear enough to any audience. The model hero expounds a simple philosophy: 'The lives of men are measured but in years, those of nations in generations and generations.'[97] The closing words of the play, spoken by the queen of Bithynia in honour of the dead hero, sum up al-Madani's notion of the worthy ancestor: 'Let the nations learn, and history record, that there is no greatness, no honour, and no immortality, save for one who lives to struggle in the cause of freedom, and dies a martyr in the service of his nation.'[98]

Hannibal's cardinal virtue, 'love of the homeland', is illustrated and contrasted with the supreme vice, treachery, in al-Madani's earlier text, *Qarṭājanna fī arba'at 'uṣūr*, when, with Hannibal almost at the gates of

[93] On the Arabic theatre in colonial Algeria, see Bachetarzi, *Mémoires*; Roth, *Théâtre algérien*; Djeghloul, *Eléments d'histoire culturelle*.

[94] Report, Cabinet du Prefet, Algiers, 15 May 1948 no. 7741; Chief, SLNA, Government-General to Prefect, Algiers, 13 May 1948 no. 1103/NA, 'Note sur le théâtre arabe à Alger' (unsigned), Algiers, 24 November 1948; Prefect, Algiers, to Governor-General, 27 January 1949 no. 37SLNA (ADsA/4I/66/2). The breakthrough in Algerian theatre came when Alloula, one of its early stars, began to write in dialect.

[95] Algerian audiences' impatience with classical theatre is illustrated in Merzak Allouache's 1976 film *Omar Gatlato*, where a *fuṣḥa*-speaking lovelorn prince is given short shrift by the public; things might, of course, have been different in the late 1940s.

[96] Al-Madani, *Ḥanba'l*, 79.

[97] *Ibid.*, 40. Cf. al-Madani in *al-Baṣā'ir*, no. 310, 18 March 1955, ADA/4I/14/2: 'Generations pass away, one after another – the nation remains.'

[98] Al-Madani, *Ḥanba'l, 81.*

Rome, the Carthaginian aristocrats themselves, who had neglected their own city's defence and failed to support Hannibal in his campaign, find themselves attacked and call on their hero to save them:

What was greater than Hannibal's grief? And what more intense than his pain? Why did his homeland summon him with a call to abandon his hopes and his pledge . . . to destroy Rome, when he was face to face with her? He forgot that it was his homeland that had been the cause of his [earlier] defeat, through its lack of support . . . that it had abandoned and dishonoured him. He forgot that it was the men of his homeland who had thrown obstacles in his way because of their envy. He forgot that, if the men of his homeland had helped him in time of necessity, they were in the same hour, secretly in their minds, preparing to rally to Rome. They had not concerned themselves with the defence of Carthage itself. All this, the general Hannibal forgot, when before him [he saw] traced out the terrible word[s], [like] a fire devouring his heart: the homeland in danger! And could a true patriot listen to these words, and not risk everything to sacrifice [himself], rushing headlong to place himself directly in the face of terror?[99]

The theme of patriotism and treachery runs all through al-Madani's treatment of the 'great men' of history, whose impeccable virtue is made all the more radiant for its being placed in this recurrent rhetorical couple. 'Abd al-Qadir is betrayed by intrigue, division and factionalism among the Algerian tribes, and by the 'pretence' of an army fielded by the Moroccan sultan at the crucial battle of Isly in 1844.[100] The climax of Hannibal's story connects the figures of treachery/patriotism with that of 'death in the cause of freedom' in a paradigmatic destiny of martyrdom. Having sought refuge with the king of Bithynia, Hannibal is pursued by Roman emissaries who demand that his host surrender him: 'The King was afraid, and decided to surrender his guest. Hannibal now saw that the doors were closed in his face. He had for some time carried with him a deadly poison. . . he swallowed these drops and entered the judgement of History. Thus ended Hannibal the Great.'[101]

Death as martyrdom in preference to dishonour is another leitmotiv of al-Madani's narratives, embodied among others in Hannibal, in the fall of Carthage, and in the female figure of Sophonisba, the Berber queen, who is captured by the Roman general Scipio, and drinks poison rather than allowing herself to be taken in chains to Rome.[102] Jugurtha, betrayed to and captured by the Romans, is paraded in chains in Rome and, unable to bear the dishonour, becomes insane. He dies in prison, a

[99] Al-Madani, *Qarṭājanna fī arbaʿat ʿuṣūr*, 60.
[100] Al-Madani, *Kitāb al-Jazāʾir*, 51–3.
[101] Al-Madani, *Qarṭājanna fī arbaʿat ʿuṣūr*, 65.
[102] *Ibid.*, 61.

martyr 'in the cause of the independence of his nation, the liberation of his people, and the salvation of his homeland'.[103] The citizens of Carthage, who also 'preferred a noble death to a life more wretched than death [itself]' were 'determined to defend their territory in a desperate defence, the act of martyrs'.[104]

These themes, again, should not be seen as a call to arms and revolt, but as the formulation of a modern cultural idiom, reinventing a historical imagination of ancestral sanctity, and prefiguring a new kind of sanctified ancestry. As Omar Carlier observes, the 'civil religion' of Algeria after independence would be 'the worship of the dead taken to such a level of commemoration, even on the day of the *'aid*, as [to become] a sort of competition with, and displacement of, the worship of saints'.[105]

The reliquary of 'Abd al-Qādir ibn Muḥyī al-Dīn

> The revolution in Algeria began with 'Abd al-Qādir, and has never ceased since his time.
>
> Muḥammad al-Tammār[106]

Algeria marked four years of independence, in July 1966, with celebrations of the future and the past. The twin official themes of the national festivities were, on the one hand, youth – 'the rising generation, the builders of tomorrow who today are still at the school of socialism' – and on the other, history, 'our history, [which] gives us the most striking, the most touching example of patriotism, of struggle and of abnegation'. The exaltation of the young architects of the socialist future was married to 'the homage that the fatherland pays to its national hero, the emir Abdelkader'.[107] The national holiday of 5 July 1966 was declared to be 'placed under the sign of fidelity to the revolutionary traditions of Algeria and of confidence in the future . . . this day is the symbolic mark of the union of two values which are the strength of our country'.[108]

The remains of the emir 'Abd al-Qadir ibn Muhyi al-Din al-Hasani were about to be brought to Algiers, 119 years after he quit his native country for exile in France and spiritual apotheosis in Damascus, where he lived in the very house that had been, long before, occupied by the

[103] *Ibid.*, 84–5. [104] *Ibid.*, 71.
[105] Carlier, 'Civil war, private violence', 85–7.
[106] Al-Ṭammār, *Ta'rīkh al-adab al-jazā'irī*, 278.
[107] *Algérie actualité*, 3 July 1966 (BnF).
[108] *Ibid.*

master philosopher and mystic Ibn 'Arabī. The theosophical visionary, the enthusiast for freemasonry, the *chevalier de la légion d'honneur*, the saviour of the Damascene Christians in 1860, was not the figure of interest.[109] As the poet and novelist Assia Djebar would, much later, lament, 'there was no rush to publish [his] poems, to sing them, teach them, to recall the spiritual message of his last meditations . . . there was no place, yet, for the creative beauty, the intelligence and wisdom of Abdelkader! Only his name, [which was] formally confiscated.'[110] The reappropriated name and remains of 'Abd al-Qadir had a very specific role to play in 1966:

> It cannot be permitted that one should forget today that, at the same time as he valorously led the Algerian armies, the Emir Abdelkader was also, even while struggling against the colonial forces, he who introduced profound reforms destined to abolish exploitation and establish social equality: the Emir Abdelkader was also a modernist, who, understanding that a country cannot be truly strong and independent unless it possesses and develops its own industries, implanted in Algeria the first factories worthy of the name. And we should remember also, as an example of this passionate search for national independence, the creation of an Algerian currency free from dependence on that of a foreign power. Precursor of modern, free Algeria, of today's Algeria, the Emir Abdelkader is a model for our generation and for all those young Algerians who are living an exhilarating moment of our history: that of the construction of our country on virgin foundations and by the application of social and economic principles as noble as those that guided every action of the Emir Abdelkader.[111]

The two-day celebration was a remarkable ritual of commemoration and national self-fashioning. Over four days (2–5 July), the official newspaper *El Moudjahid* carried the story on its front page. An announcement was printed in newspapers on 3 July, anticipating the arrival of the emir's mortal remains, scheduled for 11 a.m. the following day and due to be greeted by a 101-gun salute and live television cameras:

> The Ministry of Information: Request to Television Stockists – Put Your Sets at the Disposal of the Public for the Celebration of 5 July. On the occasion of the

[109] Other, particularly spiritual, aspects of the emir have more recently received greater attention: Etienne, 'Quelques aspects d'une vie complexe'; Etienne, *Abdelkader*; Chodkiewicz, *Ecrits spirituels*.

[110] She adds:

> It is not true: the body of Abdelkader has not truly returned! . . . It is not true; it is an illusion; he does not rest in peace [in Algeria], or if he is truly there, I am sure, myself, that he is turning and turning again in his grave. He had, himself, in those last years, truly wished to rest in the Umayyad mosque of Damascus, where his master Ibn 'Arabi lies in beatitude. (*Le Blanc d'Algérie*, 266–7)

[111] *Algérie actualité*, 3 July 1966. The Algerian dinar had replaced the franc in April 1964.

ceremonies of 4 and 5 July 1966, marking the return to Algeria of the remains of the Emir Abdelkader, it is requested of all dealers, wholesale and retail, of television sets, to place functioning TV sets in their windows during the entirety of the scheduled programmes dedicated to this event, so as to permit the public to follow the various organised events.[112]

Through newspaper special editions, radio and television, Algerians engaged in a massive collective rite of veneration for the returned remains of their reimagined saint-protector. The coffin containing the ashes of ‘Abd al-Qadir, draped in an Algerian flag and covered with flowers, was placed on an armoured car and driven in a slow cortège from Algiers airport at Dar al-Beïda, southeast of the city, to the *carré des martyrs* in the cemetery at El Alia. After its arrival and interment there, five minutes' silence was to be observed throughout the country. The FLN's Executive Secretariat, mouthpiece of the regime installed only a year before, issued a message intended for the whole population. The day of independence was to mark

the crowning of 130 years of heroic and continuous struggle . . . The man who, for seventeen years of heroic struggle carried the flame of liberty, will henceforward repose in his land, at the side of those who, like Didouche Mourad, Ben Mhidi Larbi, Ben Boulaid Mustapha, Zirout Youcef, Amirouche and so many others, assumed the continuity of the fight for national independence . . . We shall all render, together, a vibrant homage to all our martyrs . . . Throughout the journey of the cortège, participating *en masse*, in order and discipline, in this national funeral, you will demonstrate once more the maturity of our people, and its attachment to the memory of its heroes.[113]

The emir's tomb was placed between those of Mourad Didouche and Larbi Ben Mhidi.[114] President Boumédienne's speech from the graveside emphasised the history of continuous struggle and sacrifice of which ‘Abd al-Qadir had become the exemplary founding ancestor:

The struggle he began did not end with his exile . . . the resistance that he led in 1830 did not end until 1962, with the liberation and independence of Algeria . . . His heroism was the first step in the long march to the great revolution of the first of November which realised the hopes of the emir, and of those who came after him.

[112] *Ibid.*
[113] *El Moudjahid*, 3–4 July 1966, p. 5 (BnF).
[114] Twenty-seven years old in 1954, Didouche was the youngest of the *neuf historiques* (original leaders of the FLN); first chief of *wilaya* II (north Constantinois), he was killed by the French in January 1955. Another of the *neuf historiques*, Ben Mhidi was head of *wilaya* V (Oranais) on 1 November, then political chief of the Zone autonome d'Alger during the Battle of Algiers. Captured by the paras, he was murdered in custody by French special services (March 1957).

Figure 12. The tomb of the emir 'Abd al-Qadir, el-Alia cemetery, Algiers. (Author's photograph.)

Echoing a quarrel of thirty years previously, the president adduced this history as a proof of the reality of the Algerian nation:

Should we suppose that the Algerian nation did not exist before the colonialist aggression? Arising united in the face of the colonialists throughout this period, maintaining a ferocious resistance to the strongest European army of its day, did Algeria not prove that she was a nation? The unity of the Algerian nation is older than the unity and existence of many European nations. The Algerian people is no mix of different peoples and disparate races. It is a nation, solidly unified, as its noble history and long resistance to aggression prove, as is proved by its existence in spite of so many calumnies and malicious campaigns that we have experienced in the recent past.

And a properly *salafī* conception of 'return' is employed to emplot, in the official rhetoric of Algeria's recovered history, the meaning of 'Abd al-Qadir's life, death and homecoming, and his incorporation in the grand scheme of the national past:

In the return of the emir to his homeland after more than a century, we observe an application of the great principle of *returning to the source*. Truth, sooner or later, will triumph, despite all the attempts of those who try to falsify history.

These latter have long – for over a century and a quarter – said and repeated that Algeria never existed as a nation. They thereby defied history, turned their backs on manifest reality, reality which declares that Algeria has been a nation and was a sovereign state until 5 July 1830; that is, until the colonialist aggression which temporarily ended Algeria's existence as a state, believing this to be definitive, that such a state of affairs would last forever. They did not know . . . that nations never die.

In thus defining the 'reality' of past and present, the chief spokesman of independent Algeria spoke as if directly to the sainted 'Abd al-Qadir, newly enshrined among the revolution's martyrs as the inviolable *genius loci* not only of the capital but of the whole territory now united, through the printed and broadcast word, under its aegis:

We exalt in you the high virtue and the noble soul that have made you our well-beloved guide . . . Your noble soul glides now over our proud and happy heads, surrounded by the souls of millions of our heroes and martyrs, pure and eternal. They surround us to bless this flag, which flies over our dear land with dignity and pride as a living witness to the sacrifices of all our martyrs and heroes. This witness, in particular, directs the young to follow their example, and the road that they have traced out towards greater dignity, greater glory, progress, and prosperity. Our great hope, O great guide, as we celebrate also today the Festival of Youth, is that our rising generations will know how to take their example from you.[115]

Boumédienne's language, mobilising history, spirituality, science, socialism and revolution, and the integrative, televised ritual of the return of 'Abd al-Qadir, symbolically united Algerians in the worship of the nation and its virtues. It all occurred in a striking reformulation of the cultural idiom of sainthood. The celebrations were marked, around the country, by acts of communion fusing history, nationalism and Islam. In Constantine, 'religious vigils' were organised in every mosque; in Oran, after the five minutes' silence, fifteen minutes of Qur'anic recitation were broadcast on regional television; at Tlemcen, a vigil was held at the principal mosque and lectures given there on the theme 'The Life and Resistance of the Emir Abdelkader'. At Batna, on the eve of the funeral, 'hundreds of the faithful met in the town's mosques to read verses of the Qur'an in memory of the emir', and following the noonday silence the next day, prayers 'in homage for the great *mujahid*' were said in the crowded mosques.[116] The official, national Islam of the new Algeria had not eliminated sainthood but had re-enabled it in new forms, producing new kinds of venerated ancestors. Nationalism's rituals of

[115] *El Moudjahid*, 6 July 1966 (BnF).
[116] *El Moudjahid*, 5 July 1966 (BnF).

reinscribing history and its actors, reshaping the past in the new causes of the present, reinstituted a vision of Algerian inviolability in the form of the deep-rooted, perennially resisting nation, valorous, true to itself and unchanging. A new form of saint-worship, a newly imagined common ancestry, was an essential part of this new cultural politics.

The old forms, too, returned soon enough, in a muted form, perhaps, without all their old confidence, and in a transformed environment that would change their meanings.[117] Nonetheless, Jacques Berque, driving through Algeria in the summer of 1971, was struck by the *qubba*s (domed mausoleums) studded about the countryside. These little shrines, 'which one might have thought condemned to disuse . . . had undergone a change of fortune of late'. Immediately after independence, many were seen repainted in an apparently secular fashion, green and white, the colours of the national flag. *Et voici*, Berque notes, 'their whitening with chalk reigns anew, and everywhere one glimpses a careful, and no doubt lucrative, upkeep of hagiology'.[118]

In the early summer of 2002, a candidate for election to the Algerian national legislature went, with his supporters, to the shrine of a once-prominent Oranais saint, in a locality racked by unemployment and terrorism, 18 kilometres from the regional government centre of Ighil-Izane (Relizane). The candidate, a deputy for the RND,[119] confidently expecting to be returned to the assembly's palace on boulevard Zighout Youcef, nonetheless sought the saint's assistance in his enterprise. The saint, and the impoverished township that bears his name, was Sidi M'hammad Ben 'Aouda, the lion-taming *walī* and legendary guest of Sidi 'Abd al-Rahman al-Tha'alibi. The mayor of the little town met the candidate's party and offered them a *zarda*. 'Couscous and *petit lait* against a promise of peace, bread, and water. What better could be hoped for by a place as poor and naked as Sidi M'hamed-Benaouda?'[120]

[117] Andezian (*Expériences du divin*, 167–9) gives an instructive example: a ceremony of the 'Isawiyya in Tlemcen in 1982, billed by a hotel as a 'show' (which pleased neither the audience nor the 'performers').

[118] *Intérieur du Maghreb*, 15. Many *qubba*s, and mosques, can be seen in Algeria today (save in the south, where shrines are overwhelmingly chalk-white) painted white and a pale green – the green is now, however, said to be simply that of Islam, a reference shared with, rather than to, the national flag.

[119] Rassemblement national démocratique – the electoral vehicle of former President Zeroual, created in 1997 and at the time of this episode the dominant coalition partner, but the biggest losers in the 30 May 2002 election.

[120] *Liberté*, 27 May 2002. Having regained their visibility in the 1980s, the *ṭarīqa*s created a national association, whose first congress, in May 1991, was highly mediatised and attended by leading regime personalities. The *zawāyā* as support networks were very prominent in the re-election campaign of President 'Abd al-'Aziz Bouteflika in the

Commenting on the eviction of the saints, and their internally diverse version of orthodox Islam, by the *pensée unique* of the reformists, Fanny Colonna observed that their inheritance, one at least as old as the presence of Islamic brotherhoods in the Maghrib, was 'a cognitive universe of plurality . . . a very old practice of plurality'. This inheritance, subdued by colonialism, excoriated by *iṣlāḥ* and 'forgotten for a century', might yet nonetheless, she suggested, provide Algerians with 'ancestors who would no longer be ferocious, as Kateb Yacine said, but cosmopolitan – *autogestionnaires* of their own thought'.[121] If the recent 'return' of the saints has been embedded in – potentially constricted by – politics, it might still be possible to discern a recovery of Algerians' everyday, shared and locally rooted plurality, and their capacity for 'self-management', in such older cultural forms, older ancestors whose powers, in the absence of the freedom, peace and dignity once promised by the monolithic nation, are once more looked to for hopes of comfort, cohesion and safety – for a rediscovered inviolability. At the same time, however, issues of local culture and of national plurality have also proved liable not only to political manipulation, but to open conflict.

spring of 2004. The opprobrium still attached to the brotherhoods, however, was clear in press reports on Bouteflika's campaign (e.g. S. M. Haouili, 'La moubayaa des zaouias', *L'Expression*, 11 February 2004), and in the comments of rival candidate and heir of the reformists, Ahmed Taleb Ibrahimi (e.g. *El Watan*, 19–20 March 2004).

[121] Paper presented at the Centre culturel algérien, Paris, March 1994.

5 Arabs and Berbers?

In any event, one cannot deny, as a certain propaganda has done, the existence of Berbers in North Africa.
Jacques Berque[1]

There are no Berbers in the Arab Maghrib. . . for the Berbers have become completely Arabised.
Fadil al-Wartilani[2]

On 18 April 2001, a high-school student, Massinissa Guermah, was shot by gendarmes in the Kabyle commune of Beni Douala. He died shortly afterwards in custody. Twenty-one years after the 'Berber Spring', and in an Algeria racked by ten years of atrocious civil conflict, a wave of protests and confrontation broke out, along the Soummam valley and in the mountains, between young civilians and the state's police and gendarmerie. The riots of Kabylia's 'Black Spring' turned into a wider movement, dubbed *la protesta*, continuing through the summer and into the autumn of 2001, with a series of marches on the capital and sporadic violence in Kabylia. The legislative elections of 30 May 2002 were boycotted in the region, with two major parties (the RCD, Rassemblement pour la culture et la démocratie, and FFS, Front des forces socialistes), whose principal constituencies are in Kabylia, abstaining from fielding candidates. Unrest simmered on into the spring of 2004.[3]

A common interpretation of these protests hung on the notion that this, yet again, was a conflict of 'Berbers' (the Kabyle civilians) against 'Arabs' (the Algerian state), that this was only the latest expression of a primordial split in Algeria between antagonistic ethnicities, languages and cultures that the transition 'from tribe to nation' had, after all, failed to overcome.[4] Arabs *and* Berbers, Arabs *or* Berbers? Conflicts over, or

[1] Berque, *Maghreb entre deux guerres*, 238.
[2] *Al-Wartilani, Al-Jazā'ir al-thā'ira*, 49.
[3] See Roberts, 'Towards an understanding of the Kabyle question', for the 1980 Berber spring. On the *printemps noir*, see International Crisis Group MENA report no. 15, 'Unrest and impasse in Kabylia' (10 June 2003); Roberts, *The Battlefield*, chs. 18, 19.
[4] Cf. Gellner and Micaud, *Arabs and Berbers*.

Figure 13. 'No, I am not an Arab!' – Kabyle demonstrator at a Berber Cultural Movement rally in Algiers, May 1994. (Photograph by Nazim Touati.)

articulated through, these names have periodically broken out with much violence in the cultural and political life of Algeria, and at the beginning of the twenty-first century once more demonstrated their undiminished ability to articulate a number of different struggles. This question, perhaps more than any other, is immediately, acidly emotive in contemporary Algeria. It is steeped in a dense saturation of history frequently experienced by those concerned with an extraordinary affective intensity. What place did *salafī* history accord 'the Berber'? I use the word here both to condense the various notions of 'Berber substratum', 'Berber question', '*fait berbère*', and so on, and as a direct translation of the essentialised personal signifier '*al-barbarī*' which occurs in the writings of Tawfiq al-Madani. But in fact this 'Berber' must be more fully contextualized, not least because the word itself is far from being generally acceptable.

Indeed, most of the constituent groups of today's 'Berberist' movement in the Maghrib and among communities abroad (especially in Canada and the USA, as well as in France) would probably now prefer the term *Amazigh* (often transliterated *amaziɣ*, pl. *imaziɣen*,) a term whose history is itself revealing. Now a general, self-designating ethnonym shared by disparate berberophone groups throughout North Africa and the diaspora, the term is well attested in various forms in the names given to African populations in antiquity (Maxues, Mazax, Mazices. . .), and is the only self-designation known among berberophones in central Morocco and the Tuareg (*imūhaɣ* in the Ahaggar and Tassili in the Algerian far south; *imâjeɣen* further south in Mali, Niger, the Aïr). In contrast, more northerly Algerian berberophone societies in the Aurès, the Mzab and Kabylia did not, it seems, know the term,[5] and its generalisation to these regions, (as, thereafter, in the diaspora) occurred only in the period since 1945, particularly under the impulse of nationalist militantism among Kabyles.[6] *Amazigh* here was a national signifier, first, for the mobilisation of Kabyle youth, particularly in the Muslim Boy Scout movement,[7] through songs such as 'Kker u mmi-s amazigh' ('Arise, son of Amazigh'[8]). 'Amazigh' is almost always, in its contemporary usage by Berberist writers, understood to signify 'free man' – indeed, it could be argued that the semantic texture of the word is, in the current language of Berber cultural and political groups, entirely and densely woven with the notion of 'liberty'. Its etymology, though, is much less certain than the frequent reiteration of this meaning suggests: according to Chaker, who traces it to the sixteenth-century geographer Leo Africanus, from whom it was repeated by no less an

[5] Chaker equivocates as to whether it had existed here, too, in Antiquity, and was effaced by Arabisation – and, indeed, as to whether the general use of the term in Antiquity can be assumed among indigenous populations or is only ascertainable as a Latin literary usage (Chaker, 'Amazigh', 564–5).

[6] *Ibid.*, 565; Benbrahim, 'Mouvement national'.

[7] Encouraged from the 1920s onwards by the reformist *'ulamā* and frequently run from the mid-1940s by PPA militants.

[8] Benbrahim, 'Mouvement national'.

authority than Gsell,[9] 'it is, however, certainly unfounded and appears to be an undue extrapolation of accurate, regionally specific data',[10] i.e. the *restriction* of the signifier 'amazigh' among berberophone groups of rigid and complex social stratification (Tuareg especially) to 'high-caste' individuals, 'free men, perhaps the "noble" or "suzerain"', in contradistinction to other berberophones of black African or mixed descent and 'inferior social status (slaves, descendants of slaves . . . specific professional groups: musicians, butchers)'.[11]

These very few elementary observations begin to place us at the heart of the matter: it is, once again, in conflicts over naming, and the meaning of naming, over the appropriation of symbolic goods that serve to construct the categories by which social self-definition, as community and nation, can occur, that 'the Berber question' is meaningful and instructive. In particular, given the cultural, and especially linguistic, politics of independent Algeria, and before it of Algerian nationalism, it is worthwhile asking what was the formulation given 'the Berber' by the principal architects of Algerian nationalism's cultural doctrine, the reformist *'ulamā*? What place did 'the Berber' have in their thinking? And how does this relate to their overall project of asserting the 'essentially Arab-Islamic'[12] national identity of a renascent Algeria and a resurgent 'Arab Maghrib'?[13]

Colonisers from Canaan

According to a recent study of the ancient Maghrib, it remains the case that 'very little can be said confidently of prehistoric Algeria'. The proto- and early historic eras (roughly 1500 to 150 BCE) are 'only a little better documented. The Greek historians and geographers who mention the region clearly knew almost nothing about it . . . much of what Herodotus has to say about the north African interior is demonstrably untrue.'[14]

The surviving indigenous evidence, inscriptions, usually on funerary stelae (although building inscriptions also exist, including the sole

[9] Stéphane Gsell (1864–1932), the most outstanding historian of the 'Algiers school', expert on the ancient history of the Maghrib.
[10] Chaker, 'Amazigh', 567.
[11] *Ibid.*
[12] Merad, *Réformisme*, 93.
[13] A term often avoided in Berberist literature. Recently, the term *tamazgha* has been used to denote 'the Amazigh land' – understood to extend from the Canary Islands to Siwa in western Egypt, and from the Mediterranean to the sub-Saharan fringe, or as far as Lake Victoria.
[14] Cherry, *Frontier and Society*, 9, 10, 20.

datable text, which belongs to 139 or 138 BCE[15]) is impressive testament to a language 'at best, imperfectly understood'[16] today. These samples of the ancient language that contemporary prehistorians and classical scholars generally term 'Libyan', and which Berberist writers (following colonial ethnographic and epigraphic scholarship[17]) identify with 'Berber'/Tamazight, denoting the complex of (not always mutually intelligible) dialects spoken and written today, are generally untranslated and frequently indecipherable. This remains true of the inscriptions found at the spectacular rock-painting sites in the Tassili n'Ajjer, in the extreme south-east of Algeria, as of the texts collected before independence by French archaeologists in the north (particularly in the area between 'Annaba – colonial Bône – and the Tunisian border). Contemporary local Berber speakers have found these inscriptions legible, but not meaningful. The precise status and nature of Libyan in antiquity, read only from the surviving epigraphic record, is arguably uncertain. A leading classical historian argued of Libyan that 'it remains to be shown that it was a language in current ordinary use at all . . . The fact that it is known solely from funerary stelae makes it impossible to say whether or not the language was spoken, or if so by what sections of the population.'[18] Libyan characters (or at least, eastern and Saharan variants of the several attested forms of this alphabet[19]) survived to become the script today called *tifinagh*, long used among the Tuareg, and, at least among some Moroccan berberophone communities, in magic (inscribed upon amulets, for example), a function shared with Hebrew script.[20] This division of scriptural labour between Arabic, the language of revealed and orthodox religion, and Tamazight, is indicative; Islamic texts (including the Qur'an) have also, of course, been written in Berber – but generally in Arabic script.

It seems, then, that we can say little for certain about this enigmatic language, and whoever might have spoken (or at least inscribed) it. The most cautious scholarly position has held that ancient Libyan 'may, or may not, be the, or an, ancestor of present-day Berber' and that 'the

[15] *Ibid.*, 11–12; Jean-Baptiste Chabot, *Receuil des inscriptions libyques* (Paris, Impr. nationale, 1940–2), no. 2.
[16] Cherry, *Frontier and Society*, 10.
[17] Cf. Camps, *Berbères*, ch. 4, 'Permanence berbère'.
[18] Millar, 'Local cultures', 129, 133. Specialists in Berber linguistics, however, have been less cautious than ancient historians in attributing continuity to the language. If, as Millar argues, Libyan inscriptions do not represent a language of 'high culture', it seems difficult to imagine that they do not stand for a contemporary vernacular – unless their use was strictly formulaic or 'liturgical'.
[19] Camps, *Berbères*, 276–7.
[20] I am grateful to John Shoup for this point.

precise connection between the two may perhaps never be known'.[21] To contemporary self-designating Amazigh communities, of course, all this is anything but an academic question. The revival and promotion of *tifinagh*, like the identification of Imazighen as an *ethnos* and Tamazight as a linguistic unity, together, more recently, with an Amazigh flag[22] and calls for 'Amazigh sovereignty' in Tamazgha,[23] are notable developments in the ongoing recreation of Maghribi historical imaginations.

It is, however, important to situate such contemporary developments against the background of how little 'we really know' of the origins and antiquity of 'the Berber', just as this background is necessary to the main focus of our inquiry. Important, too, to maintain a principled ignorance of 'what we cannot (presently) know', and to differentiate this awareness of scholarly ignorance from the object discourses of 'Berber identity' and its 'other', 'Arab(-Islamic) identity'. Conflation of the one into the other – retranscription as 'sociological reality' of the terms of a particular social imaginary, or of a particular construction of the 'national subject' – is precisely the error that analysis of this question should avoid. The danger is self-evident: that in attempting to unmask the ways in which a dominant worldview imposes its definition of social reality, disinterring suppressed, discrepant alternatives, we merely substitute one essential 'authenticity' for another, as if excavating 'superficial' topsoil to reveal a substratum of bedrock 'reality'. This has, indeed, been an image all too frequently employed in writing on this particular issue. The intention here, to borrow again from Prasenjit Duara's work on Chinese historiography, is 'not to recover an uncontaminated, originary history . . . but to locate the site[s] where narratives, indeed layers of narrative, seek to appropriate or wrestle with the historical real, which, of course, cannot be meaningfully known except through narrative symbolizations'.[24]

21 Millar, 'Local cultures', 128–9. As far as I am aware, no more recent research has shed any more definitive light on this question.

22 A horizontal tricolour of blue, green and yellow (representing the geography of Tamazgha from north to south: the Mediterranean, the mountains and the desert), with the *tifinagh* letter *aza* (z), now the ubiquitous sign of Amazigh identity, in red across the centre. This flag can now be seen regularly at demonstrations in Algeria and in France (it was carried in anti-fascist popular marches during the 2002 French presidential election), and the sign *aza* can be seen incorporated into Kabyle domestic and municipal architecture (e.g. in monuments to the victims of the 2001 Black Spring).

23 Final declaration of the second World Amazigh Congress (Agraw n Imazighen n Umad'al), Brussels, 7–9 August 2000; www.tamurt-imazighen.com/tamazgha/agraw/decl_bru_080900.html, 20/11/2000.

24 Duara, *Rescuing History*, 27.

North Africa's sociological reality was represented in colonial scholarship at a basic level in terms of a number of recurrent structural oppositions: nomadic/sedentary, orthodox/heretical, the East/Europe, stagnation within/civilisation from without, despotism/democracy, 'Arab'/'Berber'. By 'the Berber' was principally understood (parodying only very slightly) a sedentary, agriculturalist mountain countryman speaking a dialect of a language family eventually classified as one branch of the 'Hamito-Semitic' group,[25] and practising a 'superficially' Islamic, but 'in reality' multi-millenary culture particularly distinguished by its primitive direct-and-republican democracy. This Berber, so defined, had been elected the 'true' autochthonous North African, possibly even a distant cousin of 'our ancestors the Gauls', but in any event a fascinating, beguiling embodiment of a socio-political idyll long lost to industrial, imperial Europe – and having little in common, indeed everything in contrast, with his neighbour 'the Arab'.[26] This definition of the Maghrib's sociological reality had to be countered by a nationalist history whose keystone would necessarily be the historical–cultural unity of all Algerians (indeed, of all North Africans) in the face of the coloniser; national history would have to refute 'the complete opposition in organisation, habits, legislation, which separates the Arab from the Kabyle race',[27] and (one supposes, in principle) from other 'Berbers' in the Aurès, the Mzab and the Sahara, as well.

But simply writing off the category 'Berber' was evidently not an option. Nor, of course, could al-Madani et al. proceed by noting the much more mundane and (now) uncontroversial fact that, given the numerical weakness of attested migration from the Arabian peninsula, the majority of the Maghrib's inhabitants might reasonably be described as predominantly Arabic-speaking Muslims of ultimately Berber extraction. The rhetorical couple of 'Arab' and 'Berber', conceived on the basis of observed, existing speech-communities but swiftly worked up in the French literature (and in all discussion for ever after) into a densely woven mass of thickly textured images, myths and prejudices, was much too entrenched a fact, in the descriptive imaginary of Algeria's sociological reality, to be ignored.

[25] The label 'Hamito-Semitic' has more recently been replaced by 'Afro-Asian'; Berber is one branch, the others being Egyptian, Semitic, Chadic and Cushitic.

[26] For influential statements along these lines, see Daumas, *La Kabylie*, 38–50; Gautier, *Passé de l'Afrique du nord*. An analysis of the persistence of these stereotypes, and their place within a Mediterranean and 'Hellenic' model of society governed by the paradigm of Fustel de Coulange's *Cité antique* (a model still much in favour in Gellner's later writing), is Colonna, 'Modèle de *La Cité antique*', esp. 221–2. See also the discussion of binary stereotyping in Lorcin, *Imperial Identities*, and especially her conclusion.

[27] Daumas, *Kabylie*, 47.

On the contrary, a total national history had to concern itself *specifically* with 'the Berber'. A new, Arabic knowledge of the Maghribi past had to compete with the legitimate knowledge of modern science and the pedigree of the coloniser's nation (and undercut the appropriation of the colonial 'Berber myth' by upwardly mobile Kabyle '*évolués*' such as Hocine Hesnay-Lahmek). For this, it would be necessary to put the ancient history and prehistory of the region, which had been excavated, written about and testified to in museums by the French and in French, into Arabic. A *pre-Islamic* 'national' past, the history of a 'Berber' Maghrib before the coming of the Arabs, had to be stitched into a historical worldview that would nonetheless be anchored in Arabic and Islam. The 'Berber' problem, then, for *salafī* historiography was, briefly, this: 'the Berber' had to be recovered, reappropriated from colonial knowledge and from dangerous assimilationist fantasies, and sacralised in unity with 'the Arab', thus circumventing colonial ethnography's categorical division of the two and setting up an irreducible 'national identity' as a present truth grounded in history. Thus 'the Berber' must be, above all, defined by an essential, irreducible *inassimilability* – a theme conveniently borrowed from French arguments which had held that Berber speakers were only superficially Islamised and Arabised – *and assimilated* with 'the Arab' in one 'authentic' nation whose 'essence [is] Arab and Islamic'.[28] 'The Berber' must be irreducibly unique *and* entirely reduced into one, Arabic and Islamic, nation. And to achieve this *coup* of paradoxical logic, the 'deep antiquity' of 'the Berber', so beloved of the colonial era's pastoral idylls – the Shawi shepherd playing on a reed pipe and the Kabyle *thajma'ath* (village assembly) preserving the democratic virtues of ancient Greece – had to be *rooted* elsewhere.

Investigating the local emergence of a nationalist social imaginary among the tribes of the Balqa in Jordan, Andrew Shryock privileges 'genealogical imagination' as a central explanatory principle in local memory, and in conceptions of history and legitimate social knowledge. He sees this, moreover, as reflecting a more general epistemic model in Arab societies, in which

> there is widespread acceptance for the idea that authentic forms of human community, and . . . the most reliable forms of human knowledge, are reproduced genealogically, whether in biological pedigrees or intellectual chains of transmission . . . Islamic learning, which transcends the world of biological ties, has traditionally been depicted as an inheritance whose authenticity is safeguarded by the accurate, lineal, face-to-face transmission of sacred Arabic

[28] Merad, *Réformisme*, 93.

utterances and authoritative texts, in other words, by legitimate 'genealogical' succession.[29]

This approach, he rightly insists, does not 'exoticise' the system studied, but rather takes seriously, and accords proper weight to, the ways in which forms of knowledge and worldview are culturally modelled and locally specific. In his observations of the development of rural social structure in his early work on Algeria, Bourdieu noted the importance of a certain 'capital of power and prestige', self-reinforcing and self-attracting, in the system of 'tribal' agglomeration observed between disparate social groups. This system, he wrote, proceeds from 'an initial capital that is, it appears, nothing other than the *name*, and the ancestor which the name confers upon the group [and not *vice versa*] that carries it. Thus is the genealogical phenomenon explained.'[30] He continues:

'Particularly today, when the exploits of the first conquerors, magnified by their distance [in time], have been popularised in song and poetry, in a landscape where almost every remarkable accident of relief calls to mind their memory, there is no shepherd who does not loudly and sincerely pride himself on his descent from the *hilali* warriors.' We are in a country where certain names are epic poems.[31]

This latter point is especially true of the Banū Hilāl, the Arab nomads who migrated to Ifriqiya in the mid-eleventh century and whose *taghrība* (migration to the west) is both part of a popular oral and written epic cycle in North Africa and the Middle East, and the root of a long-standing historiographic wrangle over the Arabisation of the Maghrib. The 'colonial vulgate', on the basis of Ibn Khaldūn's celebrated description of a 'spreading swarm of locusts' (*jarād muntashir*), emphasised the calamitous effects of an invasion of destructive warriors who laid waste the lands of the peaceful and sedentary Berbers.[32] In contrast, the desirability of Arab ancestry, resting on the prestige of the conquerors

[29] Shryock, *Genealogical Imagination*, 16.

[30] Bourdieu, *Sociologie de l'Algérie*, 85–6.

[31] *Ibid.*

[32] The Hilali 'catastophe' is still present, for example, in the work of a scholar as eminent as the late Gabriel Camps, who wrote of a 'Bedouin scourge' (*Berbères*, 136), 'the worst catastrophe the Maghreb had known . . . this flood of invaders . . . spreading pillage and destruction' ('Comment la Berbérie est devenue le Maghreb arabe', 16). Partly in reaction to the colonialist instrumentalisation of the catastrophe thesis, later studies sought to refute it. Poncet ('Mythe de la "catastrophe" hilalienne') gives an account of the social and economic conditions in the mid-eleventh century Zīrid state preceding the arrival of the Hilalis, and Brett ('The flood of the dam and the sons of the new moon', ch. 9, and 'Fatimid historiography: a case study. The quarrel with the Zirids', ch. 8, in his *Ibn Khaldun and the Medieval Maghreb*) proposes a textual history of the myth itself which, however, omits the contemporary account of Hilali destruction in the *Jamharat*

and bearers of Islam, and on the repute of 'heroic saga . . . repeated in oral tradition'[33] of which the Hilalis were the subject, is a marked feature of the social model described by Bourdieu and widespread, according to the medieval historian Michael Brett, from the ninth century onwards in the Maghrib.

The genealogical principle of knowledge-transmission and community-formation, *isnād* (chain of transmission) and *nasab* (ancestral lineage), provided Tawfiq al-Madani, in approaching the pre- and ancient history of the Maghrib, with a powerful epistemic framework for dealing with the vexed question of Berber origins. His answer to the question is clear from the initial chapter of his *Kitāb al-Jazā'ir*, which opens with the sub-heading 'The Berbers and the Canaanite colonies': 'All the Berber races came by migration from Asia, and crossed Egypt and Libya; they are of the stock of Mazigh, son of Canaan son of Ham son of Noah, and so the Berbers are the cousins of the Arabs and the Phoenicians.'[34] Later in the same work, he elaborates on this: 'Ibn Khaldun affirms for us that . . . their origin is in Mesopotamia in Asia, that they migrated in very ancient times to North Africa, whether from fear or ambition, just as a great number of Bedouin Arabs would later migrate from the Egyptian desert to the [lands of the] Ḥammādid state [in the eleventh-century central Maghrib], and settle there.'[35] A more elaborate discussion, drawing equally on Arabic tradition and the scientific authority of the French, leads to the same conclusion in *Qarṭājanna fī arbaʿat ʿuṣūr*: 'We can conclude that the Berbers come from the East, and reconcile the Arab historians with modern theories supported by evidence. And we can say that they are of the Semitic race, and that they came from Asia. They settled in Egypt for a while before coming [into North Africa].'[36] Against this truth, though, are 'some historians and scholars [who] have taken great strides towards absurd fantasies' in this regard; their political motivations have

ansāb al-ʿarab of the Andalusi scholar Ibn Ḥazm (d. 456/1064). I am grateful to Michael Cook for discussion of this.

33 Brett, 'Ibn Khaldun and the Arabisation of North Africa', 14.

34 Al-Madani, *Kitāb al-Jazā'ir*, 9.

35 *Ibid.*, 97. The reference to 'Bedouin Arabs' is to the Hilali 'invasion' (note 32 above).

36 Al-Madani, *Qarṭājanna fī arbaʿat ʿuṣūr*, 17. Al-Madani carefully avoids the other branch of medieval scholarship's family tree of Noah, which would make the Frankish descendants of Japheth just as much cousins of the Berbers as the Arab descendents of Shem. The key point for him appears to be establishing an ancestral link to the east. The disorderly reconstruction of racial genealogy seems to borrow simultaneously, and selectively, from European ideas of racial scientificity and from much older ideas contained in medieval Arabic scholarship.

committed a horrendous outrage against history and . . . wishing to serve political schemes, have attacked and effaced historical facts; they have said that the Berbers are of Germanic or of Latin origin, that they migrated to Africa from Europe. Those who make such statements have no aim but to influence the Berbers, to distance all that is Asian from them and to convince them that they are of European origin; that they must return to Europe and to all that is European.[37]

There is an immediate opposition here between those 'who are allies of history . . . *who truthfully investigate and purify* it'[38] and their 'politically' motivated opponents – with 'the Berber' as the passive object of knowledge and of their struggle over knowledge. A colonialist historical politics, for al-Madani, has committed an 'outrage against history', has muddied the limpid waters of historical truth, and the *salafī* historian is one of those who restore their clarity, who purify. His self-ascribed role is as one of those 'who bring forth the sincere truth, though the boastful hate it'.[39] If there is a quasi-religious overtone, there is equally a perfectly positivistic assertion of scientific objectivity as against the 'meddling' distortion of politics. 'The true history' of the Berbers is there to be discovered, lying 'like the statue of Hercules in the veins of the marble',[40] ready-made; only prejudice has obscured it. 'The Berbers' themselves are abstracted out of the contest over their origins and nature; a blank space signified by a strictly *meaningless* onomatopoeia[41] around which the limpid language of the truthful historian weaves webs of significance.

Al-Madani's portrait of the essentialised Berber is, from the outset, complicated by his conception of the symbolically dense relationship between east and west. 'Our land of North Africa', al-Madani says in an article published in 1930, 'was isolated, in ancient times, from the rest of the world. Its people, the Berbers, lived in it a life of innocent simplicity, preserving some of their customs and traditions which they had brought from the east at an unknown date, or which they acquired from among the elements of Egyptian religion and culture.'[42] Already,

[37] Al-Madani, *Kitāb al-Jazā'ir*, 97.
[38] *Ibid.*, emphasis added.
[39] *Ibid.*
[40] Ricoeur, *Contribution of French Historiography*, 6.
[41] English *Berber*, and French *berbère* traditionally derive from Latin *barbarus*, pl. *barbari*, from Greek *barbaros*, pl. *barbaroi*. Camps (*Berbères*, 86–7) was unconvinced by this etymology, preferring to see a generalisation from Latin *bavares*, assimilated in time to *barbares* (but not *barbari*), attested in five ancient authors (whom he does not name) as the name of a tribal group among the *mauri*. His alternative is of marginal significance, however, even if accepted, since the Arabic verb *barbara* certainly has the same force as the Greek *barbaróô*: to be inarticulate, jabber meaninglessly.
[42] Al-Madani, *Taqwīm al-Manṣūr* 5, 70.

here, there is an uncomfortable tension apparent between the notion of indigenous permanence and the constant pull of the Mashriq, towards which, as to a massive centre of gravity, everything attributed to the 'originary-Maghribi' Berber in one breath falls irresistibly back in the next. 'Their own' customs come from the east – although their land is isolated from the rest of the world – and those they acquired on their way to the (isolated) Maghrib are rooted in the prestigious soil of ancient Egypt. These descendants of Canaan have crossed (somehow), in the most distant past, to the *jazīrat al-Maghrib*, the 'island of the West', and taken permanent root there, but their originary attachment to the Mashriq is constantly reaffirmed.

The same uncomfortable tension is evident again in the treatment of differentiated Berber 'types'. In *Qarṭājanna fī arba'at 'usūr*, al-Madani categorises four 'basic' groups of Berbers distinguished by physiognomy: blond; tall (to 1.7 m); of medium height (to 1.63 m) with 'short, broad faces . . . prominent cheekbones and broad, crooked noses'; and of medium height (to 1.63 m) with 'round heads . . . and curved foreheads, short, fat noses, wide mouths'.[43] The first group, 'the fair Berbers', are supposed to be 'the remnants of stone-age man'.[44] No more precise origin in time or space is attributed to them – they arise in the text *ex nihilo* from the caves of the prehistoric Maghrib. The migration out of Mesopotamia in this instance concerns only the latter three groups, qualifying his later assertions (four pages later in the same text, and in his other writings) of the arrival of 'all the Berber races' from the Mashriq. This intriguing first group is described in the *Qarṭājanna* passage at some length:

> They lived in caves and grottoes, and buried their dead there also . . . These first [inhabitants] believed in sorcery, and the practices of magical prophecy grew up among them. They believed vipers, apes, and rams with great horns to be sacred animals. As for their food, they ate the meat of wild animals and their bone marrow, and the insects of the land and sea, the fruits of trees and some roots and plants.[45]

The 'sole riches' of these people, he says, came from raising livestock. Agriculture was not unknown to them – they grew beans 'from the earliest times'. Wheat, olives and wild vines were also known in prehistory. In the next breath, however – on the same page – this account is undermined by the arrival 'at an unknown date' of the 'other' Berber groups from the east:

[43] Al-Madani, *Qarṭājanna fī arba'at 'uṣūr*, 14.
[44] *Ibid.*, 15. [45] *Ibid.*, 19–20.

> As for cattle, sheep, goats and donkeys, it is supposed that they came from Egypt . . . And the agricultural knowledge of this people also came to them from Egypt. We think that the Berbers who came from the east to this country were the ones who brought everything that came from Egypt, animals as well as fundamental knowledge [of agriculture].[46]

The questions of how prehistoric agriculture was practised before the introduction of agricultural knowledge, or of what livestock was raised before the introduction of livestock, remain to disrupt this attempted closure of the 'origins' question. It is clear, in fact, that 'the blond Berber' is nothing but a residual category, inherently problematic in his inappropriate physiognomy and thus left in an ill-defined 'indigenous' space because no obviously legitimate geographic or temporal origin can be found for him. He is credited with agriculture and animal husbandry only to have even these 'sole riches' at once taken from him, to be returned *almost*, but not *quite*, at once, as a gift from the eastern origin and gravitational centre of the narrative (and of civilisation). The initial distinction set up differentiates the 'blond' type, appearing from the primordial caves of Africa, from the others, rooted firmly (on the authority of Ibn Khaldun) in Mesopotamia and attested (on the authority of Hamito-Semitic comparative linguistics) in Egypt. This distinction is reduced *almost* to nothing by setting the migration of the posited 'other' groups in the furthest distances of antiquity. Still, the discomforting gap remains in al-Madani's text.

Five years after *Qarṭājanna*, in composing *Kitāb al-Jazā'ir*, his argument would be different. Abandoning the problematic classification of Berber 'types', he states in the later work that after passing through Egypt on their way from the Levant, 'all the Berber races . . . settled in North Africa, *and swallowed up its original inhabitants who have become in every respect unknown to us, and they themselves became the original race ('unṣur aṣlī)* known to history in North Africa'.[47] Here too, as one *'unṣur aṣlī* replaces another – stretching the capability of the word itself somewhat beyond semantic breaking-point – there opens up a disruptive margin of absence, that of the evoked-and-instantly-suppressed first 'original inhabitants' (*sukkān aṣliyyūn*). They, whoever they are, are acknowledged and glossed over in two rapid phrases.[48] The difficulty

[46] *Ibid.*, 20.

[47] Al-Madani, *Kitāb al-Jazā'ir*, 98, emphasis added.

[48] Al-Mili's *Ta'rīkh al-Jazā'ir*, I, 39–50, gives an account of the 'ancients' in the Maghrib that deals with their genealogy through Japheth son of Noah (whose descendents are said to have moved through Egypt and North Africa before some of them crossed over to Europe) and insists that 'the people of the stone age [in Algeria] are not the Berbers'

of reconciling indigenous perennity with arrival from the east leads the writer, again, to a strategy that must minimise a distance that he himself has created, but cannot quite eliminate it.

These revealing ambiguities, antinomies never quite resolved, are traces of the difficulty facing the writer in formulating his own exposition of what he believes to be historical truth. The tension between permanence, rooted authenticity (*aṣl, uṣūl, aṣāla*) in Africa and the gravitational mass of the Mashriq whence legitimate ancestry (*nasab*) springs is visible in these disruptions. The writer wishes to locate 'the Berber' as an originary, unassimilable North African *and* as a wandering Canaanite from the east who can only become the 'originary' North African by replacing another – an all but invisible other of whom history has nothing to tell us. In his own mind, and in those of his readers, he perhaps achieved his aim, but not without leaving in his text the marks of the difficulty of the enterprise.

'The Berber' who arises/settles in the Maghrib is a cultural blank page, a 'noble savage' in a pristine state. He is, says al-Madani, noble, generous, fearless and brave, steadfast 'to the utmost limit of resolve', caring for his homeland with the utmost degree of love, 'hard to satisfy, such that he accepts no idea or belief save with difficulty, but once he takes it up and is imbued with it, he will fight in its cause as he would for his own children'.[49] He is frugal, thrifty, 'saving, as they say, from his youth for his old age, his strength for his [hour of] weakness, his fullness for his [time of] want'.[50] Besides this, 'he is distinguished by his implacable resentment and impatience towards any offence', and by the consequent vendettas pursued in defence of honour, giving rise to 'a chain of acts of vengeance to which no limit can be set'.[51] This is allied to a 'great capacity to assume the difficulties and hardships of life', a nobility towards guests and the defence of those who seek refuge.[52] The theme of purity, austerity and immovable constancy is an important leitmotiv. Whether manifested in unshakeable attachment to the land, reluctance to embrace new beliefs, unflinching sacrifice in defence of liberty, or in bloody and aberrant feuds, this notion of *ṣalāba, taṣṣalub* ('solidity', unyielding constancy), may usefully be seen as the key condensation symbol[53] of Berber virtue.

(I, 48); the latter, as for al-Madani, originated in the Levant and migrated in prehistoric times to North Africa (I, 62–4).

49 Al-Madani, *Kitāb al-Jazā'ir*. 99.

50 *Ibid.*

51 *Ibid.*, 100.

52 Al-Madani, *Qarṭājanna fī arba'at 'uṣūr*, 18.

53 Ortner, 'On key symbols'.

This stern, moral inflexibility combines with a 'life of simplicity' to tie 'the Berber', thus 'thickly' constituted, to his Arab cousins: 'The morality of Berbers and Bedouin united [them] in a simple and virtuous way of life . . .united [them] in the Bedouin character.'[54]

Genealogy and salvation

wa-jā'a al-inqādh min al-sharq.
And salvation came from the east.
Tawfiq al-Madani[55]

It is here that the full significance of the organising principle of eastern genealogy comes into play, in the key relationship of pure ancestry, civilisational affinity and a common destiny in Islam and the language carrying it, that this *salafī* historiography establishes between 'the Berber' and 'the Arab'.

Al-Madani's Berbers 'knew from the inception of history that they formed an independent race with its own customs, morality and language'.[56] They are 'the original race known to history in the Maghrib, a race of outstanding nature who surpassed other peoples in many priceless qualities, the most important of which are a total [devotion to the] defence of their existence, and constancy in defence of their independence. At no time were they assimilated to any other race.'[57]In brief, 'the Berber mingles, but is not mixed'.[58] The construction in these texts of 'the Berber' as a strongly defined, positively valorised figure, solid (*taṣṣalub*) and unswerving, irreducible in his 'essential self' (*kiyānuhu*), is the perhaps neglected face of the reformists' approach to history and 'the Berber question'. Much of this is surprisingly reminiscent of a Boulifa, or of more recent Berberist manifestos. We might expect, in texts produced by the reformist movement, something closer to the more usual arguments that produced the official Arab-Islamism of the independent Maghribi states, and the relation of domination and, at times, suppression experienced since independence by Tamazight,[59] as a direct continuation of the *salafyya* movements' outlawing of linguistic and cultural

[54] Al-Madani, *Qarṭājanna fī arba'at 'uṣūr*, 160.
[55] Al-Madani, *Hādhihi hiya 'l-Jazā'ir*, 53.
[56] Al-Madani, *Qarṭājanna fī arba'at 'uṣūr*, 17.
[57] *Ibid*, 13.
[58] Al-Madani, *Kitāb al-Jazā'ir*, 99.
[59] This perception should be nuanced, and is no longer (as of the late 1990s) as justified as it was in an earlier period (the 1960s–80s) of either Algeria or Morocco, but see Chaker, 'L'Émergence du fait berbère', 475–6, 'Quelques évidences sur la question berbère', 105–6.

plurality during the construction of Maghribi nationalisms from the 1920s to 1950s. This is also true, but neglects the importance of the substantive role that 'the Berber' *does* play in the reformists' historiography, if, indeed, not in their socio-cultural ambitions. It remains to be shown how their recovery of 'the Berber' as national signifier in prehistory and antiquity leads to their suppression of 'the Berber' in a twentieth-century cultural project of Arab-Islamic nationhood.

The principle, set up as a maxim, of the Berber who 'mingles but is not mixed', summarising the 'solid' constitution of the essentialised, primary 'Berber' figure, is attenuated to the point of collapse by the simultaneous narrative structure of genealogical kinship, which guides the whole conception of *salafī* history, and which leads to the reinscription of 'Berber' and 'Arab' not as oppositional, nor as complementary, but as *identical.* In its *salafi* formulation, the nation in Algeria – and in North Africa as a whole – *was* indeed represented by a 'Berber' reality. But this reality is structured by a very particular logic of genealogy and salvation that governs the entire span of the history of the Maghrib.

> The whole of North African history comprises two great ages. The first is the purely Berber age, which begins with the first knowledge of history and runs to the arrival of the Arabs. The second age begins when the sons of Ya'rab and the sons of Māzīgh shook hands. The Maghrib became an Islamic country inhabited by the conjoined race of the Berbers and Arabs.[60]

This overarching, two-stage structure is fundamentally defined both genealogically, in terms of race, and culturally, in terms of civilisation. There is a parallel throughout al-Madani's *Qarṭājanna fī arba'at 'uṣur* between national destiny plotted as racially and as civilisationally determined, and the two are constantly linked, with the Berbers inherently predisposed to eastern – Phoenician and Arab – civilisation, and fundamentally opposed to that of Rome (and, by extension, modern Europe).

By setting up this structure as the 'total meaning' of North African history, al-Madani accomplishes at least three things. First, all of classical and late antiquity up to the Islamic conquest is reinscribed as 'the purely Berber period', decentring colonial historiography's fundamental notion of a Latin North Africa in the long Roman–Byzantine era. This was a notion much relied upon by the ideologues of colonisation as a civilising work seen not only as bringing the Maghrib into the modern, enlightened age, but also as returning it to its authentic history, with France as the natural heir of Rome, creating a new Mediterranean 'Latin race', a conception widely propagated in the late nineteenth and early

60 "*Unṣur mazīj min al-barbar wa 'l-'arab*' (*Qarṭājanna fī arba'at 'uṣūr*, 8).

twentieth centuries.[61] Second, the categorical division made by colonial ethnography of the Maghrib's inhabitants into 'Arabs' and 'Berbers' is appropriated and turned against its originators, the canonical uniqueness and immutability of 'the Berber' being accepted in order to make Berber history the first 'great age' of a tri-millennial national past, *continuous* with the complementary history of Berbers and Arabs 'conjoined' after the coming of Islam. Instead of the ethnic and geographical distinction made by French scholars, in which Arabs and Berbers are found throughout the contemporary Maghrib, divided across space, al-Madani introduces a historical distinction: the Berbers, already closely linked to the Arabs, existed separately only in the past. There is one, undivided Muslim nation in the contemporary Maghrib, heirs of the fusion of Arabs and Berbers (and the enlightenment and salvation of the latter by the former) consummated in the Arab-Islamic conquests. Hence the third achievement, with the Islamic conquest itself being placed at the very centre of the story, an archimedal point around which the destiny of the nation turns. Such centrality for the *fatḥ* is, perhaps, predictable (although its meaning, as we saw, is far from classically orthodox). It is the 'first age' that represents a crucial innovation for the reformists' understanding of 'national' history.

The ancient past, recovered from the writings of the colonial academic establishment, is the privileged site of the Berbers' role in Maghribi national history: 'These were the days of the Berbers, proud sons of Mazigh. They inhabited the plains of this land and its hills. And they acquired, from all who came to them, the lights of civilisation.'[62] The Berbers are here in their 'pure' state; initially 'in the shadows', they are progressively 'civilised' by their genealogical cousins from the east. Acquiring the rudiments of knowledge from the ancient Egyptians on their prehistoric migration, they are first acquainted with 'civilisation' in the form of the Phoenicians who found Carthage, and finally by the Arabs, who complete the Punic civilisational mission with the light of Islam. The colonial constitution of the native subject as racially/culturally 'fenced in' since earliest times, as immutable, insensible to the penetration of 'European' influence and 'progress', is subversively redeployed here as a 'proof' of Arab–Berber unity. The insistence on the essential, genealogically predestined and immutable inassimilability of the North African shares, while inverting its values, the beliefs of colonial racism,

[61] E.g. in the work of Louis Bertrand, director of the review *Afrique latine*. On Bertrand, see Lorcin, *Imperial Identities*, ch. 9; on 'Latin Africa' generally, see Berque, *Maghreb entre deux guerres*, 242–3.
[62] Al-Madani, *Qarṭājanna fī arba'at 'uṣūr*, 8.

where Europeans and Africans occupy a (genealogically – we might say, genetically) predestined place in a recurrent struggle of civilisations. Simultaneously, and as we already saw in the previous chapter, the Western myth of civilisation is perfectly inverted by a narrative of an uninterrupted *mission civilisatrice* from the Mashriq. Inassimilability and fusion coexist in a conception of history that refigures 'the Berber' as an irreducible essence, but one which is by nature akin to its cousins, the 'oriental' races of Arabs and Phoenicians. The difficulties already observed, however, regarding the establishment of 'the Berber' as both eternally indigenous and as an oriental migrant, are repeated in the problematic representation of his eternal irreducibiliy and destiny of fusion with Arabic and Islam. The notion of genealogy and salvation, borrowing both from a scientific vocabulary of evolution and from the sacred one of Islam, is the mechanism by which this problem is addressed.

The Phoenicians, as we already saw, are for al-Madani a vanguard of Arabism, bearers of a civilisation rooted in eastern ancestry that they share with the Berbers. 'The Phoenicians were from among the sons of Canaan and are related to the Arabs by close kinship; [hence] the Phoenicians and the Berbers, indeed, are of one sole race, the offspring of the same stock.' For the Berbers, the Carthaginians are

> the teachers who brought instruction in civilisation . . . and their civilisation was one of the greatest in the world. The Berbers, before the arrival of their cousins the Phoenicians, were like them in their innermost character, and they had not mixed with any other nation since their coming from the East. When the rule of Carthage spread, [and] her towns multiplied, the Berbers mixed with the new arrivals, and took from them all the civilisational instruction which they brought. This imprint of rule and custom has never disappeared [from among them]. And this new, flourishing civilisation mixed with [the Berbers' culture] of lesser quality, [and swallowed up the latter, whose adepts began to follow the new] so that it became their custom, and they forgot the old.[63]

The Berbers' own 'great degree of intellectual and material progress'[64] (indicated by the *tifinagh* alphabet, which the Berbers invented 'at the dawn of history') is superseded by the Phoenicians, a 'second Canaanite wave'. The Berbers 'became inhabitants of [Phoenician] centres of civilisation such that there was no division in any respect between them and the original Carthaginians'.[65] The Berbers' language 'was completely assimilated' with that of the Phoenicians to form

[63] *Ibid.*, 34.
[64] Al-Madani, *Kitāb al-Jazā'ir*, 73.
[65] Al-Madani, *Qarṭājanna fī arba'at 'uṣūr, 34.*

the Carthaginian national language . . . and we can easily understand this assimilation when we remember that Punic and Berber [languages] are from the same origin and that the Semitic tongue comprises them both. *And there is no doubt that this Carthaginian language paved the way for the supremacy of the Arabic language in these regions* . . . The influence of this civilisation, deeply rooted in the hearts [of the people] has not ceased to exercise its apparent effect up to our own day.[66]

Indeed, he claims that agricultural, craft and social practices visible in Kabylia in the first decades of the twentieth century 'all go back to the influence of Carthage'. If the Berbers already knew the plough before the Phoenicians' arrival, they 'knew nothing of cultivation; it was Carthage who gave them the idea of growing trees, and particularly olive-trees, vines, figs and pomegranates'. More crucially, 'the Berbers had not known the meaning of unity, and had not understood the idea of a state. It came to them through the influence of Carthage that they themselves could begin to erect great Berber states.'[67] Carthage, indeed (not Greece or Rome, nor the 'primitive communism' of the Kabyle *thajma'ath*), is the originator of democracy and representative government in North Africa: 'It was she who first established constitutional life and a representative political order in the world, at a time when all the countries of the world submitted to the despotism of kings and absolute rulers.'[68]

In the religious field, though, there is a crucial problem. Most of the Berbers, rather than adopting Phoenician–Canaanite religion, 'continued to protect their ancient religious customs: the worship of the forests and woods, and of natural powers and *jinn*, and these customs still abide in the Berbers' identity to this day, despite the passing of the Christian age and the coming and fixed establishment of the rule of Islam'.[69] Berber religion is still, in part, *jāhilī*. Moreover, the civilisational greatness of Carthage stops at the door of religion, where we encounter a terrible barbarism, adroitly exploited by al-Madani in his narrative of the exemplary heroism of Carthage's destruction. The final moments of the city, at the narrative crux of the book, are seen through the desperate patriotism of the wife of a Carthaginian general who, as the citadel is put to sack by the Romans, has given himself up to the enemy:

She stared at him, with eyes filled with Carthaginian fury, and shouted out at him: 'Go, in servility, you coward! Let the victors boast of your captivity!' Then she strangled to death, with her own hands, her own two children, and threw

[66] *Ibid.*, 34–5, emphasis added. Again, different Afro-Asian languages are here assimilated to the Semitic branch.
[67] *Ibid.*, 35. [68] *Ibid.*, 33. [69] *Ibid.*, 35–6.

them, and herself immediately after them, into the midst of the blaze [of the burning temple]. Rather the flames than shame.[70]

This particular incident, closing the story of Carthage, is noteworthy for its accomplished narrative skill and the moral force implicit in its symbolism; this 'final page in the history of Canaanite Carthage'[71] is an echo of earlier references to the pagan flaws of this heroic era. While the Berbers are guilty merely of idolatry (sun- and moon-worship), the Carthaginian/Canaanite religion is horribly flawed by the practice of child sacrifice. This is the most clear-cut expression of the ambivalent role played by Carthage in the text – the fall of the city, while narrated as a heroic act of patriotic martyrdom in defence of the homeland and against the evils of imperial Europe, is also implicitly emplotted as divine judgement against this terrible practice, a Qur'anic apocalypse of 'danger from which there was no escape for them'.[72] It thus points to the incompleteness of the civilisational influence of Carthage for the Berbers, who await the salvific *dénouement* of their history in the coming of Islam. The echo here, in the sacrifice in the flames to honour, the homeland and the cause of freedom, unites the respective terrors of Carthage's life and death, finally transcending the barbarism of *jāhiliyya* in patriotic martyrdom, and sublimating the horror of the city's ruin in a great and terrible epic history whose 'grand violence' connects God's judgement upon Carthage with its enduring, exemplary heroism.

Islam, the perfecting salvation of the Berber race, brings to this people, already distinguished by their illustrious history of struggle and sacrifice, the true and final 'moral' or 'spiritual' civilisation of which the Arabs are the bearers. This 'spiritual Orient' is counterposed to the 'material civilisation' exemplified by Rome (also a figure for France) and which, as '[a] civilisation of theatres, palaces, and towering buildings . . . was removed by the greatest distance from the morality of Berbers and Bedouin', united, as we have seen, in one, austere 'character'. From the point of view adopted in *Qarṭājanna fī arbaʿat ʿuṣūr*, and as we saw in the previous chapter, the conquest is not, as we might tend to think of specifically Arab-Islamic historiography, the beginning of history, but rather an end of history, a *telos* in which the perfection of 'the Maghribi nation' is achieved, and, by implication, after which no more meaningful

[70] '*Al-nār wa lā al-ʿār*' (*ibid.*, 75). The story of Hasdrubal's wife is briefly mentioned in Polybius 38.20 and Livy, *Per.* 51; the lines quoted by al-Madani are from Appian, *Punica* 19: 131.

[71] Al-Madani, *Qarṭājanna fī arbaʿat ʿuṣūr,* 75.

[72] *Ibid.*, 25. This is, I think, the only phrase in the text which clearly echoes a specifically. Qur'anic theme. (cf. the apocalypses of Q. 11, *Ṣūrat Hūd*).

change is possible. Thereafter, history is only the further expansion of the nation's glory, or its long struggle to return to this age of purity. This is precisely the message of the final part of the book:

Arabs and Berbers . . . became one nation, without the Berbers having greatly changed their ancient customs or the Arabs adopting those of the Berbers – they were brought together by their unity of religion, of morality and of interests . . . The two peoples were of one inclination and one sentiment, and they shared a love of honour and glory, a passion for freedom, and the custom of greatly honouring guests. This commonality of inclination and morality broke through the barriers that the Romans, Vandals and Byzantines were unable to pierce. The Berbers became the strongest auxiliaries of the army of Islam.[73]

This spiritual kinship, binding Arab and Berber together, is what creates the strength of the army of Ṭāriq ibn Ziyād, with whose conquest of southern Spain in 710 al-Madani opens the concluding passage of his ancient history.[74] The 'conjoined race' (*'unṣur mazīj*) of Arabs and Berbers becomes one Islamic nation, the culmination of a long, evolutionary process of 'moral and material improvement' suffused with a sacred history of destiny-in-salvation, the whole narrative unfolding under the inexorable sign of genealogy: 'This was the result of the Islamic conquest. It created the nation of North Africa and its [single] complete civilisation on the ruins of extinct civilisations. And God made the Arabs and Berbers conversant with one another, and they became, by his favour towards them, brothers.'[75]

The absurd death of the Aztecs

'The price of [linear, nationalist] History', writes Prasenjit Duara, 'has . . . been very dear, not because the narrative has actually succeeded in extinguishing different modes of being and time . . . but because . . . the closures of modernity and History have not enabled a language that can recognise and negotiate with that which has been dispersed and repressed.'[76] The 'repression' of 'the Berber' in Algerian *salafī* historiography was not the last word. Its particular attempt at the formulation of a closed and totalising national history could not, ultimately, obliterate, nor fully appropriate, the category 'Berber' – but neither could it recognise it as having a legitimate existence in the present, as a category in which communities might recognise themselves, and through which they would seek to negotiate their place in a new Algerian society and in the 'recovery' of its sovereign history.

[73] *Ibid.*, 161. [74] *Ibid.*, 159. [75] *Ibid.*, 161.
[76] Duara, *Rescuing History*, 50.

The denial of a distinct, contemporary 'Berber reality' in North Africa, a central plank in the unifying cultural doctrine of *salafī* nationalism, was based on more than a simple Arab ethnocentricity or wilful 'blindness' to the multiplicity of Algerian society. Al-Madani and his colleagues took considerable trouble and expended considerable ingenuity in addressing the 'Berber question'. Their solution was to adopt the 'the irreducible Berber' as a strongly constituted, heroic and genealogically legitimate national signifier, and then to fix this figure into a closed, *historicised* space, inextricably tied to the eastern origin of Arab and Islamic civilisation and predestined by nature to absorption in their salvific embrace. 'The Berber' was exalted, and thereby better dominated; depicted with brilliance in the space assigned him, he would so much more easily, thereafter, be made invisible. This essentialised figure emerges in al-Madani's texts as another totemic, primordial ancestor, incarnation of the ideal virtues of an unswerving, unassimilable nation committed to its independence, its 'authenticity' and rootedness (*aṣāla, uṣūl*) both in the Maghribi soil and in the moral and sacred geography, and legitimate ancestry, of the Mashriq. *This* 'Berber' is at the base of a national past stretching back into 'the dawn of history' and whose story reaches an apotheosis in the consummation, *bi-ni'mat Allāh*,[77] 'by the grace of God', of the united Maghribi nation in Arabic and Islam, narrated as the achievement of a preinscribed genealogical, civilisational and sacred destiny. No other 'Berber' could legitimately exist in either Algeria's history or its present.

The *salafī* programme was perhaps, though, bound to continue, beyond the controlled domain of textual knowledge-production, to have a problematic relationship with 'the Berber'. The reformists' religio-cultural doctrine of Algerian nationalism, and the nationalised official culture (particularly, of course, the language policies) of the post-independence state, set out to create in reality the Algerian nation whose myth they had already constructed. 'We are Arabs, Arabs, Arabs!' declared Ben Bella on his return from French captivity in 1962, to which an aide is famously said to have quipped, *sotto voce*, 'Ça va finir par être vrai!' ('Given time it might come true'). The first Algerian Arabisation programme was presented to the Arab League in Cairo, as early as 6 August 1962, one month after independence, by Tawfiq al-Madani, who would shortly become a minister in Ben Bella's first government.

It is significant that, despite the considerable attention paid to 'the Berber' and to ancient history in the texts of the historians linked to

[77] Al-Madani, *Qarṭājanna fī arba'at 'uṣūr*, 161.

the movement, history classes in AUMA schools seem to have drawn almost exclusively on classical Arab and Islamic history focused on the Mashriq. At a congress of teachers from the schools established or supported by the Association, in October 1937, the delegates expressed their need for books dealing in depth with North African history and geography, asserting that 'an Algerian must know his [own] country before [he knows] the East', although they agreed that their needs in general literature could amply be met by Mashriqi texts 'to which nothing can be added'.[78] Al-Madani's *Jughrāfiyyat al-quṭr al-jazā'irī* ('Geography of the Algerian region') was in fact prescribed in AUMA schools in the late 1940s, and a revised edition produced specifically for use in their classrooms. The use of *quṭr* (region), rather than *waṭan* ('homeland', 'nation') in the title echoes pan-Arabist terminology; in this text, Algeria is part of 'the great Maghribi homeland', itself a subdivision of the 'the Arab nation', but Algeria is also cartographically privileged as lying at 'the heart of the world'. The prescribed texts in history, however, when the Association set about the centralised organisation of its school network in the late 1940s, were those produced by the Egyptian Ministry of Public Instruction. Pupils in their fourth and fifth years of elementary education[79] were to have two lessons each of history and geography, the texts prescribed being, for the fourth year, an Egyptian *Mudhakkirāt fī ta'rīkh al-khulafā' al-rāshidīn min kitāb al-ta'rīkh al-islāmī* ('Episodes from the History of the Rightly Guided Caliphs, from the Book of Islamic History'), and in the following year a second volume of the same collection.[80] Historically themed speeches by AUMA leaders similarly appear to have eschewed pre-Islamic 'national' history. At celebrations of the *mawlid al-nabī* (the Prophet's birthday) in 1945, held at a cultural circle in Algiers, a number of senior reformists elaborated the lessons of history, evoking the life, trials and achievements of the Prophet, the age of the Arab conquests and the golden age of Arabic learning at the great Islamic universities of Andalusia.[81]

The heart of the reformists' pedagogical project was set in the *ṣadr al-'urūba*, the 'heart of Arabism', in the vivifying stream of classical Arabic

[78] Prefecture, Algiers, 15 Oct. 1937, ADA/4I/13/3(2F).

[79] It is, however, difficult to establish how many pupils there were at this level, and more difficult to know to what extent the prescriptions of the AUMA leaders were realised in its schoolrooms.

[80] AUMA school timetable, Arabic MS and translation, with Note, SLNA, Algiers, 27 Dec. 1948 no. 1216 SLNA, ADA/4I/13/2(2C). The texts of al-Madani and al-Mili were probably produced in too small a quantity for instructional use.

[81] Report, PRG, Algiers, 26 Feb. 1945 no. 1004, ADA/4I/14/9.

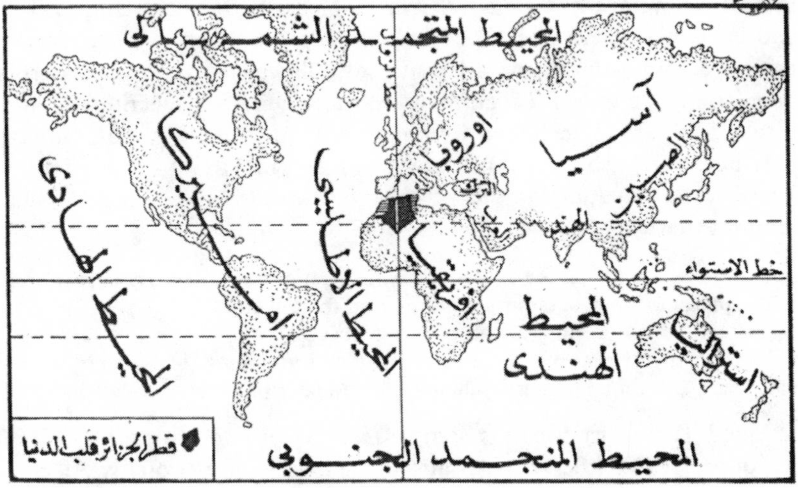

Figure 14. 'Algeria, the heart of the world', from al-Madani's geography textbook, *Jughrāfiyyat al-quṭr al-jazā'irī*. (BnF.)

achievement and 'in the path of universal Islamic renaissance'.[82] Their fascination with the Mashriq (complemented, in the opposite direction, by nostalgia for Andalusia) doubtless proceeded both from a general preoccupation with origins and a sense of the east as a 'place of beginnings', and from their awareness of the volatile events in the Middle East, its powerful currents of ideology and mobilisation, and its powerful states, as acutely important to the 'greater whole' of which they considered themselves a part, namely both the 'Arab nation' and the Islamic ecumene.[83] The predominance of an eastward-facing, strictly

[82] Al-Madani, *Kitāb al-Jazā'ir*, 373.

[83] As we saw in Chapter, 1, a certain interest continued to be concentrated on the Ottoman state up to 1918, and then on republican Turkey, at least until the abolition of the caliphate. Egypt, a focal point already in the 1870s, appears to become more important from 1919, and crucial after 1952. In parallel, the emergence of the independent and Islamically rigorous Sa'udi state may have largely filled the void left by the defunct caliphate. Al-Madani, who wrote a portrait of Mustafa Kemal in 1922, published in the first number of his *Taqwīm al-Manṣūr*, moved on to Ibn Sa'ud in the third volume (1924) of the same publication (*HK*, I, 322–3). From the interwar period onwards, Algerian reformists were also much exercised by events in Palestine. Al-Madani apparently wrote frequently on the subject (*HK*, II, 305–14). He was also in touch with the Association of Muslim Youth in Cairo, for whom he was thought to have distributed a number of illustrated pamphlets (*Fire and Ruin in Martyred Palestine*) in Algiers in July

'Arab-Islamic' worldview in the official culture of independent Algeria, in part a development of the AUMA project, in part its manipulation, and in part an echo of Ba'thist ideas, has more recently been roundly criticised, not only by the advocates of cultural pluralism and Berber linguistic and cultural recognition, but more generally by critics of what is seen as a paradoxically *un-Algerian* orientation in policy, most particularly in the state's schools. In a study of history textbooks printed in the 1980s for use in Algerian secondary education, Rédouane Ained-Tabet remarks that

> no history text is concerned exclusively with Algeria, from antiquity or prehistory to the present. No programme is centred on the History of Algeria . . . Hence, pupils are furnished no general, comprehensive account of their country . . . [The] teaching of history does not contribute to the rooting [of children] in their native soil and thus to their psychological, and later political, stability.[84]

Ained-Tabet criticises his sample-texts as promoting an ideological discourse of 'Middle-Easternisation', their lack of a properly Algerian national 'rootedness' leaving, he says, the student with 'his feet in the Djurdjura, his roots in Mesopotamia and his heart in the Middle East! – So where is his head?'[85] Worse, such 'Ba'thist ideological manipulation [predisposes] highly vulnerable adolescents to become Arabo-Islamists or "integrists" by sociopolitical "drift", and not, first and foremost, Algerian citizens.'[86] Official national historiography, in this view, is paradoxically guilty of a calamitous *anti*-nationalism,[87] responsible for laying the ideological foundations of an alienated, un-Algerian and imported Islamism.

A notable aspect of this 'un-Algerian' discourse on Algeria, according to Ained-Tabet, is what he terms 'la berbérité "arabisée" ' ('the Arabisation of Berber identity').[88] One of the books examined covers 'the civilisations of Antiquity', among which, in four lessons, is discussed 'bilād al-Maghrib al-'arabī wa al-mujtama' al-amāzīghī' ('the land of the Arab Maghrib and Amazigh society'). A map illustrating 'the emigration

1938 (Intelligence note, CIE, Government-General, Algiers, 22 July 1938 no. 1029, ADA/4I/28/6).

84 Ained-Tabet, 'Manuels d'histoire et discours idéologique', 43.

85 *Ibid.*, 44.

86 *Ibid.* Cf. Djeghloul, 'Crise de la conscience historique'.

87 The eminent intellectual, writer, diplomat and former minister Mostefa Lacheraf similarly denounces what he calls 'the supra-nationalist . . . *qawmiyya* [as opposed to] the liberating nationalism of the martyred Algerian people' (*Des noms et des lieux*, 90), 'the Ba'thist *qawmiyya* [that makes] the school an alien institution; if not alien to our "identity" (as superficially proclaimed) yet to our veridic national being' (*Ibid.*, 161).

88 'Manuels d'histoire et discours idéologique', 43–4.

of the *Amazighiyyin* to the Maghrib' is supported, in the text in question, by the assertion (denounced by Ained-Tabet as 'historical untruth') that: 'the Amazighiyyin migrated from the direction of Mesopotamia (Iraq), passed into Egypt and settled there for a short while, and then continued their journey into the Arab Maghrib'.[89] As Ained-Tabet dryly notes, 'the Maghrib is presented as having been already "Arab" even before the arrival of the Arabs!' What is most interesting here, however, is that, in concluding his critique of these school texts, Ained-Tabet observes that, with this contemporary 'Ba'thist' ideology, 'we are a long way from the 1930s, when the Association of *'ulamā* . . . proclaimed itself officially *Algerian*, and when two of its members, Mubarak al-Mili and Tawfiq al-Madani, each composed a history of Algeria'.[90] But in fact, the short passage on the Mesopotamian origin of the Berbers and their prehistoric migration via Egypt, so vigorously denounced, is nothing more than an exact restatement of al-Mili and al-Madani's treatment of the same theme. Their 'truly national' history, adduced here as a corrective to the deviations of pan-Arabism, was very likely the direct textual source used by the 'Ba'thist' writers of the criticised schoolbook.

This example illustrates how the search for definitively 'legitimate' history can lead back to ever-unresolved questions. This is not because there is nothing 'really' present in such debates besides a chaos of texts and intertexts, but because narratives of Algerian history too have an actual social life, are embedded in contested worldviews and cultural politics. Made to bear immense weights of legitimisation and counter-legitimisation, historiographic texts (which remain relatively few in number) are invoked against each other and even against themselves. Once examined critically, and in the light of their own conditions and logics of production, these texts emerge in their own proper significance. It turns out to be vain to look to a foundational nationalist historiography for a 'true' history of Algeria and the Berbers, because the historiographic logic of nationalism itself, no less than the colonialist scholarship excoriated by al-Madani or the 'Ba'thist' school texts of the 1980s, was caught up in a necessarily political claim to name and define the community and its culture. Nationalist historical writing obeys specific epistemic injunctions that exhort the community to 'know itself' in a particular, highly determined way.

In this dominant, doctrinal collective self-view, according to the prominent activist-scholar of Berber linguistics Salem Chaker, '*Berbérité*

[89] *Ibid.*, 43. [90] *Ibid.*, 45.

is excluded, ignored, and at best consigned to the distant past – in particular among the intelligentsia of the Islamic reformist movement. It is from them that springs the thesis . . . reactualised by President Chadli [at the FLN congress of December 1983] of "Our ancestors the Berbers"!'[91] In the view of recent Berberist/Amazigh cultural and political writing, the dominant 'Arab-Islamic ideology, totalitarian by nature', systematically and wilfully 'excludes Berber language and culture from the Algerian political field', since 'it cannot recognise other cultures, other languages [as legitimate within the nation]'.[92]

A revisionist history, no less 'national', represented in particular by Mahieddine Djender, has begun to readdress the same questions posed by the *salafī* historians in the 1920s–30s, with the same aim of recovering 'the total and authentic historical reality'[93] of the Maghrib. This is understood as implicating all of North Africa well beyond the flashpoint of Kabylia, since

> [there is a danger of] regionalising a Berber reality whose dimensions are in fact national, extending even from Mauritania and the Canary Islands to Libya and southern Egypt. [Without a general consideration of Berber history[94]] we risk reducing [this reality] to the limits of one part of [Algeria]; this is precisely what the adherents of the Arab-Islamic doctrine wish, since *they fear that by teaching or simply divulging history, the true nature and identity of the country will be revived.*[95]

This 'true nature and identity' (at a more immediate level than the utopian reformulation of pan-Maghribi ideals in terms of a revived Tamazgha), is that of *Algérie algérienne*, 'Algerian Algeria', the eloquent tautology associated since the PPA's so-called 'Berberist crisis' of 1948–9 with opposition to the socio-cultural pre-eminence of an exclusively 'Arab-Islamic' Algerian national self-definition. This latter definition was of course central to the programme of the Association of *'ulamā*, and also predominated among the radical-populist revolutionary activists of the PPA. To proponents of pluralism generally, and berberophone linguistic and cultural rights in particular, this definition (the reformists' truth) is patently false: the doctrinaire Arabism and Arabisation of 'official culture' are nothing more than a 'wish that that which *is not* should *be*'.[96] The ultimate aim of the revisionist, anti-'Arab-Muslim'

91 Chaker, 'Langue et identité berbères', 173. The notion of 'the Berber' as belonging to a closed historical space was reiterated with particular force by Mazouni, 'Cultures et sociétés', esp. 151–2, and *Culture et enseignement*.
92 Yefsah, 'L'Arabo-Islamisme', 106–7.
93 Djender, 'La Berbérie', 62.
94 The formulation is striking: 'l'histoire générale *de la Berbérie*' (*ibid.*, 55).
95 *Ibid.*, emphasis added.
96 *Ibid.*, 56, emphasis added.

history is 'to give a final definition of Algeria . . . complex by its history, unitary by the effort of its people: an Algerian Algeria, the description that is finally most appropriate'.[97]

This search for a final self-definition that ends in tautology points to the particular symbolic struggle, the idiom in which these conflicts are played out. Djender's account of national history varies considerably from al-Madani's. Djender speaks of a 'Romano-Berber society' flourishing up to the fifth century, while al-Madani privileges Carthage and insists on Berber resistance to Roman tyranny.[98] For Djender, Algeria is 'the product of Mediterranean civilisation' shared by Egyptians, Phoenicians, Romans and Greeks,[99] where al-Madani's historical imaginary of the Mediterranean is highly determined by a moral geography that bisects this Braudelian world, sharply dividing east/south from west/north. Finally, to Djender, 'an imperishable Berber identity' ('la berbérité, impérissable') remains essential, while for al-Madani, as we have seen, the 'Berber substratum' was a closed and historicised reality whose own destiny lies in fusion with (pure) Arabic and (pure) Islam, achieved already in the seventh century and demanding reassertion in a contaminated and alienated present. Both use strikingly similar language in expressing their aims and intentions. Both speak of historical truth, which only 'politics' and 'ideology' distort, both seek 'to see what Algeria is and to define it'. Both insist that 'above all [they] respect the facts, and respect history'.[100]

Both the reformist vision, expressed in al-Madani's texts, which was to become nationalist orthodoxy, and the later challenges to it, remain caught in a contest over the definition of historical truth, over the symbolic goods of representation, definition and naming. The eloquent tautology of *Algérie algérienne*, too, fails, in its very assumption of formulaic comprehensiveness, to appreciate that it is itself an open-ended restatement of the question, and can never be a 'definitive' answer – for there can never be one. Rather than a simple conflict between an unproblematic, stable reality, whether 'Arab' or 'Berber', however defined, and its ideological distortion, these disputes mark one latest instance of very long-standing 'symbolic struggles for the power to produce and impose the legitimate world view . . . in which agents clash over the

97 *Ibid.*, 57.
98 *Ibid.*, 61–4; cf. al-Madani, *Kitāb al-Jazā'ir,* 74.
99 Djender, 'La Berbérie', 78. The divergence has obvious parallels in similar debates over the 'eastern' or 'Mediterranean' history, destiny and identity of both Egypt and Lebanon, from (at least) the 1920s to the present, or the persistent question over whether Turkey 'belongs' to the Middle East or to Europe.
100 *Ibid.*

meaning of the social world and their position within it, the meaning of their social identity'.[101]

The emergence of a Berber cultural movement since the late 1970s has been seen as a 'reaction to the denial, prevailing in independent Algeria, of the Berber dimension [of the nation]'.[102] But this is not because such a (stable, permanent) 'Berber dimension' is a suppressed, but irrepressibly self-manifesting, fact. It is rather, perhaps, that the Algerian state's Jacobin insistence on 'the [exclusively] Arab identity of Algeria', Ben Bella's 'thundering proclamations, including the famous: "We are Arabs, we are Arabs, ten million Arabs!" '[103] and the clumsy and doctrinaire implementation of linguistic Arabisation, among other factors, all of which have served particular purposes and agenda within successive regimes since independence, have *made* 'Berber identity' into one of the most sensitive and volatile sites, or idioms, of contest and opposition in independent Algeria – Islam being the other.

It was, perhaps, assumed for too long that the unanimist state could maintain its monopoly over religion, after its hold on language and 'ethnicity' had been challenged by the students of Tizi Ouzou and those who followed them onto the streets in the 1980 'Berber Spring'. But whether the Islamist 'alternative' will be able to reassert itself as a credible vehicle of opposition after the transition, in the late 1990s, from unrestrained to residual violence, remains to be seen.[104] What is more undoubtedly striking is the vigorous return, as of April 2001, of grassroots mobilisation, bypassing the political parties, centred on Kabylia, and expressing itself largely through 'Berberist' demands and symbols, but certainly articulating grievances and demands common to the broader population, as the most vocal expression of a civil society opposed to the perennisation of the status quo. Banners carried by demonstrators in Bejaïa, eastern Kabylia's main city, in June 2001, read: 'Regime, Islamists – one struggle against both' ('Pouvoir, Islamistes, même combat'). In the Kabyle *protesta*, a potentially democratic, pluralist

[101] Bourdieu, 'Social space', 201–2.
[102] Chaker, 'Langue et identité berbères' 173.
[103] *Ibid.*, 174.
[104] The fate of Ahmed Taleb Ibrahimi's Wafā' party – not legally recognised, and unlikely to be – is indicative of the intractability of the 'red line' henceforward banning a serious (however enlightened) Islamist opposition from the political arena, notwithstanding the toleration of the 'moderate', entryist parties, MSP/HAMAS (Ḥarakat mujtama' al-silm, Movement of Society for Peace (formerly Haraka li-mujtama 'islāmî, Movement for an Islamic Society)), MRN/Islah, Movement for National Renewal, and al-Nahda. One of the major successes of 'Abd al-'Aziz Bouteflika as president since 1999 has been the reabsorption of the ex-FIS' Islamist constituency into his own support base.

alternative re-emerged, mobilised around the issue of cultural and linguistic pluralism most obviously embodied in the 'Berber question', particularly among specifically Kabyle opponents of the system. This was no more because Kabyles are 'inherently democratic' than it was because Arabs are 'inherently despotic' – despite persistent tropes to this effect in the French media – but because of the contemporary configuration of the terms of an ongoing struggle over the nature of Algerian community and its expression in the institutions of the state.

In this struggle, a reinvigorated notion of Berber identity, reimagined in opposition to the doctrinaire unicity of Arab-Muslim nationalism, has become a powerful expression of dissidence. This struggle for self-definition and self-determination has been in part, no doubt, about exactly what it has claimed to be about: the right to exist as a community (of language, culture and history)[105] and to freedoms of expression and representation. This demand itself, however, also crystallises and vehicles grievances and concerns common to all Algerians: the cost of living, privatisation and unemployment, the allocation of state resources, the accountability of the security forces, and the experience of *hogra* ('contempt' shown by the rulers to the ruled, a recurring theme in ordinary Algerians' expression of their relationship to the state). The inability of the movement to spread significantly beyond Kabylia, and its internal failure to assume genuinely democratic forms, however, were most likely the result of the regime's effective management of the protests, and of the protestors' own self-isolation, as *specifically* Kabyle, or 'Berberist', dissidence – as a 'regionalism' threatening the unity of the nation on the one hand, and as an ethno-culturally specific, rather than political and generalised, mobilisation on the other.[106]

It is instructive to compare the insistent language of *berbérité* with other notions from previous centuries. Arab ancestry – sharifian, Himyarite or Hilali – was an eminently desirable and key feature of substantial social transformation in the medieval Maghrib, as noted earlier: 'At different times in different places, among literates and illiterates, townsmen and countrymen, princes and poor peoples, descent from all of these has been claimed . . . for the sake of prestige.'[107] The

[105] A red-haired young man with Amazigh signs painted on his face, interviewed in Algiers by French television in the summer of 2001, insisted: 'On existe, on veut exister officiellement' ('We exist, and we want to exist officially').

[106] The emergence of the *'aarush* (local delegations), whose deliberations excluded women, as the organising force of the protests, and the resort to violence and intimidation in enforcing the boycott of elections, undercut the claim to represent a genuine 'citizens' movement'.

[107] Brett, 'Ibn Khaldun and the Arabisation of the North Africa', 14.

numerous Arab genealogies of Berber groups reported by Ibn Khaldun are testimony to the flourishing industry in Mashriqi origin myths pursued by medieval Berber dynasties anxious to secure 'their place in known, legitimate History',[108] i.e. in history known in Islamic and Arab(ic) terms. The medieval Arabic literary *mafākhir al-barbar* ('glories of the Berbers') also valorised the *ahl al-Maghrib* (indigenous Maghribis) within the Arab and Islamic ecumene: the world is like a bird, says one anecdote, of which the Maghrib is the tail (the East the head, Iraq the chest, Syria and Yemen the wings) – a Maghribi in the assembly retorts: 'The bird is a peacock!'[109]

In the recent past of Algerian nationalism, 'the Berber question' served, too, as an idiom of contest and competition, not simply as a contest in itself. The PPA's 'Berberist crisis' of 1948–9, in which one faction of the party purged another under the indictment of 'Berberism' (condemned as a divisive, ethnic sub-nationalism) was, according to Harbi, initiated by 'criticism of the anti-democratic functioning of the party, [which later] spread to the rejection of the Arab-Islamic conception of Algeria, to finish by posing, under the cover of the question of cultural pluralism, that of the territorial organisation of the party on the basis of the criterion of language'.[110] In a highly sophisticated re-reading of this episode, Omar Carlier suggests that

> the Arab/Kabyle relation, which feeds the 'Arabism-Berberism' couple through which the protagonists of the 1949 crisis read their contradictions, and which belongs to a multisecular practice of spontaneous ethnology that colonial policy tried innumerable times to instrumentalise . . . in fact permits the illumination of an extreme complexity of relations of interaction and imbrication between the social, the cultural, and the political.[111]

It is thus neither an Arab nor a Berber 'authenticity' in itself that is at stake, but the terrain of legitimate self-definition and political representation that is contested, in ongoing processes of social struggle, through the cultural resources of historical imagination.

[108] Shatzmiller, 'Mythe d'origine berbère', 148. Shatzmiller argues, *pace* Brett, that such myths, tying 'the Berber' to 'the Arab' and Islam, 'remained the [exclusive] spiritual inheritance of a restricted [lettered, elite] sector of the population, the masses of which, in general, did not in any respect share it' (*ibid.*, 153). It would not, indeed, be surprising if the 'legitimate history' of the rulers were not congruent with the histories and self-identifications of the ruled, in any case at this period, although both Brett and Bourdieu suggest otherwise in this case.

[109] Anon., *Kitāb mafākhir al-barbar*, quoted in Norris, *Berbers in Arabic Literature*, xxiv.

[110] Harbi, 'Nationalisme algérien et identité berbère', 33.

[111] Carlier, 'Production sociale', 348.

Similarly, the specific socio-political and cultural situation of colonialism that framed the conditions of possibility and production of al-Madani's texts – the colonial knowledge that he both borrowed and contested, the social programme of pedagogy and 'renaissance' that he believed himself to be serving – provides the keys to an explanation of the particular ways in which he framed his own historical knowledge, presented as the 'true national past'. It is in relations of power and bids for power in the interconnected web of society, culture and politics that the *salafī* reading of 'the Berber' becomes illuminating. Al-Madani's refiguring of the Berber as national signifier, and his fixing of this figure in a historicised and superseded role, was an accomplished exercise in effective political cultural symbolisation. This reading of history was the foundation of a would-be legitimate definition of Algerian reality that has ever since been locked in the struggles of hegemonic process that have constituted the political life of independent Algeria. Analysis of this textual production reveals 'the *historicity* of an identity presumed to be originary, exclusive and cohesive, [and belies] the claims of those who would harden the boundaries of society in the name of cultural authenticity. This is an authenticity that lacks the capacity for tolerance and interdependence, because it will not admit of the Other within itself.'[112]

Such narratives of 'originary identity', in their struggle for legitimate representation of the historical real, fail ultimately by their own historicity. The impending language-death and ethnocide feared by the Berber poet-professor Mouloud Mammeri, an impoverishing assault on Algeria's plural reality, which he opposed and lamented as another 'absurd death of the Aztecs',[113] and which for al-Madani was already an accomplished historical destiny, has not in fact occurred. A newly reimagined Amazigh subjectivity is alive and more vocal than ever, expressing complex struggles and complex webs of interests, demands and desires.[114] In the symbols and narratives through which such expression occurs, surprising faces reappear. Among the articles in an Amazigh magazine produced in France in 1996, readers could discover 'My compatriot, Saint Augustine'.[115] Si Amar Boulifa's history of

[112] Duara, *Rescuing History*, 236.

[113] *La Mort absurde des Aztèques* (Paris, Perrin, 1973).

[114] See Silverstein, 'Martyrs and patriots', for the ongoing 'reinvention of Kabyle political subjectivity'.

[115] Wynna Nat Iraten, in *Tifinagh* 9, Spring 1996, 59–60. Anti-globalisation and autochthonous rights movements (Basque, Breton, native American sovereignty) in the 1990s have also influenced the morphology of the contemporary Berberist movement. The World Amazigh Congress's Brussels declaration of August 2000 (note 23 above)

Kabyle resistance and democratic struggle, *Le Djurdjura à travers l'histoire* of 1925, was republished by a small firm outside Algiers in 1999. The conflict over a legitimate definition of social reality continues, recreating, as it shifts into new phases, the categories through which is expressed 'l'aspiration à une Algérie réelle'.[116]

stressed that 'the Amazigh struggle is part of the vast movement of resistance to globalisation, which is a movement that is in essence against cultural identities'.

116 Youcef Rezzag, in *Le Matin*, 19 July 2001, after sixty days of rioting, to which security forces in Kabylia were again responding with live ammunition.

Epilogue: Algiers, 2001

In the first year of Algerian independence, an event of major symbolic significance took place in what had been the centre of old, pre-colonial Algiers. In a ceremony presided over by the minister of *habous*, Tawfiq al-Madani, the former colonial capital's cathedral was re-dedicated as a mosque. Four decades later, Ben Badis Square (ex-place Lavigerie), on whose western side the Ketchaoua Mosque, with its distinctive twin octagonal minarets facing the sea, stands behind its iron railings, is a busy area where small shops and street traders crowd in beneath the high arcades of colonial architecture along the roads that feed into what was still, until the 1930s, the heart of the city: rue Bab Azzoun, rue de la Lyre, rue Bruce.[1] The little square which formerly celebrated the proselytising archbishop of Algiers, now aptly renamed for shaykh Ben Badis, sits one block behind Martyrs' Square (sāḥat al-shuhadā / place des Martyrs), formerly Government Square, a parade ground carved out of the lower Casbah by French engineers in the first years of the conquest to remedy the lack of an open space sufficiently large for the orderly mustering of troops.

To make room for the ranks of the colonial army, one of Ottoman Algiers' finest buildings, the Sayyida Mosque, was demolished in 1831, as (later, after its partial destruction by fire) was the Janina palace, formerly the residence of the dey. The Ketchaoua Mosque, a few yards away up the gentle slope that, just beyond it, sharpens into the first of the Casbah's famous stairways, stood at the logistical and symbolic centre of the pre-colonial city, at the meeting-point of the roads that led from the lower Casbah out to the city's five gates, in a district of splendid family palaces occupied by the commercial and political élite of the Ottoman Regency. A mosque had stood on the site, according to some sources, since the fourteenth century, although the first extant attestation is a notarial act of 1612. The Ketchaoua was rebuilt, 'in unparalleled beauty' according to the commemorative inscription, by Hasan Pasha at the end

[1] Berque, *Maghreb entre deux guerres*, 16–17.

Figure 15. Place du Gouvernement, Algiers, early 1900s. The dome in the foreground is that of the Ottoman New Mosque (Jami'a al-jadid, known in French as the Mosquée de la pêcherie. The cathedral is in the right middle ground. The dome in the centre is the Synagogue. (Postcard, author's collection.)

of the eighteenth century. In 1832 it was consecrated as a church, which became the St Philippe Cathedral in 1838. In 1840, Marshal Valée, the conqueror of Constantine, had a cross placed atop the building.[2]

As colonial Algiers spread outwards across the hilltops inland to the districts of Bouzaréah, el-Biar and Hydra, and down the curve of coastline to the south-east, the centre of things moved from the old lower Casbah into newer European quarters further down the waterfront, to the tower block of the Government-General above the marble-paved expanse of the 'Forum', where de Gaulle would appear, arms outstretched in miraculous fraternity, in 1958, to announce that he had understood. . .[3] Today, the centres of power and decision are elsewhere, and Martyrs' Square, with its broken flagstones and subdued bandstand, its crowded, dusty bus station and crowded, dusty buses, its jostling press of small stallholders, has a certain air of worn-down, downward mobility. Few might suppose that the smaller, more modest Ben Badis Square behind it, a small opening between the ranks of colonial arcades marching along the waterfront and the condensed mass of the Casbah itself that rises up the hillside, might be a densely symbolic centre of contemporary Algiers. Compared to the grand sweep of boulevard Zighout Youcef where the National Assembly sits, the wooded heights of el-Mouradia, site of the presidential palace, or the commanding hilltop at Riyad al-Fath where a winding road leads up to the massive *maqām shahīd*, the Martyr's Memorial that dominates the skyline from the sea, the Ketchaoua in its crowded little square is not obviously a place of major symbolic importance.

It stands, nonetheless, as an exemplary site of memory, a monument in which the history of Algeria might be read. The mosque-turned-cathedral stood, through the colonial era, as a symbol of Algeria's alienation in the most basic sense – the ownership of a material estate appropriated by another. As a central sacred space, the Ketchaoua was, perhaps more importantly, symbolic of the alienation of Algerian culture, in the deeper sense of *becoming other*; of the conquest of a central cultural symbol by an invasive cultural and political system which transformed the meaning of the building and its function, as well as its physical fabric, in terms of a newly imposed code. In the aftermath of liberation, in the triumphant creation of a new historical memory of the nation-at-arms in reconquest of its sovereignty, the restitution of the Ketchaoua to Islam stood, correlatively, for the reconquest of Algeria's authenticity, as a supreme symbol of the nation's recovery of its integrity.

[2] Klein et al., *Feuillets d'El-Djezaïr*, 22–5; Çelik, *Urban Forms*, 19.
[3] The famous speech of 4 June 1958: 'Je vous ai compris. . .'.

Figure 16. The Ketchaoua Mosque as the St-Philippe Cathedral, early 1900s. (Postcard, author's collection.)

Figure 17. 'The Ketchaoua mosque recovered, supreme symbol of our aspirations.' (Illustration by Abu Bakr al-Sahrawi, cover of *al-Aṣāla*, May–August 1973, reproduced from Deheuvels, *Islam et pensée contemporaine en Algérie*. By permission of CNRS Editions.)

On the front cover of the May–August 1973 edition of the Ministry of Religious Affairs' official periodical review, *al-Aṣāla* ('Authenticity'),[4] there appeared a gorgeously coloured depiction, in the style of a fine, nostalgic miniature, of the Ketchaoua imagined in its pristine, pre-colonial splendour as a place of piety and learning. Above the illustration was printed, in calligraphy, a line by the poet Moufdi Zakarya: 'And the Ketchaoua mosque recovered, supreme symbol of our aspirations.'[5]

The 'time of corruption' whose advent the historian Ahmad al-Nasiri had perceived was thus at an end: the land, its sacred spaces, its history, culture and sovereign selfhood were recovered, and the future lay open for a revolutionary society to go on to the conquest of progress and freedom. In 2001, all that hope lay already in a far distant past. In the 1930s and 1940s, Algerian spokesmen had created a domain of liberty for themselves in the expression of their own personality, nationhood and citizenship, out of the space of their exclusion from the citizenship of the colonial state. But walking near the French embassy in Algiers, in the summer of 2001, I was stopped by someone who urgently inquired whether I happened to know if Algerians born before 1962 retained a right to French citizenship. For many Algerians in the 1990s, a French passport became a precious means of escape from the worsening crisis. The Ministry of Justice in Paris, at the same time, had a massive backlog of inquiries from Algerians seeking after 'naturalised' family members from the colonial period, whose imagined existence in the ex-metropole's records might furnish such an escape.[6]

Bourdieu, in his first work, echoed Berque's comments on 'the life of words' by remarking of the sociology of groups and toponyms in rural Algeria that it was a name, and the history of a name, that provided the central point for the articulation of group relations and cultural self-identification: 'The name in itself constitutes a [cohesive] power.'[7] In the immediate aftermath of independence, the struggle to define the meaning of newly independent Algeria, and of its victorious revolution, began. In August 1962, the Fédération de France du FLN, the revolutionary organisation in the ex-metropole which had itself suffered some of the struggle's worst internecine fighting as well as vicious state repression,[8]

4 Deheuvels, *Islam et pensée contemporaine*.

5 The line is taken from Zakarya's 'Algerian Iliad', *Nashīd al-anāshīd aw ilyādhat al-Jazā'ir*. Zakarya, the accredited poet of the revolutionary movement, was the author of 'Qassaman', Algeria's national anthem.

6 I am grateful to Laure Blévis for this point.

7 Bourdieu, *Sociologie de l'Algérie*, 86.

8 The struggle between the FLN and MNA was fiercest in France and Kabylia. Repression against the emigrant community reached its notorious peak with the massacre of 17 October 1961 in Paris.

issued a call for a secular constitution in the new republic, a proposal advanced by the committee charged with drafting the new constitution in Tripoli.[9] The AUMA had ceased to exist, but a declaration in the name of 'the *'ulamā* of Islam and the Arabic language' was published, protesting that the secularist proposal 'denies the very principles of our revolution'. The war over, it was time to ask why it had been embarked upon:

> If certain people were asked this question, the answers . . . would be diverse: we fought because we were oppressed and we refused humiliation, because we were impoverished and wanted wealth, because we were in tutelage and wanted sovereignty . . . We were unhappy and . . . wished to be happy . . . For ourselves, we say no to all of this . . . We are Algerians and this means that we are a people with its own personality. This personality appears in its language, its manners, its tradition, in its history.[10]

This conception of the purpose of the revolution, and of the overriding nature of Algeria's singular 'personality', announced in the first months of independence, is instructive. It was the reformists' investment in, and their claimed authority over, the crucial discursive resources of history and culture that gave them their symbolic strength relative to their rivals who lacked the cultural capital to claim this space as their own domain. The reformists had established a single, undifferentiated vision of Algeria's national 'selfhood', and this ideological *tawḥīd* in the fields of history and culture paralleled the ruthlessly unifying and centralising operations of the FLN in its birth from the factional struggles of the PPA/MTLD, in the unfolding of the revolution, and in the consolidation of the army's power in its aftermath. The reformists, with their centralising proselytism, their denunciation of cultural plurality and of the people's ignorance and incapacity for self-direction, had produced a propitious environment for the reinforcing of the political culture of monolithic, authoritarian and prescriptive unanimism that had emerged from the exigencies of clandestine political organisation and the prosecution of a revolutionary war. After independence, the regime would happily redeploy the reformists' 'national culture', under the banner of 'authenticity', as an instrument of control to assert the dominance of the 'unanimist' state in the religious and cultural fields. The reformists themselves, incongruously represented, in 1962, by their one leading personality in the councils of state, al-Madani on the steps of the Ketchaoua Mosque, were for the most part content to accept this state of affairs.

9 A secular constitution was favoured by the Tripoli programme committee, but Ben Bella quashed the proposal.

10 'Un Appel des ulemas de l'Islam et de la langue arabe au peuple algérien', *Dépêche d'Algérie*, 22 August 1962, repr. in *AAN* 1 (1962, second edn. 1972), 712.

Through their service to the FLN, beginning in Egypt and the Mashriq in 1956, they became part of the central apparatus of the republic.[11] Under Ben Bella, certainly, the ex-AUMA was suppressed, and Bashir al-Ibrahimi openly opposed the regime on his return from Cairo. Nonetheless, the overall trajectory, including that of those who found themselves dissidents from 1962 to 1965, was towards incorporation in the unitary apparatus of the state, not towards the creation of autonomous public spaces for religion, culture and self-expression.[12] In the new dispensation, the *'ulamā* remained 'dead' – they

> left empty the place of the *'ālim* whose duty is to speak the good and the ill in this world and the next . . . thinking that they themselves were the intermediaries *par excellence*, when they were bound hand and foot to the power of the state . . . More incorporated in the state than embodying the Qur'an, they . . . left empty this space, into which Islamism has flooded.[13]

This, of course, does not even begin to explain all that has occurred in Algeria since 1962, a task which is impossible here, and no part of my intention. The point has not been to establish another genealogy of contemporary Islamism, nor to account for Algeria's post-independence 'destiny' (which was never predestined), but to explore the ways in which the production of 'authentic selfhood' has itself been a bid for, and an instrument of, power, one whose failures have been as significant as its achievements. If the reformists created the cultural conditions for unitary, prescriptive definitions of post-colonial 'Algeria', it was more their failure – to re-establish an autonomous, depoliticised religious sphere, to construct an open public culture in competitive tolerance with other forces, both religious and secular, to preserve their own, and others', independence of thought, and, ultimately, to appreciate the part of colonial history that was their own inheritance – than their success that is represented in the turns taken by a politicised Algerian Islam since its restitution to sovereignty. What appears most clearly in the Algiers of a new century is the troubling inheritance of the necessary violence of revolutionary nationalist emancipation, and of the limits set to that emancipation, both by the political form it ultimately took, and by the cultural code in which it was expressed – the reformists' language of an invented authenticity.

[11] Colonna, *Versets de l'invincibilité*, 354, for the importance of the passage via Cairo.
[12] This sometimes ran counter to their intentions, notably in the incorporation of the reformists' cultural–educational apparatus into the state by the decree of 8 October 1977, which integrated the 'original education', *al-ta'līm al-aṣlī*, schools of the Ministry of Religious Affairs, the heirs of the AUMA schools of the 1930s–50s, into the purview of the Ministry of National Education (*ibid.*, 349–53).
[13] *Ibid.*, 356, 364.

The invention of authenticity

> I am a cultural hybrid. Cultural hybrids are monsters. Interesting monsters, but ones without a future. I therefore consider myself condemned by history . . . Why? Because the future is going to be made on the basis of a past which will be reappropriated, recovered, and we do not know what the projection of this past into the future will bring. Bear in mind that it may be that Algerians, in future, will indeed, collectively, be the sort of hybrid that I am. I do not know . . . Since one of the principal objectives of the Algerian revolution is to recover the Algerian selfhood [l'être algérien] occluded by colonisation, the past will be a significant force.
>
> Jean el-Mouhoub Amrouche[1]

An emblematic figure of our history: 'L'Algérie, c'est moi!'

Jean Amrouche said of nationalism that it was nothing but an 'expression of the tragic need to have a name. A name that is recognised, that one can fill.'[2] If a nationalist historian is, at least in his own conception of his practice and his intentions regarding its ends, the producer of the genealogy of that name, and of the meanings with which it is endowed, he is also himself remade in and through that very practice. His own historical subjectivity is produced in the recreative act of self-fashioning by which he objectifies and institutionalises the story of the past that, he declares, he shares with all those compatriots joined with him, through it, in a common community of origins, inheritance and destiny. The writer is not only a consciousness and agency prior to and outside writing – in writing history, conceived also as his story, through which his own place in the world is understood and in the telling of which his own position as spokesman of the truth of the community is established, he constitutes

[1] *Un Algérien s'adresse aux Français*, quoted in Liauzu, 'Disparition', 121.

[2] Amrouche, *Un Algerien s'adresse aux Français*, quoted in Liauzu, 'Disparition', 120. Amrouche (1906–62) remains an iconic figure of francophone and berberophone Algerian culture. His mother's autobiography (Fadhma Aït Mansour Amrouche, *Histoire de ma vie* (Paris, Maspero, 1968)) is also a primary document of Maghribi history. The mother and son, together with Jean's sister, the singer Marguerite Taos, form a celebrated trio of twentieth-century berberophone poets.

himself as a particular kind of individual, as the consciousness (or conscience) of 'his people' and agent of their 'self-awareness', the voice of their authenticity. The consciousness of this self-constitution is explicit in Tawfiq al-Madani's writing:

O Algerian Muslim, my friend, noble brother . . . You know, O Muslim youth, my friend, that I am not one of those who deceives his conscience, nor one of those who will sell their pens, nor one of those who say with their mouths what is not in their hearts. All that you read in this book proceeds in truth from integrity and sincere faithfulness – you will read here no burning criticism that does not truly stem from righteous honesty. I have said nothing but that which I firmly believe to be the truth, have given no opinion but that which I believe holds the good of this nation and [may serve to] lead it by the hand in the way of the universal Islamic renaissance.[3]

The nationalist historian sets himself up as the speaker of the nation's name, and in so doing takes that name upon himself, making himself the representative of the nation whose true story he tells. The *ego*, Husserl said, constitutes itself in the unity of a *Geschichte*[4] – a story, or history. 'The nation' is spoken of, and for, as the collective selfhood of dead, living and future generations tied together in the linear unity of a narrative, the ineluctable progress of the nation's self-manifestation.

Such a narrative seeks emancipation – the recognition of an active name speaking with its own dignity, in which people denied self-expression might finally escape from the repressive spaces of silence constituted for them by the fixing vision, language and laws of dominant others.

You are the son of heroes and in your veins runs the blood of the greatest of men, so raise high your Algeria and be glad because of her . . . And whenever people shout with acclamation of the life of their nations, then raise your head proudly, your heart full of glory and honour, and shout over the heads of the crowd in a voice that all might hear, 'Long Live Eternal Algeria!'[5]

The name thus proclaimed, however, is not simply that of a whole, homogeneous community wherein all think, and are, alike, nor is it an open field which every previously silenced voice can freely fill with his/her own meanings. 'The nation' is a contested space, a terrain of conflict between competing claims for hegemony. The resources of meaning-creation are not equally distributed – each would-be spokesman seeks to shape the world through a particular 'legitimate language', a particular order

[3] Al-Madani, *Kitāb al-Jazā'ir*, 373.
[4] *Cartesian Meditations*, quoted in Carr, *Time, Narrative and History*, 104; cf. Ricoeur, *La Mémoire, l'histoire, l'oubli*, esp. part 3, 'La condition historique', and his 'Life in quest of narrative'.
[5] Al-Madani, *Kitāb al-Jazā'ir*, 373.

of words. The emancipatory name is formed and expressed in, and bound around with, very specific forms of language, words seeking to structure the world, to imagine community, past and present, in a specific, programmatic way. Such language cannot be equally articulated by everyone. If it frames and enables a new way of acting in and on the world, it also imposes forms and frameworks that define and limit the meanings of 'self' in new ways.[6]

Some forms are more successful than others in the struggle for dominance. If no hegemony is ever total, much less final, the words that come to form and fill the social world nonetheless have a definite shape, a syntax, accidence, and range of meanings bound up in the social struggle to speak with authority. Languages of history and selfhood become effective as they are institutionalised as discursive formations shaping and shaped by the material conditions of actual social life – that is, as they themselves acquire material form in social and cultural practices, the disciplining of minds and bodies, the rituals of religion and state, the policing of boundaries and enforcement of laws. As such, they enter into the web of forces and resources by and through which the order of the social world is made and constantly reproduced; they enter into the complex of 'durable dispositions' and unchosen conditions into which new generations of men and women are born and have to make history. The emancipatory name of 'nation' may be forever reappropriated, remade as a new cry for freedom, but it may equally become one more, particularly powerful, sign of the tradition that weighs down, inescapable as a nightmare, on the mind of the living.

Jean Amrouche, poet, 'one hundred percent Algerian in [his] blood', of Kabyle parents and 'the greater Muslim family' but brought up in Catholicism, whose 'first language' was French but whose mother tongue was not ('I can only weep in Kabyle'), was also one of those 'who worked for [Algeria's] emancipation, if sometimes with an awareness that it would condemn them'.[7] With heartbreaking acuity, Amrouche saw his own condemnation by history in the very 'recovery' of the Algerian past that he saw manifested in the revolution, in the assertion of an Algerian selfhood that colonialism had occluded and

[6] Such frameworks are, of course, subverted and inflected, the power exercised through them contested, as James C. Scott's work has shown. The point is reinforced, though, in that the arts of resistance have to operate *in terms* of the system shaping the world within which people act. There is no autonomous space of pure freedom beyond the realm of power – rather, every point in the system is at once a point of enforcement and contention.

[7] Liauzu, 'Disparition', 113.

Figure 18. Speaking for the nation: Tawfiq al-Madani at Cairo University, 1 November 1960. (From al-Madani, *Ḥayāt Kifāḥ*, vol. III.)

denied but that was soon to irrupt into life as a vision of the past hurled into the future.

Among the spokesmen of that particular past/future, Tawfiq al-Madani, orator for the FLN in Cairo and Baghdad, minister of culture and religious affairs in its first provisional government and later in Ben Bella's first cabinet, ambassador for his country throughout the Middle East, could surely not have seemed more different. He had created himself as the speaker of the nation's past and true self; its first major historian, instigator of the founding of the AUMA, awakener of Algeria when it slept, he who had 'made a school of his thought', whose whole life had been the struggle of the nation. It was he – so he declares – who, in 1936, in response to Ferhat Abbas's 'La France c'est moi!', wrote the *kalima ṣarīḥa*: 'For our part, we have consulted the pages of history, and we have consulted present circumstances, and we have found the Algerian Muslim nation.'[8] He, almost exactly twenty years later, would serve as translator for Ferhat Abbas's adherence to the revolution, a

[8] Merad speaks initially of 'a solemn declaration of the reformist leadership', noting that the article is unsigned (*Réformisme*, 398), but elsewhere lists the text among Ben Badis's

revolution that neither man had wanted or made but that would itself be narrated in a language that al-Madani spoke – one of perennial struggle, heroic martyrdom and unanimous destiny. Abbas had been 'mistaken', and Amrouche was a monstrous 'error of history'; al-Madani was the voice of Algeria's reconquest of itself. He had diagnosed its mortal ignorance ('The Arab sons of Algeria are totally ignorant. . . But they do not live, who live ignorant. . .'), remedied it by placing the truth before the people's eyes and in their hands ('. . . here am I to prepare the way for you, that you might be able to undertake the study of your homeland . . . *I place your country in your grasp*. . .'[9]). He prophesied the coming 'glorious day' at the very foot of the Aurès days before 1 November, close to where the FLN's first armed actions would take place: 'Pointing to the lofty Aurès . . . as if prophesying what was shortly to occur, [I said]: "From these proud mountains, the raging voice of the people has arisen for thousands of years, to eradicate the oppression of tyrants and destroy the might of the occupier." It was a true prophecy'.[10]

Al-Madani's *Life of Struggle* announced him as the integral spokesman of the nation: 'I was created a revolutionary. Wherever revolution was, there was I. And wherever I was, there was revolution . . . I realised . . . the independence of the nation . . . *I was born on the first of November*'.[11] Incarnation of the nation's history, a son of unyielding resistance who never himself ceased to resist, guardian of the pure Arabic language and of pure Islamic culture, emblematic figure of a *salafi* 'Algeria' whose life was devoted to returning the people to their ancestral grandeur, al-Madani's own self-view, as he writes it, is thoroughly heroic, thoroughly *self-same*.

own writings (*Ibn Badis*, 240). Al-Madani (*HK*, II, 61–3) gives his account of the text's origins in a conversation between himself and Ben Badis, claiming its authorship for himself. He notes that, Julien (*L'Afrique du Nord en marche*) having attributed it to Ben Badis, others had followed this assertion. The truth of the matter is probably unimportant; al-Madani might well have penned the article, but it was in any case intended as a collective statement. What is interesting is his later claim on the text as part of his own self-representation.

9 Al-Madani, *Jughrāfiyya*, preface.

10 Al-Madani, *HK*, II, 410–11, emphasis added. The speech was made at the opening of a reformist school in Batna. Al-Madani says that the event took place in October 1954. Reports mentioning the ceremony give the date as 5–6 September ('L'Association des oulama d'Algérie', Synthèse des renseignements généraux, Direction de la Sûreté nationale en Algérie, Algiers, 26 Oct. 1955 no. 6442SNA/RG3 (45 pp. plus appendices), ADA/4I/14/1, pp. 7, 14, 24).

11 Al-Madani, *HK*, I, 5, 8, 13. 'L'Association des oulama', (note 10 above), Annexe VI, gives his date of birth as 16 June.

The sovereignty of our truth

> 'All these questions of *identity*, as we so foolishly say nowadays . . . Our question is still identity. What is identity, this concept of which the transparent identity to itself is always dogmatically presupposed by so many debates on monoculturalism and multiculturalism, nationality, citizenship, and, in general, belonging?
>
> Jacques Derrida[12]

Tawfiq al-Madani's 'self-generating', and simultaneously self-effacing, autobiography reflects something about his historiography, and the broader project within which both were situated, namely the creation, and institutionalisation in a new legitimate language of history and culture, of a 'rediscovery of ourselves', forging individual and collective nationalist subjectivities, produced from reworked and reappropriated cultural materials, endowed with particular, prescriptive, meaning, and erasing the 'inadmissible' complexities and uncertainties that had in fact constituted them. As the composition of *Ḥayāt Kifāḥ* reinvented its subject, casting his life as a linear, heroic epic and smoothing out its inconvenient complications, so *Kitāb al-Jazā'ir* and other works illustrate a broader reinvention of the meaning of 'Algeria'. Not that these texts themselves (as in the straightforward reading of cultural nationalism to which I objected at the outset) actually changed Algerian society, either by 'awakening the nation' or by imprisoning it. Their reception was limited and their direct influence, on the whole, and with the exception of certain specific questions (such as that of Berber origins discussed in chapter 5), marginal at best. Their importance lies rather in the extent to which the shape of newly authoritative historical and cultural imaginations, brought about by the vast and complex effects of colonialism, modernism, Islamic reform and war, are legible in the stories they tell. Their narratives, like the much vaster cultural changes involved in the production of the nation and its 'truth', are closed, doctrinaire narratives of destiny.

All kinds of futures hung in the realm of the realisable for a new, liberated Algeria, 'this land, henceforward free and rich in every possibility' as the young, revolutionary intellectual Mostefa Lacheraf called his country in 1963.[13] At the same time, he warned that 'we have not been colonised with impunity; we have not been deprived . . . for 130 years without feeling the consequences . . . our cultural problems must therefore be handled with the greatest care'.[14] Not only, in fact, had

[12] Derrida, *Monolingualism*, 10, 14.
[13] Lacheraf, 'L'Avenir de la culture algérienne', 740.
[14] *Ibid.*, 739.

colonialism – triumphalist rhetorics of purity to the contrary – had real effects, fashioned a profoundly different 'Algeria' to the one(s) whose world(s) had ended after 1830, but the struggles to reconquer 'Algeria', to remake it in a new image, were unable to permit the free opening of that space, of that name, to the liberation of its new citizens' free self-determination, in either the cultural or political spheres.

Massively complex, internecine plays of power had necessarily gone into the making and sustaining of the revolution; they would persist in the making of its state. In assessing the relationship of the *salafiyya* movement, and its durable consequences, to nationalism and the revolution, it is not sufficient to posit a 'contribution' – however one assesses that posited contribution – that would be falsely embodied in a totalising scheme under the controlling, unidirectional closure of 'the national movement'. The revolutionary movement was made, and for the most part made its revolution, without the *'ulamā*. Within this delicate and violent game, the reformists managed to preserve themselves by rallying to the just cause at the opportune time. They also held cards that others did not. Their struggle to gain recognition as the spokesmen for Islam and 'national culture', Islam and 'the national past', Islam and 'the national personality', and their mastery of that language, meant that, to a certain extent – and if only, in the intentions of at least some among its leadership, for pragmatic, instrumental reasons – the revolution did have to 'abide by the terms of their requirements', had to accept their definition of 'national identity', culture and belonging.

Nothing symbolised this more strikingly than al-Madani's place at the Cairo microphone, at the side of Ferhat Abbas – or, for that matter, of Ahmed Ben Bella, of whose Arabic he was patronisingly scathing.[15] More than simply an eloquent tongue in which the (dialectically incomprehensible) revolutionary Maghrib could speak, with appropriately classical modulation, to its Mashriqi brothers, however, al-Madani expressed the newly legitimate cultural and intellectual language of pure, recovered, Arab-Islamic Algeria. The FLN's concession (in the commercial sense) to the reformists, after the revolutionary movement had successfully superseded and broken up the AUMA, absorbing its most useful elements into its own ranks, under its own discipline, was the field of cultural and religious authority in which the *salafi*s had most invested before things had got out of hand. The imperatives of the war tied them inextricably to the FLN and its state, within whose mythically unifying history they would henceforward have to reimagine themselves.

[15] Al-Madani, *HK*, III, 124.

The franchise they gained, however, on authorised versions of national personality, history and culture, if not the most obviously lucrative aspects of the enterprise, gave them considerable control of the symbolic capital that the AUMA had amassed before 1954, and that the ALN *maquisards* would greatly multiply in their own radically Jacobin, mobilising deployment of Islam as Algeria's code of revolutionary purity and solidarity.[16]

Some of the radical austerity of this Islam might well have discomfited Tawfiq al-Madani, who had worked for a tobacco company, who wrote plays (while also sitting on the Algiers Prefecture's censorship committee for the Opéra's Arabic season), who, like other leading reformists, sent his children to French schools, and who was famously reputed to be fond of whisky. After independence, as an energetic minister of religious affairs, said to have created seventeen different Islamic institutions of state, he was lampooned by sterner *salafi*s as *tnāfiq al-madāni*, 'al-Madani the hypocrite'. It was even recognised *argot* in the well-heeled districts of Algiers to 'commander un toufiq' when asking one's host for whisky. He, nonetheless, was himself a speaker of the language of purified self-knowledge, and perhaps he later felt the need to live down the reputation: writing his memoirs in the mid-1970s, he chose to highlight a canonical abstemiousness, reproducing *in extenso* his first newspaper article of 1914: 'Alcohol is the first minister of death'.[17]

The monumental document of al-Madani's life – the very fact of his writing three volumes is indicative – clearly seeks to constitute, in the minds of his readers a generation after 1954, the author's life as an integral narrative of the nation's struggle to rediscover and realise itself/its self. Its episodic construction, placing in successive spotlights his presence at the key places, interviews with the leading figures and action in the watershed events of colonial history and nationalism, the constant intercalation of 'proof-texts' (letters, photographs, reproduced articles), the word-for-word reported conversations and correspondence of forty or fifty years previously with the journalistic, political and religious leaders of the Arab world serve to bear out the truth of the book's title, establishing the author's name 'among the names of those who have struggled and fought [for the nation] in their different ways, names that

[16] Kamel Chachoua observes that in Kabylia the ALN 'did more to propagate the reformist spirit than did the movement's own principal institution, the *médersa*' (*Islam kabyle*, 251–5, 269). The instrumental deployment of Islam as disciplinary code was also particularly marked in the Fédération de France, whose later, belated rallying to the secular constitutional proposal at Tripoli therefore rang rather hollow (Harbi interview, Paris, 2004).

[17] Al-Madani, *HK*, I, 69–70.

future generations might perhaps hear'[18] – fixing his legitimate place in history.

That history was one which, against all expectations, especially those of the *'ulamā*, had eventually been made by workers, peasants and shopkeepers, and in which the learned doctors of religion themselves had had to scramble for a place to rescue what they could of what they had supposed to be their natural social authority. 'The land', al-Madani believed, 'had been emptied of its true guides', and '*the salvation of Islam and of the nation was an absolute duty that had been laid upon my shoulders*'.[19] To substantiate that unlikely claim, an exorbitant influence had to be ascribed to the reformist movement, one significantly other than that which it had really had, or wished to have. Rivals, opponents of the revolutionary movement for leadership of the community in the social struggles of pre-revolutionary Algeria, the AUMA, and particularly Ben Badis, became after 1962 the acknowledged 'spiritual leaders' of the revolution they had mostly not wanted. This suited the new rulers who had emerged from the *jaysh* (the ALN) of the frontiers, eclipsing the indigestible heritage of Messali and the unforgivable 'assimilationism' of Abbas along with those 'brothers' of the interior maquis who – if not dead and safely sanctified – had had to be suppressed in the hot and bloody summer of 1962. It also suited the ex-AUMA leaders and their *protégés* returning from universities in the Mashriq, where they had spent the revolution imbibing heady notions of *'urūba* (Arabism, Arab-ness) and Ba'thist pan-Arab ideals. From their new seats on the margins of power they could, at last, exercise the sovereignty of their truth through the organs and institutions of state. The dominant language of history and culture, in the public domain, would be substantially spoken in the *salafi* idiom of a rediscovery of ancestral purity, 'authenticity' and *thawābit*, 'les constantes nationales'. Even so heterodox and cosmopolitan a character as al-Madani (Tunisian, Ottomanist, 'anticolonialist Frenchman',[20] pan-Maghribi idealist, scholar, playwright, journalist. . .) not only could not escape the power of this narrative, but sought to make himself its epitome.

The perhaps neglected potency of this language was that it provided a means for closing off the creative possibilities of newly liberated Algeria in the restatement of a dominating, total societal 'truth', an authentic substantial 'Algeria' that would insist that Algerians be, not what they might freely, creatively wish to become through the constant recreation

[18] *Ibid.*, 8.
[19] *Ibid.*, 24, emphasis added.
[20] Personal communication.

of their own religious, linguistic, artistic and historical imaginations, but what the 'deep reality' of (newly invented) ancestral tradition showed they 'truly were'. Barely freed from the fixing essence imposed by colonialism, Algerians could be immediately reimprisoned in another, imposed this time by dogmatic definitions operating in the name of their own ancestors. In the political culture of the new state, already under Ben Bella but more markedly after 1965, the reformists' religious *tawḥīd* ('unicity') served as the model for a political community in which 'diversity of status and opinion is denounced as deviance . . . Community is placed under the sign of unicity while society itself unceasingly produces diversity.'[21] While 'national culture' was enthroned as sovereign at the 'centre', the local specificities of culture, language and history were silenced, their own creative potential suffocated, by the impossibility of democratic debate between mutually respected, autonomous voices,[22] leaving the field of culture, and cultural politics, to competing, and culturally impoverished, authoritarianisms. It was not even, in fact, that a single, coherent and 'genuinely' national (i.e. common) culture was created out of the cultural 'patchwork' that was pre-colonial and 'French' Algeria – the patchwork was torn up and never reassembled.[23] The culture of nationalism may have ended up simply as absence, and the rhetoric of authenticity. But the rhetoric was powerful enough.

Was this, then, already Algeria recolonised? As another child of colonial Algeria has it: 'All culture is originarily colonial . . . Every culture institutes itself through the unilateral imposition of some "politics" of language. Mastery begins, as we know, through the power of naming, of imposing and legitimating appellations.'[24] The *salafī* project aimed precisely at authority over the name, and the meaning of the name, of 'Algeria'. To establish this authority in the present, its spokesmen hoped to reappropriate the past – a pristine, uncontaminated and homogenising past – and, as Amrouche foresaw, to project it into the future, into which future he could not see, but in which he could not see himself. Lacheraf, also passionately concerned with Algerian culture and Algerian emancipation, knew precisely what part had been played by whom in the making of the revolution. He looked forward to the disappearance of self-legitimisation with regard to it, 'now that the revolution . . . has equalised everyone's opportunities and everyone's merits . . . [in] a

[21] Carlier, 'D'une guerre à l'autre', 134.
[22] Colonna, *Versets de l' invincibilité*, 68–9; Colonna, 'The nation's "Unknowing Other"', 163–7; Benrabah, 'Arabisation and creativity'.
[23] The image is Mohamed Harbi's (interview, Paris, 2004).
[24] Derrida, *Monolingualism*, 39.

genuinely collectivist society whose untapped resources are within our grasp and require rather the serene and effective conquest of the future and of progress than the fraudulent return to a past on whose basis the messianisms of certain groups wish to perpetuate themselves'.[25]

And he warned that 'what messianism projects into the future is not an emanation, a logical consequence of the present, but a past restored in its presumed authenticity'.[26] This language of 'presumed authenticity', the *salafi* conception of a national past to which al-Madani's texts give an early expression, despite this 'eminently likeable man'[27] and his joyously human contradictoriness, in spite, almost certainly, of his own intentions, would impose on Algeria a conception of itself that repressed the extraordinary diversity of its history and culture in a fraudulent 'return' to a single, newly created and artificial (in Derrida's term, 'prosthetic') origin. This 'authenticity' was in fact its exact opposite, an *alienation* of Algerians from their own imaginations of themselves, fixing them into a closed and homogeneous destiny, fabricating a new (and dangerous) collective memory of purity and exalted struggle,[28] forgetting diversity with 'division', complexity with 'collaboration', and producing a society not only victimised by colonialism but also 'culturally ransacked by its own voluntary amnesia.'[29]

'. . .And they have not been changelings who change'[30]

> . . .as if, more than by its content, an ensemble were to be defined by its sign.
>
> Jacques Berque[31]

This language of authenticity, like the conditions of its production and most vividly like Tawfiq al-Madani, was itself, no less than the poetry and person of Jean, Fadhma or Taos Amrouche, a child of the colonial world. Albert Hourani's classic work on Arab cultural and intellectual history spoke implicitly, just after Algeria's independence was realised, of modernity as a power-complex 'by the very nature of its institutions compelling men to live in a certain way',[32] and of the complex relationship between such compulsion and the traditions of all those dead generations, inherited, reinterpreted and continuously, innovatively

[25] Lacheraf, *Algérie, nation et société*, 43.
[26] *Ibid.*, quoting Vladimir Jankélevitch, *Tradition et traditionalisme: Le mythe de l'origine.*
[27] Lacheraf interview, Algiers, 2001.
[28] Soufi, 'Fabrication d'une mémoire'; Remaoun, 'Pratiques historiographiques'.
[29] Personal communication.
[30] 'Wa-mā baddalū tabdīlan' (Q 33.23), epigraph to al-Madani, *HK*, I.
[31] Berque, 'Ça et là dans les débuts du réformisme', 494.
[32] Hourani, *Arabic Thought*, 161.

reproduced. This relationship and its difficulties, in whatever manifestation, have continued to provide the focus of much study of the contemporary history and politics of North Africa and the Middle East – indeed, of the formerly colonial world more generally, wherever it has been thought that 'events . . . have been translations of a basic cultural debate over the value of a leap to "modernity" versus a return to "authenticity" as a model for polity and society'.[33] Zartman suggests that it is the dialectical relationship between these two terms, seeking viable synthesis, that is the key to cultural debate and political dynamics in such societies and states.[34] But 'authenticity' is not a condition of being, nor even a slogan of self-sufficiency; not the persistent longevity of ancestors constantly returning with redoubled ferocity, nor a 'substantial self' immutably true at its point of origin to which present generations are constantly summoned to return. There is no fixed pole of 'tradition' in the past corresponding to another of 'modernity' in the present, between which extremes two-thirds of the world would somehow be caught forever in an irresolvable flux. 'Authenticity' is itself an invention of thought in the colonial world, an expression of the dislocating stresses of modern power on cultural and political practices of self-understanding and worldview, languages of truth, value and legitimacy, that are forever transformed in a radically reordered world.

'The West' and modernity, after the conquest, are inescapable, pervasive, insidious. But, precisely through their cataclysmic thoroughness, they no longer stand over 'the non-West' as 'an absolute and devastating exteriority, nor as an eternal mastery'.[35] To suppose so would merely be to reproduce the old, monologic account of the West's sovereign agency, the 'narcissistic projection of the Western will to power'.[36] Instead, in Asia and Africa 'Europe . . . troubles our intimate being . . . inhabits it as a difference, a conglomerate of differences'[37] through which (i.e. both *by means of*, and *to cope with*, which) people in the colonial world themselves have struggled, acted and spoken. Nationalism did not arise from some ancient and indestructible life-force drawn from inexhaustible, secret wells of perennial Being, 'this will-to-be rooted in the depths of time'. 'Authenticity' did not precede 'modernity'. It was an artefact painstakingly created, a doctrine elaborated out of the differences and divisions opened up in the social world, in political order and cultural

[33] Zartman, 'Political dynamics', 20.
[34] *Ibid.*, 35.
[35] Khatibi, *Maghreb pluriel*, 12.
[36] Wolfe, 'History and imperialism', 412.
[37] Khatibi, *Maghreb pluriel*, 11–12.

hierarchy, in conceptions of civilisation and science, in the mapping out of space and time, by the operations of modern, colonial power itself. Algerians, like Indians and Africans, took up their 'native status' and the idioms in which it was defined, and reworked it: *la personnalité algérienne*, *Hindutva*, *négritude*. Established cultural forms and the internalised gaze of the coloniser were refigured together and put back into circulation in new forms, as the authentic past of the nation that pointed the way to its modern future. In a radically reshaped world, such practices seeking anchorage, seeking 'the consoling play of recognitions',[38] all too naturally expressed themselves as authenticity/'originarity' (*aṣāla*), as bearers of inalienable heritage (*turāth*), as the recovery of the past and the return to it (*salafiyya*). Historians should see through such cultural artefacts and recognise them for what they are:

> The return to the past is either the return to something so remote that it has to be reconstructed, a 'rebirth' or 'renaissance' . . . or, more likely, a return to something that never existed at all, but has been invented for the purpose . . . Nationalism could not conceivably be a return to a lost past . . . It had to be revolutionary innovation masquerading as restoration. It had, in effect, to invent the history it claimed to bring to fruition.[39]

As we began by recalling, the past 'does not shape the present simply by *persisting* in it. It enables the transformation of the present and in that transformation is itself much transformed.'[40]

As the expression of a past reimagined and suffused with sacred splendour, as the site of the community's lost 'true self', the *salafiyya* claimed to bring a message of unrefusable reality, the 'deep reality' of community and selfhood to which, if they were to be truly free, Algerians must be true. They too might have said: 'The narration of reality ("le récit des faits réels") is for us a matter of doctrine.' But as de Certeau insists, 'such a narrative deceives because it wishes to impose its own law in the name of "reality" '.[41] The *salafīs*' narrative of national self was not the revelation of ancient truth but the making of a new law, ready to rush in and fill Algeria's future with the meanings of 'messianism'. They could not have foreseen – al-Madani perhaps least of all – what such a language of unrefusable truth would become in the context of the social, political, demographic and economic crises of Algeria's 1980s and 1990s. The 'resurgence' of a radical Islamism and the terrible forms

38 Foucault, 'Nietzsche, genealogy, history'.
39 Hobsbawm, *On History*, 34–5.
40 Duara, *Rescuing History*, 76.
41 De Certeau, *L'Ecriture de l'histoire*, 5.

taken by its new contests (and the manipulation and repression of those contests) were not inevitable results of their doctrines. Nonetheless, 'we know, henceforth, that no society can cultivate the myth of purity and remain unscathed'.[42] This statement should be all the more forceful in light of the fact that the very discourses which most stridently speak of 'authenticity', when examined for a moment, reveal themselves to be, not echoes of time immemorial, but contingent practices of creation, dyed through with their own historicity, assembled from the complex products of history's collisions and transformations. The call to singular purity itself speaks in dissonance and heteroglossia.

Al-Madani numbered himself among those who had held fast, through the alienations of history, to originary truth, one of those who 'have not been changelings who change'. Such stress laid on Algerian changelessness, unanimism and unitary selfhood was itself perhaps an enabling condition of liberation. It was also a convenient means of outlawing pluralities, of occluding possible futures. Now more than ever we might seek to recognise in Algeria, and in the Maghrib, not some unitary 'national identity', however defined, but 'the active plurality of its utterances'.[43] Historians above all, Berque said, should not be labouring to predict what has passed, but should 'seek in the aborted, hidden past the multiple possibilities of yesterday and today'[44] that Mostefa Lacheraf saw abounding at the dawn of independence. If it is true that the tradition of the dead generations has seemed to weigh nightmarish on Algeria, speaking to new generations in authoritarian, demagogic and utopian tones instead of enabling the creative, and inescapably complex, transformation of its future, Algerians are not thereby condemned forever grotesquely to repeat the tragedies of their forebears. Novelist Yasmina Khadra observes that 'we are accustomed to hear Algerians only through their sobbing',[45] but their futures, too, are open, can still be conquered in a new polyphony of expression, in newly creative words creating new, and freer, histories. 'The history of people is first of all that of words'.[46] Abdallah Laroui wrote: 'The only antidote to tradition is hope, that is, the perspective of an open future – and that is the profound meaning of revolution, whatever name it may bear.'[47]

[42] Liauzu, 'Disparition', 121.
[43] Khatibi, 'Diglossia', 158.
[44] Quoted in Liauzu, 'Disparition', 120.
[45] Roundtable at the MMSH, Aix-en-Provence, 29 April 2002.
[46] *Ibid.*
[47] Laroui, *Crise des intellectuels arabes*, 57–8.

Archival sources

France

Centre des Archives d'Outre Mer, Aix-en-Provence

- *Archives du Gouvernement Général de l'Algérie*

Series H: Affaires musulmanes

1H Affaires extérieures: Arabic press and brochures, 1914–18
9H Police: political surveillance, 1877–1946
10H Etudes et notices (education, *madrasa*s, AUMA etc.), 1931–40
11H Political situation: periodical reports, 1914–56
15H Periodical analysis of the Algerian press, 1935–56
25H Tunisia: political questions, 1923–46
26H Tunisia: press, 1934–60
29H Muslim countries: notes, press, 1914–18; pan-Islamism, 1920–44

Series X: Acquisitions diverses (private papers, print, ephemera)

9X Press and printed brochures

- *Archives du Département d'Alger*

Series I: Administration des indigènes

2I Reports from *Communes mixtes*, 1889–1956, Muslim associations, censorship, press, theatres, religious affairs, mosques, etc., 1910–62
4I CIE and successors: Muslim associations, Muslim Congress, cultural life, theatre, mosques, education, press and publications, political parties and movements, 1923–61

- *Archives du Département de Constantine*

Series B: Cabinet du Préfet

B2 Sûreté générale: police reports, 1875–1914
B3 Affaires indigènes: press and publications, Muslim associations, cultural and political movements and parties, religious affairs, students and intellectuals, AUMA, 1875–1940

• *Library – press and periodicals*

Alger républicain, Attakadoum/le Progrès, al-Baṣā'ir, La Défense, L'Echo indigène, L'Entente, L'Ikdam, al-Islāḥ, al-Muntaqid, al-Najāḥ, al-Shihāb, La Voix indigène

Bibliothèque nationale de France, Paris

• *Press and periodicals*

Alger républicain, al-Najāḥ, L'Ikdam, al-Shihāb, al-Muntaqid

Ministère des affaires étrangères; Archives diplomatiques, Nantes

• *Fonds Tunisie, 1er versement*

Grandchamps papers

Tunisia

National Archives, Tunis

• *Archives Générales du Gouvernement Tunisien*

Series MN: Mouvement national (classification in progress)

Institut supérieur de l'Histoire du Mouvement national, La Manouba

• *Fonds du Quai d'Orsay (ISHMN/MAE), 1882–*

Fonds nominatifs (private papers): Augustin Bernard papers

Series K, Afrique, 1918–40: Affaires musulmanes

Series n.s. Tunisie, 1882–1917: Press, 1906–11, Zaytuna, political movements, press, censorship, 1911–16

Series Guerre 1914–18: Affaires musulmanes, German–Ottoman propaganda effort

Series Tunisie 1917–40: Sûreté publique, control of travel, expulsions, internments, 1917–29, Dustur, delegations, press, 1919–20, biographical notices, Dusturi delegations to France, 1920–24, press and publications, 1917–29

• *Fonds de la Résidence Générale de France à Tunis (ISHMN/Résidence), 1920–56*

(n.s.)1700–4: Police, Dustur, war in the Rif, 1921–6

(n.s.)1712: Algerian and Tunisian nationalists, press, 1934–8
(n.s.)2242: Dusturi press, biographies of Dusturi leaders, 1925–8

Algeria

Archives of the wilaya *of Constantine*

- *Press and periodicals*

al-Shihāb, *L'Entente franco-musulmane*

- *'Archives saisies' (perquisitions in the aftermath of 8 May 1945)*

Papers of shaykh Muhammad al-Ghassiri

Archives of the wilaya *of Oran*

Series I: Affaires musulmanes
Muslim private education, Qur'anic schools, 1877–1931; AUMA local activity, 1944–61

Bibliography

Abbas, Ferhat *La Nuit coloniale,* Julliard, 1962
Autopsie d'une guerre: l'aurore Paris, Garnier, 1980
De la colonie vers la province. Le Jeune Algérien Paris, Garnier, 1981 (2nd edn) [Paris, La Jeune Parque, 1931]
L'Indépendance confisquée Paris, Flammarion, 1984
Abrams, Philip 'Notes on the difficulty of studying the state', *J. Hist. Sociol.* 1, 1 (March 1988) [1977]: 58–89
Ageron, Charles-Robert 'Le Mouvement "Jeune Algérien" de 1900 à 1923', in Jacques Berque et al., *Etudes maghrébines: Mélanges Charles-André Julien* Paris, PUF, 1964, 217–43
'L'Emir Khaled, petit-fils d'Abdelkader, fut-il le premier nationaliste algérien?', *ROMM* 2 (2nd semester 1966): 9–49
'L'Emigration des musulmans algériens et l'exode de Tlemcen (1830–1911), *AESC* 22, 3 (1967): 1047–66
Les Algériens musulmans et la France, 1871–1919 (2 vols.), Paris, PUF, 1968
'Ferḥat 'Abbās et l'évolution politique de l'Algérie musulmane pendant la deuxième guerre mondiale', *Rev. Hist. Maghr.* 4 (July 1975): 125–44
'Du mythe kabyle aux politiques berbères', in Moniot et al., *Le Mal de voir,* 331–48
Histoire de l'Algérie contemporaine, vol. II: *De l'insurrection de 1871 au déclenchement de la guerre de libération (1954)* Paris, PUF, 1979
'L'Algérie algérienne' de Napoléon III à de Gaulle Paris, Sindbad, 1980
'Lectures du nationalisme algérien', *Relations internationales* 28 (Winter 1981): 515–24
'Pour une histoire critique de l'Algérie de 1830 à 1962', in Charles-Robert Ageron (ed.), *L'Algérie des Français* Paris, Seuil, 1993, 7–13
'Un Manuscrit inédit de Ferhat Abbas: "Mon testament politique"', *Revue française d'histoire d'Outre Mer* 303 (1994): 181–97
(ed.) *La Guerre d'Algérie et les Algériens, 1954–1962* Paris, Armand Colin, 1997
Ained-Tabet, Rédouane 'Manuels d'histoire et discours idéologique véhiculé', in Ghalem and Remaoun (eds.), *Comment on enseigne l'histoire en Algérie,* 35–45
Ained-Tabet, Rédouane and Colonna, Fanny (eds.) *Lettrés, intellectuels et militants en Algérie, 1880–1950* Algiers, OPU, n.d. [1988]
Alazard, Jean et al. *Histoire et historiens de l'Algérie* Paris, Félix Alcan (coll. Centenaire de l'Algérie), 1931

Alonso, Ana Maria 'The effects of truth. Re-presentations of the past and the imagining of community', *J. Hist. Sociol.* 1, 1 (March 1988): 33–57

Amin, Samir *The Maghreb in the Modern World: Algeria, Tunisia, Morocco*, tr. Michael Perl, Harmondsworth, Penguin, 1970

Amrouche, Jean 'L'Eternel Jugurtha. Propositions sur le génie africain', *L'Arche* (Algiers), Feb. 1946: 58–70

Anderson, Benedict *Imagined Communities: Reflections on the Origins and Spread of Nationalism* (2nd rev. edn), London, Verso, 1991 [1983]

Andezian, Sossie 'Mysticisme extatique dans le champ religieux algérien contemporain', in Sophie Ferchiou (ed.), *L'Islam pluriel au Maghreb* Paris, CNRS, 1996, 323–38

Expériences du divin dans l'Algérie contemporaine. Adeptes des saints dans la région de Tlemcen Paris, CNRS, 2001

Andrew, C. M. and Kanya-Forstner, A. S. 'Centre and periphery in the making of the second French colonial empire, 1815–1920', *Journal of Imperial and Commonwealth History* 16, 3 (1988): 9–34

Aussaresses, Paul *Services spéciaux, Algérie 1955–57* Paris, Perrin, 2001

Bachetarzi, Mahieddine *Mémoires 1919–1939: Suivi de 'Etude sur le théâtre dans les pays islamiques'* Algiers, SNED, 1968

Balandier, Georges 'Les Mythes politiques de colonisation et de décolonisation en Afrique', *Cahiers internationaux de sociologie* 33 (July–Dec. 1962): 85–96

Balibar, Etienne 'Racism and nationalism', in Balibar and Wallerstein, *Race, Nation, Class*, ch. 3

'The nation form: history and ideology', in Balibar and Wallerstein, *Race, Nation, Class*, ch. 5

Balibar, Etienne and Wallerstein, Immanuel *Race, Nation, Class: Ambiguous Identities*, London, Verso, 1991

Ben Achour, Mohammed el-Fadhel *Le Mouvement littéraire et intellectuel en Tunisie au XIVe siècle de l'hégire (XIXe–XXe siècles)*, tr. by Noureddine Sraïeb of Ibn 'Ashūr, *al-Ḥaraka 'l-adabiyya wa'l-fikriyya fi Tūnis* Aix-en-Provence, Alif, 1998

Benbrahim, M. 'Le Mouvement national dans la poésie kabyle, 1945–1954', *Awal. Cahiers d'études berbères* 1 (1985): 124–43

Bencheneb, Saadeddine 'Quelques historiens arabes modernes de l'Algérie', *RA* 100 (1956): 475–99

Bendana, Kmar 'Les Ouvrages de Thaalbi, entre evidences et mystères de sa biographie', presented to the seminar 'Abdelaziz Thaālbi, l'intellectuel, le réformiste et le politique', ISHMN, Tunis, 7 May 1999

Benhabylès, Chérif *L'Algérie française vue par un indigène* Algiers, Imprimerie orientale Fontana, 1914

Bennoune, Mahfoud 'The introduction of nationalism into rural Algeria (1919–1954)', *Maghreb Review* 2, 3 (May–June 1977): 1–12

The Making of Contemporary Algeria, 1830–1987. Colonial Upheavals and Post-Independence Development Cambridge, Cambridge University Press, 1988

Benrabah, Mohamed *Langue et pouvoir en Algerie: histoire d'un traumatisme linguistique* Paris, Séguier, 1999

'Arabisation and creativity in Algeria', *Journal of Algerian Studies* 4–5 (1999–2000): 49–58

Berger, Anne-Emmanuelle (ed.) *Algeria in Others' Languages* Ithaca, Cornell University Press, 2002

Berque, Augustin *Ecrits sur l'Algérie* Aix-en-Provence, Edisud, 1986

Berque, Jacques 'Ça et là dans les débuts du réformisme religieux au Maghreb', in Jacques Berque et al., *Etudes d'orientalisme dédiées à la mémoire de Lévi-Provençal* (2 vols.), Paris, Maisonneuve & Larose, 1962, II, 471–94

Dépossession du monde Paris, Seuil, 1964

'Le Maghreb d'hier à demain', *Cahiers internationaux de sociologie* 37 (1964): 51–78

'Qu'est-ce qu'une "tribu" nord-africaine?' in Jacques Berque, *Maghreb, histoire et sociétés* Algiers, SNED, 1974 [1954]

L'Intérieur du Maghreb, XVème– XIXème siècles Paris, Gallimard, 1978

Le Maghreb entre deux guerres (3rd rev. edn) Paris, Seuil, 1979 [1962]

Bouguessa, Kamel *Aux sources du nationalisme algérien. Les pionniers du populisme révolutionnaire en marche* Algiers, Casbah, 2000

Boulifa, Si Amar *Le Djurdjura à travers l'histoire (depuis l'Antiquité jusqu'en 1830). Organisation et indépendance des Zouaoua (Grande Kabylie)* (2nd edn), Algiers, Berti éditions, n.d. [1999] [1925]

Bourdieu, Pierre *Sociologie de l'Algérie* Paris, PUF, 1958

'Champ intellectuel et projet créateur', *Les Temps modernes* 246 (Nov. 1966): 865–906

'Les Modes de la domination', *Actes de la recherche en sciences sociales* 2–3 (June 1976): 122–32

'Les Conditions sociales de la production sociologique: Sociologie coloniale et décolonisation de la sociologie', in Moniot et al., *Le Mal de voir*, 416–27

'The social space and the genesis of groups', *Social Science Information* 24, 2 (1985): 195–220

Language and Symbolic Power, ed. John B. Thompson, tr. Gino Raymond and Matthew Adamson, Cambridge, Polity, 1991

Brett, Michael 'Ibn Khaldun and the Arabisation of North Africa', *Maghreb Review* 4, 1 (Jan.–Feb. 1979): 9–16

'Legislating for inequality in Algeria. The Senatus-Consulte of 14 July 1865' *BSOAS* 51 (1988): 440–61

Ibn Khaldun and the Medieval Maghreb Aldershot, Ashgate, 1999

'Le Mahdi dans le Maghreb médiéval', *REMMM* 91–4 (2000): 93–106

Brett, Michael and Fentress, Elizabeth *The Berbers* Oxford, Blackwell, 1996

Brow, James 'Notes on community, hegemony and the uses of the past', *Anthropological Quarterly* 63 (1990): 1–6

Brown, L. Carl 'The Islamic reformist movement in North Africa', *Journal of Modern African Studies* 2, 1 (1964): 55–63

Brown, L. Carl and Gordon, Matthew S. (eds.) *Franco-Arab Encounters. Studies in Memory of David C. Gordon* Beirut, AUB, 1996

Bulliet, Richard W. 'Botr et Beranès: Hypothèses sur l'histoire des Berbères', *AESC* 36, 1 (Jan.–Feb. 1981): 104–16

Burke, Edmund III 'Theorizing the histories of colonialism and nationalism in the Maghrib', in Ali Abdullatif Ahmida (ed.), *Beyond Colonialism and Nationalism in the Maghrib. History, Culture, and Politics*, New York, Palgrave, 2000, ch. 1

Burke, Edmund III and Lapidus, Ira (eds.) *Islam, Politics and Social Movements* London, Tauris, 1988

Camps, Gabriel *Berbères. Aux Marges de l'histoire* Toulouse, Ed. des Hespérides, 1980

'L'Origine des Berbères', in Ernest Gellner (ed.), *Islam, société et communauté: Anthropologies du Maghreb* Paris, CNRS, 1981, 9–33

'Comment la Berbérie est devenue le Maghreb arabe', *ROMM* 35 (1983): 7–24

Carlier, Jean-Louis (Omar) 'La Première Etoile Nord-Africaine (1926–1929)', *RASJEP* 9, 4 (Dec. 1972): 907–66

Carlier, Omar 'La Production sociale de l'image de soi. Note sur la "crise berbériste" de 1949', *AAN* 23 (1984): 347–71

'Mémoire, mythe et doxa de l'état en Algérie. L'Etoile Nord-Africaine et la religion du Watan', *XXe siècle. Revue d'Histoire* 30 (1991): 82–91

'Culture politique et mémoire militante: "L'Etoile Nord-Africaine" et la figure de l'ancêtre fondateur', *Hespéris-Tamuda* 31 (1993): 117–27

Entre nation et jihad. Histoire sociale des radicalismes algériens Paris, FNSP, 1995

'Scholars and politicians: an examination of the Algerian view of Algerian nationalism', in Le Gall and Perkins (eds.), *The Maghrib in Question*, 136–69

'D'une guerre à l'autre: le redéploiement de la violence entre soi', *Confluences Méditerranée* 25 (Spring 1998): 123–37

'Civil war, private violence, and cultural socialization. Political violence in Algeria (1954–1988)', in Berger (ed.), *Algeria in Others' Languages*, ch. 4

Carr, David *Time, Narrative, and History* Bloomington and Indianapolis, Indiana University Press, 1986

Castoriadis, Cornelius *The Imaginary Institution of Society*, tr. Kathleen Blamey, Cambridge, Polity, 1987 [1975]

Çelik, Zaynep *Urban Forms and Colonial Confrontations. Algiers under French Rule* Berkeley and Los Angeles, University of California Press, 1997

Chachoua, Kamel *L'Islam kabyle. Religion, état et société en Algérie* Paris, Maisonneuve & Larose, 2001

Chaker, Salem 'L'Emergence du fait berbère. Le cas de l'Algérie', *AAN* 19 (1980): 473–83

'Langue et identité berbères (Algérie/émigration): un enjeu de société', *AAN* 23 (1984): 173–80

s.v. 'Amaziɣ (Amazigh), "le/un Berbère" ', *Encyclopédie Berbère* Aix-en-Provence, Edisud, 1984–, IV, 562–8

'Quelques évidences sur la question berbère', *Confluences Méditerranée* 11 (Summer 1994): 103–11

Chatterjee, Partha *Nationalist Thought and the Colonial World – a Derivative Discourse?* London, Zed/United Nations University, 1986

The Nation and its Fragments. Colonial and Postcolonial Histories Princeton, Princeton University Press, 1993

Cherry, David *Frontier and Society in Roman North Africa* Oxford, Clarendon Press, 1998

Cheurfi, Achour *Ecrivains algériens. Dictionnaire biographique* Algiers, Casbah, 2003

Chevallier, Dominique (ed.) *Les Arabes et l'histoire créatrice* Paris, Presses de l'Université de Paris-I, Sorbonne, 1995

Chodkiewicz, Michel *Ecrits spirituels de l'Emir Abdelkader* Paris, Seuil, 1982

Christelow, Allan 'Intellectual history in a culture under siege: Algerian thought in the last half of the nineteenth century', *MES* 18, 4 (Oct. 1982): 387–99

'Algerian Islam in a time of transition, c.1890–c.1930', *Maghreb Review* 8, 5–6 (1983): 124–9

Muslim Law Courts and the French Colonial State in Algeria Princeton, Princeton University Press, 1985

'Ritual, culture and politics of Islamic reformism in Algeria', *MES* 23, 3 (July 1987): 255–73

'Oral, manuscript, and printed expressions of historical consciousness in colonial Algeria', *Africana Journal* 15 (1990): 258–75

'Re-envisioning Algerian cultural history in the imperial age', *Maghreb Review* 24, 3–4 (1999): 108–15

Clancy-Smith, Julia A. 'Saints, mahdis and arms: religion and resistance in nineteenth-century North Africa', in Burke and Lapidus (eds.), *Islam, Politics and Social Movements*, ch. 4

Rebel and Saint: Muslim Notables, Populist Protest, Colonial Encounters (Algeria and Tunisia, 1800–1904) Berkeley and Los Angeles, University of California Press, 1994

(ed.) *North Africa, Islam and the Mediterranean World: From the Almoravids to the Algerian War* London, Frank Cass, 2001

Cohen, Anthony P. *The Symbolic Construction of Community* London, Tavistock, 1985

Cohn, Bernard S. *Colonialism and its Forms of Knowledge. The British in India* Princeton, Princeton University Press, 1996

Collot, Claude 'Le Régime juridique de la presse musulmane algérienne (1881–1962)', *RASJEP* 6, 2 (June 1969): 343–405

'Le Parti du peuple algérien (mars 1937–février 1947)', *RASJEP* 8, 1 (March 1971): 133–204

Les Institutions de l'Algérie durant la période coloniale (1830–1962), ed. Jean-Robert Henry and Ahmad Mahiou, Paris, CNRS/Algiers, OPU, 1987

Collot, Claude and Henry, Jean-Robert (eds.) *Le Mouvement national algérien. Textes 1912–1954* Paris, L'Harmattan, 1978

Colonna, Fanny 'Cultural resistance and religious legitimacy in colonial Algeria', *Economy and Society* 3, 3 (1974): 233–52

Instituteurs algériens, 1883–1939 Paris, FNSP, 1975

'Production scientifique et position dans le champ intellectuel et politique. Deux cas: Augustin Berque et Joseph Desparmet', in Moniot et al., *Le Mal de voir*, 397–415

'Les Débuts de l'*islāḥ* dans l'Aurès: 1936–1938', *RASJEP* 14, 2 (June 1977): 277–87

'Saints furieux et saints studieux ou, dans l'Aurès, comment la religion vient aux tribus', *AESC* 35, 3–4 (1980): 642–62
'Discours sur le nom: identité, altérité', *Peuples méditerranéens* 18 (Jan.– March 1982): 59–65
Savants paysans. Eléments d'histoire sociale sur l'Algérie rurale Algiers, OPU, n.d. [1987]
'The transformation of a saintly lineage in the northwest Aurès mountains (Algeria): nineteenth and twentieth centuries', in Burke and Lapidus (eds.), *Islam, Politics and Social Movements*, ch. 5
'Invisibles défenses: à propos du kuttāb et d'un chapitre de Joseph Desparmet', in Sraïeb (ed.), *Pratiques et résistances culturelles au Maghreb*, 37–51
Les Versets de l'invincibilité. Permanence et changements religieux dans l'Algérie contemporaine Paris, FSNP, 1995
'Le Modèle de *la Cité antique* dans les représentations des sociétés maghrébines: aux origines d'un débat toujours brûlant', in Marie-Noëlle Bourguet et al. (eds.), *Enquêtes en Méditerranée. Les expéditions françaises d'Egypte, de Morée et d'Algérie* Athens, Institut de recherches néohelléniques, 1999, 209–25
'The nation's "Unknowing Other". Three intellectuals and the culture(s) of being Algerian', in McDougall (ed.), *Nation, Society and Culture in North Africa*, 155–70
Colonna, Fanny and Haddab, Mustapha (eds.) *Méthodes d'approche du monde rural* Algiers, OPU, 1984
Colonna, Fanny and Haïm-Brahimi, Claude 'Du bon usage de la science coloniale', in Moniot et al., *Le mal de voir*, 221–41
Connelly, Matthew *A Diplomatic Revolution. Algeria's Fight for Independence and the Origins of the Post-Cold War Era* Oxford, Oxford University Press, 2002
Cooper, Frederick and Stoler, Ann L. (eds.) *Tensions of Empire. Colonial Cultures in a Bourgeois World* Berkeley and Los Angeles, University of California Press, 1997
Dallal, Ahmad 'Appropriating the past. Twentieth century reconstruction of pre-modern Islamic thought', *Islamic Law and Society* 7, 3 (Autumn 2000): 325–58
Damis, John 'The free-school phenomenon: the cases of Tunisia and Algeria', *IJMES* 5 (1974): 434–49
Danziger, Raphael *Abd al Qadir and the Algerians. Resistance to the French and Internal Consolidation* New York and London, Holmes & Meier, 1977
Daoud, Zakya and Stora, Benjamin *Ferhat Abbas. Une utopie algérienne* Paris, Denoël, 1995
Daumas, Eugène *La Kabylie* Paris, Jean-Paul Rocher, 2001 [1856]
Davis, John 'The social relations of the production of history', in Elizabeth Tonkin et al. (eds.), *History and Ethnicity* London, Routledge, 1989, ch. 7
de Certeau, Michel 'L'opération historique', in le Goff and Nora (eds.), *Faire de l'histoire*, I, 3–41
L'Ecriture de l'histoire Paris, Gallimard, 1975
Deeb, Mary-Jane 'Islam and national identity in Algeria', *The Muslim World* 87, 2 (April 1997): 111–28

Deheuvels, Luc-Willy *Islam et pensée contemporaine en Algérie. La revue* al-Açāla, *1971–1981* Paris, CNRS, 1991

'Histoire et épopée littéraire dans les courants fondamentalistes Algériens contemporains durant les années soixante-dix', in Chevallier (ed.), *Les Arabes et l'histoire créatrice*, ch. 3

Deming Lewis, Martin 'One hundred million Frenchmen: the "assimilation" theory in French colonial policy', *CSSH* 4 (1962): 129–53

Dermenghem, Emile *Le Culte des saints dans l'Islam maghrébin* Paris, Gallimard, 1954

Derrida, Jacques *Monolingualism of the Other; or, the Prosthesis of Origin*, tr. Patrick Mensah, Stanford, Stanford University Press, 1998

Desparmet, Joseph 'L'Oeuvre de la France en Algérie jugée par les indigènes', *BSGA* 55 (1910): 167–86; 57 (1910): 417–36

'Les Réactions nationalitaires en Algérie', *BSGA* 130 (1932) (parts I: 'Le Vieux génie maure': 173–84; II: 'La Vieille poésie nationale': 437–44; III: 'La Conquête racontée par les indigènes': 444–56); *BSGA* 131 (1933): 35–54 (part IV: 'Elégies et satires politiques de 1830 à 1914')

'Naissance d'une histoire "nationale" de l'Algérie', *BCAF* (July 1933): 387–92

'Les Chansons de geste de 1830 à 1914 dans la Mitidja', *RA* 83 (1939): 192–226

'Les Réformistes et l'éducation nationale arabe en Algérie', in Robert Montagne et al., *Entretiens sur l'évolution des pays de civilisation arabe*, Paris, Centre d'études de politique étrangère, 1939, vol. III, 174–182

Coutumes, institutions, croyances des indigènes de l'Algérie, vol. I: *L'Enfance, le marriage et la famille*, tr. Henri Pérès and G.-H. Bousquet, Algiers, Typo-Litho/Carbonel, 1939 [1st edn in Arabic, Blida, 1905]

Djaout, Tahar *Les Chercheurs d'os* Paris, Seuil, 1984

Djebar, Assia *Le Blanc d'Algérie. Récit* Paris, Albin Michel, 1995

Djeghloul, Abdelkader *Eléments d'histoire culturelle algérienne* Algiers, ENAL, 1984

'La Formation des intellectuels algériens modernes, 1880–1930', *RASJEP* 22, 4 (December 1985): 639–64

'Nationalisme, Arabité, Islamité, Berbérité: la crise de la conscience historique algérienne', in Chevallier (ed.), *Les Arabes et l'histoire créatrice*, ch. 13

Djender, Mahieddine *Introduction à l'histoire de l'Algérie* (2nd rev. edn), Algiers, ENAL, 1991

'La Berbérie, la Kabylie à travers l'histoire', in Yacine (ed.), *Les Kabyles*, 53–79

Djerbal, Daho 'La mémoire des acteurs de la guerre de libération et l'enseignement', in Laamirie et al., *La Guerre d'Algérie dans l'enseignement*, 23–7

'La guerre d'Algérie au miroir des écritures: Texte écrit et texte oral', in Rivet et al., *La Guerre d'Algérie au miroir des décolonisations françaises*, 529–42

Donham, Donald L. *Marxist Modern. An Ethnographic History of the Ethiopian Revolution* Berkeley and Los Angeles, University of California Press/Oxford, James Currey, 1999

Dournon, A. 'Kitâb tarîkh Qosantîna par El Hadj Ahmed El-Mobarek', *RA* 57 (1913): 265–305
Duara, Prasenjit *Rescuing History from the Nation. Questioning Narratives of Modern China* Chicago, Chicago University Press, 1995
Duby, Georges 'Histoire sociale et idéologies des sociétés', in le Goff and Nora (eds.), *Faire de l'histoire*, I, 147–68
Eickelman, Dale F. *Moroccan Islam. Tradition and Society in a Pilgrimage Center*, Austin, University of Texas Press, 1976
'The political economy of meaning', *American Ethnologist* 6, 2 (May 1979): 386–93
Elvin, Mark 'A working definition of "modernity"?' *Past and Present* 113 (1986): 209–13
Entelis, John P. *Algeria: The Revolution Institutionalised* Boulder, Westview, 1986
'Islam, democracy and the state: the reemergence of authoritarian politics in Algeria', in Ruedy (ed.), *Islamism and Secularism in North Africa*, ch. 13
Etienne, Bruno 'Le Vocabulaire politique de légitimité en Algérie', *AAN* 10 (1971): 69–103
L'Algérie, cultures et révolution Paris, Seuil, 1976
'Abdelkader. Quelques aspects d'une vie complexe', *Parcours, l'Algérie, les hommes et l'histoire* 4 (Summer 1985): 9–21
Abdelkader. Isthme des isthmes (barzakh al-barazikh) Paris, Hachette, 1994
Etienne, Bruno and Leca, Jean 'La politique culturelle de l'Algérie', in Vatin et al. *Culture et société au Maghreb*, 45–76
Feierman, Steven 'Africa in history. The end of universal narratives', in Prakash (ed.), *After Colonialism*, ch. 2
Foucault, Michel *L'Ordre du discours. Leçon inaugurale au Collège de France prononcée le 2 décembre 1970* Paris, Gallimard, 1971
'Nietzsche, genealogy, history' in Michel Foucault, *Language, Counter-Memory, Practice* Ithaca, Cornell University Press, 1977, 139–64
'L'Ecriture de soi', *Corps Ecrit* 5 (1983): 3–23
Gadant, Monique *Islam et nationalisme en Algérie d'après "El-Moudjahid", organe central du FLN de 1956 à 1962* Paris, L'Harmattan, 1988
Gautier, Emile-Félix *L'Islamisation de l'Afrique du Nord. Les siècles obscurs du Maghreb* Paris, Payot, 1927
Gellner, Ernest *Nations and Nationalism* Oxford, Blackwell, 1983
Muslim Society Cambridge, Cambridge University Press, 1995 [1981]
Nationalism London, Phoenix, 1998 [1997]
Gellner, Ernest and Micaud, Charles (eds.) *Arabs and Berbers. From Tribe to Nation in North Africa* London, Duckworth, 1973
Georgeon, François 'Un Manifeste de l'occidentalisation dans la Turquie kémaliste: *Üç medeniyet (Trois civilisations)*, 1928', *REMMM* 95–8 (April 2002): 43–54
Ghalem, Mohamed and Remaoun, Hassan (eds.) *Comment on enseigne l'histoire en Algérie* Oran, CRASC, 1995
Gilsenan, Michael *Saint and Sufi in Modern Egypt. An Essay in the Sociology of Religion* Oxford, Clarendon Press, 1973

Recognising Islam. Religion and Society in the Modern Middle East (new edn), London, I.B. Tauris, 2000 [1982]

Gordon, Cyrus H. *Before Columbus. Links between the Old World and Ancient America* New York, Crown, 1971

Gordon, David C. *Self-Determination and History in the Third World* Princeton, Princeton University Press, 1971

Gouvion, Marthe and Gouvion, Edmond *Kitāb Aāyane el-Marhariba* [*The Book of Maghribi Notables*] Algiers, Imprimerie orientale Fontana, 1920

Grandguillaume, Gilbert 'Langue, identité et culture nationale au Maghreb', *Peuples méditerranéens* 9 (Oct.–Dec. 1979): 3–28

Arabisation et politique linguistique au Maghreb Paris, Maisonneuve & Larose, 1983

'Arabisation et démagogie en Algérie', *Le Monde diplomatique* (February 1997): 3

Grandguillaume, Gilbert et al. *Les Violences en Algérie* Paris, Odile Jacob, 1998

Grangaud, Isabelle *La Ville imprenable. Une Histoire sociale de Constantine au 18ème siècle* Paris, Editions de l'EHESS, 2002

Green, Arnold H. *The Tunisian 'Ulamā 1873–1915: Social Structure and Response to Ideological Currents* Leiden, Brill, 1978

Habeeb, W. M. and Zartman, I. William *Polity and Society in Contemporary North Africa* Boulder, Westview, 1993

Haddab, Mustafa 'Histoire et modernité chez les réformistes algériens', in Vatin et al., *Connaissances du Maghreb*, 387–400

'Les Intellectuels et le statut des langues en Algérie', thèse de doctorat d'état (2 vols.), Université Paris-VII (Jussieu), 1993

'Statut social de l'histoire: éléments de réflexion', in Ghalem and Remaoun (eds.), *Comment on enseigne l'histoire en Algérie*, 15–34

al-Ḥafnāwī, Abū 'l-Qāsim Muḥammad *Ta'rīf al-khalaf bi-rijāl al-salaf* [*Forebears Made Known to the Men of the Present*] (2 vols.), Beirut, Mu'assassat al-risāla/ Tunis, al-Maktaba al-'Atīka, 1982 [Algiers, Fontana, 1907–9]

al-Ḥafnāwī, 'Amayriya 'Ṣāliḥ al-Sharīf (1869–1920). Niḍāluhu wa-mawāqifuhu ithnā' al-ḥarb al-'ālamiyya 'l-ūlā' ['Ṣāliḥ al-Sharīf (1869–1920). His struggle and positions during the First World War'], *Rawāfid* (Tunis) 4 (1998): 226–51

Hannoum, Abdelmajid 'Historiography, mythology and memory in modern North Africa: the story of the Kahina', *Studia Islamica* 85, 1 (February 1997): 85–130

'Historiographie et légende au Maghreb. La Kāhina ou la production d'une mémoire', *AHSS* 54, 3 (May–June 1999): 667–86

Harbi, Mohamed *Aux origines du FLN: le populisme révolutionnaire en Algérie* Paris, Bourgois, 1975

'Nationalisme algérien et identité berbère', *Peuples méditerranéens* 11 (April–June 1980): 31–7

Le FLN: mirage et réalité, des origines à la prise du pouvoir (1945–1962) Paris, Jeune Afrique, 1980

(ed.) *Les Archives de la révolution algérienne* Paris, Jeune Afrique, 1981

1954, la guerre commence en Algérie Brussels, Complexe, 1984

L'Algérie et son destin: croyants ou citoyens Paris, Arcantère, 1992
Une Vie debout. Mémoires politiques, vol. I: *1945–1962* Paris, La Découverte, 2001
Harbi, Mohamed and Meynier, Gilbert (eds.) *Le FLN, documents et histoire* Paris, Fayard, 2004
Haroun, Ali *et al Messali Hadj, 1898–1998. Parcours et témoignages* Algiers, Casbah (coll. Réflexions), 1998
Heggoy, Alf Andrew 'The origins of Algerian nationalism in the colony and in France', *The Muslim World* 58 (1968): 128–40
Heine, Peter 'Salih ash-Sharif at-Tunisi, a North African nationalist in Berlin during the First World War', *ROMM* 33, 1 (1982): 89–95
Henry, Jean-Robert 'France–Algérie: assumer l'histoire commune', *Confluences Méditerranée* 19 (Autumn 1996): 17–28
Hesnay-Lahmek, Hocine *Lettres algériennes* Paris, Jouve, 1931
Hobsbawm, Eric 'Peasants and politics', *Journal of Peasant Studies* 1 (1973–4): 3–22
Nations and Nationalism since 1780: Programme, Myth, Reality Cambridge, Cambridge University Press, 1990
On History London, Abacus, 1998
Hobsbawm, Eric and Ranger, Terence (eds.) *The Invention of Tradition* Cambridge, Cambridge University Press, 1983
Horne, Alistair *A Savage War of Peace. Algeria 1954–1962* (rev. edn) London, Macmillan, 1996 [1977]
Hourani, Albert *Arabic Thought in the Liberal Age, 1798–1939* (2nd edn) Cambridge, Cambridge University Press, 1983 [1962]
A History of the Arab Peoples London, Faber & Faber, 1991
Huntington, Samuel P. *Political Order in Changing Societies* New Haven, Yale, 1968
Ibn Khaldūn, 'Abd al-Raḥmān b. Muḥammad *Kitāb al-'Ibar (Dīwān al-mubtada' wa-'l-khabar fī ta'rīkh al-'arab wa-'l-barbar) [The book of Exemplary Histories]*, ed. Jalil Shehadeh (9 vols.), Beirut, Dar al-Fikr, 1996
Ibrahim, Amr 'Egypte: luttes pour l'appropriation de certaines représentations communautaires', in C. Vieille and P. Veauvy (eds.), *La Communauté en Méditerranée*, special issue of *Peuples méditerranéens* (Jan.–March 1982): 77–99
Ibrahimi, Ahmed Taleb *De la décolonisation à la révolution culturelle, 1962–1972* Algiers, SNED, 1973
Joseph, Gilbert M. and Nugent, Daniel (eds.) *Everyday Forms of State Formation: Revolution and the Negotiation of Rule in Modern Mexico* Durham, NC, Duke University Press, 1994
Julien, Charles-André *Histoire de l'Algérie contemporaine*, vol. I: *La Conquête et les débuts de la colonisation* Paris, PUF, 1964
L'Afrique du nord en marche: nationalismes musulmans et souveraineté française (3rd edn), Paris, Julliard, 1972 [1952]
Kaddache, Mahfoud *La Vie politique à Alger de 1919 à 1939* Algiers, SNED, 1970
L'Algérie dans l'antiquité Madrid, SNED, 1972
L'Algérie médiévale Algiers, SNED, 1982

L'Emir Khaled: documents et témoignages pour servir à l'étude du nationalisme en Algérie Algiers, OPU, n.d. [1987]

L'Algérie durant la période ottomane Algiers, OPU, 1991

Histoire du nationalisme algérien. Question nationale et politique algérienne, 1919–1951 (2 vols.) (2nd edn) Algiers, ENAL, 1993

Kaddache, Mahfoud and Sari, Djilali *L'Algérie dans l'histoire,* vol. V: *La Résistance politique (1900–1954); bouleversements socioéconomiques* Algiers, OPU, 1989

Kayali, Hasan *Arabs and Young Turks. Ottomanism, Arabism and Islamism in the Ottoman Empire, 1908–1918* Berkeley and Los Angeles, University of California Press, 1997

Keddie, Nikki R. (ed.) *Scholars, Saints and Sufis. Muslim Religious Institutions in the Middle East since 1500* Berkeley and Los Angeles, University of California Press, 1972

Kerrou, Mohamed (ed.) *L'Autorité des saints. Perspectives historiques et socioanthropologiques en Méditerranée occidentale* Paris, Ministère des Affaires Étrangères/Tunis, IRMC, 1998

Khatibi, Abdelkebir *Maghreb pluriel* Paris, Denoël, 1983

'Diglossia', in Berger (ed.), *Algeria in Others' Languages,* ch. 7

Klein, Henri *et al Feuillets d'El-Djezaïr* (2 vols.) (2nd edn) Blida, Editions du Tell, 2003 [Algiers, Chaix, 1937]

el-Korso, Mohammed 'Politique et religion en Algérie. L'islah: ses structures et ses hommes. Le cas de l'Association des 'ulamas musulmans algériens en Oranie, 1931–1945', thèse d'histoire (2 vols.), Université Paris-VII (Jussieu), 1989

Koulakssis, Ahmed and Meynier, Gilbert *L'Emir Khaled, premier za'īm? Identité algérienne et colonialisme français* Paris, L'Harmattan, 1987

Laamirie, Abdeljelil *et al La Guerre d'Algérie dans l'enseignement en France et en Algérie* Paris, CNDP, 1992

Lacheraf, Mostefa 'Colonialisme et féodalités indigènes en Algérie', *Esprit* 213 (April 1954): 523–42

'Le Patriotisme rural en Algérie', *Esprit* 224 (March 1955): 376–91

'L'Avenir de la culture algérienne', *Les Temps modernes* 209 (Oct. 1963): 720–45

L'Algérie, nation et société Paris, Maspero, 1965

Des noms et des lieux. Mémoires d'une Algérie oubliée Algiers, Casbah, 1998

Lanasri, Ahmed *La Littérature algérienne de l'entre-deux-guerres. Genèse et fonctionnement* Paris, Publisud, 1995

Laroui, Abdallah *La Crise des intellectuels arabes. Traditionalisme ou historicisme?* Paris, Maspero, 1974

The History of the Maghrib. An Interpretive Essay, tr. Ralph Mannheim, Princeton, Princeton University Press, 1977

Launay, Michel *Paysans algériens: la terre, la vigne, et les hommes* Paris, Seuil, 1963

Le Gall, Michel and Perkins, Kenneth (eds.) *The Maghrib in Question: Essays in History and Historiography* Austin, University of Texas Press, 1997

le Goff, Jacques and Nora, Pierre (eds.) *Faire de l'histoire* (3 vols.), Paris, Gallimard, 1974

Lerner, Daniel *The Passing of Traditional Society. Modernizing the Middle East* New York, Free Press, 1958

Liauzu, Claude 'Disparition de deux hybrides culturels', *Confluences Méditerranée* 19 (Autumn 1996): 113–23

Lorcin, Patricia M. E. *Imperial Identities. Stereotyping, Prejudice and Race in Colonial Algeria* London, I. B. Tauris, 1995

Lüdke, Tilman 'Jihad made in Germany – Ottoman and German propaganda and intelligence operations in the First World War', D.Phil. thesis, University of Oxford, 2001

al-Madanī, Aḥmad Tawfīq *Taqwīm al-Manṣūr* [*The Almanac of al-Mansur*] Algiers, Maṭba'at Muḥammad al-Mūhūb, vol. 5, 1348/1929–30

Kitāb al-Jazā'ir. Ta'rīkh al-jazā'ir ilā yawminā 'hādhā [*The Book of Algeria*] (1st edn) Algiers, al-Maṭba'a 'l-'arabiyya fi 'l-jazā'ir, 1350/1932, (2nd edn) Cairo, Dar al-ma'ārif (distr. Dar al-kitāb, Bulayda [Blida]), 1382/1963

al-Muslimūn fī jazīrat ṣiqiliyya wa-janūb Italyā [*The Muslims in the Island of Sicily and Southern Italy*] Algiers, al-Maṭba'a 'l-'arabiyya, (distr. Maktabat al-istiqāma, Tunis), n.d. [1365/1946]

Jughrāfiyyat al-quṭr al-jazā'irī li 'l-nāshi'a 'l-islāmiyya [*The Geography of Algeria for Islamic Youth*] (2nd edn) Algiers, al-Maṭba'a 'l-'arabiyya bi 'l-jazā'ir, 1952

Hādhihi hiya 'l-Jazā'ir [This is Algeria] Cairo, Mu'atammar al-khirrijīn al-'arab/Maktabat al-nahḍa 'l-miṣriyya, n.d. [1956]

Ḥanba'l. Ma'sa ta'rīkhiyya [*Hannibal. A Historical Drama*] (2nd edn) Algiers, SNED, February 1969 [Algiers, al-Maṭba'a 'l-'arabiyya bi 'l-jazā'ir, 1950]

Ḥarb al-thalāthimi'at sana bayna 'l-Jazā'ir wa-Isbānyā, 1492–1792 [*The Three Hundred Years' War: Algeria and Spain, 1492–1792*] Algiers, SNED, n.d. [1972?]

Qarṭājanna fī arba'at 'uṣūr, min 'aṣri 'l-ḥijāra ilā 'l-fatḥ al-islāmī [*The Four Ages of Carthage: from the Stone Age to the Islamic Conquest*] (2nd edn) Algiers, ENAL, 1986 [Tunis, 1927]

Muḥammad 'Uthmān Basha, dey al-Jazā'ir 1766–1791: sīratuhu, ḥurūbuhu, a'māluhu, niẓām al-dawla wa-'l-ḥayāt al-'āmma fī 'ahdihi [*Muhammad Uthman Pasha, Dey of Algiers, 1766–1791. His Life, Wars, and Works; the State and Life of his Age*] (2nd edn) Algiers, ENAL, 1986 [Algiers, 1356/1938]

Ḥayāt Kifāḥ. Mudhakkirāt [A Life of Struggle. Memoirs] (3 vols.) (2nd edn) Algiers, ENAL, 1988 [1977–81]

Mémoires de combat, tr. by Malika Merabet of *Ḥayāt Kifāḥ*, vol. I, Algiers, OPU/ENAL, 1989

Mahiou, Ahmed 'Les Forces politiques en Algérie entre les deux guerres mondiales', *RASJEP* 11, 4 (Dec. 1974): 7–10

Mahsas, Ahmed *Le Mouvement révolutionnaire en Algérie de la première guerre mondiale à 1954* Paris, L'Harmattan, 1979

Malek, Réda *Tradition et révolution. Le Véritable enjeu* Algiers, Bouchène, 1991

El Mansour, Mohamed 'Maghribis in the Mashriq during the modern period: representations of the Other within the world of Islam', in Clancy-Smith (ed.), *North Africa, Islam and the Mediterranean World*, 81–104

Marçais, Georges 'Sidi 'Abd er-Rahmane, patron d'Alger, et son tombeau', in Klein et al., *Feuillets d'El-Djezaïr*, 151–64

Martinez, Luis *La Guerre civile en Algérie, 1992–1998* Paris, Karthala, 1998

Masud, Muhammad 'The obligation to migrate: the doctrine of *hijra* in Islamic law', in Dale F. Eickelman and James P. Piscatori (eds.), *Muslim Travellers: Pilgrimage, Migration, and the Religious Imagination* London, Routledge, 1990, ch. 5

Mazouni, Abdellah *Culture et enseignement en Algérie et au Maghreb* Paris, Maspero, 1969

'Cultures et sociétés: le cas de l'Algérie de 1962 à 1973', *RASJEP* 12, 1 (March 1975): 147–59

McDougall, James '"Soi-Même" comme un "Autre". Les histoires coloniales d'Ahmad Tawfiq al-Madani (1899–1983)', *REMMM* 95–8 (2002): 95–110

(ed.) *Nation, Society and Culture in North Africa* London, Frank Cass, 2003

'The *Shabiba Islamiyya* of Algiers: education, authority, and colonial control, 1921–1957', *Comparative Studies of South Asia, Africa and the Middle East* 24, 1 (2004): 18–25

'S'écrire un destin: l'Association des 'ulama dans la révolution algérienne', *Bulletin de l'Institut d'histoire du temps présent* 83 (1st semester 2004): 38–52

'Etat, société et culture chez les intellectuels de l'*iṣlāḥ* maghrébin (Algérie et Tunisie, c.1900–1945), ou, la réforme comme apprentissage de l'arriération', in Odile Moreau (ed.), *La Réforme de l'état dans le monde islamo-méditerranéen aux XIXème–XXème siècles*, Paris, Maisonneuve & Larose/Tunis, IRMC, forthcoming

Meijer, Roel (ed.) *Cosmopolitanism, Identity and Authenticity in the Middle East* Richmond, Curzon Press/European Cultural Foundation, 1999

Memmi, Albert *Portrait du colonisé* Paris, Gallimard, 1985 [Ed. Corréa, 1957]

Merad, Ali 'La Formation de la presse musulmane en Algérie (1919–1939)', *IBLA* 105 (1964): 9–26

'L'Enseignement politique de Muhammad Abduh aux Algériens (1903)', *Confluent* 42–3 (1964): 643–89

Le Réformisme musulman en Algérie, 1925–1940. Essai d'histoire sociale et religieuse Paris and The Hague, Mouton, 1967

'Islam et nationalisme arabe en Algérie à la veille de la première guerre mondiale', *Oriente Moderno* 49, 4–5 (April–May 1969): 213–22

Ibn Badis, commentateur du Coran Paris, Librairie Orientaliste Paul Geuthner, 1971

Meynier, Gilbert *L'Algérie révélée: la guerre de 1914–1918 et le premier quart du XXe siècle* Geneva, Droz, 1981

Histoire intérieure du FLN, 1954–1962 Paris, Fayard, 2002

al-Mīlī, Mubārak b. Muḥammad *Ta'rīkh al-Jazā'ir fī 'l-qadīm wa-'l-ḥadīth* [*History of Ancient and Modern Algeria*] (3 vols.) (2nd edn), Algiers, Maktabat al-nahḍa 'l-jazā'iriyya, 1963 [Constantine, 2 vols., 1929–32]

Risālat al-shirk wa-maẓāhirihi [*Treatise on Polytheism and its Manifestations*] (2nd edn) Algiers, Maktabat al-nahḍa 'l-jazā'iriyya, 1966 [1937]

Millar, Fergus 'Local cultures in the Roman empire; Libyan, Punic and Latin in Roman Africa', *Journal of Roman Studies* 58 (1968): 126–34

Moniot, Henri et al. *Le Mal de voir. Ethnologie et orientalisme: politique et épistémologie, critique et autocritique* Paris, Université de Paris-VII/Union des éditions générales, 1976

Murtāḍ, 'Abd al-Malik *Nahḍat al-adab al-'arabī al-mu'āṣir fī 'l-Jazā'ir, 1925–1954* [*The Renaissance of Contemporary Arabic Literature in Algeria, 1925–1954*] Algiers, SNED, n.d. [1969]

Muṭabbaqānī, Māzen Ṣāliḥ Ḥāmid *Jam'iyat al-'ulamā' al-muslimīn al-jazā'iriyyīn wa-dauwruhā fī 'l-ḥaraka 'l-waṭaniyya 'l-jazā'iriyya* [*The Association of Algerian Muslim 'ulamā and its Role in the Algerian National Movement*] Beirut, Dārat al-'ulūm, 1988

Muwā'ada, Muḥammad *Muḥammad al-Khiḍr Ḥusayn, ḥayātuhu wa-āthāruhu* [*Muhammad al-Khidr Husayn, his Life and Works*] Tunis, STD, 1974

Nadir, Ahmed 'Le Mouvement réformiste algérien. Son rôle dans la formation de l'idéologie nationale', thèse de doctorat de IIIème cycle, Université Paris-III, 1968

'Le Mouvement réformiste algérien et la guerre de libération nationale', *Rev. Hist. Maghr.* 4 (July 1975): 174–83

Nāṣir, Muḥammad *al-Ṣuḥuf al-'arabiyya 'l-jazā'iriyya min 1847 ilā 1939* [*The Algerian Arabic Press, 1847–1939*] Algiers, SNED, 1980

al-Nāṣiri, Abū 'l-'Abbās Aḥmad b. Khālid *Kitāb al-istiqṣā li-akhbār duwwal al-maghrib al-aqṣā* [*Thorough Enquiry into the Annals of the Dynasties of Morocco*] (9 vols.), Casablanca, Dār al-Kitāb, 1956

Norris, H. T. *The Berbers in Arabic Literature* London, Longman/Beirut, Librairie du Liban, 1982

Nouschi, Andre *La Naissance du nationalisme algérien* Paris, Minuit, 1962

Ortner, Sherry B. 'On key symbols', *American Anthropologist* 75, 5 (1973): 1338–46

Perkins, Kenneth J. '"The masses look ardently to Istanbul": Tunisia, Islam and the Ottoman empire, 1837–1931', in Ruedy (ed.), *Islamism and Secularism in North Africa*, ch. 2

Pervillé, Guy 'The *Francisation* of Algerian intellectuals: history of a failure?', in Brown and Gordon (eds.), *Franco-Arab Encounters*, 415–45

Poncet, J. 'Le Mythe de la "catastrophe" hilalienne', *AESC* 22, 5 (Sept.–Oct. 1967): 1099–120

Prakash, Gyan 'Writing post-Orientalist histories of the Third World: perspectives from Indian historiography', *CSSH* 32 (1990): 385–408

(ed.) *After Colonialism. Imperial Histories and Postcolonial Displacements* Princeton, Princeton University Press, 1995

Another Reason. Science and the Imagination of Modern India Princeton, Princeton University Press, 1999

Qasim, Mouloud 'Inniya wa aṣāla/Identité et Authenticité', opening address delivered to the Fourth Seminar on Islamic Thought, Constantine, 10 August 1970, *al-Aṣāla* (Algiers) 1 (March 1971)

Randau, Robert with Fikri, Abdelkader *Les Compagnons du jardin* Paris, Domat-Montchrestien, 1933

Remaoun, Hassan 'Le Fait maghrébin dans le mouvement socio-historique. Contribution à une critique de l'approche essentialiste', *RASJEP* 25, 2 (June 1987): 417–43

'Enseignement de l'histoire et conscience nationale', *Confluences Méditerranée* 11 (Summer 1994): 23–30

'Sur l'enseignement de l'histoire en Algérie, ou la crise identitaire à travers (et par) l'école', in Ghalem and Remaoun (eds.), *Comment on enseigne l'histoire en Algérie*, 47–68

'Pratiques historiographiques et mythes de fondation: le cas de la guerre de libération à travers les institutions algériennes d'éducation et de recherche', in Ageron (ed.), *La Guerre d'Algérie et les Algériens, 1954–1962*, 305–22

'La Question de l'histoire dans le débat sur la violence en Algérie', *Insaniyat* (Oran) 10 (Jan.–April 2000): 31–43

Renan, (Joseph-) Ernest *Qu'est-ce qu'une nation?* Paris, Calmann-Lévy, 1882

Ricoeur, Paul *The Contribution of French Historiography to the Theory of History* Oxford, Clarendon Press, 1980

Temps et récit (3 vols.), Paris, Seuil, 1983–5

The Reality of the Historical Past Milwaukee, Marquette University Press, 1984

Soi-même comme un autre Paris, Seuil, 1990

'Life in quest of narrative', in David Wood (ed.), *On Paul Ricoeur. Narrative and Interpretation* London, Routledge, 1991, ch. 2

'L'Ecriture de l'histoire et la représentation du passé', *AHSS* 55, 4 (July–Aug. 2000): 731–47

La Mémoire, l'histoire, l'oubli Paris, Seuil, 2000

Rivet, Daniel et al. *La Guerre d'Algérie an miroir des décolonisations françaises. Actes du colloque en l'honneur de Charles-Robert Ageron, Sorbonne, novembre 2000* Paris, Société française d'histoire d'Outre-Mer, 2000

Roberts, Hugh 'Towards an understanding of the Kabyle question in contemporary Algeria', *Maghreb Review* 5, 5–6 (Sept.–Dec. 1980): 115–24

'The FLN: French conceptions, Algerian realities', in George Joffé (ed.), *North Africa: Nation, State and Region*, London, Routledge, 1989, ch. 8

The Battlefield. Algeria, 1988–2002. Studies in a Broken Polity London, Verso, 2003

'North African Islamism in the blinding light of 9/11', LSE Development Studies Institute working paper 34, October 2003, http://www.crisisstates.com

Roff, William R. (ed.) *Islam and the Political Economy of Meaning. Comparative Studies of Muslim Discourse* London, Croom Helm, 1987

Roseberry, William 'Hegemony and the language of contention', in Joseph and Nugent (eds.), *Everyday Forms of State Formation*, 355–66

Roth, Arlette *Le Théâtre algérien de langue dialectale, 1926–1964* Paris, Maspero, 1967

Rouadjia, Ahmed *Les Frères et la mosquée. Enquête sur le mouvement islamiste en Algérie* Paris, Karthala, 1990

Ruedy, John *Modern Algeria: The Origins and Development of a Nation* Bloomington, Indiana University Press, 1992

(ed.) *Islamism and Secularism in North Africa* London, Macmillan/Washington DC, Center for Contemporary Arab Studies, Georgetown University, 1994

'Chérif Benhabylès and the Young Algerians', in Brown and Gordon (eds.), *Franco-Arab Encounters*, 345–69

Sa'adallah, Abū 'l-Qāsim 'The rise of Algerian Nationalism, 1900–1930', Ph.D. thesis, University of Minnesota, 1965

al-Ḥaraka 'l-waṭaniyya 'l-jazā'iriyya [*The Algerian National Movement*] Beirut, Dār al-ādāb, 1969

Abḥāth wa ārā fī ta'rīkh al-Jazā'ir [*Research and Opinions on the History of Algeria*] (4 vols.), Beirut, Dār al-gharb al-islāmī, 1990

Sa'd, Fahmi *Ḥarakat 'Abd al-Ḥamīd ibn Bādīs wa-dawruhā fī yaqẓat al-Jazā'ir* [*The Movement of 'Abd al-Hamid ibn Badis and its Role in the Algerian Awakening*] Beirut, Dar al-Rahab, 1983

Sahli, Mohammed Chérif *Le Message de Yougourtha* Algiers, Impr. générale, 1947

Décoloniser l'histoire. Introduction à l'histoire du Maghreb Paris, Maspero, 1965

Sayadi, Mongi *al-Jam'īya al-khaldūniyya (1896–1958), la première association nationale moderne en Tunisie* Tunis, MTE, n.d. [1974]

Sayer, Derek 'Everyday forms of state formation: some dissident remarks on "hegemony"', in Joseph and Nugent (eds.), *Everyday Forms of State Formation*, 367–77

Scott, James C. *Weapons of the Weak: Everyday Forms of Peasant Resistance* New Haven, Yale, 1985

Sebti, Abdelahad 'Au Maroc: sharifisme citadin, charisme et historiographie', *AESC* 41, 2 (March–April 1986): 433–57

Shatzmiller, Maya 'Le Mythe d'origine berbère. Aspects historiographiques et sociaux', *ROMM* 35 (1983): 145–56

Shinar, Pessah 'The historical approach of the 'ulema in the contemporary Maghreb', *Asian and African Studies* (Jerusalem) 7 (1971): 181–210

'Some observations on the ethical teachings of orthodox reformism in Algeria', *Asian and African Studies* (Jerusalem) 8, 3 (1972): 263–90

Shryock, Andrew J. *Nationalism and the Genealogical Imagination. Oral History and Textual Authority in Tribal Jordan* Berkeley and Los Angeles, University of California Press, 1997

Silverstein, Paul 'Martyrs and patriots: ethnic, national and transnational dimensions of Kabyle politics', in McDougall (ed.), *Nation, Society and Culture in North Africa*, 87–111

Smith, Anthony D. *The Ethnic Origins of Nations* Oxford, Blackwell, 1986

National Identity London, Penguin, 1991

'The Golden Age and national renewal', in Geoffrey Hosking and George Schöpflin (eds.), *Myths and Nationhood* London, Hurst, 1997, 36–59

Soufi, Fouad 'La Fabrication d'une mémoire: les médias algériens (1963–1995) et la guerre d'Algérie', in Ageron (ed.), *La Guerre d'Algérie et les Algériens, 1954–1962*, 289–303

Sraieb, Noureddine (ed.) *Pratiques et résistances culturelles au Maghreb* Paris, CNRS, 1992

St-Calbre, Charles 'Constantine et quelques auteurs arabes constantinois', *RA* 57 (1913): 70–95

Stedman Jones, Gareth *Languages of Class. Studies in English Working Class History, 1832–1982* Cambridge, Cambridge University Press, 1983

Stoler, Ann L. 'Rethinking colonial categories: European communities and the boundaries of rule', *CSSH* 31, 1 (January 1989): 134–61

Stora, Benjamin *Messali Hadj, pionnier du nationalisme algérien (1898–1974)* Paris, L'Harmattan, 1986

Les Sources du nationalisme algérien: parcours idéologiques, origines des acteurs Paris, L'Harmattan, 1988

La Gangrène et l'oubli: la mémoire de la guerre d'Algérie, Paris, La Découverte, 1991

Histoire de l'Algérie coloniale, 1830–1954 Paris, La Découverte, 1991

'Algérie: Absence et Surabondance de Mémoire', Grandguillaume et al., *Les Violences en Algérie,* 143–54

al-Ṭammār, Muḥammad ibn 'Umar *Ta'rīkh al-adab al-jazā'irī* [*A History of Algerian Literature*] Algiers, SNED, n.d. [1969]

al-Temīmī, Abd al-Jalīl 'Min a'lāminā 'l-bārizīn wa'l-munasiyyīn: al-shaykh Ṣāliḥ al Sharīf al-Tūnisī' ['An eminent and forgotten *'ālim*: shaykh Salih al-Sharif al-Tunisi'] *Rev. Hist. Maghr.* 23, 4 (November 1981): 345–62

al-Tha'ālibi, 'Abd al-'Aziz *La Tunisie martyre, ses revendications* Paris, Jouve, 1920

al-Tha'ālibi, 'Abd al-Aziz, Sebaï El Hadi and Benattar César *L'Esprit libéral du Coran* Paris, Ernest Leroux, 1905

Touati, Houari 'Algerian historiography in the nineteenth and twentieth centuries: from chronicle to history', in Le Gall and Perkins (eds.), *The Maghrib in Question,* 84–94

Tozy, Mohamed 'Monopolisation de la production symbolique et hiérarchisation du champ politico-religieux au Maroc', *AAN* 13 (1979): 219–34

Turin, Yvonne *Affrontements culturels dans l'Algérie coloniale. Ecoles, médecines, religion, 1830–1880* Paris, Maspero, 1971

'La Culture dans "l'authenticité et l'ouverture" au Ministère de l'Enseignement originel et des Affaires religieuses', in Vatin et al., *Culture et société au Maghreb,* 96–105

Turner, Victor *Dramas, Fields and Metaphors. Symbolic Action in Human Society* Ithaca, Cornell University Press, 1974

Vatin, Jean-Claude 'Conditions et formes de la domination coloniale en Algérie (1919–1945)', *RASJEP* 9, 4 (Dec. 1972): 873–906

'Nationalisme et socialisation politique: de quelques conditions du regroupement national entre 1919 et 1945', *RASJEP* 11, 4 (Dec. 1974): 43–52

'Questions culturelles et questions à la culture', in Vatin et al., *Culture et société au Maghreb,* 43–16

'Sur l'approche des mouvements nationaux maghrébins en général, et sur l'Algérie des années trente en particulier', *RASJEP* 14, 2 (June 1977): 229–63

'Science historique et conscience historiographique de l'Algérie coloniale. I: 1840–1962', *AAN* 13 (1979): 1103–22

'Popular puritanism versus state reformism: Islam in Algeria', in James P. Piscatori (ed.), *Islam in the Political Process,* Cambridge, Cambridge University Press, 1983, ch. 6

L'Algérie politique. Histoire et société (2nd edn), Paris, FNSP, 1983 [1974]

'Seduction and sedition: Islamic polemical discourses in the Maghreb', in Roff (ed.), *Islam and the Political Economy of Meaning,* ch. 7

Vatin, Jean-Claude et al. *Culture et société au Maghreb* Paris, CNRS, 1975

Vatin, Jean-Claude et al. *Connaissances du Maghreb: sciences sociales et colonisation* Paris, CNRS, 1984

Venture de Paradis, Jean-Michel *Tunis et Alger au XVIIIème siècle*, ed. Joseph Cuoq, Paris, Sindbad, 1983

von Sivers, Peter 'The realm of justice: apocalyptic revolts in Algeria (1849–1879)', *Humaniora Islamica* 1 (1973): 47–60

'Insurrection and accommodation: indigenous leadership in eastern Algeria, 1840–1900', *IJMES* 6 (1975): 259–75

'Les Plaisirs du collectionneur: capitalisme fiscal et chefs indigènes en Algérie (1840–1860)', *AESC* 35, 3–4 (May–Aug. 1980): 679–99

'Rural uprisings as political movements in colonial Algeria, 1851–1914', in Burke and Lapidus (eds.), *Islam, Politics and Social Movements*, ch. 3

Wansborough, John 'The decolonisation of North African history' *JAH* 9, 4 (1968): 643–50

al-Wartilānī, Faḍīl *al-Jazā'ir al-thā'ira* [*Algeria in Revolt*] Beirut, Maṭba'at al-'abād, 1956

Washbrook, David A. 'Orients and Occidents: colonial discourse theory and the historiography of the British empire', in Robin W. Winks (ed.), *The Oxford History of the British Empire* Oxford, Oxford University Press, 1999, vol. V, ch. 38

Willis, Michael *The Islamist Challenge in Algeria: A Political History* Reading, Ithaca, 1996

Wolf, Eric *Europe and the People Without History* Berkeley and Los Angeles, University of California Press, 1982

Wolfe, Patrick 'History and imperialism: a century of theory, from Marx to postcolonialism', *AHR* 102, 2 (April 1997): 388–420

'Land, labor, and difference: elementary structures of race', *AHR* 106, 3 (June 2001): 865–905

Wuthnow, Robert *Communities of Discourse. Ideology and Social Structure in the Reformation, the Enlightenment, and European Socialism* Cambridge MA, Harvard University Press, 1989

Yacine, Tassadit (ed.) *Les Kabyles: éléments pour la compréhension de l'identité berbère en Algérie* Paris, Groupement pour les droits de minorités, 1992

Yacine-Titouh, Tassadit *Les Voleurs de feu. Eléments d'une anthropologie sociale et culturelle de l'Algérie* Paris, La Découverte/Awal, 1993

Chacal ou la ruse des dominés. Aux origines du malaise culturel des intellectuels algériens Paris, La Découverte, 2001

Yefsah, Rachid 'L'Arabo-Islamisme face à la question berbère', in Yacine (ed.), *Les Kabyles*, 105–25

Young, Robert *White Mythologies. Writing History and the West* London, Routledge, 1990

Zakarya, Moufdi *Nashīd al-anāshīd aw ilyādhat al-jazā'ir/l'Iliade Algérienne* [*The Hymn of Hymns, or the Algerian Iliad*], Arabic text with French tr. by Tahar Bouchouchi, Algiers, Ministry of Original Education and Religious Affairs, 1972

Zartman, I. William 'Political dynamics of the Maghreb: the cultural dialectic', in Halim Barakat (ed.), *Contemporary North Africa*, London, Croom Helm, 1985, ch. 2

Zerrūqī, 'Abd al-Rashīd *Jihād Ibn Bādīs ḍidd al-isti'mār al-firansī fī 'l-Jazā'ir, 1913–1940* [*The Struggle of Ben Badis against French imperialism in Algeria, 1913–1940*], Beirut, Dār al-shihāb, 1999

Index

Cambridge Middle East Studies 24

1 PARVIN PAIDAR
Women and the Political Process in Twentieth-Century Iran
2 ISRAEL GERSHONI AND JAMES JANKOWSKI
Redefining the Egyptian Nation, 1930–1945
3 ANNELIES MOORS
Women, Property and Islam: Palestinian Experiences, 1920–1945
4 PAUL KINGSTON
Britain and the Politics of Modernization in the Middle East, 1945–1958
5 DANIEL BROWN
Rethinking Tradition in Modern Islamic Thought
6 NATHAN J. BROWN
The Rule of Law in the Arab World: Courts in Egypt and the Gulf
7 RICHARD TAPPER
Frontier Nomads of Iran: The Political and Social History of the Shahsevan
8 KHALED FAHMY
All the Pasha's Men: Mehmed Ali, his Army and the Making of Modern Egypt
9 SHEILA CARAPICO
Civil Society in Yemen: The Political Economy of Activism in Arabia
10 MEIR LITVAK
Shi'i Scholars of Nineteenth-Century Iraq: The 'Ulama' of Najaf and Karbala'
11 JACOB METZER
The Divided Economy of Mandatory Palestine
12 EUGENE ROGAN
Frontiers of the State in the Late Ottoman Empire: Transjordan, 1850–1921
13 ELIZ SANASARIAN
Religious Minorities in Iran
14 NADJE AL-ALI
Secularism, Gender and the State in the Middle East: The Egyptian Women's Movement
15 ROGAN/SHLAIM EDS
The War for Palestine: Rewriting the History of 1948
16 SHAFIR/PELED
Being Israeli: The Dynamics of Multiple Citizenship
17 A.J. RACY
Making Music in the Arab World: The Culture and Artistry of Tarab
18 BENNY MORRIS
The Birth of the Palestinian Refugee Crisis Revisited
19 YASIR SULEIMAN
A War of Words: Language and Conflict in the Middle East
20 PETER MOORE
Doing Business in the Middle East: Politics and Economic Crisis in Jordan and Kuwait
21 IDITH ZERTAL
Israel's Holocaust and the Politics of Nationhood

22 David Romano
The Kurdish Nationalist Movement: Opportunity, Mobilization and Identity
23 Laurie A. Brand
Citizens Abroad: Emigration and the State in the Middle East and North Africa

LaVergne, TN USA
21 July 2010
190253LV00003B/50/P
9 780521 103671